This Book is About SCHOOLS

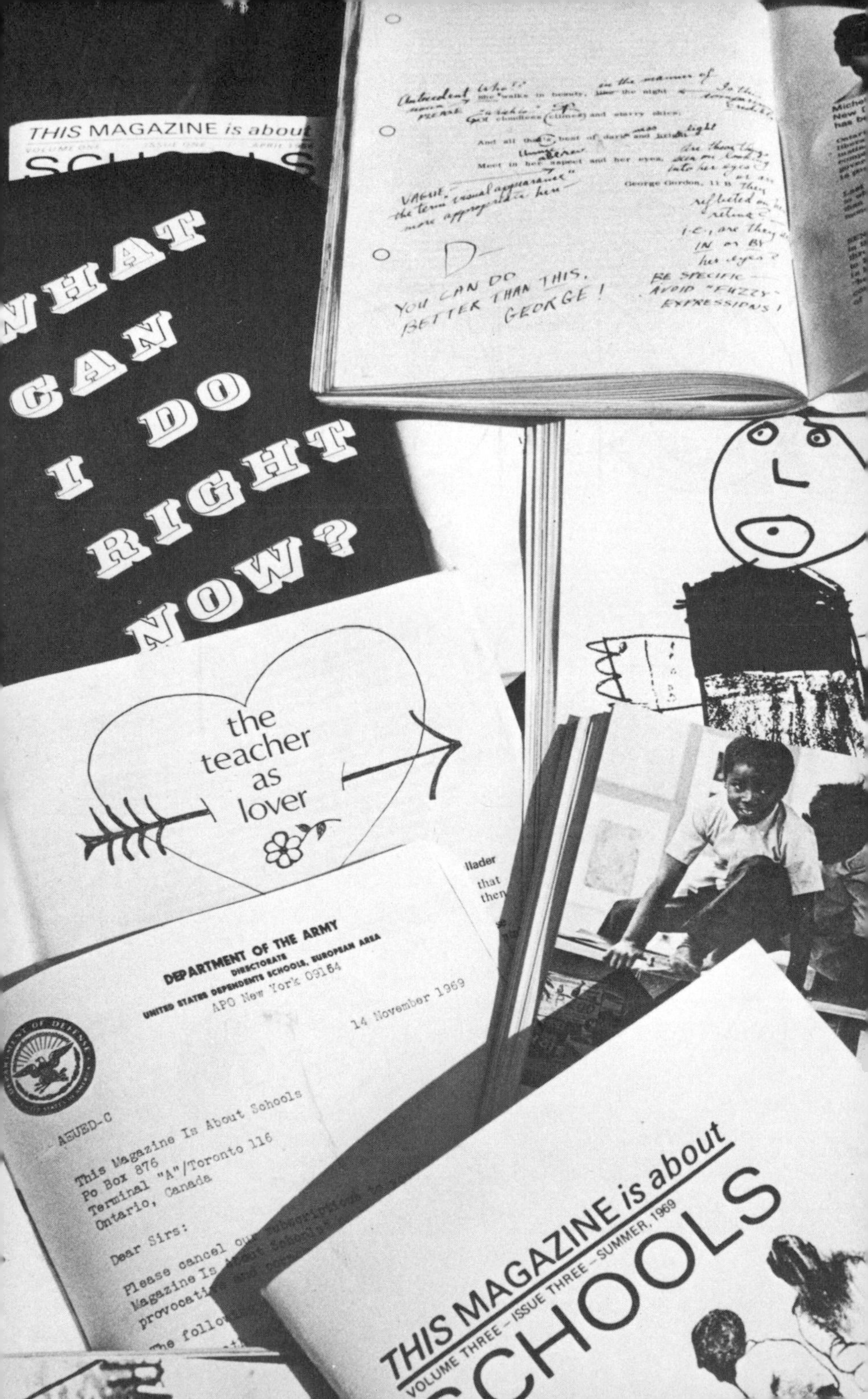
THIS MAGAZINE is about
WHAT CAN I DO RIGHT NOW?
D–
YOU CAN DO BETTER THAN THIS, GEORGE!
BE SPECIFIC — AVOID "FUZZY" EXPRESSIONS!
George Gordon, 11 B
the teacher as lover
DEPARTMENT OF THE ARMY
DIRECTORATE
UNITED STATES DEPENDENTS SCHOOLS, EUROPEAN AREA
APO New York 09164
14 November 1969
AEUED-C
This Magazine Is About Schools
Po Box 876
Terminal "A"/Toronto 116
Ontario, Canada
Dear Sirs:
THIS MAGAZINE is about SCHOOLS
VOLUME THREE—ISSUE THREE—SUMMER, 1969

This Book is About SCHOOLS

Edited by
Satu Repo

Pantheon Books
New York
A Division of Random House

 Published in the United States by Pantheon Books, a division of Random House, Inc., New York, and simultaneously in Canada by Random House of Canada Limited, Toronto.

These articles first appeared in *This Magazine is About Schools* from April, 1966, to July, 1969, and are reprinted here by courtesy of the magazine.
"Electronics and the Psychic Drop-Out" by Marshall McLuhan appears by permission of Harold Ober Associates, Inc. It appeared in Volume One, Issue One of *This Magazine*.
Library of Congress Card Catalog Number: 70–113720

Credits for illustrations

Frontispiece by Rebecca W. Rosenblatt.
Page 1, by John F. Phillips
Page 6, by Gail Ashby
Page 18, by Francis Kagige
Page 51, by John F. Phillips
Page 165, by Laura Phillips
Page 271, by John F. Phillips
Page 276, by John F. Phillips
Page 277, by John F. Phillips
Page 279, by John F. Phillips
Pages 280–281, by John F. Phillips
Page 284, by John F. Phillips
Page 312, by Charlie Berry
Page 314, by John F. Phillips and Darlene Rowe
Page 316, 317, by John F. Phillips
Page 323, by Darlene Rowe
Page 381, by John F. Phillips
Page 390, by John F. Phillips
Page 404, by John F. Phillips

Manufactured in the United States of America
by H. Wolff, New York

First Edition
9 8 7 6 5 4 3 2

INTRODUCTION

I can't remember how I first heard of *This Magazine is About Schools*. It might have been from Bill Ayers when he was at the Children's Community in Ann Arbor, or from John Holt, or perhaps from some graduate students in education at the University of California in Berkeley. I do remember however that all of a sudden a few years ago people throughout the country who were involved in changing the public schools or creating new schools were passing copies of the magazine from hand to hand and talking about how cool it was to have a voice at last.

What first impressed me was an ad run in the first few issues inviting the readers to participate in the making of the magazine. The editors were serious when they said:

SEND US
your articles
your letters
your pictures
your comments
about children
about schools
about television
about transistors
about your own
school days
about drop-outs
about stay-ins
this magazine
life, society
the universe
everything

SEND US
humor
cartoons
kid's poems
subscriptions
SEND US

The invitation was tempting and I wanted to test the seriousness of the editors. I sent them a copy of a review of Robert Cole's *Children of Crisis* that I had written a while before. George Martell sent back a letter rejecting the review for the best of reasons. He explained that my review was essentially academic and that it added nothing to Cole's own report of his experiences. On rereading the review I agreed and was relieved and surprised at the openness and candor of the comments. Martell went on to point out that *This Magazine* was more interested in direct accounts of experiences that could be of use to other teachers, than in reviews by so-called experts. In fact it encouraged many people who had never written seriously before to take the step and tell of their lives and work without the fear of academic judgment if they felt some other individuals could learn from their successes or failures.

My next personal experience with *This Magazine* was when a friend showed me a letter printed in the magazine that dealt with *Teaching the Unteachable,"* a pamphlet I had written. That letter was printed in its entirety and without comment or introduction. I wrote a reply which was reproduced in the next issue even down to the offset copying of the letterhead and my signature. The format in which the correspondence was reproduced is characteristic of the magazine. It is informal, sprawling. Typographical errors aren't corrected. There is an immediacy to the look of the letters that the magazine reproduces. The magazine is alive and not posed.

A sense of life, both complex and uncertain, pervades the pages of *This Magazine is About Schools.* The letters reproduced in the exact form they were submitted is only one example of the feeling of participation and urgency that the magazine conveys. In each issue there are pictures taken at schools or on the streets. The pictures are candid, and the cameras are not in the hands of professionals who are trying to prove a point or make a pretty picture. One can experience these schools through the eyes of students and teachers who are actually involved in the work.

As well as pictures there are poems, impressions, drawings, fragments of essays, diaries. In each issue one can experience the work of many different people of different age and perspective. The magazine is fun to look at and full of the unexpected. It is serious but not so serious that it can't be silly at times or just plain outrageous. One of my favorite pieces published in the magazine is about pigeons:

> I hate pigeons because they're one of the dirtiest birds in the world. In Harlem where I live all you see is Pigeon shit, and its so dirty. One day when I was in the fifth grade a bird (a pigeon) was flying over me and a couple of seconds later some pigeon turd was on my shirt. Also in Harlem Pigeons just keep flying around you, they annoy you because they fly so low and just keep dropping it all over the place. If it was up to me I'd kick a Pigeon straight up its god dam ass just as long as they didn't shit on me.
>
> —Christopher Gamble
> (in Vol. 2, issue 4, p. 57)

There are useful things that teachers and others concerned with schools can find in *This Magazine*. It is filled with guerrilla tactics for teachers, with suggestions on where to get materials cheaply, on how to maximize one's resources, on where to find allies, and on where to go when one is fired. There are paste-ins that excerpt some of the more absurd public statements made by school officials about change in the schools as well as lists of free schools in Canada and the United States. There are suggestions about curriculum, about spatial reorganization of the schools, about the use of contemporary media. Every issue is a mixed bag of criticism, vision, and practical suggestion. The issues have served me as texts to use with my students as well as sources of ideas and personal pleasure. The editors don't even suggest that the magazine ought to be used in certain ways or that specific conclusions ought to be drawn from its contents. For once there is a magazine for teachers that assumes that people who teach are intelligent, sensitive adults capable of making judgments for themselves and not dependent childlike beings who need to be told what to do and how to do it.

Last summer I discovered that *This Magazine is About Schools* is much more than a magazine—it is also a community of people who work in real schools. Four young men from Toronto pulled up to my house in Berkeley California and said in an accent I barely understood that George had sent them and that he had assured them that I would find a place for them to stay. I tried to rack my brains for a George I knew who would send me young people to put up and finally I got up the courage to ask one of the young men, who turned out to be the writer and filmmaker Clay Borris (see "Cabbagetown"), "George who?" Clay replied, "George Martell, you know, from Point Blank." I had never met George Martell and still haven't met him. Yet I knew *This Magazine* and was flattered that he had thought of asking me to put up some of the students from his school. I know I would assure our students at Other Ways in Berkeley that George would put them up in Toronto without ever having met him. We are in the same life and have similar priorities and commitments.

This Magazine is About Schools is real and important because the people who put it together are involved in the day-to-day struggle of trying to create new forms of schooling and new ideas of communal existence in a mad and too frequently hostile environment. The magazine, without publicity or money, has reached young teachers and students throughout the continent because we were ready and looking for it.

HERBERT KOHL

FOREWORD

How do you change things? For years a group of us in Toronto had been arguing about this in our communal living rooms and in local taverns. Most of us made a living in either teaching or in some kind of social work, and the argument often centered around how to change the institutions that shape kids, and particularly the school system. Should we do political organizing? There was eloquent talk about getting together pressure groups of the powerless in education—students, teachers and parents—around demands that they have some say in what happens in the schools. Others argued that unless it can be shown that there are better ways of learning and relating to each other and the world, organizing in itself will not accomplish much. These were the people who were reading A. S. Neill and thinking seriously about setting up small free schools. When Bob Davis quit his high school teaching and started to round up people who were interested in starting a magazine on education, he had in mind a publication that would act as a forum for both kinds of activities.

In the initial stages of the magazine, we all agreed that an analysis of the educational system and a detailed description of its texture were both necessary in a journal of education. Some of us were interested in clarifying our own experiences and trying to make sense of our own process of growing up. Others wanted to look at what exactly the schools were doing and to expose some of the myths of public education.

This Magazine is about Schools has attempted to do these things, but not always with equal success. To a great extent we have been disappointed in our hopes for reform—or even rebellion—within the school system. Furthermore, few people seem to have been able to write well about their experiences within the established schools. Most of our writers have been people who have been committed to developing radical alternatives and have not found it possible to combine this with working in the regular system.

The editors themselves have spent a great deal of time setting up new kinds of schools. Bob Davis is one of the founders of Everdale, a school community fifty miles outside Toronto. He is teaching there now for the fourth year. Gail Ashby has taught both at Everdale and Superschool, a free high school organized by some Toronto students who didn't want to go back to their old school. Sarah Spinks has worked as a community organizer in downtown Toronto and is involved with the Women's Liberation Movement Day Care Center. This Center works in co-operation with parents and is also concerned with a serious re-evaluation of the nuclear family, current child-rearing practices and sex roles in our society. George Martell and I are members of Point Blank School, which is attempting to build a neighborhood-based free school in a poor downtown area.

What moves people towards attempting these kinds of alternatives, which so often tend to be small, fragile, short of funds, and take a tremendous amount of energy and determination to keep going? Some people come because they feel pretty strongly that meaningful learning will only take place in an atmosphere of freedom. Others are there because they know in their gut that something very destructive is happening to individuals in the regular system. Nobody starts those things with much of a sense of community, simply because it is rare to have had a communal experience in one's past. Uppermost in people's minds is a wish to be free to pursue their own interests and at the same time have an opportunity to relate meaningfully to others. Strong liberal impulses. Thus the name "free schools" tends to stick to these experiments.

The actual experience of participating in a school community usually turns out to have less liberal freedom than people expect; often it is more like becoming a member of a big, intense clan which is at many times unwilling to leave you alone to pursue your own thing at your own convenience. It does not take long before different temperaments and life styles begin to clash and people discover that their utopias do not match nearly as well as they did in earlier bull-sessions. Common responsibilities emerge, and there is a lot of arguing about how to look after these. "This is the second time David has refused to feed the guinea pigs. I think it is time we had a serious meeting," says my ten-year-old daughter. Seven-year-old David, however, has a very different story to tell. Confrontation and long, intense community meetings become ways to settle disagreements and plan future action. Some people find this kind of community of peers more demanding than the authorities they wanted to escape, and withdraw in disappointment. Others are dismayed by the chaos and inefficiency and leave convinced that human selfishness is an insurmountable obstacle in attempting to create a community where there is no imposed order. Some experiments falter from the very beginning because there is not enough social energy in the group to create a center of life. People find that they can be as lonely living together as by themselves. When the garbage gets too high and the crashers start pouring in, they quickly pick up their things and leave.

Some, however, decide to hang on and struggle to create a new way of living and learning together. For most members, adults and children alike, the most significant experience so far has been that they have started to feel like citizens for the first time in their lives. The new places have become their own, and they experience new dignity in feeling responsible for them and knowing that they are taken seriously by the community as a whole. The result is often the release of new energies in an individual: he may get involved, for the first time perhaps, in serious creative activity or become curious about the world and interested in participating in larger political events. A significant, although still haphazard, educational process is beginning to take shape.

Four school communities have emerged around Toronto in the past couple of years: Everdale, Superschool, Point Blank, and Rochdale (to a lesser extent), and others are on the way. All, however, are so recent that it is hard for us to evaluate them, and much of what we say on the subject is still a bit like whistling in the dark. People that have been engaged in building these communities are convinced of their importance, yet few seriously hope that they can have a significant impact on the educational system unless some fundamental changes take place in the cynical and fragmented society that surrounds them.

A good part of the writing in this collection is by people who are either engaged in developing alternative educational institutions (in which we would include Browndale and the experimental ward at Penetang) or who hope, or have hoped, they might carve out space within the established school system for something approaching a free-school environment. Much of the intent of our authors has been to clarify their own and their contemporaries' experience: both as members of particular communities or as people who have grown up inside the socializing institutions of North America. They are looking for ways to survive as individuals and at the same time to stay relevant as members of society. We have also included some theoretical articles on those socializing institutions (particularly the educational ones): these examine in a general way the tension between individual self-fulfillment and the goal of mass integration within our schools.

The book presents few conclusions and perhaps more bravado than wisdom. It reflects the views of people who are pursuing a rather desperate search for life forces in our civilization. Whether it will be possible for us to combine our strong heritage of bourgeois freedom with the interconnectedness necessary to create a viable human community no one knows. The world may be pushing us too hard, forcing us to shift our priorities in such a way that the will to keep our schools together gradually is dissipated. But at the present time they give one answer—maybe too sane an answer—to the question: "What Can I Do Right Now?"

This Magazine is about Schools
56 Esplanade Street East, Suite 301
Toronto 1, Ontario
Canada

—SATU REPO
JANUARY 18, 1970

CONTENTS

PART I

GROWING UP IN AMERICA

Gail Ashby

the child I was

1

What was important? I'm somewhere deep and long ago this week because my father is in the hospital and, for awhile, I thought he was dying. "Smell the air," he would say after a rain. "Look at the stars." "Listen to that wind." "See how the little tree is growing." "There's a bee's nest in the lilac bush. Come and listen." It was a world where I was free enough to feel things, and I was grateful for that. But it was also a world in which my father and my mother were still fearful. Full of the Depression. Hollow fear. The fear of hard-working people who were careful with their feelings, because that's the way they knew how to survive. Thrift, politeness, morality, discipline. When my father punished us it was always "something that had to be done." No one wanted it; it was out of his control. No one asked "Says who?" or "Why?"

School was like that too. An unpleasant necessity. The important things were the other kids. Tapping maple trees. Picking wildflowers. Collecting tadpoles. Having recess. Going home for lunch. Skipping. Marbles. Boyfriends. We went to school in a four-room brick schoolhouse, where the principal was authoritarian and worshipped brains and gave the strap. But he also believed in children learning all they could take, which was nice for me . . . in the beginning at least. Because I liked to learn, and I was eager for everything. Eventually the reward became important too, and about the fourth grade I grew anxious to learn. Not eager, anxious. My parents' fear got to me too.

But it didn't get to me thoroughly, and I began what I thought at the time was a pretty liveable double life. Polite, quiet, smart at school and at home, I was smart-alecky, seductive and daring with my peers. I was terrified of getting the strap and terrified of failing in school. But in the schoolyard and the backyard, I bullied the little kids, wrote blatantly provocative notes to the boys I liked, led daring snowball attacks on the tough kids everyone else was afraid of, read forbidden books behind the chesterfield, and introduced my friends to the delights of the senses.

I was eleven years old when I started high school. I turned twelve at the end of September. I was also very small for my age. I had no breasts at all, only tenderness where I ardently expected them to be. I knew what being in love was like and I thought about boys and my physical self and sex most of the time. That was nothing new. It had been going on for years. But that last summer before high school I remember vividly. It was the last of something. Something I lost trying to be a member of society, and something I'm trying to get back to.

I grew up in a little village on the outskirts of Ottawa. Until I was fifteen or sixteen that village hardly changed. My friends stayed the same, and when we moved that summer when I was eleven, we moved two blocks away.

There was a river we walked to barefoot at least three times a day all summer. There was a railway track with a path running along beside it through deep grass, which we used as a short cut from school in the daytime and where we flirted outrageously with the boys in the evenings.

I played dolls with my friends quite passionately. That was a strange changing time. We moved easily and naturally, and just as passionately, from dolls and making little dresses for them and playing house to dressing like teen-agers with Veronica Lake hairdos, shoulder purses filled with used lipsticks, combs and empty cigarette boxes . . . to paper dolls that wore the most suggestive clothing, that dressed and undressed each other, postured and finally fucked . . . to erotic, quite realistic drawings of people screwing and saying lewd things to each other complete with gigantic penises and marvelously hairy cunts . . . to hot afternoons in a friend's attic wearing the wild costumes from her mother's theatrical trunk, painting our lips and our little nipples with bright red greasepaint, blueing our eyes and taking turns dancing, discussing each dance and its power to excite and seduce, matching breasts and counting pubic hairs and talking about how we would treat our husbands when we were married.

To all outward appearances we were gangly, freckled little girls. We even wore pigtails and bows occasionally. But our playing and even our playing house had taken a quite different turn from our appearance. Our fantasies included boys or "husbands." And our games slid back and forth from pretend to reality. We fought once be-

cause two of us wanted the same real boy for the same pretend husband. The boys were never there, understand. Only in the evenings were they really there, but in our games we were playing to them. We looked forward to growing up. Because it would mean all those things which were so important to us, which we desired constantly and talked about so openly—sex and having babies, wearing seductive clothes and perfume, and so on.

We had one place where we sometimes shared these feelings with two or three of the boys we had grown up with. We used to meet spontaneously in a little patch of scrub and bush in plain sight of several houses and two streets. We sat under one very large, tangly bush and talked and displayed ourselves and handled each other quite seriously. I remember our seriousness with amazement, and our honesty. "How does that feel?" we would often say. "Do you like that?" and an honest answer would follow and we would try something else. We didn't attempt to make love. We knew all about it, but we weren't too sure about babies and anyway the boys we felt comfortable with sort of put us off that way. They were too familiar.

What got killed, of course, was our honesty. We already led a double life in relation to our parents and our school teachers. Some of our drawings got found, and we acted out being abashed and ashamed while our mothers acted out being horrified and stern. They actually had a good laugh over them, I could tell, and perhaps there was even a hint of admiration in their faces when they lectured us. But for a short time we kids were straight with each other. About what we wanted. About what we felt. About what was important. Significantly, the important things had nothing to do with school or jobs. For the girls, being desired was important. Being beautiful. And touchingly enough, we were certain that we were beautiful. We weren't shy about our bodies or our looks. We expected to be movie stars someday.

I don't think we were wrong. I don't think we had a mistaken idea of reality. We were reality.

It had something to do with our growing up, our childhood. We all had a lot of freedom. Freedom of space. Freedom to play and to be with each other without the interference of adults. But the adults were there. We knew their names and their faces and their weaknesses, and they didn't change or move away. Gardens and fields remained just that, day after day, and houses were always there the next morning.

But that summer when I was eleven and a child, alive and growing, it changed for me. I went away too soon, too fast. And "everybody," the adults, egged me on. Nobody stopped me as I went to High School.

2

Being a teen-ager was terrible. Especially one that was only eleven years old, four feet, eleven inches tall and flat-chested.

My high school was on the outskirts of Ottawa, the city, and I had to leave my familiar village to go to it. On the terrifying brink of being judged and judging myself as a potential woman, I found myself completely alone and friendless in a huge, confusing building filled with hundreds of strangers—none of whom were eleven years old, four feet, eleven inches tall and/or flat-chested.

I was not prepared for this devastating change in my life. Nor did anyone around me appear to understand it. I was terrified. Literally. My heart pounded, and my hands and knees shook. I didn't know where the auditorium was. I sat in the wrong section of seats. The teachers and the principal sitting stiffly on the stage were a far cry from Miss Davis and Mr. Stiles winding a gay march out of the old victrola in the main hall as we filed by. Nobody smiled at me. And the glamorous older students who knew where to sit and what to do breezed by and wouldn't be caught dead speaking to a ninth grader. Of course, there was a morning ritual in assembly, and by the time it was done and no one had explained it to me, and I had stood up and sat down at all the wrong times and gotten lost again on the way to my home room I felt immeasurably guilty. I dared to peep around me only after I found a seat and discovered one of my brotherly loves of the house in the bushes. We had seen, stroked and discoursed on each other's genitals, but now we only nodded to each other distantly. The class was silent. The teacher talked at us. We copied our timetable from the board. He told us we were class 9A, vaguely where to go next, what his name was, read ours from a list, and ticked us off unsmilingly as we acknowledged our own presence. There were about twenty-five of us. From that day on, we spent all day, every day, together for a year, moving from class to class. We had English together, Math together, History, French, Latin, Music, Home Economics or "Shop" together, Phys. Ed. together. We undressed in the same room, smelled each other's sweat, used each other's combs, ate each other's lunches, but we never talked to each other. Never as a group and only rarely one-to-one while we were at school. And we separated when the school day was over. We had no desire to be together. We never got to know each other. I spent five years with at least ten of those same young people and didn't feel any more comfortable with them five years later than I did the first day of school.

The most important things, according to the adults in my life, were attendance, marks, what I was going to do when I "got out" of high school, whether I talked in class or not, whether or not I did my homework, whether or not I was late for school, whether or not I could "do"

Math, History, English, Latin, Science, Music, Home Ec. and Phys. Ed. and get good marks.

The most important things to me and to the other kids were still basically the same. More painful maybe and more secret, but the same. How we looked. What the other kids thought of us. But there were important differences too. How we looked the year before had concerned my face, my hair, and my naked body. How we looked now became a little more dishonest. It was how we dressed. We didn't agonize much about whether or not we knew the countries of Europe or the date of the American War of Independence, until it came to exams and marks and then we agonized a little. What we were constantly tortured about, however, what we were anxious about all those hours of this and that, was how we looked. Whether or not our stocking seams were straight. Whether or not our clothes were "right." Whether or not our skirts were tight enough or our hair in place. Whether or not Bill Dickson was looking and liked me and would he ever ask me for a date. Would I ever have breasts like Elizabeth Purdy? They sort of turned up at the points. Did she fuck? The boys seemed to think she did. And even the male teachers allowed a gust of whistles and suggestive laughter when she walked up to the front. There were dirty girls and girls who weren't. Mary White, for instance, fainted in Home Ec. and some of the girls were laughing afterwards. Was she pregnant? And what about Neil? He never speaks to me any more. Has he told the other boys about us sitting in the little house in the bushes showing ourselves to each other? My stomach would shrivel at the thought. Sex was all-powerful, most important, blatant in everything we laughed at, were afraid of, in every motion and gesture of the class but never acknowledged openly.

We cared desperately day after day what the others thought of us. We never thought to ask. Asking was unheard of. Talking was unheard of too. Particularly about sex, about ourselves. We became more and more afraid of each other sexually. And sex became a weapon. I was used to boys and liked boys, but simple horseplay or joking or any kind of open courtship was a source of laughter. Of course, we laughed away our own fears and our own desires, our uneasiness. But then, and by then, we didn't know what we were about, nor that there was any other way to be or to feel.

We created rules of behavior as we went along. Oh, there were already rules imposed on us. No talking. Ask to leave the room. No chewing gum or swearing. No horseplay. No physical affection displayed in the halls or the classrooms. But our own rules were tighter and fiercer. They had to be. And the punishment more devastating.

We judged each other by the clothing we wore. We loved by the rules of dress and rejected by the same rules. We classed and labelled each other by dress. I realize now that it was the only way we had of judging, of making contact. Visual contact was allowed. No other form of interaction was. Significantly enough, the desirables in terms of dress were the cleanest, the neatest, the most conventional, and the least sexual.

Gone were my dreams of Veronica Lake hairdos and sensual shrugs and tossings of my long, silky hair. If I wanted to be where it was at, some changes would have to be made. God knows I tried. By the beginning of my third year I looked just like everybody else. I even had breasts. But I knew it was a lie even if nobody else did; and I could never quite bring it off—being bright, and clean, and sterile.

I now led a double life even in terms of clothing. Banished to utter privacy about my feelings, not daring to share with any friend who might use my sexual honesty against me, I painted provocative faces on myself in the bathroom mirror, postured nakedly (not without guilt) before the long mirror in the hall when my parents were out and wore red blouses with deep V-necks. I also did not have dates, was not desirable socially, and had no one to ask about it, and because of this I began to suffer severe doubts, about ever being loved or even liked.

The feeling of separation was immense. In terms of where I am now in the present I know it was not just because I started out too young. I wasn't the only person I knew who felt alone. But I can't remember witnessing one expression on the face of any teen-ager I knew of love, fear, anger, loneliness, though we suffered these things all the time. It wasn't allowed. Not anywhere. Not at home, not at school, not even two by two.

We had an accepted language that we spoke, derisive about our own feelings as well as the object of them. I don't remember daring to be visibly moved by anyone or anything past the age of eleven, unless it was death.

On most things we exaggerated our feelings to the point of being ludicrous. "Isn't he cute!" Sigh! Sigh! A dialogue out of a comic book, but it was standard, acceptable behavior. And the boys, though I would have to guess at their dialogues, postured and derided in much the same way. Didn't we all fall heartbreakingly in love, and blush and stutter when the beloved walked by? You'd never know it to hear it. Or see it? Poetry was mush, hand-holding was a signal for loud hoots and hollers, desire was a dirty joke, and we avoided being alone. The girls protected themselves with a gaggle of girls and the boys were sternly guarded by boys.

So afraid were we of our bodies and our desires, we were vulnerable to and hounded by the most deadly feelings of embarrassment.

Far from being understood or reassured by the adults in our lives, our fears and our vulnerability to embarrassment, both physically and emotionally, were used to manipulate us to perform intellectually. There was no worse threat than being singled out in a class by a teacher who "joked." The jokes were always derisive, always pertaining to physical appearance or affectionate behavior. We accepted it. We even liked the teachers who "joked" the best. At least we could laugh and relieve some of the tension. We accepted the most outrageous ridicule and violations of our self-respect as our due. No wonder we practiced the same disrespect on ourselves and each other.

Feeling it out, how it was back there, I wonder how on earth the whole school didn't explode. So much violence and love. Such a force of brand-new sexual feeling. The intellectual activity, the charade of learning, was paper-thin. So many dreary hours of sitting in rooms with dreary people to talk to us about dreary subjects. While we lived in deep fantasy, not allowed a richer, more real outlet, and all that violence and love burnt itself out. Worse still, we never knew. No one ever told us we were brave, or honest, or creative, or beautiful. And we didn't dare to tell each other. Either we were smart, or we weren't. And we racked our heads and hearts at the ages of thirteen and fourteen with what "we would do" when we finished school. That counted. Every year we made decisions affecting "what we would do" and every year the fateful day got closer. We didn't get a chance to practice any of the activities we were choosing as our "vocation" or talk to anyone involved in those activities. It seems incredible now that so much pressure was put on us at that time to clearly decide what we would spend a lifetime doing. With so little information to go on and when so much of real importance was denied us. Like the simple opportunity of talking to each other. Or of just being.

The pressure we put on ourselves to perform socially was just as incredible. Somehow we knew there was a real world to reckon with. It appeared to be a place where having a "vocation" and having someone to love you and be loved were of tremendous importance. It began with having "dates." Having "dates" was more important than how you felt about the person you went out with or how he made you feel. The person didn't exist. Clothes did, or looks, or intellectual or physical prowess, and the real catch was the one who had them all. We simply bought and sold each other.

A teen-age dance was like being up for auction. It was also the first step out of the gaggle and away from the guardians. Oh, they were there, but no longer offering safety or protection. I wanted to be wanted. I wanted to dance, but I felt like a robot and somebody had lost the key. I wanted to be asked, but I didn't have the answer. I wasn't even sure I had a voice. And the moment I stepped out of it, the gaggle would pronounce judgment on me.

I wore lipstick and powder, and my hair fell accidentally over one eye, and my sweater bumped out where it was supposed to and it was the right shade of blue. The room was dark, and sexual expectation dense. If you danced, you would kiss. If you kissed, you would pet. You had physical contact before you exchanged names. Nervous and sweaty and ungainly as hell I danced and flirted with boys I didn't know, might never see again, and found physically repulsive. I allowed them to touch me, hold me, press their faces into my hair, and I came back to the gaggle a heroine. My soul rebelled. (My soul always rebelled.) It rebelled against the humiliation of standing along the wall, of looking eager, of acting eager in the first place, let alone being handled by someone I didn't know. And how many souls rebelled along with me? But I never dared to express it and neither did they. And I never dared to stay away or refuse. Neither did they. We all came home from dances and from frantic dates with stomach-aches, bragging about the wonderful time we had.

The next step out of the gaggle was the group of four or six couples, and more rigid sexual and social expectation. The movement from the group to a one-to-one relationship was a jump. There was no courtship; it wasn't allowed. There was no space or time to explore ourselves. We made our love choices visually and jumped. When we got there we hugged and kissed and petted. What else could we do? Love and desire were still dirty jokes unless you were married, engaged or going steady. We were obliged to "fall in love" before we were allowed the questionable relief of declaring our affections openly. Hopefully we still had some feelings left to express.

3

I'd like to tell you why I began this article.

At present I am teaching at a new free school here in Toronto called Superschool. [Superschool is a free school organized by a number of Toronto high school students unwilling to go back to the regular system. In its second year of operation, it is organized like Everdale, with a limited number of boarders.—EDITOR.] For two years before that I was at The Everdale Place in Hillsburgh. [Everdale is a school community fifty miles outside Toronto. Students and teachers "live in." It is a non-hierarchical community, operating on a consensus basis. All classes are voluntary.—EDITOR.] And I now know that in a free school it can be different for kids than it was for me.

At Superschool we have a very relaxed Open House every week. It's a party at our home—for teen-agers, adults and even occasionally very young kids. When they come to the Open House the teen-agers show little interest in the adults, but I have the impression that they're glad we're there. They seem free to talk, to play, to be with each other, to enjoy being pretty or handsome, to create emotional attachments without the old pressure to perform sexually. Over the months I've seen them growing and having fun. Those have been good evenings for me.

One night a camera crew came to Open House to start filming us for a TV program on the school. They'd spent the day before talking us into it. We'd been pretty disillusioned by the publicity we'd had in the fall, but they promised us a "sensitive" observation and a copy of the film for our own use. After hours of bargaining, we bit.

The camera crew began filming in our kitchen on Open House night. There was a wild game of "Pit" in progress. It's a card game which involves lots of yelling and arm-waving. Then one of the boys began to sing and play guitar, and the camera tuned in on him. Usually he plays and sings alone. Sometimes he's listened to. Often not. There are so many other things to do. This night he was surrounded by kids, all singing their lungs out. The feeling in the air was frantic and competitive and loud.

It was worse the next morning.

My young kids were as high as kites. The peacefulness we had been experiencing disintegrated, and under the influence of the camera's search for excitement, violent music blared from the common room. Our small kids danced wildly for the camera against our perpetual backdrop of sparse furniture, shabbiness and dirt. Wonderful stuff on a free school for television land.

Joey and Alex, who are nine and ten, dumped powdered paint all over the work table in their room. The cameraman was on hand. About two o'clock in the afternoon he photographed the same kids sitting on the same table helping a six-year-old with her reading. I asked him to. He looked out of the window most of the time.

The "sensitive" producer breezed in and asked one of the teen-agers in my presence if the staff were drop-outs too.

One of the girls was crying because she had encouraged the little kids to dance on the cameraman's advice, and the other teen-agers were disappearing into their rooms. I wanted to disappear too, or throw everybody out.

"You can't do that now," I said to myself. "They've been promised a film."

So I joined the discussion underway in the common room, and, primed by the day's irritations, stepped right into the first trap.

"One of the questions people ask about a place like this is how will kids fit into society when they leave? Won't they be misfits?"

I heard myself mouthing the same old reassuring stuff, like at the beginning of the year. Convincing, convincing. "My God, they've all been to the same announcer's school," I thought. I reeled off an appropriate catechism I'd gotten pretty good at, too.

"Isn't this just a 'hippie haven'?" he asked. And again I bit.

But I felt sick and outraged and humiliated. There were now some questions I wanted to ask of society, the society that came to make a "sensitive" film of us and didn't ask us how we felt or what happened, that threw loaded questions at us "to turn us on" and believed that people had to be wheedled and needled to turn on to anything, and that asked us to justify ourselves.

I heard myself reassuring that society about "our kids" and just about vomited.

I knew suddenly and dangerously that I didn't want them to "fit in." And I was very angry. For the child I was, and for other kids.

Childhood in an Indian Village

Wilfred Pelletier

GOING BACK as far as I can remember as a child in an Indian community, I had no sense of knowing about the other people around me except that we were all somehow equal; the class structure in the community was horizontal. There was only one class. Nobody was interested in getting on top of anybody else.

You could see it in our games. Nobody organized them. There weren't any competitive sports. But we were involved in lots of activity (I was not like I am now; I was in pretty good shape at that time) and we were organized, but not in the sense that there were ways of finding out who had won and who had lost. We played ball like everyone else, but no one kept score. In fact, you would stay up at bat until you hit the ball. If somebody happened to walk by on the street, an old guy, we'd tease him and bug him to come over and try to hit the ball, and he would come over and he'd swing away. If they threw us out on first, we'd stay on first anyway. We ran to second, and they would throw us out there, and sometimes we'd get thrown out all the way around.

We had a number of other games we used to play. There was one where we used to try and hit each other between two lines with a ball. It didn't really make any difference if you got hit or whether you stayed in the center and tried to hit the other guy or not. But it was very, very difficult to hit these guys. I remember standing between these two lines, and all of a sudden the guys would take off, and you could be two or three feet from them, and you would have to throw the ball at them, and you just couldn't hit those guys. They were really terrific.

It was later on in life that I began to realize that what we were really doing was *playing*. Very much like animals play. When you observe the bear, the adults, the male and female are always playing with the cubs. The otters do the same thing. None of the kind of play we had was really structured and organized. That came after the recreation directors from the outside world came in and told us that we had a problem in the community, that we were not organized, and they were going to introduce some.

They introduced them all right, and the tremendous competitiveness that went with them. It's not as bad on Manitoulin Island, where I'm from, as it is a lot of other places where competitiveness is rolling in. I'm glad I can remember that as a kid I was able to become involved with a community with others and nobody was competing. Even if we did formally compete in the games we played, no one was a winner though someone may have won. It was only the moment. If you beat someone by pulling a bow and arrow and shooting the arrow further, it only meant that you shot the arrow further at that moment. That's all it lasted. It didn't mean you were better in any way whatsoever. It just meant that at that particular time the arrow went further; maybe it was just the way you let the bow go. These kinds of things are very important to me and that is why I am talking about them and, probably, exploring while I'm talking, now. When I get the opportunity to listen to myself the odd time, I try to explore those kinds of things that I can remember as a child.

One of the very important things was the relationship we had with our families. We didn't always live at home. We lived wherever we happened to be at that particular time when it got dark. If you were two or three miles away from home, then that is where you slept. People would feed you even if they didn't know who you were. We'd spend an evening, perhaps, with an old couple, and they would tell us stories. Most of these stories were legends, and they were told to us mostly in the winter time. In the summer people would generally take us out and we would do a number of things which in some way would allow us to learn about life and what it was all about: that is, by talking about some particular person and demonstrating what that person did. At no time, in all the years I spent there, do I ever remember anyone teaching us anything.

I have been to numerous communities across Canada and I still do not find where Indians teach. All young children were allowed to grow, to develop, to learn. They didn't teach you that this was mommy, daddy, desk, ash tray, house, etc. We learned about these things by listening to the words adults spoke, what they said when they were talking, and built our own kind of relationship with the article. If you observe your children now you will see a child turn a chair over, cover it with a blanket and use it for a house. He can relate many ways to a chair. As we get older we have only one relationship and that is to stick our rear ends on that chair. It's for no other purpose, and, in fact, we tell our kids that that is what it is, and it belongs in a corner and don't move it out of there.

These things I remember very well. We were brought up to have a different relationship to a house and to all the things that surrounded us. That is, the values that adults placed on things in the community did not necessarily carry over into their child and lead him to place the same values on them. Children discovered the values of these things on their own, and developed their own particular relationships to them.

This is very closely related to the religion of the community, which centered entirely on man. One of the practiced ethics of the community was non-interference. No one interfered with us, and this way of living still exists today. If you go to an Indian home the kids don't come up and bug you while you are talking to someone else. They might come and stand by you quietly, just as an adult might. If you observe Indians someplace, they will stand quietly, and only when they are acknowledged will they speak. If they get into a group session, they will act the same way. They will sit and listen to people talk, and when they get the opportunity they will speak, but they won't cut you off or interfere. There are some who do this now, but not very many. Most of them will just wait. The whole background in the educational system was that of observing and feeling. This is how they learned.

It was a very different kind of learning situation that we were in as children. In fact, all of the things we did related to our way of life. Everything had to fit into the whole; we didn't learn things in parts. As an example: if we watched someone running an outboard motor, we would learn everything that was involved in working that motor. If someone taught someone here to do that, after he was finished he might add a safety program on top of it. This would be an additional thing. The way Indians learned it, they built in a safety program while they were learning through their observations and because their very lives depended on their doing it right.

And just as we didn't separate our learning from our way of life, we didn't separate our work from it either. The older women, for example, who used to work all day at whatever—tanning hides, etc.—didn't really think of it as work. It was a way of life. That's the real difference between the kind of society we have now where we equate these kinds of things with work and yet will go out and play sports and enjoy it, and the kind of society I'm talking about. Here, we go and work and use maybe half or a quarter of the energy we spend playing sports, but we call it work and we feel differently about it altogether. These are the kinds of differences that exist. Indian people who had a way of life and who felt it was their way of life didn't call it work. It was part of the way they provided for their families; and they "worked" very hard.

One of the reasons, of course, why they didn't call it "work" was that they didn't have any foremen. As I mentioned before, there wasn't any kind of a vertical structure in the community. In these communities, what existed was a sharing of power. In spite of what everybody says, we really didn't have chiefs, that is, people who were bosses. We had medicine men, who were wise men. The rest were leaders in particular ways. They weren't leaders as we look at them today. It was a different kind of leadership in that the person who was leader had special abilities, say in fishing or hunting. He took the leadership that day, and then discarded the leadership when he was finished with the job. He had power only for the time he wanted to do something. That power came in all forms of all the things he did in the community, so that he used power only for the things he wanted to do, and then he immediately shed it so that someone else could pick it up. It could change hands several times in the community in a day or a week or whatever.

Only in times of war and disaster was a vertical structure used. The war chief would designate various jobs to various people and use that vertical structure. This was only in times of danger. Otherwise, it was horizontal. My grandfather one time told me this, although it didn't sink in until just a few years ago, that to have power is destructive. You'll be destructive if you have power because if people don't join you, then you will destroy them. I forgot this and dug around for power and began to lose friends. I was making decisions for people even with the background I have. Now I have such a problem fighting this thing off, because people are always putting me in a position where I have power. They say I am director of the Institute of Indian Studies. This is not true. I'm just at Rochdale College. [Rochdale College is a residential anti-university. Not much is happening academically, but the creative arts flourish. The College contains an Indian Institute which holds seminars and does some organizing in Canadian Indian communities.—EDITOR.] Where I am everyone makes up their own minds in terms of what they want to do, and they do those things, and if I can be of assistance, then I assist. I've got my own thing that I hope to do. One of the things that I'm interested in is the kind of lives that the young Indian people now at Rochdale live—what is happening to them in the city.

The city has special problems for them as it had for me. For many of them were raised in Indian homes, where the attitude is that no child ever should be rejected. In an Indian home, if a child's face is dirty or his diaper is wet, he is picked up by anyone. The mother or father or whoever comes into the house. He is never rejected. And they don't stick children in cribs, where they can only look in one direction—up. The child generally sits or stands (often tied in), so he can relate to the world in all directions. And children are fed whenever they are hungry. They are never allowed to be in want. Whatever is wanted is given to them. If a child wants to play with something, it is always placed in his hand. No one would think of putting a rattle slightly out of reach, so he would try to grab it and be aggressive. No one would think of feeding the baby only at set times. What follows this approach in terms of attitudes and way of life is immense. The child's nature is very strongly influenced in the first four or five years. The children become very noncompetitive. They have no need to compete.

The whole situation changes, however, when they go out into the world, where the attitudes and values are totally different. A world, further, in which their values are not acceptable. Where for many of us as children we were not even permitted to speak our own language. Of course, we still tried to speak our own language, but we were punished for it. Four or five years ago they were still stripping the kids of their clothes up around Kenora and beating them for speaking their own language. It is probably still happening in many other institutions today. I was punished several times for speaking Indian not only on the school grounds but off the school grounds and on the street, and I lived across from the school. Almost in front of my own door my first language was forbidden me, and yet when I went into the house my parents spoke Indian.

Our language is so important to us as a people. Our language and our language structure related to our whole way of life. How beautiful that picture language is where they only tell you the beginning and the end, and you fill in everything, and they allow you to feel how you want to feel. Here we manipulate and twist things around and get you to hate a guy. The Indian doesn't do that. He'll just say that some guy got into an accident, and he won't give you any details. From there on you just explore as far as you want to. You'll say: "What happened?" and he'll tell you a little more. "Did he go through the windshield?" "Yep!" He only answers questions. All of the in-between you fill in for yourself as you see it. We are losing that feeling when we lose our language at school. We are taught English, not Indian, as our first language. And that changes our relationship with our parents. All of a sudden we begin saying to our parents "you're stupid." We have begun to equate literacy with learning, and this is the first step down. It is we who are going down and not our parents, and because of that separation we are going down lower and lower on the rung because it is we who are rejecting our parents; they are not rejecting us. The parents know that, but they are unable to do anything about it. And we take on the values, and the history of somebody else.

And part of the reason our parents say so little is that that's their way. They don't teach like white people; they let their children make their own decisions. The closest they ever got to formal teaching was to tell us stories. Let me give you an example. We had been out picking blueberries one time, and while sitting around this guy told us this story. The idea was that he wanted to get us to wash up—to wash our feet because we had been tramping through this brush all day long. He talked about a warrior who really had a beautiful body. He was very well built, and he used to grease himself and take care of his body. One day this warrior was out, and he ran into a group of other people whom he had never seen before. They started to chase him. He had no problem because he was in such good shape. He was fooling around and playing with them because he was such a good runner. He ran over hills and over rocks, teasing them. Then he ran into another group. The first group gave up the chase. But now he had to run away from this other group, and he was fooling around doing the same thing with them. All of a sudden he ran into a third group. He ran real hard and all of a sudden he fell. He tried to get up and he couldn't. He spoke to his feet and said, "What's wrong with you? I'm going to get killed if you don't get up and get going." They said, "That's alright. You can comb your hair and grease your body and look after your legs and arms but you never did anything for us. You never washed us or cleaned us or greased us or nothing." He promised to take better care of the feet if they would get up and run, and so they did.

This is one of the stories we were told, and we went up and washed our feet right away and then went to bed. Maybe this happens among other ethnic groups, I don't know, but this is the kind of learning we had. I will never forget the kinds of things we learned, because to me it all belongs to me. It isn't something that someone says is so; it's mine. I'd want to go hunting, and the guys would know I couldn't get across the stream because it was flooded, but they wouldn't say anything. They'd let me go, and I'd tell them I'd see them later where the rocks are, and they'd say O.K. knowing all this time I couldn't get through. But they wouldn't tell me that. They'd let me experience it. And I'm grateful to these people for allowing me to have this kind of exploration/learning situation. Secondly, of course, the fact is that maybe I could have gotten across where they couldn't, discovered something different, a method that was new. I think this kind of learning situation is one of the really important things that Indians have today and which could contribute to the society we have today. That is, a learning situation *for people,* instead of teaching or information giving.

All these things—the various ways Indian life differed from that of our present society—I didn't learn until after I left the reserve community later on in life. Then I could understand how very differently structured the two communities are. While it didn't have a vertical structure, our community was very highly structured. So highly structured that there wasn't anything that could happen that somebody couldn't almost immediately, in some way, solve, whatever problem arose. Without any given signals or the appearance of any communication whatsoever (there were no telephones) the most complex social action used to happen. If somebody died in that community, nobody ever said: We should dig a grave. The grave was dug, the box was made, everything was set up . . . the one who baked pies baked pies. Everyone did something in that community, and if you tried to find out who organized it, you couldn't.

It's exactly the same way today. You cannot find out who organizes these things. In 1964, Prime Minister Pearson came up to the reserve. He had a cocktail party in the hall, and at the same time there was a big buffet organized for him. This was organized by a woman from Toronto. She went up there and set this whole thing up. He had been coming there every year. This was his riding. Every year they turned out a beautiful meal for him, and he never knew who to thank because it was just all of a sudden there; it was done. The people just got together. There was no foreman or boss. There was no vertical structure, and it just happened. You should have been there in '64. It was chaotic. There were no knives, no desserts, nobody had cut up the heads of lettuce that were all over, because this woman came there and gave orders, and the people wouldn't do anything until she told them what to do. She got so busy that she couldn't tell everybody what to do, and she had four or five turkeys all over the town in different people's ovens, and that's where they sat. They had to go and tell the women to bring the turkeys down because they wouldn't do it on their own. There was someone in charge. Had there not been anyone in charge it would have gone off fine. It was a real mess. This is the difference. Here you organize, and you know those kinds of structures, and they mean something to you. You instinctively behave in certain ways to those things.

But it's more than that too. As I see it, organization comes out of a need for immediate order—say in war. When it develops this way so that people say let's organize, and they get together and create a vertical structure, and place somebody up at the top and then it becomes a power group, and from there on it filters on down until after a while you have somebody running that organization, two or three people or maybe eventually just one, and all the rest of the people get suppressed, pushed down, and held down by that very thing they formally sought. You give power to someone and suppress others.

I don't know if a different kind of structural organization can exist today. I know some people are trying to make a different one—some people in Rochdale College and I suspect in many places where people are getting together and trying to live communally. I remember as a child a different kind of organization existing, and I have come to call it now "community consciousness." That community can exist and function and solve all its problems without any kinds of signals, like a school of fish. All of a sudden you see them move; they shift altogether. That is exactly the way most Indian communities function. And yet we have the Department of Indian Affairs coming and telling us we have no organization. The local priest or minister will come and tell us we have to be organized. The Recreation Department will come along and say there's no organization in this community. And when they come it's like shooting a goose in a flock of geese. When you hit him you disrupt the pattern. So every time somebody comes into the community they disrupt the pattern. Every time you remove a resource person from the community you disrupt the pattern. You break it up, and they have to reorganize. But in a lot of communities this is very hard to do, and some of them have been too hurt to make it. Indian resource people begin to drop out of sight and white organizers take over, making it even more difficult for Indian people to function. I know that in one community where there are 740 people (about two-thirds of them children), there are eighteen organizations. There are three churches that all have two or three organizations, and there is also a community development officer who has a number of organizations behind him, and they are in such conflict that the community cannot function. It's just sitting there, with people at each other's throats. The people who come in can't understand that if a guy is sitting under a tree and doing nothing but observing the stars or the clouds in the daytime or the birds flying, he is running through a recreational pattern and at the same time he is learning. These are all parts of a whole. Most Indian people deal with wholeness. It is much different than the way we deal with things where we segment them and deal with them only in parts.

It is also very difficult to know what to do now—now that the organizers have come in. The dependency is so great and government and outside resources have created this dependency. They have removed most of the human resource and certainly all the economic base from most Indian communities and there is very little left. Yet the Indian relationship to that dependency is much different from ours in this society. Indians may receive welfare, but most of them feel it is a right. They don't look down on people who are on welfare. Drawing welfare doesn't change the nature of the person. In the same way, if they walk into a room that is messy they don't say the woman is sloppy. They say the room is sloppy. A lot of them don't paint their houses. That is because they don't have the same relationship to that house that we in this society do. Clothes don't make the man. Relationships are built on something that is not materialistic. The same thing applies to money. If you observe your children when they have money, they want to get rid of it right away. How long do children stay mad at one another? A moment. All of these behavior patterns that you observe in children are very much related to adult Indians. Your history books say that when the white men first came here they noted that the Indians were very child-like. That is very true in many ways. But if you look at it, how beautiful to be child-like and yet be mature. Here we say that you mustn't show feelings. I don't agree with that. If a man can cry, then he has feelings. Indians cry all the time. We get together and sing songs, and we cry in these songs. But this society is very machine-like, and so we begin to act like machines and then we become machines.

Because of this approach Indians don't really want to fight for their rights. They really don't want to get into the society at all. In this way they are probably different from the black people on this continent who are a much larger group, and have no choice but to fight for their rights. When they get these rights, what they are doing in essence is moving into society. When they do get in, they might make the changes they want in terms of their cultural background or how they look at things, or whatever, and these changes may give them the freedom to practice or do those things they want to do.

But the Indians have fundamentally rejected society as it now is. The Indians are expert at making all programs that the Indian Affairs Branch has ever come up with, a failure by withdrawing. The Indians embrace everything that comes into a community. If you want to build a church, that's fine. We'll help you build that church, etc. Then once they see that they can't relate to that church in any way, they withdraw and the thing falls apart. If you want to build a road, they'll help you build one, with the result that some reserves have roads running all over the place, but nobody uses them. The Branch has a history of complete failure. The Indians have always rejected it. We have a society here where we must win. For everything you do you must end up fighting—fighting for your rights, good against evil, war against poverty, the fight for peace. The whole base of Western culture has an enemy concept. What would happen if you remove the enemy? How then do you defeat somebody who is on your side? I suspect that if you remove the enemy the culture might collapse. The Indian can't fight on your terms. For a start he doesn't even have the numbers, much less the inclination. So he withdraws. And he pays a certain price. He suffers poverty in many ways.

But maybe the future is with the Indian. Marshall McLuhan says that the only people living in the twenty-first century are the Indians, the Eskimos, some French people and the Japanese. All the rest, because they deal with history, live in the nineteenth century because they deal with the past and not the present. The pan-Indian movement, with the Native American Church, recognizes this and there are various Indian cultures that are moving closer and closer together. It's a spontaneous thing that just happened. It's just growing and there isn't anyone who is heading it up. It's a movement. And it's made me much more hopeful.

SARAH SPINKS

A LITTLE GIRL learns to be attractive and gentle. "Isn't Stephanie pretty? Say 'pretty,' pretty Stephanie." And we lead her off to look in the mirror to see for herself how pretty she is. The girlish tricks of lowering her eyes, and sighing and whining when she wants something.

Coquetry, not sexuality, is what we encourage. We mystify a small girl's experience of her body by telling her that her sexual organs are for having babies, or that babies grow in mummy's tummy, not in her womb. With most of her sexual organs hidden, her sexuality is diffused and mysterious. But we diffuse it more by talking about her as mother and not as a woman. When asked what sex means we say, "Sex is about mummies and daddies and having babies."

The little girl follows us around the kitchen, helping to stir a cake, setting the table, or helping with the baby when her mum is busy. Even at this age, the girls are expected to be better helpers, more natural substitutes for the parents than the boys.

The toys help this too. Mothers all do the same thing; fathers do many things. Sitting in a corner of the kitchen, the little girl bakes her cake in her easy-bake oven, puts on a little eye shadow from her miniature cosmetic set or puts one of her countless dolls to bed. Maybe, since it's 1969, she's a modern kid who plays with a Barbie doll and she puts her in a four-poster bed in a diaphanous yellow nightgown.

Her brothers, on the other hand, are expected to be "men." They play with GI Joes and building sets. Instead of ovens and dolls they have trains and chemistry sets. Their toys orient them up and out. They are moving toys, loud toys, and they take the boys outside the house for action and adventure.

Books contain the message too—books like *I Want To Be A Dentist* by C. Greene:

> "I think I will be a dentist when I grow up," said Johnny.
>
> "Johnny liked to work with his hands. He carved animals out of soap. He made things out of clay. He put together a space-ship model."
>
> "Betsy couldn't read, so Johnny made some signs for her with pictures on them."
>
> "Then one day, Johnny had an idea. He said to Betsy, 'You can be a dentist's nurse.' "
>
> "I'd like that, said Betsy." [1]

or this one, entitled *Whom Shall I Marry?:*

> "Primrose was playing house. Just as she finished pouring tea for her dolls she began to think. She thought and

[1] Carla Greene, *I Want To Be a Dentist* (Chicago, Children's Press, 1960).

> thought and she thought some more: 'Whom shall I marry?' "
>
> "Whomever shall I marry?"
>
> "I think I shall marry a mailman. Then I could go to everybody's house and give them their mail."
>
> "Or I might marry a policeman. I could help him take the children across the street."
>
> "But if I marry a fireman it will be exciting. I'll ring the bell real loud and everybody will get out of the way. Maybe though I ought to marry a doctor. I would be his nurse and we would help people be strong and healthy."
>
> "Or perhaps a man who owns a bookstore. Then I could find the most wonderful books for my friends to read." [2]

Perhaps her bedtime story may be more subtle and full of fantasy. Instead of a dentist's nurse or an ice-cream man's helper, she can be a beautiful maiden or an ugly witch. She can be Rapunzel, Snow White or Sleeping Beauty. She can be a witch wreaking havoc all over the forest or a stepmother who sets traps for people by poisoning apples. But most of all, she is the one who is given life by a man. Sleeping Beauty and Snow White, of course, are actually brought back to life by the kiss of a princely adventurer.

Many children don't read much any more. They are television watchers. They understand the life of Betty and Fred Flintstone as well as we knew about Nancy Drew and Ned, her boyfriend, who drove a yellow roadster. But besides Betty Flintstone and Lucy of the "I Love Lucy" show, there is "Bewitched" and "The Flying Nun." These women have new powers which are at once anti-scientific, anti-technical; a part of their own history, as witches and fairies. The men on television are private eyes and space adventurers, who are doing the killing. The women, however, must leave the house more surrep-

[2] Arnold Spilka, *Whom Shall I Marry?* (New York, Holiday House, 1960). Copyright © 1960 by Holiday House. Reprinted by permission.

titiously: they don't go out after the dishes are done; they make them disappear.

If I was a witch
I would turn the princess into a giant . . .
Then I would make her tear down
The whole world.
I would rule the land.
Everyone who would come to me
I would cut off their heads
Or turn them into fruits
For the giant to eat them . . .
When everybody is dead
I will turn into the Princess
And do what I want . . .

—CATHY BISO, 11

The toys and the books and television programs say to a little girl: you have no worth in yourself. A girl-child exists in relation to a boy or a man. She is a dentist's nurse, an ice-cream man's helper, or the woman who gives sleepyhead Flintstone a hand with his shave in the morning.

Now, people aren't born with egos. They get their sense of themselves through analyzing and feeling an experience and trying to imagine and feel another person's experience of the same situation. If we are sensed by others as inessential, as existing only in relation to another, then we do not exist otherwise. We are genuinely unreal. Alone, even fleetingly, we fantasize that we are persons above ourselves, looking down upon us, watching us move mechanically. We become schizophrenic.

On the surface, schools don't seem to teach girls that they're different. But they do. They do it overtly by giving them different subjects like home economics and shop and by dividing them into different classes for gym and health education. But it is the complicated web of many subtler things that is more important: mother is the shopper in arithmetic problems, the cozy town family in the Dick and Jane readers, the cozy inner-city family of the Bank Street Readers, the encouragement of "feminine" qualities of neatness and docility. The point of feminine dependence is made indirectly. As Friedenberg says in *This Magazine is About Schools:*

> In the schools, more than in most of the other mass media, it is indeed true that the medium is the message, which is one reason that I haven't said a word about curriculum. What is taught isn't as important as learning how you have to act in society, how other people will treat you, how they will respond to you, what the limits of respect that will be accorded to you really are.[3]

The message of thc school never seriously questions the sanctity and necessity of the nuclear family; or the "natural" role of a woman as eternal mother and housewife.

The little girl reacts very sanely to this situation. She begins at the age of ten or eleven to look for a man. She perceives very clearly that that is what she is supposed to do and so she goes ahead.

She begins to be very attentive to her clothes and hair styles. She begins to fantasize about movie stars, about Pierre Trudeau, and about her future husband.

But she's rather dismayed, having made her hair shiny with Londonberry Hair Shiner, to go to the school dance and find that the boys are not the slightest bit interested in dancing with her. The boys are off in a corner, fooling with doughnuts and orange drinks. They're boisterous as they run up and down the stairs of the school. They're not very aware of what the girls are up to. "The boys," say the girls to each other, "are so immature." "They just act

[3] Edgar Friedenberg, "What The Schools Do," *This Magazine,* III, No. 1, Issue 9 (1969), p. 33. This article appears below pp. 391–404.

stupid; they're not interested, you know, 'cause they're a couple of years behind us." She internalizes a definition of maturity which is the early acceptance of quietness, obedience, and poise. Because these are character traits instilled in her from the time she is one, and because they correspond to the demands of the school system, she often does better at school. Which is why she's called more mature. She also accepts and feels her social position earlier than boys for he will be most seriously oppressed as a producer, and the full force of that oppression hits him later.

But to return to the kids at the dance. There is a subtle game going on which builds on the sexual quality of the little girls as witches and princesses. The game has many names. It is called "You have the control," or, "Let's just be friends." On the one hand, the girls are temptresses—they push to have the boys dance with them. On the other hand, they are the princesses—white and pure—they are counselled not to kiss a boy on the first date. Boys are portrayed as sexual and lustful. Girls are the ones that react with reason and logic. When, later on, they are asked to make love, they answer in societal terms, "I can't sleep with you, because we're not married." And the more mystified version, "I'm only going to sleep with the man I love and he'll probably be the man I marry."

Of course, children are becoming freer about sex. The girls are losing their repression, but not their sexual oppression. The sexual hierarchy within the hippie and rock communities is still strong. The language is indicative. People "ball." Girls are "balled." The supreme compliment for a girl is, "she has balls."

Balling is a game, like dating. It is a status game with the target being to ball the man with the most status, usually a musician. If you ball Country Joe then you're a "chick" with status. If you ball a little fish then you're a little fish yourself. There are many gradations of this chick status, but it doesn't look much different from the phenomenon of the gang girls who wear "I am Buster's" on their black leather jackets. The hippie girls, at their most sophisticated, those frcm Los Angeles, New York and San Francisco, call themselves groupies, which means that they hang around the rock groups like the Jefferson Airplane and the Grateful Dead or The Doors. The groupie girls are supposed to keep hip. A girl in these circles should know the difference between the bass and lead guitar. She should know the music, but she should know better how to be an outrageously good screw. This way she can get to the top. In *The Rolling Stone,* a well-written folk rock magazine, a groupie named Henri says:

> Musicians should pay a lot more attention to the good thing they have going for them—groupies, I mean. After all, a groupie is a non-profit call girl. Like a Japanese geisha in many ways, and a friend and a housekeeper and pretty much whatever the musician needs.[4]

or Anna:

> It's nice when people come into the store now and mention so-and-so is coming into town and you can just drop a bomb on them, you know. Like you say I'm going to ball so-and-so. And later on, that person comes to town and they go backstage and there you are. It's kind of fun. It's like *I told you so*. Those are games. Those are beautiful, beautiful fun games . . . Some of the limelight is on you, too. You're in the room. You're involved . . . Spending three or four days with one person, you, uh, . . . under those circumstances meals are served on carts and photographs are being constantly taken and you can leech off the feeling and it's a gas.[5]

[4] Burks, Hopkins, & Nelson, "The Groupies and Other Girls," *The Rolling Stone,* No. 27 (San Francisco; February 15, 1969), p. 11.
[5] *Ibid.,* p. 23.

As Dr. David Smith, head of the Haight-Ashbury Medical Clinic, says in the same article:

> Within a certain subculture in San Francisco, rock is the basic art form . . . It's the same as straight culture in a way where bankers are attractive to young girls. They've got the money and power. In this community, rock musicians occupy that role.[6]

Now it is doubtful that many young girls are turned on to bankers. Bankers lack "bizazze"—they have no element of risk about them, they have no style. In a straight community, a girl is more likely to be turned on to a lawyer who takes on some civil rights cases, one who appears to be beating the system with the system's own tools. But the point that Smith makes about the hierarchy is valid. The high priestess, someone like Janis Joplin, is a lone woman amongst the priests: The Grateful Dead, The Mothers, The Rolling Stones, and Country Joe and the Fish. The models of the rock community are male.

But the girl in the hip community does experience a sense of liberation in the fact that she can not only consummate her sexual relationships but she can also initiate them. The dating gamesmanship goes. In this way, the hippie culture is less repressive. The ideology of the community does not accept competitive ethics either in work or in play. It is unfortunate that the kids must sell their dope at a high profit to stay alive.

The culture of the rock community is based on sensuality and passivity. It is a culture of music and drugs. Girls can get stoned. They can roll their own joints. They participate in a grand dressing-up, a costuming that blurs sexual differences. The costumes are part of the theatre of the absurd. The kind of extravaganza that the Rochdale-Yorkville kids wear has a duality. It protects them from

[6] *Ibid.*, p. 12.

unreality. It reminds them that they exist. In a visual culture, they are what they dress up as. The younger girl in a mountie hat, a studded vest and psychedelic bell-bottoms is responding to and creating a media image.

But, despite, her feeling of being plastic and consumptive she is also giving a repressive culture a good kick in the face. She outrages the authorities who try to control the length of her skirt and the length of her hair and the neighbors who despise her messiness. Although she assumes her traditional role by dressing up, her new front is a serious affront to the established order.

The experience of The Everdale Place, a free school near Toronto, is interesting in that it combines a hippie fluidity and a solid geographical community.

At the school the students can do pretty much what they want. It is a communal existence—all the students and staff share equally in the decisions. It emphasizes directness and it encourages people to defend their opinions on matters of school policy. Within this freer atmosphere, most children flourish. It is interesting, though, to note that it is the girls in the school who seem to be the leaders. They are the ones with the most verve, anger and aggressiveness, and I think they are for a number of reasons.

The sexuality that the male staff feel toward the female students is direct and open. It is expressed in touching, dancing, wrestling and cuddling. But it is understood clearly by both students and staff that they do not sleep with each other. This gives the kids the chance to be direct and safe in the understanding that they will not get into a situation they cannot handle. At the same time, the attraction of the young girls for the male staff means that the girls get a lot more attention than the boys.

The boys, on the other hand, are faced with a rather formidable challenge, for at least half of the eight male staff members are extremely competent in traditionally male pursuits. Three of the men have designed and built two buildings on the property. Three or four of them are good mechanics. All are rugged and physically strong. With the physical aspects of the school being so central to its existence, the boys find themselves competing in a field crowded by experts, and they are forced to form their image of themselves in an area in which there is little chance for initial success. The girls, who are not expected to do the heavy wiring and construction work, can take part with the assurance that any effort on their part will be highly praised. . . . Of course, the mood of Everdale is so fluid and unpredictable that I make these observations with no sense of finality.

But, to get back to the schools and the straighter kids . . . . We have recently witnessed in Ontario a resurgence of sex-segregated classes. The reasons for dividing up the boys and girls vary in the minds of the administrators and teachers. The two that I hear most are these: Since most elementary school teachers are women, the little Canadian boy is getting "a prissy grade school education." Secondly, the girls mature faster than the boys so they have to split them up. This distortion of the meaning of maturity I've already dealt with. As for the prissy education the boys are supposed to be getting—the fact is, though the women are teachers, the men are principals, and the authority patterns are quite clear to the children. If the kids are going to be emasculated, then that will happen because school sees its duty as being to quantify and to package. Its predisposition to neatness and its destruction of the boy's mind is the enemy, not the female teacher. And the boys will be made impotent when they realize that the promise of a creative and human future is a lie.

But the girls aren't even laboring under the liberal illusion that the society has a place for them apart from their role as a man's wife or a child's mother. They don't get the chance of being undercut, for they start out by having their minds colonized. In terms of the black struggle, the problem looks like this: It is accepted by many that part of the reason why children can't be educated is because they have few successful models with whom to identify. Further, their models of success are white men and they can strive to be like the white man, but they never lose their black skin. In a racist society, that means they can never be successful; in an individualist society, it means they blame their lack of success on themselves. In the same way, women cannot be successful because we live in a society that sees women being inessential to production. . . . Now our oppression is more comfortable. We are allowed more than watermelon and rhythm. We are allowed houses and gadgetry and for many of us, physical comfort. But our minds have been colonized in much the same way. We cannot conceive of ourselves as childless. The thought of being single at the age of thirty horrifies us. We cannot conceive of ourselves with a project or a future which is important for itself. Most girls when faced with the possibility of pursuing difficult studies and jobs, back down like the girl whom Betty Friedan interviewed:

> I loved it. I got so excited about my work. I could sometimes go into the library at eight in the morning and not come out until ten at night. I even thought I might want to go to graduate school or Law School and really use my mind. Suddenly, I was afraid of what would happen. I wanted to lead a rich, full life. I want to marry, have children, have a nice house. Suddenly, I felt, what am I beating my brains out for? So this year I'm trying to lead a well-rounded life. I take courses, but I don't read eight books and still feel like reading the ninth. I stop and go to the movies. The other way was harder and more exciting. I don't know why I stopped. Maybe I just lost courage . . .[7]

[7] Betty Friedan, *The Feminine Mystique* (New York, W. W. Norton & Co. Inc., 1963), p. 155.

It is the feeling that many young girls experience—that to be excited about their work is to forfeit their femininity. Despite a real passion to learn and to act, there is always the lingering doubt, this implicit disbelief in their own abilities, that makes them drop their commitments when they find a man. They say, like the college girl quoted above,

> Well, I guess I just lost courage . . .

It is pretty hard to maintain your courage when you are constantly faced with comments like this: "Well, you know so-and-so, she's a very castrating woman." When girls start to get stronger, they get written off by therapists as neurotic, too demanding and dominating of the men around them. People say, "Be tough, but don't lose your femininity."

The comments about castration are a popularized form of Freudianism. Various child psychologists like Erik Erikson, educational reformers like Edgar Friedenberg and Paul Goodman, and most psychiatrists in America today are Freudian-based. I have two reactions to Freudian psychology. One is an anger over his theories on femininity; the other is more complex. It is a feeling that this is the very time in history that we need a psychology which places its emphasis on *the structure of society* rather than on the individual apart from that structure. Right now, numerous people in America—students, workers and professional people—feel that there is no place for them in the society. If they work at factories or secretarial jobs, they simply work to live. They earn money and have no time to enjoy the things they spend it on. And no sense of purpose or creativity about their jobs. And, if they are mothers, their satisfaction lies in the vicarious status they get from their kids' marks at school or their child's possibility of a good job.

What I am arguing is that we must go much beyond Freud; indeed we have to change our emphasis. The potential of the technology of the late sixties, the potential of American capitalism to determine our environment and *our responses to it* makes a different approach to psychology mandatory.

But let's get back to exactly what Freud said—particularly about little girls. He seems to base his theories about human identity on a person's inborn and innate characteristics. His primal estrangements and inner dynamic. A child is born with an individual historical sense of primal man, original sin, and the Eden of the womb. The nature of man—his rationality, his emotions and sexuality—is largely determined by childhood experience, particularly sexual experience. For little girls, the central childhood experience involves the castration complex, or penis envy.

> The castration complex of girls is also started by the sight of the genitals of the other sex. They at once notice the difference, and it must be admitted, its significance too. They feel seriously wronged, often declare that they want "to have something like it too" and fall a victim to "envy for the penis," which will leave *ineradicable* traces on their development . . .[8]

Later on, Freud repeats, this wish for a penis is sublimated into trying to achieve like a man—pursuing a career, deciding not to have children.

> The wish for the longed-for penis, eventually, in spite of everything, may contribute to motives that drive a mature woman to analysis and what she may reasonably expect from analysis—a capacity, for instance, to carry on an intellectual profession—may often be recognized as a sublimated modification of this repressed wish.[9]

[8] Sigmund Freud, *New Introductory Lectures on Psychoanalysis* (New York, W. W. Norton & Co. Inc., 1965), p. 125.
[9] *Ibid.*, p. 125.

According to Freud, when little girls discover their castration, they are lifted out of their closeness to their mother whom they blame for their lack of a penis. They also renounce clitoral masturbation in envy of the "boy's superior equipment" and turn to their father as love object. They see their mother as also castrated and start to fantasize about having their father's baby. The wish for the baby begins to replace the wish for the penis which they hope to possess vicariously by having a boy. The girl enters the Oedipal stage. Her true rivalry with her mother, hidden when she was younger, is intensified. But, unlike the boy who transcends or sublimates his libidinous feelings for his mother, the girl, Freud believes, remains in a romance and dependence on her father. The boy must abandon the Oedipal situation for fear that his mother will castrate him. In transcending and repressing this complex, the boy develops a super-ego which pushes him outward upon the world. The same super-ego does not exist in the girl and for this reason she finds it difficult to play other than a passive or immanent role.

How is one to question this? It seems like such a neat and tidy explanation of feminine passivity. But where the fallacy lies in both the Freudian approach and in the work of behaviorists is that little girls, as I have tried to show in the rest of this paper, learn their roles very young. And there is a reason that they are trained into this role. If a child is brought up to believe that she can be nothing more than a wife and mother, then her admiration may well go to a boy who she perceives to have a more challenging life. If she sees that other people expect more of boys—allow them to be more violent and sloppy and selfish, then boys are treated with envy. If, in fact, childbearing had the same importance in our society as production, then we may well experience the reverse of penis envy. Boys would envy their sisters who could produce the coveted child. Unfortunately, despite the mystification of childbearing and motherhood, having babies does not compare in status to having a job. And despite efforts of women's rights groups, if the economy of a country cannot operate with more than a certain percentage of its labor force employed, then there is a structural reason that the popular psychology of women's magazines places them in the home.

So when we're trying to discover our identities, we must look primarily at our relation to the rest of society, to production and not search so hard for our "inner selves."

We also have to look closely at the function of the family. Laurel Limpus has already written well on this topic in *This Magazine is about Schools,* but I would like to elaborate on a particular point that she makes. It is the rather subtle mechanism by which mothers absorb the personality of their children. The child is all the mother has and she is around most of the time. What happens is that she destroys the child's autonomy by pre-empting his natural curiosity. She seeks to explain things to him before he has experienced them. She shows him that combs are for running through one's hair, not for dragging along the edge of the table and making a funny noise. Everything the child does is turned into a "learning experience." The mother in fact becomes a professional mother. She begins to use the withdrawal of her affection, *in a benevolent way,* to make the child conform to her wishes. She acts *always in the best interests of the child.* And if the child protests that what she does is not in his interest, he is likely to be termed deviant, or "going through a stage." These are ways of invalidating children. Look at this dialogue between mother and daughter:

MOTHER: Well, that's how it appeared to us—that you were selfish.

MARY: How was I selfish?

MOTHER: Well, I can't remember now, but I do know that—

MARY: No, you won't tell me now, so I don't know how —so if I get better again I won't know if I'm right or wrong or when I'm going to crack up again or what I'm going to do.

MOTHER: Now that's what I call selfishness, thrusting your opinions on me and not listening to mine.

MARY: Well, you were thrusting your opinion on me and not listening to *mine*. You see it works both ways.

MOTHER: I know.

MARY: But I always have to take it when I'm at home from you, because *you're my mother. See—I can't be selfish—but if you're selfish that's not wrong. You're not ill because you're selfish, you're just my mother and it's all right if you can do it.*[10]

Education reformers like Paul Goodman perpetuate a basically Freudian view of girlhood. Goodman is the most blatant. In the introduction to *Growing Up Absurd,* he states:

(I say "the young men and boys" rather than the "young people" because the problem I want to discuss in this book belongs primarily in our society, to the boys: how to be useful and make something of oneself. A girl does not "have" to, she is not expected to "make something" of herself. Her career does not have to be self-justifying, for she will have children, which is absolutely self-justifying, like any other natural or creative act. With this background it is less important, for instance, what job an average young woman works at 'till she is married)[11]

The mistake Goodman makes is first of all assuming that all women are going to have children and second of all, assuming that it is a natural act which is self-justifying. In fact, there are few natural acts which are not now per-

[10] R. D. Laing and A. Esterson, *Sanity, Madness and the Family* (New York, Basic Books, 1965), p. 206.

[11] Goodman, Paul, *Growing Up Absurd* (New York, Random House, 1960), p. 13.

verted. Sexuality is exploited to make us consume more. Our children grow up in an isolated family unit which is oppressive to its members. As to the self-justifying nature of procreation, the large numbers of women who are meeting across this country are not doing so because they find their "woman's lot" self-justifying.

Friedenberg, at least, is more self-conscious of the problem. Berated by Bettelheim for ignoring the plight of girls in his book the *Vanishing Adolescent,* he attempts to talk about girls in a later essay. But in the end, Friedenberg is in love with the adolescent boys, "the hot-blooded minority," the Finnys and Holden Caulfields. And as a man with profound respect for a Freudian like Erik Erikson, he ends up wanting to protect gentlemanly virtues. He wants to protect the autonomy of individuals. He wants private and aristocratic men with a fine sense of irony. This view is naïve and hurtful. Not only because Finny and Holden don't articulate a *feminine* sense of outrage, but because the call for autonomy and privacy—the civil libertarian stance—is an immoral and impossible wish on a continent dissolving before our very eyes.

The insanity that is distant, cool and apart is far worse than the madness that makes us act with passion. It is the first insanity that the society applauds. It is the coolness of the Trudeaus. Instead of wishing for privacy and autonomy, we must be public people acting in the world. The more we act politically, the more we will be defined as deviant and neurotic. Bettelheim recently said that the student rebels were acting out of "intense guilt feelings." People look for lesbians in the women's liberation groups. But we can reject those definitions. We can stop looking inside ourselves, for ourselves. We should accept the fact that we are becoming "the people our parents warned us against."

It is sad that any person must struggle so hard to do what he wants to do. It is a lonely struggle, and young girls find it even lonelier and harder than boys. It is a fundamentally alienating experience for both sexes. I understood better when I was in Cuba last summer the small but concrete ways this alienation manifests itself.

The buses in Cuba are crowded with people. You are lucky to make it to the door for your stop. When I'd ask directions from someone, everyone in the bus would start arguing and gesticulating about the quickest and simplest route. But it wasn't just the spontaneity, the laughing and aggressive pushing and touching. What impressed me more was that women, standing with babies in their arms, could quite freely put their child down in the lap of the person sitting in front of them. They weren't afraid. They didn't have to struggle alone, like we do in Toronto subways, hoping that our child won't cry. In Cuba, the women didn't have to be urban guerrillas—constantly watching for washrooms, seats and tables.

I went into day nurseries, filled with *chicorroticos,* little ones, brought by their mothers on the way to the field and the office. They were tiny, some of those babies, and they looked not a bit neglected.

And I worked in the fields with some of their mothers. They had a clear sense of working to build a communal society in which everybody could share heavy physical work and tough political decisions. And it was experiencing and seeing how deeply they incorporated the nation's necessity to survive, that I understood *emotionally* and not intellectually, our oppression. For we have not only been robbed *as women* of a place in the world, we have been robbed *as people* of a cultural identity and a national purpose.

watching my children watching TV

SATU REPO

THERE IS NO DOUBT that my eight-year-old daughters are better informed, more skeptical, and more irreverent than I was at their age. Yet the kind of education they are receiving is not noticeably different from the one I had. I think it has something to do with all the TV they watch.

Recently they were competing at who could draw more pictures of people in different countries. They drew Arabs with tents and camels, tribal Africans, Indians in saris and turbans charming snakes in stone vessels, Chinamen surrounded by pagodas and Japanese sipping tea in kimonos, Eskimos, Laplanders, Dutch people, Englishmen—all coming with some characteristic detail that made them easily recognizable. I asked them how they found out how all these people looked and they said on TV, of course.

And if you ask them where they learn most about the world, they put TV on the top of the list. Talking to adults is next; then comes books; and lastly, school. Even after finishing grade one they had not yet begun associating school with learning. "School is a place where they teach you manners and rules and things like that," one of them said to me.

These girls of mine have been avid TV watchers ever since we got an old TV set three years ago. There are no restrictive rules about watching it in our household; there is only a deadline for going to bed.

The first six months I was greatly bothered by their attempt to pressure me into buying various products ad-

vertised on TV and their endless curiosity about any product mentioned on TV.

I attempted to undermine their faith in commercials by pointing out that this and that product was really quite different from what the man said on TV. It never cut any ice with them until once when they were inspired to do some testing on their own hook. They were watching a commercial on *All Bran* cereal, which was reputed to have unusually fine qualities in taste, food value, etc. One of the twins remembered that we had a box of the stuff in our cupboard and she brought it into the living room to taste it. "It tastes like dried-up grass," she said very indignantly and gave a sample to her sister, who agreed with her. The next moment they were steeped in a cartoon and the incident seemed to be forgotten.

The next afternoon I caught them in the kitchen having a very heated discussion with some of their friends. Sylvia and Marya were maintaining that TV commercials lied, and the other kids did not believe them. It ended up with my girls passing around the *All Bran* box. After munching it quietly for a few minutes the kids had to admit that it did taste like dried-up grass, irrespective of what the nice man said on the screen. I don't know whether this was a revelation to the other kids in the neighborhood, but it seemed to have a lasting impact on Sylvia and Marya. They no longer were pushing for Name Brand products.

Six months later I was sitting with them in the living room when an education message flashed on the screen. A serious man, looking like a principal, wearing an earnest suit and horn-rimmed glasses, was urging youngsters to stay in school until graduation and learn proper skills in trade schools afterwards. I asked Sylvia whether she was going to follow that advice. "Not me," she said, turning up her little nose, "*I* don't believe in commercials."

Sylvia and Marya have become increasingly skeptical about information given to them. Over a year ago I intervened in a noisy argument they were having about how the world was made. They were arguing about the details of the creation myth in the Bible, again after a TV show. I thought it was just the right time to get a little rational science into the picture, and launched into a lecture about galaxies and solar energy and the formation of the earth as a planet and then gave them a quick run-down on the Theory of Evolution. The girls listened patiently, but finally Marya interrupted me. "But Mummy," she said, "how do people *know* about these things, if they happened so far away and long before there were any people here?" "Besides," chimed in Sylvia, "it seems just as hard to show you're right than it is to prove God created the world." "Why do you think your story makes more sense?"

Totally caught off guard, I had to admit that I had only the sketchiest notion of *how* we had systematic information about distant galaxies and the evolution of man. The explanations had become self-evident to me, just like religious truths had for other generations. I had to excuse myself and scramble back to my college textbooks.

For various reasons adults seem less formidable to Marya and Sylvia than they did to me at the same age. I recall adults as all-powerful creatures, who carried on a great deal of incomprehensible conversation with each other and did not have much time or patience with children. In primary school I often did not have the slightest idea why the teacher wanted us to do or learn some particular thing; yet it would never have occurred to me to question her. I understood the world at that point in terms of power. The teacher was telling us what to do *because* she was an adult and a teacher. *She* did not have to make sense, but *I* did, or otherwise I would get punished.

Sylvia and Marya react more strongly to "unfairness" in teaching and parents and insist that things make sense. They are almost never overawed by adults, and are in general fairly accepting of weaknesses in them. I cannot help but feel that TV has had something to do with that. For years now they have watched grownup men and women very courteously appeal to them to buy this or that underarm deodorant or floor wax, patiently explaining why it is the best one to use. Panel discussions, news, commercials, interviews and most documentaries all seem to be talking directly to the person watching, and they are rarely above the comprehension of an alert seven-year-old.

The school, however, seems to remain (whatever the decorations) as authority-oriented and rule-ridden as ever, and continues to puzzle my girls. One of them, after complaining for a week that her new teacher was not very "sensible" and kept punishing and rewarding kids in a very arbitrary way, making everybody angry, finally asked her teacher whether she enjoyed being a teacher. The young woman was apparently not too happy about the question, and told her in no uncertain terms that she did, and asked her to get back to her work. "I said it to be kind to her," said my girl the next day, "but instead I seemed to have hurt her feelings. Do you think I should draw her a picture?"

Myself, I don't watch TV much. I find the medium so merciless, like an X-ray into people and social attitudes; just a little too much reality to bear. The live shows jar me especially; the meaning that gets communicated to me is often so complex and ambivalent and contradictory. "The voice is Jacob's, and the hands are Esau's." A watchful child will learn a lot of things nobody intended him to.

Take, for example, a recent Ontario Department of Education telecast—a half-hour documentary on "How We Organize." They were on to parliamentary procedure, and to illustrate this revered national ritual they showed a group of well-scrubbed suburban kids attempting to act out the problems of democracy by organizing a puppet club. They were all so keen and had memorized their lines with such energy that their faces were left blank and their bodies limp. I disliked them the instant they appeared on the screen.

Although various parliamentary procedures were clearly illustrated—setting up a constitution, electing officials, delegating authority, making decisions—all that came across was the overwhelming irrelevance of these procedures for a bunch of kids who wanted to make puppets. Who, for Christ's sake, would put up with a pedant of a neighborhood kid forever saying, "Will the meeting please come to order," when one was busy comparing one's marionettes with the other kids'?

Finally, like an evil parable of the nation-state, the procedures grow and grow and take over all the time, space and energy available. One no longer sees kids making puppets but hovering together in small clusters, buttering each other up, and asking each other who they think should be the next president of the club, debating how election campaigns should be conducted and whether the kids should be divided up geographically or according to interests.

But it was a recent high school telecast on Hemingway that really got my head swimming. The MC was a buttoned-up teacher with all the sincerity and enthusiasm of a used-car dealer. He was telling us about the good points in Hemingway's writing and urged us to let history make the final judgment. There were a couple of large blow-ups of a demented-looking Hemingway and a few quick quotes: "If people bring so much courage to this world the world has to kill them to break them, so of course it kills them. The world breaks every one and afterwards many are strong at the broken places. But those that will not break it kills. It kills the very good and the very gentle and the very brave impartially. If you are none of these, you can be sure it will kill you too, but there will be no special hurry." *

Then it's back to the modern world interviewing Joseph Heller, who looks like an ex-Marine, and tells us he likes to write because he can make more money in writing than any other way and with less effort. "I also like writing because of the kind of ec-s-tasy involved," he says and looks you in the eye. He stumbles over the word ecstasy and a flicker of shame or self-consciousness or some other human feeling comes to the surface, and he looks like a big kid caught in the cookie jar and you are almost prepared to like him.

Then come the critics who have the final say in determining the literary worth of Ernest Hemingway. There's Leslie Fiedler, cherubic face and nicely trimmed beard, who begins to describe his last visit with Hemingway shortly before the old man committed suicide. "It did not take me long to realize that Ernest was pretty disturbed, hostile and suspicious and lonely," (I am quoting from memory now) says Leslie, who pauses and gives us a big Liberace smile. "A tortured man; he kept pleading with me to tell him whether he had got it right, whether he was relevant to the modern world—I mean if *he* doesn't know, who does"—a little shrug of the shoulders and another flash of teeth and dimples. Like always, the other message is coming through and I have forgotten all about Heller, and I am shouting to myself, "Fiedler, you bastard, don't let me hear any more of that shit about pot and humanism. If you're a humanist, so is L.B.J."

I also wonder what kids make of all these adults dressed up as children or fairies or giants—Dress-up Man, The Friendly Giant. Stolid and benevolent, they stand all-powerful, playing with cuddly animal toys; who are al-

* Ernest Hemingway, *A Farewell to Arms* (Scribner Library ed.; New York, Charles Scribner's Sons, 1929), p. 249.

lowed outrageous license in being pig-headed, mean, pouting, irrational, and in the end very lovable because they take so many chances—emotionally and physically—just like cartoon characters. Do the children conclude that there is a Christopher Robin in every adult? Or do they think that even when you grow up it is not safe to express your real feeling in human relations but only in fantasy, that only the toys are free and therefore only the toys can be trusted.

DINOSAURS AND BABIES

Nomi Wall

I WAS DELIGHTED that I got that job. The reason I was so enthusiastic was because I was hired on the basis of what had happened at the New Play Society Drama School. I lost that job during the Selma civil rights demonstration at the American Consulate building in the spring of 1965. I was teaching drama on Saturday mornings to two classes at that school, and I spent an hour and a half with each group every Saturday morning.

I started sitting-in at the Consulate around Monday of one week and I was there all night the next Friday, and that Saturday morning I had to go teach my classes. I sort of felt it was stupid to have spent all that time at the Consulate and not bring it up in the class. So we discussed it, we dramatized it, actually—we did it as actors and actresses. In other words, each person played a different role. And it was all stereotyped so if there were any criticism that the principal might have laid down I can understand that she might have objected to that. The kids had a certain picture in their mind of what a bigot was, and what a liberal was, and what a Negro was, and what a demonstration was. And they assigned each other these roles. I just watched. And it was really beautiful to watch them do it. And I thought it was valuable as an acting lesson as well, but the secretary, who was listening in, reported it to Mrs. Moore.

The thing that really lost me my job was that the kids went to the demonstration after the class to see for themselves what it was all about. When one father, who was a lawyer for a foundation which supported Mrs. Moore's school, came to pick up his son after school, he wasn't there. This father called the principal that evening at home and she had me into her office the very next weekday, Monday, and she fired me. The reason she gave was that I was a menace in any classroom and she would see to it personally that I never would be able to work with children again.

But there was an ad in the paper for this small private school, and it advertised itself as a nice, small (small classrooms) progressive school with an accelerated curriculum. It sounded perfect, and it was right around the corner from where I lived, so I went for an interview.

Anyway, to make a terribly long story short, I went to the Spadina Road School and I got the usual kind of interview. I was very honest about the kind of teaching I was going to do and the way I felt about kids. She was a very, very honest woman, extremely honest and frank, very, very British, but with enough Welsh in her to be dynamic. And I was on my way out when she said she would call me after she checked my references, and I very impulsively turned to her and said, "I'm going to tell you something I wasn't going to tell you. But I'm going to tell you because I think that you should know." And I told her what happened at the drama school. And she was thrilled. She said, "Oh you're just what we need here"—and she thought it was a funny story. She *was* pleased that I told her and she was pleased that I was at the demonstration, I think.

I can honestly say that for four months I did nothing, and I fell into my method of teaching those kids purely by accident. And it wasn't until I'd been doing this for six months that I realized that I had actually hit upon the best way of teaching them. Suddenly, after Christmas, I looked up and realized that I had created a beautiful second grade monster—fifteen of them, beautiful monsters—and I had done it by doing nothing. It wasn't because I had said, "I'm going to let them be free." They had to be free because I just, I just abdicated.

I didn't want to follow a curriculum. But I had had very little teaching experience with children that age, and I didn't have anything to replace what I wanted to throw out. If somebody had asked me, "Well, you don't like this curriculum but what are you going to do instead?" I couldn't have said anything except, "It's a terrible curriculum and I'm not using it." I had absolutely nothing to replace the curriculum I wanted to throw out. So I panicked. The thing that I was afraid of, the thing that impresses me most about kids, really young kids, is how naturally free they are. There's nothing these kids are afraid of, and the thing that horrified and frightened me more than anything else was that I would damage their freedom, make them afraid to be natural. You and I have to work so hard at being free. And they just don't; they have to work hard *not* to be.

Well, up until Christmas, I didn't know what to do and so I did nothing. So the kids took over. Around that time I got sick and was off for four days and they had to replace me. I was out from Tuesday to Friday and it was obvious during that week that my class didn't exactly lend itself to substitute teaching. I couldn't teach them arithmetic. Since then I got very smart about arithmetic. I discovered a kid in the class who was a genius and he taught us all arithmetic, including me. Anyway, the substitute teacher had them do a lesson in arithmetic, and their performance was abominable. So she took their papers with her to the principal and told her everything. She was very upset at how they had behaved with her.

When I got back on Monday, the principal called me in and asked me to eat lunch with her. The principal told me that there seemed to be a complete breakdown of authority in the classroom. The kids didn't seem to know the function of a teacher; they didn't seem to understand that certain things were allowed and certain things weren't; they were rude, they were fearless—that was the word, fearless—they were audacious, and obstinate.

Apparently the teacher had tried for two days to stick to the schedule and each time, she would say, "All right, now it's time for a lesson, so get your nature workbooks," and some kids would, and some kids would get something else, she would say, "It's *nature* workbook time. Get your *nature* workbooks." "Oh well, when Mrs. Wall's here we don't have to do nature if we don't want to—some people who want to do nature do nature, and people who don't want to do nature don't do nature, and that's the way Mrs. Wall does it."

And when the principal was telling me all this, I was saying to myself, that's not the way Mrs. Wall does it, that's the way the kids have been doing it, and it was all a revelation to me because it was all so accidental. The reason some of the kids would do nature and others would do something else was not because I had said—which was what I *should* have said—"Do what you want."—it was because I hadn't said anything.

There was one comment that I'll never forget, and that determined my future in that classroom. She said, "If I walked into that classroom I wouldn't be able to tell which one was the teacher." And it suddenly struck me that I had accidently created the most beautiful classroom imaginable—when you walk into a classroom and you can't find the teacher.

So I promised the principal that I would change my method, and this was a terrible, an immoral thing for me to do—I was taking credit for something I hadn't done. What I should have said was, "This isn't *my* fault; *I* didn't create that classroom." But I didn't. I took credit for the situation, said I would change and promised her that they would pass their achievement tests in June—I promised absolutely they would pass.

And I understood her feelings about this. She said that the children had to transfer to other schools after fourth grade and if they weren't up on their academic subjects, how could she justify the school to the parents. And I understood her position completely. I hadn't done any serious academic work with those kids.

So I walked back into my classroom and, you know, I don't believe in these metamorphoses taking place overnight or anything, but I really was like a different person. I suddenly developed this marvelous sense of humor with them and they didn't scare me anymore. After that things just got better and better. I knew what was happening. And I could even appreciate some very good things that had happened before Christmas.

We always had news, because it was on the schedule. Every Monday morning—it was supposed to be for fifteen minutes, from 9:00 to 9:15—they were supposed to come up, one by one, if they wanted to, and give their news. And I used to take that opportunity to wake up after the weekend. I never listened to their news and it never ended at 9:15. You know, I was just about the laziest teacher imaginable. I sometimes think that's why I like this freedom bit—because I sometimes confuse freedom with doing nothing.

Sometimes I'd appoint someone who wanted to take charge of news and some kid would stand up there. They love calling on people, so they raised their hands and this particular news-day I noticed that a little girl—who had maybe given news once before—she just didn't like talking in front of the kids, very shy—she was very agitated, she was wiggling around in her chair, and she was waving her hand around. She wanted desperately to give her news, so I suggested to the kid calling on them, "I think you better call on Rose because she looks like she's going to pass right out."

So Rose ran up to the front of the classroom, and as soon as she got there I stopped listening to her and I started doing something. I vaguely heard her say something about she and her mother and father and sister and brother got into their car that morning (this was the weekend after Hallowe'en) to go to school and the kids had been around "trick or treating." And they'd written a nasty, nasty word all over the driveway and on the windows of the car, and on the bricks of the house—they'd written a *nasty* word. And I was sort of half listening, and she said, "The word was *fuck*." It was fuck, fuck, fuck all over the driveway and fuck, fuck, fuck all over the windshield of the car, and they even wrote a great big fuck right on the bricks of the house. And, you know, that sort of caught my ear. And I turned to her and I said—what I actually said was, "Oh? Oh? They did what?" And she said it again. She said they wrote this nasty word.

There was not even a ten-second pause while the kids waited for me to do something. I looked very quickly around the class, and running through my mind was, "Oh, it's a brilliant opportunity. I can't tell her to shut up. I've got to use this; what am I going to do?" And again, it was because I didn't come up with any ideas, and they ended up doing it, that it was beautiful.

There was this one kid in the back of the class who was peeing in his pants, he was laughing so hard, but he was the only one who was, and I said to myself, "Sandy knows that word, this kid knows that word, and he's waiting for me to pounce on this girl." I knew he knew a lot of other words that most of the kids didn't know, and I knew he was more sophisticated in that way, than most of these kids were. He has an older brother. But he was obviously killing himself waiting, you know, for me to take a ruler and hit her hard on top of her head. But I didn't . . . I was just looking at him. And he was . . . he was like an adult, laughing. He was laughing in a sort of lecherous way, waiting for something to happen.

And while I was watching him and wondering what to do, a kid in the back of the class said, "What does that mean? What's that word mean?" And I didn't say anything. Rose said, "I don't know," and then another kid said, "How do you spell it?" And Rose said, "It rhymes with duck." And this impressed me right away, because I think the reason that the word impressed Rose so much, even though she had probably never heard it before, considering the neighborhood she lived in and the home she came from, was that kids that age *love* rhymable words. And fuck, I mean let's face it, it's a beautiful-sounding word. And it's just a great word for phonics, when you're learning words. And it's such a simple word and it does look just like duck, you know; it looks like so many other words: luck, suck, muck and all this stuff. So she said, "It rhymes with duck, except with an 'f.' It rhymes with duck, except with an 'f'."

And then, suddenly they were all yelling at me: "How do you sp— What does it mean? What does it— Who uses that word, I never heard that word before, is that like poop? Is that a dirty bathroom word? Why did they write *that* word?" But mostly, "What does it mean?" Because there are other dirty words they understand, you know, and first of all they know why they're called dirty words because they all have to do with the bathroom. To kids that age, everything's the bathroom. Their whole life centers around what they do in the bathroom and the *worst* thing a six-year-old can say to another six-year-old is "doody" or, "you're full of diarrhea," or something. The really brave ones might say "shit" but it's not the way *we* would say it; its got to do with what you do in the toilet and that, to them, is just the biggest thrill these kids could get.

Anyway that was one of the big questions—they wanted to know what it meant. One of the kids wanted very much to know if it fitted into this bathroom repertoire they had. So I decided I'd have to do something. I *had* to do something, I mean, I either had to tell them what it meant or I had to divert them, or I had to tell them to shut up and go on to something else—because they were addressing their questions to *me*. And it reached a point where I couldn't leave it in their laps anymore, 'cause it wasn't going to go away, obviously. And I didn't really want it to go away; I just hadn't found a creative way of handling it. I decided that I wasn't going to tell them what it meant because, for Christ's sake, we don't *use* it that way. We don't use it because we literally mean what it means; we use it to mean so many hundreds of different things.

So I asked them why they thought people used them, because it was a good question and I wasn't sure they'd come up with it. So I said, "Why do you think people use these words, like the one Rose used?" And they said *they* used them when they wanted to hurt somebody's feelings and when they felt anxious. That wasn't the first time I had heard them use the word anxious. It wasn't just one or two isolated kids that used this word. It was like all the kids in my class used it and a lot of other kids in other classes of the school used it. And they used it a lot. I don't know where they picked it up. Maybe they had parents, you know, I mean it's the most famous word of the century, among middle-class people. I think everybody's got anxieties, and everybody's anxious, and it's a word they knew and they loved, and they used it to explain all their feelings and all their anxieties. This was why they said that people used these words when they wanted to hurt people's feelings and when they were angry and anxious.

And that also led to a little talk about why, not only were their particular bathroom words called dirty words because what you do in the bathroom is dirty, but the nastiest thing you can do, they decided, is to hurt someone's feelings. They know a lot about feelings and getting feelings hurt because, you know, when you start going to school that's when you really begin to get your feelings hurt. If you come from a fairly comfortable home and your feelings don't get hurt too much there, if you have nice parents, and nice sisters and brothers, it's when you start going to school that your feelings really begin to get damaged. And they had been experiencing this kind of rejection, by their friends, and being accepted and not accepted, and getting their feelings hurt by their teachers. Feelings were very, very important to these kids.

I don't know how many times my kids would come in during recess crying, not because they fell down, but because so-and-so wouldn't play with them or so-and-so wouldn't be their best friend anymore. And that's why dirty words are important to them; it's a very easy or quick way to do it—to hurt someone's feelings—you know.

Just say, "kaa-kaa" to somebody or, "you're full of diarrhea," and you've just put him down for the day and it's only taken one little word to do it.

Anyway, they were still asking what the original nasty word, fuck, meant. So I explained to them that it meant a lot of things, just like when they say "doody" or "kaa-kaa" or "diarrhea." They don't really mean that; they're using it to describe the way they feel about something.

I kept saying, "It's a word grown-ups use, you know. When they feel a certain way, the way they say 'hell' or 'damn.' And sure enough, one of the kids wanted to know —did grown-ups have their own little group of dirty words—and kids have *their* own group of little dirty words? Were they two different languages, grown-up dirty words and kid dirty words? So I said the best way to find out was to hear as many of *their* words and then see if we could think of any of the grown-ups' words and see if there were any similarities or any common words. So they started throwing them out and it became a real free-for-all. I said, "So that we're not all screaming at once, if you have one that is meaningful to you or that you've heard that you want to tell us about, raise your hand." But after a while, there was this barrage of words filling the air and I could just see somebody walking into the classroom and being greeted with "prick," you know, out of the mouth of a little six-year-old boy. One kid said, "Um, well, grown-ups say, 'god damn,' but we don't. Kids don't usually say that; kids say 'darn' and 'gosh darn,' most kids, and they probably sort of mean the same kinds of things." Some of the words these kids came out with were just beautiful. *"Plop,"* one kid said, the dirtiest word in the world was "plop," you know. And that's the sound a bowel movement makes, plop. They really love words like that, and "bum," the thing you sat on was dirty.

Finally one little guy raised his hand—beautiful, one of the most beautiful children you've ever seen, I mean, a physically gorgeous child—and he said that *he* knew THE DIRTIEST WORD IN THE WORLD! It was so dirty he wouldn't say it. He would have to tell *me* and if I thought it was all right, I could tell them, but he didn't think that I'd think it was all right. And I said, "All right then, you can tell me. Whisper it." And he said, "You've got to promise you won't get mad, because you don't know what this word is, and when you hear it, you're just going to . . . you're just going to be very angry because it's such a dirty word." And I said I'd take that chance. He *begged* me *not* to tell the class the word unless I *really* thought is was all right. And I promised. And he came up and he whispered, whispered his dirty word, "Statistics."

Nobody heard it but me because, I mean, I barely heard it myself. As soon as he said it he drew back and put his hand over his mouth, because he was sure, you know, that the devil was going to come with a pitchfork (I'm sure that's what he felt) and stab him. And I started to laugh. The whole experience had been so euphoric anyway, you know, that that was really all I needed. I started to laugh, and while I was laughing I was looking at all these faces waiting to hear this word, and their mouths were hanging open. They were just *dying* to know whether or not I was going to tell them the word. So I told them. I said, "David said the word 'statistics.' " Some of the kids I'm sure had heard the word someplace. I got no reaction from them at all. They didn't laugh, they didn't say anything. They just looked at me and I looked at David and I said, "Uh, what makes you think that's a dirty word?" And he said, "Well, my daddy's always saying 'those god damned statistics.' " So I laughed some more, and I later found out from his mother that his father works for a radio station and his job depends a great deal on the ratings his program gets and he's always worried about them. Whenever his father uses the word "statistics" it's always when he's in a terrible temper. His mother told me that in fact her husband, at least six times a night, gets up from reading one of these reports and goes bellowing through the house, "Those god damned statistics!" So that was one of the things.

Another news period I wasn't listening or paying any attention again. This kid Stuart. He was all boy, if you know what I mean. He was just healthy and happy. I mean, to spoil this child, to frighten him in any way would have been a real crime because this kid just loved life and everything about it. There was nothing this kid didn't want to know about . . . totally uncompetitive, he couldn't have cared less. It was just the thrill of getting up every morning and knowing that the whole day stretched out in front of him and there were millions of things he could learn that day.

Anyway, he got up to tell his news, and he said, "My mom was bleeding last night," and I sort of heard him and I said, "Oh, that's too bad Stuart. Did she cut herself?" He looked at me as though I must be absolutely *dumb*. That's the kind of kid he was. He looked at me as if to say, "Would I be up here, you know, telling news at news-time, an important time, would I be telling that my mother cut herself?" And that's the kind of kid he was, you know. I knew that that wasn't what he was talking about as soon as he gave me that look. He certainly wouldn't be wasting my time and everybody else's telling us that his mother cut herself.

So he said, "Oh no, my mum's bleeding from *here,*" and he pointed to his crotch. He *showed* us exactly from where his mommy was bleeding, and waited, because he was very clever, he waited for a reaction. You don't just say something like that and expect everyone to sit there and say "Oh yeh, what else is new?" and he waited for a response.

And he got one, boy. This little girl. She. . . . (First of all this requires a little explanation to understand why she was so horrified. She was a very sexually precocious girl.

She was always having these mock-wedding ceremonies during recess, and she identified strongly with her mother, who was a very young, vivacious, beautiful woman.) This little girl knew where Stuart was pointing, and she knew that it's very unlikely to cut yourself there, and he just said his mother didn't cut herself, and she wanted to know exactly why anyone would bleed from there. I think she actually felt the sensation of bleeding from there, and so she asked me, "Mrs. Wall, why would a lady bleed from *there?*" And I decided right then and there, *I* wasn't going to explain it because I would probably make the mistake my mother made when I was six years old when I asked the usual question about "where did I come from" and in her effort to be progressive she gave me much too much information so that I lost all interest and wasn't interested again until I had some personal experiences. This little girl did NOT want to know about the menstrual cycle, and how babies are made, and all this crap. She wanted to know why was his mother bleeding at *that* particular time from *there*.

And I figured, knowing Stuart, if he had caught his mother changing a pad or something, he wouldn't have left without an explanation. He would have insisted on *some* kind of explanation, and knowing his mother I was sure she had given him one. I knew damned well that Stuart wouldn't be up there unless he had a big story to tell us. He wasn't the kind of kid who just got up and had one line of news. He usually had three or four hours. So I said, "Stuart, can you tell her why your mother was bleeding from there?" And he said, "Oh, YEH! My mother told me. She was bleeding from there because that blood is food and if there's a baby growing inside, the blood feeds the baby, but if there isn't a baby growing inside, then the blood can come out because nobody needs it."

And that was his explanation. I waited for other questions. I was sure this was going to lead to a marathon discussion on sex and what was I going to do then, because *I* didn't know how to handle that. But the thing that was beginning to upset me at that point was not that I *wouldn't* handle it if I had to, but that, again, I wouldn't know how to do it the best way. And, because I was sitting there thinking about it, *they* handled it. I mean, all you really have to do is shut up and these kids teach themselves.

Sure enough, there were one or two kids in the class who had gotten *some* education on this subject at home and they provided the explanation in their own language, that everyone understood. The thing that excited them more than anything else was that blood is food and this had never occurred to them before. To them blood was always something that was awful and terrible and came out of you when you were cut and crying.

So one kid said, "You mean babies eat blood?" And Stuart said, "Yeh, they eat the blood that's, uh, the mommy has this blood in there and that's what they eat." "Well, how do they get it?" and Stuart didn't know that. So we had a little, very, very elementary lesson in physiology because I didn't really know myself, *exactly* how babies got the blood. We talked about the umbilical cord. I said, "You know your belly button," and they all roared 'cause "belly button" *almost* qualifies as a dirty word. I said, "Well, that used to be a LONG cord and at the other end of that long cord was your mommy and that blood that fed you when you were inside your mommy, growing, went through that cord from your mommy's body into *your* body." And this wasn't even accurate, but it fascinated them, absolutely thrilled them. I didn't know enough about the placenta, (I didn't know anything about this *really* until I got pregnant myself) but I had some vague recollection that the thing they cut must have been the thing you were attached by, and that must have been how you got your food. It's amazing how much you don't know until it happens to you. And that's the basis on which you teach kids—you let it happen to them.

So anyway, they wanted to know what happened to that cord because all they had left was this little stubble—some stick out and some stick in but there's no cord there. I told them how it got cut, and they wanted to know, did that hurt and what happened to all the blood. At one point I was saying to myself, you're giving them a lot of phony information, you know. I mean, I was only guessing half the time but I figured it really didn't make that much difference. By the time they needed to pass an exam they'd have got the right information. And I have never known a course offered anywhere in sex education where you have to pass exams.

That was a beautiful lesson, that news session. It must have lasted two hours because we just went from one thing to the next. And the thing that amazed me was there was absolutely *no* basis for my fears whatsoever. Any question that they asked, they could have answered themselves. Any question, any explanation at all that they could have offered would have been far superior to anything I would have been able to tell them.

We'd already spent a great deal of time—three-fourths of that year, I'm sure—talking about dinosaurs. These kids can't get over dinosaurs because everybody tells them dragons are make-believe, and then they pick up a science book, a grown-up science book, and there are pictures of dragons in there and the science book says there really were these dragons and they may call them by other names, but THEY LOOKED LIKE DRAGONS. This fascinates them, and the more interested they become, the more ready they are to accept the fact that they were not in fact DRAGONS. I mean, they all love dragons, but these are interesting for reasons other than that they are dragons.

So we did dinosaurs inside out. I asked for two trips to the Royal Ontario Museum because they wanted to see them again and again. And the stories they wrote—I really turned them on one day. I told them that the Spadina Road School actually at one time had been a haven for dinosaurs and that the garage in the back was a dinosaur restaurant. It's amazing how they'll believe anything, the great ones will (the really imaginative kids *want* to believe everything you tell them). And I told them that I was one of the people who founded the Spadina Road School many, many hundreds of years ago. The odd kid would say, "Oh, the Spadina Road is only four years old," and "Dinosaurs lived millions of years ago," and I said, "Well, the Spadina Road School's only four years old maybe *you* think, but actually it's much much older than that. That garage out there was where the dinosaurs used to go for Pepsi-Colas." And some of the kids actually believed it and wanted to know more—had we found any bones, how did I know they drank Pepsi-Cola and I said I had come upon two dinosaurs' skeletons with the straws still in their mouths, sitting at the counter, drinking their sodas.

Anyway, they loved dinosaurs more than they loved their own mothers—they just *adored* dinosaurs, particularly the plant-eaters because plant-eaters were big and fat and cuddly. They were sure that if they ever came upon a brontosaur that it would be the most, the gentlest of all. It was the terrible meat-eaters that did all the damage but the brontosaurs just wanted to be left alone in their lakes. The kids loved them—the bigger and the fatter the dinosaur, the more cuddly he probably would have been.

From the dinosaurs, of course, they wanted to know about other animals. And we talked about mammals and why mammals were so very, very different from dinosaurs, and, they decided, *better*. Mammals certainly make better mommies and daddies. They had to admit even the cuddly plant-eaters would lay the eggs and just leave them and when things really got bad and the meat-eaters were eating the plant-eaters and they'd eaten up all the plant-eaters, the meat-eaters began to eat their own eggs. And what worse thing can a mommy and a daddy do than lay the egg and then eat it so that the poor baby dinosaur never even gets born? So in this way mammal mommies and daddies are much, much better, especially mammal mommies because mammal mommies *feed* their babies from their own bodies, and they don't have to go around getting their own food.

So one day—I guess it was the beginning of May—I was beginning to show, and I had on a maternity dress, and I was looking very pregnant; I walked in and I said, "Let's talk about animals." This one kid didn't want to talk about dinosaurs because, "That's all we ever talk about. Let's talk about some other kind of animal." And this little girl said she thought he *liked* dinosaurs. Why didn't he want to talk about them, and he said, "Because, they . . . they weren't nice to people and they ate their own babies." And another kid said, "There weren't any people around then, and they ate their own babies because they were hungry, because there wasn't anything else around to eat." And this same kid—John, his name was—he said, "Well, that was all fine, but even when mammals get hungry, they don't eat their own babies."

And Francis said—he was looking at me this whole time, really eyeing me up and down—he suddenly said, "Mrs. Wall, are you going to do it the way the cows do?" And I said, "Do what, Francis?" And he said, "Feed your baby when it comes out, are you going to feed your baby the way the cows feed their babies?" And I said that I was *thinking* about it. I certainly wanted to very much, but that there are lots of human mothers who didn't because humans were *so* smart that they had found another way of doing it. They had bottles. And some of the kids said, "Yeh, that's the way I was fed—by bottles." And Andrea said that she wasn't fed by a bottle; she was fed from her mommy's "titty." That's exactly the way she put it, very, very proud.

Meanwhile Francis is still looking *all* over me. I really felt like I was on show at the Victory Burlesque or something. I am a bit flat-chested so he said, "Well, where? *Where* are you going to do it from?" I said "Uh . . ." and while I was saying "uh" Andrea said, "Oh, Francis, Mrs. Wall's going to do it from *here,* from her titties." And Francis looked at Andrea and said, "Andrea, *I* got them just like *you.*" And Andrea said, "You may have them like me *now* but when *I* get big I'm going to have *great big* ones like Mrs. Wall has." Suddenly the fourteen kids in the class all turned and looked at me, trying to find these great big ones that I was supposed to have. And they were looking at me so intently. It was almost pitiful because they wanted me to suddenly be a *cow* for them. They really did. They wanted to *see* them. They expected udders (I don't know how many they expected) and some of them of course *knew*. Andrea, of course, thought the whole conversation was *ridiculous* that Francis wouldn't *know* these things. That impressed her as being *dreadfully* stupid of him. But finally the topic just sort of dropped. They were satisfied that I was going to do it, and if I said I had them and Andrea said I had them they must be there *someplace* you know, though they couldn't see them anywhere.

But the thing I got a big kick out of was that, before this conversation, Francis had taken a good enough look at Andrea even through her dress to see that her chest looked NO different at all from his, and when she should so conceitedly point to her *own* to say, "Mrs. Wall is going to feed her own baby from a chest like mine," Francis would immediately begin to wonder what Andrea had that was so special because she looks just like *he* does.

We had a number of discussions about my baby, especially in June when I was in my sixth month and he was beginning to move. They were constantly coming up to feel my stomach. And I've never heard such delicious squeals. I *know* for a fact that many of them had had pregnant mothers when they were much younger and probably wouldn't have taken a very keen interest. They were at an age now, though, where they were . . . where pregnancy was interesting to them. Andrea was one of the few in the class who had had any of this explained to her, or had ever really intently watched a woman go through pregnancy. But the first time the baby kicked in class I said, "The baby is kicking, would anyone like to feel it kick?" and they lined up—very co-operatively—there wasn't this mad rush with everyone putting his hand on my stomach at once. When kids *know* that . . . that something's being offered that they *really* want, they'll devise their own way of organizing things so that they'll each get it. But they were delighted with feeling the kicks and we *did* spend much of the last part of the term talking about having babies.

What I would *really* like to do—I don't think I'm going too far at all when I say this—I would *love* to take David to the school and feed him with those kids. 'Cause it *is*, I mean, I don't care *how* civilized and sophisticated we are, it *is* just like the cows do it. And if you can keep the simple things simple for those kids so that breast-feeding never becomes anything *more* than what the cows do, or what the pussycat does to the kittens, you know, it won't take on all those ugly connotations later.

But of course, that's out of the question.

I'm trying to remember some of the other things that happened with those kids. Oh yes, this one thing. Toward the end of the year I was trying to figure out what I had done; maybe it wasn't necessary but I sort of wanted to. I didn't want to look back on that year of teaching and say I've done nothing. Then this little girl came up to me —she was leaving Toronto altogether and I'd never see her again—and gave me a big kiss and she said, she said, "I love you," and I said "Oh. I love you too." She said, "Oh, I *know that.*" And I asked, "How do you know that?" And she said, "I just *know* that, Mrs. Wall, I mean, I just know it, that's all." And she walked away and I decided that I didn't have to know what I'd done, that if she knew that so well that she could get angry at me for asking then maybe I'd be better off not knowing what I had done, because I'd try to do it again, and once you start trying to repeat something you've already done, it never quite comes off that way.

UNWANTED PREGNANCY

an issue out of focus

a review of current writing on the unwed mother & sex education.

by SATU REPO

TO HAVE A CHILD out of wedlock has always been an inconvenience and often a disgrace. In the past the social reaction to the girl who found herself in this predicament was a reasonably reliable barometer of the sexual mores of the times. In the twentieth century there has been an attempt to look at this phenomenon in a scientific and objective way, but our prejudices have, as a rule, outweighed our detachment. Sexuality has been so closely linked with sin in the Western world, that the social consequences of unwed motherhood have often been overshadowed by the moral issue: why did she go wrong? Illegal abortions, unwanted children, forced marriages, school drop-outs have all received less attention than this basic problem of morals.

As there has been a major terminology switch in our century, the problem is now expressed in psychoanalytic and sociological rather than theological language: what are the causes of this kind of socially deviant behavior? Are they internal, resulting from emotional disturbance, or external, reflecting social disorganization? The theories have tended to oscillate back and forth, and through various methods of selective sampling, each position in turn has been made to sound plausible enough.

In the 1920's, for example, researchers gave a genetic explanation for the unwed mother. She was presented as a "moral imbecile" (we might call her a "psychopath" today). Either she had a weak character and was influenced by bad companions, or she was mentally defective and lacked judgment. One had only to search rescue homes and charitable institutions to find ample evidence.

By 1930, explanations had shifted to environmental causes. Broken homes, poverty, and disorganized neighborhoods were seen as the major reasons for illegitimacy. And again, there was no problem about finding evidence. You had only to look at the descriptions of unwed mothers in domestic court files, police records, welfare agencies, and homes for wayward girls. They all had the same social background—poor homes and bad neighborhoods.

In the early 1940's there was something of a shift in the approach as anthropologists took a crack at the problem. Illegitimacy was explained as a cultural pattern, a way of life among certain subcultures. Most of the evidence came from descriptions of Negro unwed mothers in the southern United States. This approach never became very popular, it seems. I suspect it didn't have enough implied moral judgment to provide emotional comfort for the adults concerned with the problem.

By 1950 the psychological and psychiatric theories had taken over, and we were back to the explanation that the girl who gets pregnant is sick. Out-patient clinics and maternity homes, staffed with psychiatric social workers, gave detailed descriptions of emotionally disturbed, inadequate and friendless girls who had "inner needs" to get pregnant in "working out" their personality problems.

Today the pendulum is swinging back to the view that it's society who should be seen as the patient. The sociologist is aiming his searchlight at the deviant behavior of the middle class. We are snowed under with descriptions of white-collar crime, payola adults, and the delinquent youth of suburbia. And when it comes to unwed mothers, we are now told of a stream of "college educated" girls going off to be attended by physicians in private practice. The girls are seen as the accident toll of a new freewheeling sexual morality.

I shall examine the psychoanalytic and the current sociological positions in some detail and then move on to an even more perplexing subject: the prevention of illegitimacy known euphemistically as "sex education."

THE UNWED MOTHER AS "DISTURBED GIRL"

Leontine Young is a psychiatric social worker and the author of *Out of Wedlock,* the first book-length treatment of this problem. It was published in 1954 and expresses the orthodox psychoanalytic view that unwed mothers are emotionally sick women with unresolved childhood conflicts.

Miss Young discusses her theme in classic Freudian language. She makes the following central point:

> The roots of the psychiatry of unwed mothers are deeply embedded in those powerful emotions of early childhood which form the basic pattern and structure for an individual's total life. Their specific problems tend to represent a direct expression of early fantasies and emotional

> conflicts. The young woman has clearly chosen one common and specific response, having an out-of-wedlock child.[1]

The girls who have chosen this response, according to Miss Young, have had an unhappy childhood. The great majority of these girls come from homes dominated by one parent, usually the mother. This parent tended to be both overpowering and rejecting, and the girl grew up, clinging and unsure of herself, but secretly resentful. As a result of being unloved but overpowered at home, these girls never developed the ability to relate well to people. This inability to get along with people handicapped them when it came to employment, and they had to put up with the humiliation of accepting jobs far below their ability or education.

One of the most frequent tendencies to be found in their personality pattern was that of self-punishment. It was significant, according to Miss Young, that they had sought out men they either did not care for or who treated them badly. The relationships leading to pregnancy were mostly brief and never happy ones.

These girls, as Miss Young sees it, didn't want a man, they wanted a child. Why? Usually to get back at their mothers. According to her, it is very significant that these girls invariably wanted to give their babies to their mothers rather than have them adopted by strangers. In essence, this is the way the situation appears to Miss Young:

> One can only assume that giving a baby to her mother represented one of those unconscious purposes. With this one action the girl expressed both her hate and her love for her mother: what better revenge against a rejecting mother than to have an illegitimate child and leave it at your mother's doorstep? And in what more

[1] Leontine Young, *Out of Wedlock* (New York, McGraw Hill, 1954), p. 39.

> complete way could she express her love for and dependency upon her mother than to give the mother her baby, a tangible evidence of her deep, unconscious tie, as well as a symbol of her own desire to be again an infant, cared by the mother.[2]

The chief merit in this position is that it allows society to treat pregnant girls more humanely by redefining their status from fallen women to sick girls. This makes it possible to spend money on their care and rehabilitation without feeling that one is promoting sin. This also makes it easier for families to accept their unwed daughters. Altogether it has made life a little easier for the pregnant unmarried girl who still has an awful lot to put up with and has every reason to feel insecure and dependent and somewhat disturbed.

Although the therapeutic position is quite entrenched, it has not lacked critics. It has been pointed out that there is an obvious self-selection in the sample used. The girl who needs counselling and material help from a social agency often has very few decent and reliable relationships, either past or present. The sample, in other words, may tell us more about the kind of girls using these agencies than about unwed mothers in general.

Even the diagnosis has been challenged. More empirically oriented therapists have argued that the emotional disturbance in these girls could be the result rather than the cause of their pregnancy. Dr. Melitta Schmideberg in her article "Psychiatric Social Factors in Young Unmarried Mothers" argues this way:

> A girl who comes to a social agency for help seems more likely to be disturbed than the girl who has the backing of her family. Naturally the girl is in a bad state and

[2] Leontine Young, "Personality Patterns in Unmarried Mothers," *Journal of Social Casework,* Vol. XXVI, No. 8 (New York, December, 1945), p. 298.

> shows her worst side. She feels humiliated, confused, distrustful of everybody and everything. She has involved herself, her family and her lover in a dilemma with which she cannot cope. A spotlight, as it were, has been turned on a forbidden act and she is overwhelmed by guilt.[3]

It also has been suggested that biological factors may contribute to the disturbance in these girls. It is well known that many women tend to be moody and somewhat unstable while pregnant. This can at least partly be attributed to hormone changes during that period. In addition many women have mixed feelings about having a child and many irrational fears that they hardly admit to themselves which affect their behavior.

The sociologists have questioned the validity of Miss Young's position on technical grounds. We have no way of knowing that girls visiting social agencies are representative of all unwed mothers. Only by matching these girls with a group of non-pregnant girls that have a similar family background could we possibly get some clues about why some mother-ridden, inadequate girls get pregnant and others seem to find different solutions to their problems.

THE FUN SOCIETY

According to the sociologists you have to look at the whole web of social mores and practices to understand how present day sexual freedom is a cause of increased illegitimate pregnancies. Dr. Clark Vincent, a California sociologist, examines our ambiguous values in his massive study, *Unmarried Mothers*.[4] A characteristic of

[3] Melitta Schmideberg, M.D., "Psychiatric-Social Factors in Young Unmarried Mothers," *Journal of Social Casework,* Vol. XXXII, No. 1 January, 1951), p. 5.

[4] Clark E. Vincent, *Unmarried Mothers* (New York, The Free Press of Glencoe, Inc., 1961).

North America, according to him, is that we have no harmonious and agreed-upon attitudes and social practices concerning sexual or any other kind of behavior. It is typical of us to "play it by ear," to attempt to make out by living by contrasting rules of the game.

He points out that in the area of sexual behavior, for instance, we tend to have one set of standards for judging sexual relations outside marriage and another set for judging its possible results, illegitimate pregnancy. The same girl, whose sex habits may be tolerantly viewed by her friends, associates and lovers while her stomach remains appropriately flat, may be in for the severest censure when she starts stocking up on maternity dresses.

In Vincent's view there are a number of social practices that indirectly encourage illicit sex and therefore affect the increase in illegitimate births. The whole "philosophy of fun morality" as it manifests itself in education, child-rearing and personnel practices in business and industry results in the undermining of traditional sex mores.

In bringing up children the distinction between what a child needs and what he wants is made less and less frequently. If a child enjoys something, it is considered to be good for him. When he is ready for school, the educators have planned a program for him with the assumption that he will learn more and faster if he is having fun. When he becomes an adolescent and is aware of the world around him, he will read, hear and see progressively fewer denials that sex is fun. In contrast to the earlier covert treatment of sex as the source of evil (if not evil itself), the thematic patterns of novels, films and plays make it clear that sex is good for you. The stigma of *The Scarlet Letter* is replaced with the therapeutic theme of *Tea and Sympathy*.

As work has become standardized to the point that it provides very little opportunity for either creativity or competence or even the feeling that one is socially useful, the personnel managers have stopped talking about the inherent worth of work and set their pitch on providing a pleasant work atmosphere. Office parties, music in the cafeteria, expense accounts, are now the main selling points. Work, too, has become fun.

In Vincent's analysis, such social practices, when viewed collectively, are sources of learning permissive attitudes towards sex outside of marriage. The fusion of needs and wants, and the emphasis on fun and enjoyment, makes it easier for a male who is unhappy in marriage to justify, at least for himself, finding amusement outside his home. And the groovy secretaries around the office, often picked for their "presence" rather than their "performance," may further simplify his choice of fun partners.

THE GREAT DEBATE ON SEX EDUCATION

Miss Young sees the unwed mother as an emotionally starved girl; Dr. Vincent implies that she is perhaps overindulged. Where does it leave us as teachers, parents, and other concerned adults? The time has come, surely, to take a look at prevention.

The discussions about how illegitimacy could be prevented have often an even greater aura of unreality than the character sketches of unwed mothers. Most participants in this Great Debate take special pains not to define what exactly they want to prevent, illegitimate pregnancy or premarital sex. It seems that to take a stand against the former only is just a little too hip, to come down explicitly against the latter makes one squarer than one likes to appear. Thus any discussion on the matter has the appearance of being permanently out-of-focus.

The underlying problem which is rarely touched is that there is a tension between our traditional sex mores and the current, Freudian-oriented concepts of mental health. Premarital chastity continues to be an ideal, but sexual competence has also become an ideal. In addition, it is now an accepted criterion of mental health. Dr. Schmideberg, a member of the new priesthood of psychiatrists, has expressed the tension between these ideals rather poignantly:

> A girl is physically and emotionally capable of intercourse and motherhood at puberty. Our Western civilization, however, uses every type of pressure to postpone adulthood, with the average marriage taking place after the age of twenty. Hence conflict is inevitable, and whatever its outcome, the girl is bound to get hurt. If she summits to social codes, the price of adaptation is frequently paid in neuroses and inhibitions interfering later with normal married life. On the other hand, unmarried motherhood—representing failure to adapt—results in serious, often punitive social and psychological consequences both for the girl and her family.[5]

As a result of this change in values, there is more sexual freedom, but also a lot more sexual anxiety. And sexual incompetence is in the end considered to be more a serious failure than a moral failing. Any sex education program, therefore, has three aims which usually turn out to be incompatible:

1. Reinforcing traditional sex mores.
2. Emphasizing the emotional and physical satisfaction of a good sex life.
3. Giving out some basic information about human anatomy, reproduction, contraception, venereal disease, etc. with the hope that adolescents will at least learn to take certain precautions if they do have sexual involvements.

[5] Schmideberg, *op. cit.*, p. 3.

The strengthening of traditional sex mores is still considered to be the most important aim, and the rest of the facts will have to be tailored to fit it. But a peculiar thing has happened in our amorphous liberal society: if we exclude religious considerations, nobody any longer seems to have a positive reason for chastity. The reasons are exclusively negative and can be summed up as: "You will be sorry if you don't."

Here are some highlights from a typical report on a current sex education program. It took place in schools in suburban Chicago and was reported in the *Toronto Star* on November 2, 1965. The teachers take great pride, when they discuss sexual activities, in talking about Mummies and Daddies, never about men and women. Apparently this is so effective that most fifth graders simply will not believe that unmarried women can have children—biological evidence to the contrary. This may be the case, but it is hard to determine whom the joke is on in the end. I recall that some of the California physicians that Dr. Vincent interviewed complained that many of their teen-age patients had been so firmly conditioned to believe that "nice girls never get pregnant," that they were both shocked and outraged when it happened to them. We shouldn't forget that we have given them the car keys.

Another teacher on a junior high level has found an answer that satisfies her when a girl asks "why not"? She hands the girl a page of statistics whose major headings are: Venereal Disease, Illegitimacy, Early Marriage, Illegal Abortion, Divorce and Unhappy Marriages. She does not elaborate, but we have to assume that premarital sex is responsible for all these social ills. "After I have talked about VD," she tells the reporter, "anybody (in the class) with a pimple or a cold blister has just had it. Nobody will go near him. But we do not want to just scare people. What we want to emphasize are the wholesome aspects of sex."

The question is how? After you get across that sexual activities result in filthy diseases, dangerous illegal operations, incompatible marriage partners, broken homes, etc., how do you get back to the "sex is the most beautiful and meaningful human experience" theme which is usually picked up when sex-in-marriage is discussed? You are obviously attempting the impossible: either the deterrent is too good and will create adjustment problems in marriage, or it has the impact of making the adult look like a dishonest fool.

Contraceptives are invariably played down in sex education sessions. "We supply very little knowledge of contraceptives," says another Chicago educator in the same article. "If I am asked about them, as I am, I'll answer with a brief definition. I'll also say they're sold to married people. But the main thing I'll do is to stress their unreliability." This is a typical reaction and one example of how the truth is eclipsed by contradictory aims. Obviously the teacher knows that there are safe contraceptives that one can get on a doctor's prescription. But this information might further encourage premarital sex and we can't have that.

But if the statistics that are used to scare youngsters are correct—the article was filled with figures such as "41 per cent of illegitimate births are among teenagers," "teen-age marriages are up 500 per cent," "50 per cent of teen-age brides are pregnant at wedding"—it would seem both cruel and irrational to withhold this information. The human suffering caused by unwanted children, forced marriages, and school drop-outs because of pregnancy is staggering. Wrapped up as we are in our own sexual fears and inhibitions, we seem to have forgotten that it is not sexual intercourse, but unwanted pregnancy that has the objective qualities of a social tragedy. We have not made much headway in influencing teen-age morals where they have been different from ours. Why not try to see if we can at least prevent the girls from getting into trouble?

The blackmail approach to adolescent sexual problems may not have much deterrent value, but it has one predictable effect: increasing the gap between generations and the lack of trust on both sides. Our youngsters know us better than we think and they know how anxious, fearful, and embarrassed we are about sexual matters. They also suspect that we are relatively ignorant, or we wouldn't be talking such nonsense. "Sex questions embarrass 98 per cent of the population," Dr. Rich, a Toronto psychiatrist, said recently in a lecture called "The Challenges of Being a Parent." And Dr. Rich added, "Even the most enlightened parents are often too clinical." "The average man has so much anxiety about sex that he is unable to permit himself to be exposed psychologically in discussing this emotionally loaded topic with his son," states another expert in a recent mental health conference. It seems clear then that a lot of adolescents must share the experience of the high school senior interviewed in New York on the subject. "I hate to admit it," he says, "but my father simply doesn't know the answers and he is ashamed to say so. He gets even more rattled than I do."

So where is a fellow to learn about these things? The principal of a junior high school in a prosperous midwestern town is reputed to have uncovered a new secret club among his ninth graders. He called in the ring leaders, asking for some details about it. The new club was called "Look and Learn," the kids told him solemnly. Thirteen boys and seven girls belonged to it. All were under sixteen. All were competent students. All came from "good families." At their club meetings, held in a vacant apartment over a neighbor's garage, they took turns demonstrating and practicing sexual intercourse. "We don't want to be squares when we get to high school," the shocked educator was told. "If you don't know the score by the time you get up there, the other kids laugh you right off the hill." Now, if you contrast the innocent empiricism of these kids with the proverbial hysterical parent who phones the school in rage when human reproduction is taught in biology classes, you have covered the spectrum of attitudes.

But how did we get so far apart? The reasons are many, of course, and defiance of parents and a hedonistic adult society certainly plays a part in this. I would like to focus, however, on one important new development that has not received sufficient comment: the radical change in official doctrines of child-rearing in the past twenty years. The Piagets and Montessoris who were concerned with the nature of a child's intellect and his learning processes, have been overshadowed by the Freudians mainly interested in healthy psychosexual development. Parents have been urged to accept and not to hamper a child's sensuality. All early sexual tabus have been demolished. Exploring one's body, "playing doctor," masturbation, even preadolescent homosexuality have started to emerge as natural developmental phases, all necessary for successful heterosexual adjustment later in life.

The experts, realizing the parental anxiety this kind of permissiveness will create, have tried to reassure us. In the Gesell Institute's *Child Behavior,* one of the bibles of child development, we are given the following advice:

> Try to realize that it may be better for a child to show too much interest in sex than too little. Sex play at six is at least a sign that your child is developing normal sexual interests.[6]

And when the incomparable Dr. Spock cautions against too much nudity in the home, he is not worried about

[6] Francis L. Ilg and Louise Bates Ames, *Child Behavior* (New York, Dell Publishing Company, 1955), p. 206.

modesty or morality, but about an intensification of the Oedipal situation:

> A boy loves his mother much more than he loves any little girl. He feels much more rivalrous of his father and more in awe of him than he feels towards any boy. So the sight of his mother may be a little too stimulating, and the chance to compare himself so unfavorably with his father every day may make him feel like doing something violent to his old man.[7]

Conscientious, expert-oriented middle-class parents may have attempted to go along so far, but when it comes to the next developmental stage, they are definitely dragging their feet. The postponed clash between morality and sensuality is brought to the open at adolescence, but it is usually too late. The connection between body and sin which has been strong in the whole Christian era has been systematically weakened by various social forces, including our child-rearing practices, and many of our children can no longer make emotional sense out of this connection. This does not necessarily mean, as Vincent implies in his discussion of "fun" morality, that we have brought up a more irresponsible generation, but it means that criteria for morality have changed. These youngsters tend to define sin in terms of the quality of human relationships. "Sin" consists of being callous or indifferent towards a person, or taking advantage of him. "Sin" has nothing to do with the sexual act per se or with any other kind of act abstracted from human context. Thus our enterprising grade niners with their "Look and Learn" society may have felt that they had no reason for guilt. On the other hand, they would probably consider the average adult attempt to distort basic facts about sexual behavior in our society as immoral. It is, after all, attempting to take ad-

[7] Benjamin Spock, *Baby and Child Care* (New York, Duell, Sloan and Pearce, 1957), p. 379.

vantage of the adolescent's smaller knowledge and experience in these matters.

Many adults, remembering their own childhood of timed toilet visits and stern warnings about "bad habits," find this new crop of happy pagans totally baffling and not a little offensive. (To our relief, all adolescents are not like that. Our society is sufficiently heterogeneous for many child-rearing practices to co-exist. Those who are relatively guiltless sexually are probably still a minority, albeit a growing one.) For it is obvious, that in the end the whole problem of illegitimacy and even VD is somewhat of a red herring. It clearly could be tackled with good old American know-how: foolproof contraceptives and regular medical check-ups.

We don't do this because what we really resent is the adolescent's casual attitude towards sex as just another aspect of human relations. They will settle neither for "sin" nor for "fulfillment" as a label for sexual intercourse. And we, remembering the intensity, pain and guilt of the sexual explorations of our own youth, feel in some undefinable way hurt. It shouldn't be as easy as all that! The experts who have led us up the garden path have also ceased to be helpful. Aware of the conflicting values in our society and not wanting to offend anybody, they tend to be either politely quiet or obscurely critical, and they save their most explicit statements for professional journals.

And it has to be admitted that our children are right when they suspect that we are ignorant about the sexual situation they face. We do not know what it is like to have premarital sexual experiences, when you have been allowed to accept your body and enjoy it from an early age, and when The Pill can protect you against pregnancies and Penicillin against VD. We do not know whether it accelerates or hampers maturation to have early sexual experiences. We do not know what lack of sexual repression might do to a whole civilization. On the positive side, one can probably predict that pornography will disappear and cheesecake will stop selling products. But will people continue to care intensely enough for each other for marriage and family to survive as worthwhile institutions? We do not know and it is therefore not easy to give young people honest guidance in sexual matters.

Perhaps we should approach our youngsters rather humbly when we do and admit our ignorance. Perhaps we should just tell them how things were for us at their age, and not attempt to generalize too much. If we can create an atmosphere of intimacy based on the mutual admission that nobody has that much wisdom about the rights and wrongs of sexual behavior, perhaps a different, more rewarding dialogue might emerge between the generations. A closeness to our children could be our bonus after all the bewilderment that following the experts has brought us. The other alternative is to continue to reiterate that premarital sex is terrible because it is terrible. And if the kids don't believe us, we can always pull out the statistics on illegitimate pregnancies and VD.

HIGH SCHOOL

No Place to find out who you are

a review of Edgar Friedenberg's COMING OF AGE IN AMERICA: Growth and Acquiescence

George Martell

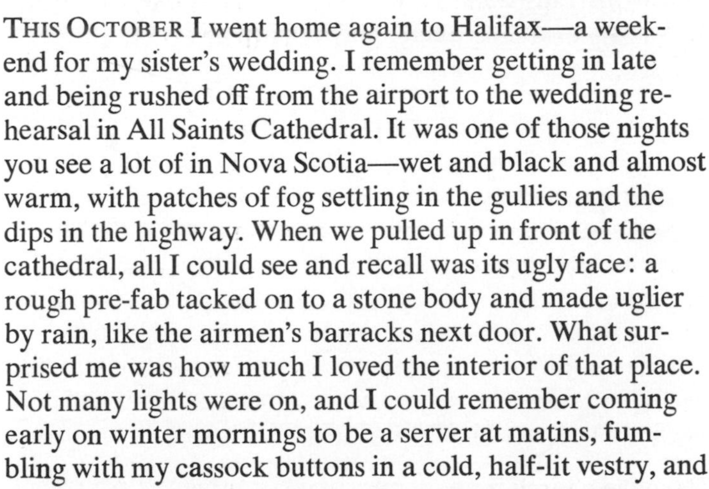

THIS OCTOBER I went home again to Halifax—a weekend for my sister's wedding. I remember getting in late and being rushed off from the airport to the wedding rehearsal in All Saints Cathedral. It was one of those nights you see a lot of in Nova Scotia—wet and black and almost warm, with patches of fog settling in the gullies and the dips in the highway. When we pulled up in front of the cathedral, all I could see and recall was its ugly face: a rough pre-fab tacked on to a stone body and made uglier by rain, like the airmen's barracks next door. What surprised me was how much I loved the interior of that place. Not many lights were on, and I could remember coming early on winter mornings to be a server at matins, fumbling with my cassock buttons in a cold, half-lit vestry, and

1 Edgar Friedenberg, *Coming of Age in America* (New York, Random House, 1965).

then going out to light the candles. At that hour the stained glass is very dark, and what you notice most are the high white walls and arches and the red carpet leading to the altar. The floor boards creak, and you can smell fresh wax and the damp of old prayer books. At the far end, near the chancel steps, I could see a little group of relatives and friends gathered around the dean. They talked purposefully and gently. There was a wonderfully subtle and almost total acceptance that even this preliminary ceremony demanded reverence. I felt as if I had never been away.

When I finally got back to my home on Oakland Road, I experienced the same childish delight I always do when I find that nothing has changed. My mother lovingly keeps the house the same; she never moves anything—not a print, not a stick of furniture. Outside, the street is covered with maple trees. When I looked out the next morning their leaves were bright, translucent gold, and their branches were black with rain. The morning sky was white-grey, and the air was soft, and I could smell the sweet smell of newly fallen leaves, wet and shiny and just beginning to decay. It smelled like Hallowe'en morning. I was home and I felt safe.

But what struck me all that weekend, was not that I was safe in my own home. I always knew that. What continuously impressed itself on me was the knowledge of how easy it had always been for me to slip in and out of the other institutions I came upon in my society. How cozy and comfortable I had found them, while at the same time feeling that I had made no contact, that they somehow left me untouched. I had always joined up when it was useful and resigned when it was convenient. That had been all there was to it.

Take the church for example. In a family full of Anglican ministers, it was unthinkable for me not to go through the rites of religious passage: in Sunday school, communion classes, regular services; they had the additional advantage of being places where I could find my friends. And, as well, the effort of turning out salved a kind of residual belief that somewhere there was a God who was capable of punishing me. Later, there was the servers' guild, whose great attraction for most of us lay in the mechanics of ritual. We got a fair-sized kick out of being on the inside of a big show. It was a show we did well. We prided ourselves on our smoothness of operation, on our *professionalism*. (There were little crosses given away for years' service.) And we had all the nonchalance and irreverence of the professional. I remember one guy especially, who had a regular feature at the big Christmas Eve service. He "called" it like Foster Hewitt. Kneeling to the side of the altar we would hear this hard nasal voice whispering: "Now, ladies and gentlemen, with only a few minutes left here in the last period . . . the crucifer . . . down at the far end . . . yes, yes, he's finally making his move. He's taken the cross now, and he's coming up with it to center aisle. You can feel the crowd stir. . . ." We all shook with laughter.

The picture of us kneeling there, and giggling as boys do, sticks in my mind as being probably the most genuine response we ever showed to a service whose content never reached us. We never stopped being boys in the church; we left before we became men. We never took it seriously, even as an opponent. (The few who attempted to do this were "oddballs," who couldn't make it anywhere else.) There was never a confrontation. When we grew older, we grew bored, and we dropped off slowly. As younger members came into the guild, it lost its appeal, and there was no other connection. One day they stopped putting my name on the schedule, and I didn't go anymore.

This pattern, I think, is a common one, and has repeated itself for me in almost every institution I have ever been in, whether it was the YMCA, or the Navy, or my school. When the time came to stop, I stopped. I had no regrets. The activity was finished, used up; at best, if recorded on paper, it might be useful in getting me a job sometime. I did my work, and I did it well. I knew people were pleased with me, and trusted me. That was what counted.

At the same time I always believed that I was invulnerable, that these institutions could neither influence me nor hurt me. I could use them as I liked, and keep my detachment and my critical judgment. I had my family and a few friends I counted on, although they were not that close. Nothing outside, I felt, could touch me. In a lot of ways I was right. My highly developed and largely intuitive sense for what authorities wanted, and for what my peers would accept, saved me from any large specific hurt and a public humiliation. But missing that kind of wound, I got another—softer and less definable. Gradually my self-respect began to disintegrate. In my mid-twenties I woke up (as many people do) to find that I had lived a third of my life and not noticed it. I knew what I had *done* in the world (I had a big list ready for scholarship committees), but I had never accepted that experience as my own and its implications as to who I was. I had no hold on my past. I felt empty and formless, like an infant responsible for a life already lived. I felt what values I had turning soft in my mouth and becoming bizarre. All abstractions seemed foreign and somehow evil, grotesquely unrelated to the human beings I was talking about.

A CONSERVATIVE CRITIQUE

In *Coming of Age in America* Edgar Friedenberg has written a very good book about formless kids like me, and the complicity of our schools in allowing us to slip through our society while making little contact with ourselves. I didn't find it quite so powerful and persuasive as his earlier work, *The Vanishing Adolescent,* which really startled me into an awareness of how my adolescence had slipped through my fingers. In many ways the second book, though more desperate and despairing, is simply a research extension of the first.

Put together, both books provide the one really substantial conservative critique of American education. They are written passionately and elegantly, and find their energy in a deep-rooted hatred of The Banal Society. (What Friedenberg cares about are its opposites—the aristocratic virtues of courage, good taste, and self-reliance . . . a mixture of early Rome and Dodge City.) But however much he hates the system, Friedenberg, like many other conservatives, feels obliged to stay within it. For many years he was a professor of education, and at the time I am writing this article, he is in the department of sociology at the University of California carrying on his old research into the functioning of the public schools. His writing, therefore, has the concreteness and precision of the alienated on the inside. In this latest book, the critical sections, which are his best, are ruthless and clear:

The school, he says, has become increasingly the "secular arm" of a mass society afraid of death, sex, and loss of control over its adolescent charges. It is without sustaining values. It can no longer rely on its past, when it had a widely accepted economic rationale, being designed to serve an expanding capitalist society. Then, there was some justification for school to be a place where a man "made something out of himself." With today's automation, however, it is no longer even useful to make some *thing* out of yourself. "The things have been quietly catching up. They are now in a position to demonstrate, conclusively, that things make better things than people do."

But if our schools are still concerned with their pupils making something out of themselves, they have rejected the individualism that went with that earlier philosophy. They are all for social harmony. They have thus become the mirrors of a society whose model is one of free-wheeling economic men functioning frictionlessly as community men. Within this model, genuine social conflict (the kind you find especially among adolescents) must be considered aberrant. There can be no honest tension between the individual and his community. Or, as the Ontario Teachers' Federation has put it: "In its broadest sense, education is the profound social process through which we acquire the ways, beliefs, and standards of society, and achieve maximum development of our personal potential."

But if education is this kind of "social process," what is it exactly a youngster learns in school? Friedenberg says he learns, first of all, which relations between himself and his society are "appropriate," and which "constitute invasions of privacy and constraints on his spirit"; and, further, he learns them as a minor, forced to go to school, with only the crudest rights as means of protection. The student also learns that the controls imposed on him have usually very little to do with his education. When this happens he learns something else: that authority is not derived from responsibility, and it soon becomes indistinguishable from power. Under these circumstances individual rights lose their meaning. What a student really needs is power, a weapon, and he doesn't have it. In this weakened position, with few personal resources, the student is easily corrupted and identifies with the more powerful forces around him. He comes to accept the school "as the way life is," and closes his mind "against the anxiety of perceiving alternatives."

One of the best things about Friedenberg's book is his uncanny empathy with students caught in this situation, but who have had the courage to fight back, however ineffectually. These are people, who have somehow retained "the capacity to attend to and respond to (their) inner life and feelings, to the uniquely personal in experience." He calls them "subjective" people:

> This is not "inner direction"—there need be nothing rigid or puritanical about it; the super-ego in such people may be so weak as to be virtually nonexistent, though it may likewise be strong and commanding. Nor does this "inwardness" necessarily make the people who have it more self-directive or truly autonomous; it may be leading them to a more vivid understanding of their existential plight, flood them with such severe and chronic anxiety as to make them almost unable to cope. Such "subjective" people are often unusually self-centered and self-indulgent, whimsical and eccentric, disagreeable and demanding. Yet in their own way, they are peculiarly trustworthy; they are present, they connect, and they treat other people as people, rather than as things, even when they treat them badly.[2]

It is this kind of person the school tries to break; and with increasingly sophisticated techniques. Very often these involve the misuse of crude theories of psychoanalysis, which can be devastating to both lower and upper-class youngsters. An angry slum kid can be given "guidance" and then be classified as "disturbed" if he protests. While smoothly defiant kids from well-to-do homes can be described as having an "authority problem" or a "compulsive drive towards pseudo-maturity." And it all goes on the record.

What is really at stake here, for Friedenberg, is our "civil liberty" and its vulnerability to clinical attack. What he cares about is warding off this attack—giving basic protection to those "subjective" people, who are going to be continuously in conflict with the school authorities. For a start, he says, the school should keep its distance; it has neither the intimacy of the family nor the resources of a

[2] *Ibid.*, p. 211–212.

private psychiatrist. It should stick to education. Like other public institutions, it should be functional and specialized: "The meshes of the law are too coarse to be worn close to the skin."

But the threat to the individual comes not only from the amateur psychiatrists in the guidance offices, it comes also from the new advances being made in the departments of curriculum.

For the lower-status youngster these advances are especially dangerous if misused. Curriculum researchers, in the past couple of decades, have amassed an enormous body of educational methodology, which recognizes the power and range of the slum kid's vocabulary, his "short attention span and higher perceptual threshold," his need for classroom reassurance, and his apathy towards the school's extracurricular activities. But, in spite of their realistic and often imaginative proposals, "their sophistication is essentially that of the research division of a competent advertising agency, which becomes more effective in selling the client's product as it becomes more astute at picturing in detail what the customers are really like, and more willing to adapt its appeals to their actual motives and life styles. What the agency does not do is question the value of the product to the client or the legitimacy of exploiting his motives." [3]

So from both sides of our schools individual liberty and dignity are coming under constant attack. What Friedenberg finds most frightening is that these techniques seem to have taken a vast toll. As the "secular arm" of mass society, the school has been overwhelmingly successful.

[3] *Ibid.*, p. 195–196.

A SURVEY OF VALUES

In order to substantiate this judgment, Friedenberg tried to do something that is enormously difficult: he attempted a survey of student values, in order to see if they matched those of the *mass* society outside the school. Along with Carl Nordstrom (a professor of economics) and Hilary Gold (a professor of education, who acted as advance man) Friedenberg spent a year testing and interviewing a carefully prepared random sample of high school students. He visited nine schools which had a wide variety of racial, social, and economic differences; in each he talked to twenty-five students.

What Friedenberg and Nordstrom did was to write six "episodes," each of which sets up a situation involving a question of moral values. Along with each episode, came nine possible responses written on separate cards. The students were asked to read the episode and then order the cards from best to worst, so making a judgment on the value of each response. Afterwards they were interviewed by Friedenberg and asked why they made the choices they did.

I want to examine one important example of the technique used in this study. First of all, because I think Friedenberg's method was a highly imaginative and at the same time a very practical way to survey something as intangible as a man's values. But secondly, because I believe that when we look at its detail, we come to see the fundamental weakness of this book—too great an emphasis on the "autonomy" of the individual, and too little understanding of the connection between individual liberty and equality.

Let's first look at an episode called "The King's Visit." It's probably the most significant of the nine, because in it students are being asked "to make judgments about what is valuable in an entire human being—or at least in a rather stereotypical description of one—which tends to reveal their set of values as a whole." Here's the episode:

> Several weeks ago, the Governor wrote to the principal of LeMoyen High School to tell him about the impending visit to Capital City of the King of a country not unlike Denmark and of the King's notable interest in spirited young people. He also informed the principal of the King's expressed desire to meet with some interesting and representative high school students during his visit. The Governor then went on to say that he had selected LeMoyen as one of the ten high schools chosen from throughout the state which were to pick several students to meet with the King when he meets the Governor at the Executive Mansion. The Governor added that the King speaks English fluently, and then concluded with the suggestion that such young people as were chosen should be persons to whom the school could point with pride as expressing what was finest and best about their school.
>
> At LeMoyen, where such things are always done as democratically as possible, the students were to have a voice in the choice. First, nine individuals and groups were nominated by a committee composed jointly of faculty members and students with the Dean of Men, Mr. Blakely, serving as Chairman. The student body was to choose from this list of nine the person or persons they thought would best represent them at the meeting with the King. This vote was not conclusive, however, but was primarily advisory, for the principal reserved the right to make the final nomination for the school, guiding himself in his choice by the committee recommendations and the student vote.[4]

Friedenberg's interviewees were given nine cards. On each one there was a character sketch of a possible candidate to represent what was "finest and best" about LeMoyen. The students were then asked to arrange the candidates in such a way that the best and worst were centered out.

[4] *Ibid.*, p. 281–282.

In analyzing their choices (and the interviews, which followed) Friedenberg finds that the vast majority of his subjects showed two things very clearly: first, their feeling that the judgment of others was more important than what they thought and felt about themselves and their world; second, their suspicion of "autonomy"—specialized personal competence operating outside the school's (or society's) control. Both these characteristics he lumps together in the students' general attitude to the problem brought up by the king's visit. Almost to a man they saw it as a technical problem; it was a simple question of public relations. They wanted someone who would make "a good impression" on the king. So they came down solidly on the side of a girl called Karen Clarke:

> Karen Clarke will be giving the valedictory at graduation for this year's class. As she should. Always well-groomed and polite, she is completely in command of herself in any situation. She is the perfect model of what a high school student ought to be. Her work is neat, correct, and unlike that of so many other students, in on time. It really has to be, because her dad, Mr. Clarke, teaches here and he makes sure Karen doesn't get any favors. He makes certain that she stands up for herself and does her work. In student activities she is treasurer of the senior class. She is also a teacher's aide for Mr. Pottipone's chemistry laboratory and a member of the Ethics Committee of the Student Government. Where others are concerned, Karen always tries to be helpful. She wants to go to a good college like Vassar or Smith, and plans everything she does carefully, with this in mind. At LeMoyen everybody feels that she has a real chance to get into the kind of college she would like to go to.[5]

Now, what surprises and disturbs Friedenberg is that the vast majority of his subjects *interpreted* this episode as a

[5] *Ibid.*, p. 55.

public relations set-up. On this point, I don't see any reason for his concern. The whole business is clearly a political maneuver. Here we have an elected politician (the governor) trying to impress an hereditary politician (the king) with a scheme being operated at the ground level by the dean of men and ultimately sanctioned by the principal—two men, Friedenberg tells us, who are "specialists in keeping an essentially political enterprise (the school) from being strangled by conflicting community attitudes and pressures." Does Friedenberg seriously believe that his students are going to be moved by the fact the governor has told them that the King "has a notable interest in spirited young people"? Has Friedenberg ever met a king who hadn't? And does he really think that any student, with even a modicum of social savvy, isn't going to know that a meeting with students at the Executive Mansion will be a "ritual public occasion"?

In my view the students have simply responded to a public relations situation they are faced with all the time. What has happened is that they have accepted this situation, just as they accept it all the time. It's a question of "acquiescence." What this episode (like all the others) shows us is not so much the total value structure of Friedenberg's subjects (as he seems to suggest) but rather certain values they will accept when presented with them. What is disturbing in this particular episode (and it's disturbing to Friedenberg too) is that very very few of his subjects rebelled at the problem being set up this way. Nobody said, "Look, this is a PR job, and Karen Clarke is undoubtedly the girl for it. But it's a very phony set-up and no way to find out what I think is 'finest and best' about a human being." Only one or two came anywhere near saying anything like this. Most thought they would like Karen Clarke.

The same kind of "acquiescence" can also be found in his subjects' response to the characters they rejected as representatives of LeMoyen High. Notice how Friedenberg sets up Scott Cowen, who was thoroughly rejected:

> Scott Cowen is supposed to be a genius. When he was twelve years old his parents arranged for him to take a special course in mathematics at the university near by and he did very well, indeed. Although all the other students in the course were either specially selected senior high school students or college freshmen, Scott came out first in the class. According to the instructor's report, "Mr. Cowen is potentially a mathematician of the first order and with proper training should be able in the future to do work of great significance." At LeMoyen, Scott has continued to do well. His entries in the Senior High School Division Science Fair won first prize both last year and this. He is a brilliant chess player and managed a draw with the state champion. And he is editor of the LeMoyen *Xantippe,* the school literary magazine. Scott's work at LeMoyen is always original and always competent, although he does tend to be sloppy. He's sloppy also in the way he dresses, and he does manage to argue with some of the teachers. If it weren't for this, he would probably be valedictorian of his class. He has the ability to be.[6]

Whatever his accomplishments, Scott Cowen is presented as anti-establishment and *out,* just as Karen Clarke was *in*. The students sensed it right away and thought of him as "a security risk—unstable and unpredictable." The passage brings up echoes of a sharp, "objective," middle-class housewife, who thinks intellectuals are all well and good, provided they don't get too close. Scott is very remote; he's "supposed" to be a genius. We have no idea what he's like as a human being. (We at least know that Karen Clarke likes to help people.) Scott is also "sloppy," an adjective right up there in the same breath with "original" and "competent." What *is* disturbing, here as with the other episode, is that practically no one attacked the *at-*

[6] *Ibid.,* p. 64–65.

titude of the writer (which is found even more extremely in the character sketch of a boy like Johnny Adams—another potential candidate). The students acquiesced in the passage's anti-intellectualism, and its implied disapproval of competence outside the control of the school.

FAINT CHEERS FOR DEMOCRACY

Friedenberg's study is valuable in that it shows us the extent to which students will accept (and I'm sure, in many cases, act on) a framework of mass society values, which in essence reflects a lack of respect for the value of the individual. The book's weakness lies in the fact that it stops here. We get no inkling of the residual, ill-formed values a student cannot articulate. (Friedenberg, I assume, has not forgotten these, or he wouldn't be in the business he's in.) What is missing, then, in his episodes is an alternative to the values of mass society which might conceivably have appealed to the inarticulate value structure of his subjects.

I was sorry, for example, that in the interviews following his tests, there didn't come a time when Friedenberg stopped saying "uh huh" and told his subjects what an insipid character he really thought Karen Clarke was. I think we might have learned something in seeing their response to a different set of values put forward by a man who appeared to be an establishment figure.

There was also nothing to stop Friedenberg from constructing a character for "The King's Visit" who exemplified some of the frontier values of "autonomy" to which he is so attached. There would be no difficulty in setting Scott Cowen up as a "rugged individualist," a young man who has "the courage to stand up on his own two feet," who has the guts not to "knuckle under" to some fink of a teacher who's putting the pressure on. Friedenberg's side certainly has enough clichés of its own for him to construct one of his admittedly "soap opera" characters. It wouldn't have been hard, for example, to mention that Scott willingly gave his prize money to his mother to help her make ends meet, or to set up a scene where he argued with dignity against a principal who was trying to censor his magazine. What then would have been the reaction of Friedenberg's interviewees? I don't think the results would have been so clear-cut for mass values as he makes out now.

In brief, I'm saying that Friedenberg has stacked his deck of cards somewhat to make his point: that student values and mass values are pretty much indistinguishable. And further, that among the "mass" of students (as among the "mass" of men) there are no residual values worth considering; there is nothing really solid in human content to count on or to develop. A small minority (the "subjectives") have somehow escaped the mass net, and the only worthwhile thing to do is to concentrate on them.

Friedenberg, like Ortega, hates mass society and "mass-man" with a passion, and has enormous contempt for the lower middle class on the way up with their eyes closed, who haven't the courage to look this "lethal way of life" in the face. So lethal does Friedenberg find it, that much of the time he leaves the impression that the only saving thing for any man is a fine sense of irony. He is very much aware of the America whose soldiers (when captured in Korea) showed a terrifying softness and lack of even the most rudimentary concern for their fellow inmates. He is sensitive to the "decent" American boy, who "learns early that devotion can be dangerous and that feeling must be sacrificed to flexibility." He knows that togetherness ends in the most degrading isolation. But somehow he knows it too well. And for all his emphasis on the value of the individual, I get no sense of what that value consists. I have no idea what it is Friedenberg thinks links men together; in what way they can be considered equals. To put this another way, there seems to be no sense of any kind of present or potential community. Between the general run of mankind there is no connection. The brave can look that right in the eye, find a few close personal friends, and hold on tight to their sense of irony. The rest are sentimentalizers. On the whole, his research starts from here.

Still, however much Friedenberg's personal view of the world has structured his research (and such structuring should be expected if the book is to have any point) his main argument comes across clearly: our high school students have largely "acquiesced" in the values of our mass society, or really in its lack of values—its tastelessness, its "disciplined expediency." But having made this point, as an educator what do you do about it? How do you set up a situation where a youth can develop his integrity, his own sense of worth?

Before you can answer this question, you must first ask where your own integrity lies. How should a man act in a society, many of whose fundamental life patterns he does not believe in? Friedenberg, himself, rejects the traditional style of the critic or rebel, who remains apart and attacks specific social ills. These ills have become too amorphous. The only alternative is to learn

> *to serve honorably on committees and to perform lovingly and penetratingly the necessary acts of administration. (A man) learns as always to respect himself and other people for their basic human qualities. . . . E. M. Forster's statement in* Two Cheers for Democracy *that "the people I respect most behave as if they were immortal and as if society was eternal. Both assumptions are false: both of them must be accepted as true if we are to go on eating and working and loving, and are to keep open a few breathing holes for the human spirit," is still the best description of integrity I know and the best reason for thinking it indispensable.*[7]

[7] Friedenberg, *The Vanishing Adolescent* (Boston, Beacon Press, 1959), p. 142.

In Canada, George Grant takes a somewhat similar position in his *Lament for a Nation,* not that Grant would go for the notion that you ought to live your life (however poetically or self-consciously) on a couple of false assumptions. What unites his conservatism to Friedenberg's is his passionate hatred of mass society combined with his deep attachment to that society's political framework—the nation-state. Friedenberg, like Grant, put all his community eggs in one national basket, and when he found out (as late nineteenth-century liberals like Forster found out) that the nation-state didn't contain a livable community life, he decided that the only alternative was to protect the individual from his society's increasing tyranny. All a man can realistically do is "to keep open a few breathing holes for the human spirit" or elect John Diefenbaker.

As an educator, therefore, Friedenberg is concerned about producing "gentlemen," an old term he brings back to life. These are men, who are content with their own tastes and way of life and who can be called upon to be "the defenders and exemplars of liberty, properly called civil." They have enough certainty of their own individuality to defend the abstract principle of freedom. In their education, the emphasis is to be first placed on "competence":

> I mean intellectual competence, particularly, since that has been slighted by the school as well as by the rest of our culture. But the need goes deeper than that. The significance of competence in developing a stable identity is that it makes the self-concept specific . . . the full human individual is he who *does* evaluate himself on specific grounds. He thinks of himself partly in terms of his particular competence and responsibilities.[8]

[8] *Ibid.,* p. 143.

What is being developed here is "autonomy," an "absolute value." The autonomous man would not neglect others, but "he makes up his own mind what he ought to do, and he makes it up alone. He is guided by the perceptions of consequences of his acts, and his respect for the people involved in them, but not by their opinions as to what he should do; except, of course, insofar as these are among the consequences for which he will be responsible."

Now, no matter how "honorably" Friedenberg serves on committees, this is the statement of a man operating very much outside his society. There is no sense for the truth in the old idea that "one becomes a man by being a citizen," though I don't think Friedenberg would deny that truth. He is responding to society where in a very real sense one must become a man before he becomes a citizen, or he doesn't become a man at all. The patterns of life demanded by the larger community are untrustworthy. But the old truth remains that maturity is dependent on a genuine community life, on an intimate relation between the individual and his society no matter how full of tension it might be. Recognizing that, at the same time, Friedenberg's principle of "autonomy" (however limited) is still very powerful. I know how much I live by it myself, because I don't get hurt so much that way.

On the other side of the coin, if "autonomy" is a limited ideal from the point of view of a mature individual, it is also inadequate for any kind of society in which men are in constant contact with one another and think of themselves as equals. Friedenberg not only hopes to produce "gentlemen," he is also looking for "aristocrats." He demands a kind of liberty for the individual that is intolerable in a society whose principles are basically democratic. It is *liberty* unconnected with *equality* and *fraternity*, if I can bring out those old words again. The words have to be connected; separated they are ineffectual. (The French didn't stick them together in a slogan for nothing.) If we expect a man to protect another's rights, I think we should also expect that man to believe that there is some fundamental way he can be considered an equal of the other; they share the right and both benefit by it. We should also expect him to believe that in some way the good of the other is his own good.

If then, in school, we expect men to protect an individual's right to a good education, we should also expect them to demand equal treatment. For me, this kind of treatment involves the assumption that all men are capable of coming to some kind of "truth" about themselves and their world. Friedenberg doesn't make this assumption. Rather, he imagines that "truth-seeking is a highly specialized function" to be carried out by an elite, and that the public schools ought to teach people "to mean the same thing by the truth; to establish in their minds similar categories of thought; to approach understanding with roughly the same unconscious predisposition to admit the same considerations as relevant."

I find this concept of public education degrading and false. When a student, attempting to make some sense of his experience, says that something is "true" for him, he doesn't think of it as a "category of thought." He means it is true in a more personal and a more general way. He believes that somehow his experience (and his reflection on it) has a kind of universal validity. That belief is at the core of his self-respect and sense of individual identity. It is up to his school to provide conditions under which that belief can be fostered. He has a right to it.

Further, it seems to me, an individual's right to a good education depends not only on real social equality, but also on the fraternity of a small community. This also Friedenberg seems to deny. On the local level, he argues, men cannot be trusted: they are "mass." Therefore, those capable of "truth seeking" (our potential cultural elite) should be removed from their own neighborhoods (especially slum neighborhoods) and placed in "aristocratically" run boarding schools for "gentlemen." The schools will have to be "imposed by a central authority."

In what "central authority" you may ask, is there a chance of such a scheme meeting approval and being given freedom to operate? Why, in none other than the "large bureaucracies of the executive branch" of the federal government.

> They are big enough to maintain officials specially trained to deal with Congress and complicated enough to shield their working personnel from having to deal with anyone else. I would favor, then, the formation of a Federal Educational Authority to control and operate such boarding schools as an open, public facility.[9]

So Friedenberg is now in the position of distinguishing between the values of the servants of a mass society and the values of that mass society itself. Somehow the bureaucrats of The Great Society are going to create a school system dedicated to demolishing the virtues their political leaders stand for, and which, incidentally, make for good bureaucrats. Whatever happened to all that celebrated irony?

But even if it were possible to develop a high degree of individual "autonomy" among students, I think it is a mistake to believe that such students can work *quietly* within our established institutions and still keep their integrity. I am thinking particularly of our schools and a boy called Stanley, who appears in Friedenberg's earlier book *The Vanishing Adolescent*.

Stanley came from a Polish immigrant family, which was solidly working-class and close-knit. Unlike most immigrant kids, Stanley was enormously successful at school

[9] Friedenberg, *Coming of Age in America,* p. 255.

—academically, in extracurricular activities, and with the administration. Why was he so successful? Primarily, says Friedenberg, because he was cool enough not to get into a power struggle with the school. His foremost qualities were his "exceptional detachment and complete lack of sentimentality." "These made it possible for him to see and accept the school for what it was, to demand nothing of it that would disturb the people who were running it, and still to use it to his own best advantage." For Friedenberg, Stanley was a picture of health. He "has the kind of mental structure people spend five years and fifteen thousand dollars to achieve through psychoanalysis. . . . He is ambitious, and aware that he is; he knows where he is going, and he is using the school to get there."

Well, Stanley may have known where he was going, but (in spite of Friedenberg's lavish praise) Stanley didn't seem to have had much idea of where he had been. His only real contact seems to have been with his home. Take a look at some of his answers to a sentence completion test:

> Girls at school like a boy who: "is a lot of fun."
> Kids who get out of line: "ought to be made to toe the line."
> Politics: "bore me."
> The kids would hang together if: "there were more things to do."
> Our student government: "is a good organization."
> Working class people are: "the average class of people."

I would like to imagine that Stanley, like Peter Pan, had never grown any older and had stayed in his sophomore year of high school. And that Friedenberg, in his random sample, had somehow run across him again and asked for his response to "The King's Visit": who was to represent "the best and finest" at LeMoyen High? Can you believe Stanley would have picked anyone but Karen Clarke?

YOU NEED IMAGINATION IN THE HOLE

Charlie Macdougal

Clay Borris, a student at Point Blank School, interviewed Charlie Macdougal on growing up in prison for a radio documentary. This article is an edited transcript of that interview. Charles Macdougal (a pseudonym) was at the time eighteen and lived in Cabbagetown in central Toronto.

1

BELIEVE IT OR NOT, I think the way it all started was over an orange. That was the critical turning point right there. An orange. Because I'd asked my stepfather for an orange and he'd said no. I had the rejected feeling already, you know, because some of my family—after I'd say something stupid—they'd all have a big giggle, and after a while it got rather sickening. So that orange was it. I was in the washroom contemplating suicide, but decided not to because I didn't like the idea of bleeding to death. So I decided I'd run away from home. They caught up with me, of course, and they put me in the Children's Aid Center. Not that there was anything wrong with my family. You know, I think maybe I was just a little bit too spoiled, and maybe a good smack on the ass might have cured me.

Anyway I was in this Childrens' Aid home with this fellow I knew. (He's dead now, and I don't want to mention his name.) I was nine then and so was the fellow I was with. The girl we ran away with was twelve, and she was staying in the girls Childrens' Aid right across from us. We decided to break out, and before I left I managed to bust every window in the place with a hockey stick because this woman who was taking care of the place slapped me in the face. I used to have quite bad fits of temper.

We started out going to Rice Lake where his cottage was, and it took us two weeks to get to Peterborough. Don't ask me how, but it did. I think we were just travelling around in circles or something; we were going up one road without knowing where we were going. One surprising thing was that we never did spend a night out in the cold. There was always someone to put us up. I don't know why the cops didn't catch us before they did.

When they did catch us, they took me to Juvenile Court and the judge says you can either go back to the Childrens' Aid or home, which I should have taken, or to training school. I'd heard my uncle use the phrase, "Why do the crime, if you can't do the time." I thought that was quite a smart saying, and I wanted to get up with my brother Bill anyway, so I said, "Why do the crime, if you can't do the time," and the judge looked down at me and he says—I can still remember—he says, "Son, there is something very seriously wrong with you. We're going to have to put you in a training school, if that's your choice." I remember Bill saying you won't find it as nice as you think you might. I remember he said you've had your cake and the icing, and you want the cherry too. You know I can still remember that. When I came back to the school the second time I ran away, they put me in Whitby Hospital to see if there was anything wrong with me, you know—a nine-year-old kid in Whitby.

The first day of training school is strange. It's like walking into a jungle because there are guys there who are just as bad or badder than you are, and they all want to play the part with each other, aggravate each other. They stick together after they've been there awhile and learn to be friends with each other. And if they don't like your appearance, they'll gang up on you or give you a hard way to go, start beating you up for odd ends, making you do things for them, stealing things off you, like your dessert. They make you do things you don't like, like being a run boy. If you're a real stooge, they make you do homosexual acts on them.

I got into a lot of fights when I first walked in, because in there the house you stay in starts from the first rock and then there's the second rock and all the way down the line like this, and you got to fit in to where you want to fit in, and you either got to fight or be known as an asshole. An asshole is a guy who's off from everybody else, and he doesn't do nothing with the group. There's this group of people around, with the assholes at the back. The guys they call wheelers are up at the front.

I was a wheeler. When you wheel, you push other people. You have to because if you let anyone push you . . . . It's like a rat race. You gotta stay in front all the time. If you don't, you'll get stepped on. Guys start thinking they're smart with you, calling you a goof. They give you a hard time to go, so you got to keep it up steadily.

Maybe I had it a little easier at the start because my brother was in at the same time. I was nine and he was eleven, and he was always one step ahead of me in the houses, and where he left friends they automatically became my friends. So he was sort of cushioning the way for me. Also I was big and I looked rough, and guys stayed away from me.

There was one time I really had to call on my brother for help. I was out in the playfield and the guard, he's been smacking around this little kid, and I said, "What a big goof," to the same kid that he was slapping around, and the kid went back and told him, and I got the severe piss kicked out of me. So I went over to the superintendent and I told him that this guard had beat me up. The superintendent came back and told the guard just what I'd said. So I got out on the field, and first of all I was invited to play a game of baseball, and I thought something was wrong there because they knew I wasn't any good at sports, but you know when you're young you don't think that quick. So I got out there, and I was playing ball, and somebody hit me on the side of the head with the ball, and somebody else beat me in the face with the catcher's mitt. Another kid hit me over the head with a baseball bat, and he split my head open, knocked me out. I was in the school yard the next day with my brother. We both picked up baseball bats, and I was kind of scared, but he made me go on walking over with him. I didn't want to hit them with a baseball bat, but it's just if they do it on you, why not do it on them? So we started swinging with the baseball bats, and after that we pretty well had an understanding there that if you took on one brother, you took on both of them. It was something like double insurance. In that fight there was about six of them. You get one guy that's got nothing in his hands and not expecting anything, well, that's fine and easy enough for six kids to jump him, but say you get one kid walking back in towards six with a baseball bat, now that makes them kind of doubtful. When you get two that puts them rather on the scared side.

I got to be a wheeler when I started showing people that I was no asshole. I started winning a lot of fights, and I got more confidence in some of the guys, and they started to be my friends. I fought with them a few times, not too regular, because if they ever had any hard times they came to me. It was equal; we came to each other. Just a certain amount of guys.

You can stay a wheeler until you become a stooge. You become a stooge if you start crossing the wrong guys or beating the wrong guys. If you start trying to beat somebody that is rougher than you, well it don't go that way because he's going to get hot and he's going to give it to you and class you as a goof, and before you know it, you'll be on the arm yourself.

When I was there, there was about ten wheelers and I was about the third, and with the other two top guys I got along good. We fought. We fought about four or five times with each other, but we had a mutual understanding. When we had a hard time we just took each other aside, had it out and got everything squared away, shook hands and we understood what we had to do.

When you want to fight you can ask the staff if you can go out in the middle of the floor. You put up your hand in the locker room, and he'll ask you what you want, and you say, "May I have such a person out in the middle of the floor." So he'll say, "all right," so you go out, and you have a little fight until one or the other quits or until the staff figures he's had his pleasure.

You fight with your bare hands, and you take off your shoes; you can use your feet, anywhere. I've seen a lot of guys get badly hurt with ruptures and broken noses.

When that happens they always use the excuse that we fell off our beds or ran into a tree playing football or these things. This is what happens when you first walk into a house at Cobourg; there are seven houses, and they vary in age limits. When you walk in there'll be a guy there who doesn't like your face, and he's been there a while, so he'll ask the staff, "Could I have that guy out in the middle of the floor." The staff wants a bit of entertainment to pass his eight hours away, so he'll say sure, and you've got nothing to say about it. You either go out there and fight, or the guy will beat the hell out of you right in your locker.

There was this one guard, one particular guy I remember quite well, and he used to like to take the goofiest-looking guy in the whole locker room and match him up against one of the roughest. It'd be no match; it just seemed like he was doing it for his own enjoyment. There has to be something definitely sick with a man who'd do something like that. Getting two kids out in the center of the floor having one scared to hell the other one will bash the shit out of him. You know you get the shit bashed out of you if you don't bash the shit out of somebody else. I was always of sufficient size, and I didn't look that goofy so I didn't have that many problems. But there were other guys that were big sizes, and maybe they might have blemishes and not really too much upstairs, and they wouldn't like one fellow. They wouldn't like some guy who say never came out from behind his mother's apron all his life. This kind of a guy might be in for playing hookey from school three times within the period of a year, and he might come from a very strict town, and so when he went in there, he was what you might call a mama's boy. I remember one of these mama's boys got into the center of the floor . . . I don't know what he was trying to do . . . I think he was trying to kill himself because he took various types of pills he'd managed to steal from the infirmary. Maybe it was his way of trying to get out of something, but he didn't take the right kind of pills.

My brother was told one time to go out and fight with somebody in the center of the floor, and he didn't do it, and the guard—the one I been talking about—got so rambunctious he broke my brother's arm for not obeying him. I don't know, it's supposed to be a training school, not a three-ring circus for their benefit.

There was nothing you could do about this kind of thing. They'd just say he fell downstairs. You might get somebody interested from the outside, interested enough to come in. Well, that's fine. They come in, and you know you're dealing with seven-year-olds right up to twelve-year-olds. They're all kids, and if somebody weighs 230 and stands maybe six foot, even five-nine, at that age it looks like you're looking at a giant. It's just like standing in front of the Empire State Building. You can't stand up to them.

Mind you, you can put in your complaint. The superintendent will mention it to the guard and investigate it, but then also you have to go back to that locker room too, and that guard will be on again. All the superintendent does is warn the guard and ask a few questions to the guys. The guys will say, "I don't know, sir, I didn't see it," or something like that because they're scared, and the superintendent will give you a blast of shit for lying and trying to get the guard in trouble. Then when you get back to that locker room the guard might make you bend over in your locker. You know, you bend down and touch your toes and stay in that position for about three hours, and believe it or not, it is quite painful after a while, being bent over like that. Or he might make you put your head down in your locker—things like that. Sometimes they even get to the stage where, when you do get back, they pound the piss out of you. They get some of the bigger fellows. The guard tells them, "I want this goof punched out." If they don't do it, they miss the show or something. The guard says, "Well, I got to go answer the phone," and you got thirty guys coming at you. Not because they necessarily want to—but because they have to, you know—or they'll get the piss beat out of them.

That's what happens to rebels. The goofs get it another way. The real stooges, like I said, they make them do homosexual acts. They'll make you play with them or suck their joint—whatever they wish to have done to them at the present. They make them do it in the bedrooms, in the washrooms or maybe out in the yard lying on the grass. I made guys do it for me, though I never really had to threaten them. These goofs, they were used to it, and they generally came to me and started it. This is one thing I got a real shock over when I walked in, because you're standing in line for your dinner, and some guy will be standing in front of you, and he'll start fumbling with your privates. For a while you tell him to get lost, but after six months to a year (I was there eighteen months the first time) you get used to it. You get used to guys doing these things, and everything comes natural because there aren't no girls around, and you got so much aggravation there. It just seems a way that you can blow everything—get it off your chest.

You get some of these goofs to do things regularly for you. They call these guys "sweet kids." This is a kid you like, more or less, and you take him and you protect him from other guys so they won't smash him around. And he does everything you want him to. If you want his dinner or his supper or anything like that, you take it. If you want him to shine your shoes, he shines them. If you want him cleaning your clothes and pressing them and folding them up, this is what he does. If you want him to do homosexual acts on you, he does them. If he doesn't, he gets punched out or you just drop him and the rest of the guys will either try to take him for themselves or start punching him out. When you've kicked a guy out there are other guys that come around. You see they want to because they get smacked around. If they're real stooges, everytime somebody sees them they give them a shot in the head. Just for nothing. A laugh. So they'll come to a guy like me and say, "Be my old man." So you take him, and he's got protection more or less.

The goofs also lose most of what they got. When you're in there you're allowed parcels, and you can also go downtown or to the beach on a pass when your parents are up for their one day a week. Some kids bring back these enormous parcels with chocolate bars, chips, coke, everything, you know. Some parents go to extremes and give their children about $20 worth of candy. I'm not kidding you, some of them did. They'd bring it all back. The superintendent did have rather a good rule: if the boy did have a lot of candy, he was supposed to share it to an extent with the others.

You know, maybe he'd take a chocolate bar and bust it in four places and hand it out. The guard would do this, not you. So that was fine, but sometimes, if you were a goof, you were lucky if you got a bag of chips out of what you had left.

2

It's been quite a while since I've been back. I think it was two years ago. No, I haven't been out that long. But when I was back to visit the training school it was the same rat race as when I was a kid. It never changed. They had new staff, mind you, but the new staff had the same ideas. I was up with a group of people to see one of the kids and to see the old place, and I was standing behind a guard, and I heard him say, "Go give that kid over there a whack in the head; he's been getting on my nerves." And this kid he was talking to walked over and hit the other kid with a baseball bat or something. It's really unbelievable.

A lot of my time I spent at the Ontario Training School at Guelph. The first time I spent ten months, and then I came back again. I outgrew the funny things that were happening around me because of how I acted. When the guard would say something I didn't want to do, I just say, "Piss on ya." So you know I was getting smacked around quite a bit before I graduated there. I had gotten smacked around quite a bit, and I decided I'd settle down and cut out of the place. So I settled down and I got my intermediate. But one day a couple of guys went AWOL. This official asked me to chase them, and I chased them all the way down to Toronto. They caught me two weeks later.

I remember this one guard in particular. In the locker room he'd start on these war stories. He'd say how he'd been collecting dog tags for his company off dead men or how he'd seen a man's fingers cut off for his rings. Then he'd tell you how he walked into a barn one time and saw these men hanging from their feet with the blood rushing to their head. The Japanese trick. I used to go to bed at night and have groovy little dreams about that. He'd go right into extreme detail about it. Like how the man's nostrils seemed to be flared out, how his face seemed purple, the look of death about him. Other things he'd do would be to ask you to get up and pull his finger and let out some very bad smells. Then he'd tell you about the green lady who's supposed to be haunting in the walls. When you're kids, you believe this kind of thing. Like one kid, I think, even went into a convulsion over this.

There were other little things:

Maybe because I was the biggest one in the room, they made me room captain. And this guy in charge of the house caught two or three guys masturbating, and he didn't want that going on. (As I found out in later years, you can become sick from it; I can understand that point.) At that time if anyone put his hands underneath the blankets you were supposed to run up and say, "Sir, this guy's got his hands underneath the blankets," or you were supposed to throw him out of the room. Then he'd get beat across the ass with a rad * broom. Myself, I didn't like the idea of ratting out on anybody nor the idea of somebody getting beaten for something I said.

One night there was a little buggery going on in the room, and somebody heard the night watchman coming. One guy jumped into his bed, and the other guy tried to get into his. But this other guy was on the bottom bunk, and he knocked himself out on the rail. So he's laying straddled out on the floor, and the guy who ran the house comes in and says, "What's been happening?" He says, "Did you see who was doing it?" Well, automatically I'm awake and supposed to be seeing it. Now don't ask me how you're supposed to stay awake until everyone is asleep, but you are, and you are supposed to report everything. On this particular night I just didn't let them know who it was. Of course, the guard knew there was something going on because there was somebody laying out on the floor. So they asked me who was the other party involved in this, and I said I didn't know. So they took me down to the locker room. There was a separate place for the head man or staff. There were four staff members there and sort of a counsellor over them. The counsellor took me in there, and he got a rad broom. He made me put my hands on the desk, and he said, "For every time you say no, you won't tell, I'll give you a smack." He started off with one. The second time I wouldn't tell him

* A broom used to clean radiators.

he gave me two. Then the third time he gave me three. I think maybe we got up to about ten times saying no. By that time my ass was well blistered and black and blue. I didn't mention anything to anybody. I couldn't sit down for a while. He went right nuts.

A little later when I was changing into my swimming trunks down at the beach when my mother came to take me out on a pass, she saw it. And she says, "I'm going to write to the superintendent and report it," and I said, "No, don't bother," and she says, "Why not?" and I said, "All you'll do is get the piss beat out of me even more." These are the kind of things that do happen. There is no unity there. Like say up in Burwash or something you can riot. But in these places you only got kids, and everybody is trying to make sure they don't get the piss beat out of them.

I spent a fair amount of time in the hole at Guelph. I used to go in there maybe fifteen to twenty days at a time. You find things to do in the hole. I don't know what anybody else does, but I masturbate quite a bit to tire myself out, so I can get away from it. Like you exhaust yourself so you can go to sleep. I do other things. Maybe I'm half stunned or something, but I'll count the cracks on the wall or lie on the bunk and start singing "love me, love me do" or something. Little things, like stand on my head in a corner. Stupid things to keep on amusing myself. I'll sit and imagine myself a pirate or a buccaneer. You know that to change what's happening right there is not within your means to realize, and you don't like to face up to that. It's just too much. So you put yourself in dreamland. Some people haven't got an imagination. Those are the people who take the hole hard.

Myself, you know, I can go on telling myself jokes and exhausting myself in my own little ways for maybe about twenty days. Even so, I'm building up to a breakdown, even though I'm holding it down. Like my unconscious, all of a sudden . . . it didn't happen in the hole in the Don, but it happened in the hole in the OTS, Guelph. I just went so berserk. They had a toilet in the room. I ripped that off the wall. Now I wasn't very strong—I was only about fourteen and I had never really done any strenuous work—but that's just how far you can go. You use every ounce of your strength to do something. I was right berserk in there. I'd bang my head out. I was underneath the bed, and I kept on looking up at them and saying, "The ceiling is falling, the ceiling is falling." That was after doing a month and a half in the hole.

That time I really deserved the hole. Because this day I got a four in my re-board, that's four months more you have to do in there. I was in with these two guys who were in for manslaughter, as kids, which sometimes does happen. There were two of them, no there were three of them, and then there was another fellow that had got a four that day, like I did. And there was also another fellow that had got a four. So we were all in quite bad moods; and these other guys who were in for manslaughter they just went along. They didn't give a shit because they were in until they were twenty-one anyway. So we started. I had saved up about a month's worth of newspapers, and we scattered them, like we were throwing them all out of our cells into the hallway. We had managed to capture a small bottle of tractor gas and we made this thing quite a plot. We threw out our sheets and mattresses and boots. We threw everything out except our jockeys, and all along the hall we threw in matches, and we all prayed.

You know, our New Testaments. Because this night watchman that was on gave them to us, saying they would help us out quite a lot. He was a bit of a religious nut. We had the hall ablaze. When the guard came the flames were about three feet high, and I yelled out, "Here you go. Hope you goddam well burn with it too, you goddam nut." So automatically I was number one on the list. They called me the shit-disturber.

After the fire subdued they bounced me around the room a bit with the fire hose at about seventy pounds of pressure. Hitting you square in the face you get your head racked up against the wall. That's all right, but that still wasn't enough to make me quite settle down. I was going to give them a fight so they'd put me in the hole. There was this one guard on—he'd been a commando in the last world war—and mind you he was a very fair man. This I must mention because he gave me more opportunities. He says, "Look son, I'm about five times stronger than you are." He says, "I've got about a hundred times more knowledge as far as fighting is concerned. So come on out of there peacefully, and it might go better on you." But I guess I wanted to be a hero or something, and so I said, "Come on and get me." He was controlling me with about two fingers down to the hole. I couldn't move except the way he wanted me to. That's how I made the hole.

The hole at Guelph isn't much different than the hole at the Don Jail. They seem to follow basically the same model. I think it must have been the same interior decorator. It's worse than fucked-up; it's just above and beyond. If I could describe it to you, then I'd have to be as mad as the goddam idiot that created it. Because I can't describe it. You have to see it to believe it.

At the Don I was thrown in the hole for refusing to scrub. I was on remand, and they say a remanded person isn't supposed to scrub. You scrub in your street clothes and you have to wear them to court and you don't want to look like a mess in them. I refused to scrub, so they put me in the hole. The hole is about six by six. It's got a steel bed and you don't get any blankets. It's as cold as hell. You don't get any sink. You got a hole in the floor that's about the size of a dish and that's what you piss and shit in. It flushes about every minute and a half, and this can drive you off your nut. The light stays on twenty-four hours a day, and it is nerve-racking. I was there this time for eighteen days.

I was in not just for not scrubbing, but for fighting. Because I wouldn't scrub, one of the staff started giving me a hard time, and he punched me, so I hit him back. When we went downstairs a couple more of the guards jumped up and they got a hold of me, and they took me downstairs to the lieutenant. The lieutenant said, "What is wrong here?" The guard said, "He wouldn't scrub piss; he hit me." I said, "I'd like to change that a bit. Fine, I wouldn't scrub, but I didn't hit him; he hit me first. And I only hit him back to protect myself because he wouldn't stop." The lieutenant says to the guard, "Is that right?" and the guard says, "No, you can ask him." So the other guard says, "Oh, yeah, that's right. This guy here went and hit him first." So I got kind of mad, and I started swinging again, and this time I got a bit luckier. I got three or four punches in before they got hold of me again and took me down to the shower room and beat the piss out of me.

They dragged me to the hole unconscious. When I woke up I was black and blue. I couldn't move. I had a pain in my stomach. I had two ribs broken. My eyes were black. My nose was cracked. I couldn't get up off the floor. I just couldn't breathe. Finally the governor came down and they made me stand when he came in. Two of them grabbed me and stood me up. The pain was so bad it brought tears to my eyes. Still, I had a bad temper, so I started using a bit of bad language. They started punching me around again. I couldn't fight back. I just lay on the floor. He said, "That will get you twenty days in the hole."

I did almost eighteen days, and I was cracking up because nobody came to see me. You can't have no cigarettes, no reading, and there is nothing to occupy your time at all. You just sit and sit and sit. You can't lay on the floor because it's too cold, and the toilet keeps you awake. You can't lay on the bed because it's too hard. There's no mattress, no nothing. As far as meals go, you get meatloaf three times a day. What meatloaf consists of is what they want to call meatloaf. It's got peas, cabbage, leftover hamburger, leftover liver, leftover shit in it. You get a cup of cold tea and you get that meatloaf on two pieces of bread. I used to always take the bread and throw the meatloaf under the door. But after eighteen days I finally went off my nut a bit. The guard looked in on me and I was talking to a fly. He got on the phone quick and got the doctor and the psychiatrist and all them down and they let me out. I blew about seventeen pounds in there. When I came back up I was scrubbing all day. But, mind you, I didn't mind scrubbing then, because I was goddam glad to be getting out of there.

You've got to have discipline. Fine and dandy, like you can't have everybody running a jail. But they go too far. You ask those guards to do you a favor like, "Have you got a pencil so I can write a letter or keep score," and they'll say to you, "Go away, don't bother me." Their attitude is so low—like they're talking to a bunch of dogs. This is exactly the way they treat you.

They put four people in a cell. You don't know the guys you're in with. They're strange. When I was in there this is what my cell consisted of. One guy was up for non-capital murder—killing a girl. The other guy was up for manslaughter—killing his wife while she was pregnant. The third guy was up for sixty-two charges of fraud or something, and here I was in for "possession over." One guy is mumbling off to himself, "I'll get her. I'll get her." She's already dead, but he's gonna get her again. And they look at you like maybe you were with her or you are her. You don't know what to think. The next thing you know you've got this pisspot and you're beating this guy over the head until he goes out cold because you're afraid to go to sleep. You don't know if the son of a bitch is going to jump you. You're just so worried.

Once when I was in the corridor this one guy came in—he was up for attempted murder—and tried to stab this other guy. And when I'm walking down at the back, all of a sudden this same guy makes a mad dash for my neck. So my buddy dinged him, and he went down. I says, "Stop it." All the guys were going to jump him, and I says, "Hang on! Let's see what's happening." So I says, "What'd you try and jump me for?" He says, "You're in with them, aren't you? You're in with that guy I tried to stab. You're a friend of his. You're gonna get me too aren't you?" This guy was automatically nuts. Why put guys like that in? They don't belong there. They belong in 999 [a mental hospital].

I spent four and a half months in the Don. Last summer I was there the whole summer. I was trying to raise a thousand dollars bail, but my family was a poor family, and they couldn't do it. I just had to stay there until my case came up. But as far as the people who come in there that are real nuts they shouldn't be in a place like that. For the simple fact that people that are up for murder, there is definitely something wrong with them. Mind you, there is something wrong with me because I shouldn't be doing things that I do. But I'm not that far gone that I have to murder somebody. Like, fine and dandy, punch them out, anything like that I'll do it. But to take a knife or a gun or to strangle a person to death—I couldn't do it. I don't think I'm crazy.

The only thing I am is . . . I drink quite a bit. I drink, and then you know, I imagine myself as heavyweight champion of the world or something. And I'm very touchy. All of a sudden somebody will say something and

I'll start with the Man Mountain Dean act. Like I just got arrested lately for a little adventure in a restaurant. Believe it or not this time I was in the right, and they were in the wrong. Still, I have to spend a week in the Don for it, and just about break down in hysterical tears in front of the judge. Before that I'd had two charges of assault causing bodily harm and the Crown mentioned that. He figures I was a nuisance to society. He must be quite an intelligent man who can just read my record and look at my face and say I'm a nuisance to society. He doesn't even know me. It had been about six months that I'd been out, and I hadn't been arrested for anything.

I've been arrested for something now. I'm on a new charge of assault causing bodily harm. I stand about a 75 per cent chance of getting convicted. About a 5 per cent chance of the judge saying he ain't too sure. The other 20 per cent says I might get off. I'll be going to Burwash or Kingston Penitentiary.

THE OPEN TRUTH AND FIERY VEHEMENCE OF YOUTH

A Sort of Soliloquy

PETER MARIN

IT IS midnight and I am sitting here with my notes, enough of them to make two books and a half and a volume of posthumous fragments, trying to make some smaller sense of them than the grand maniacal design I have in my mind. I don't know where to begin. Once, traveling in summer across the country with a friend from Hollywood and my young son in a battered green Porsche, I stopped for lunch somewhere in Kansas on a Sunday morning. As we walked into the restaurant, bearded, wearing dark glasses and strange hats, and followed by my long-haired boy, one Kansas matron bent toward another and whispered, "I bet those two men have kidnapped that little girl." I took a deep breath and started to speak,

* Originally from *The Center Magazine,* (published by The Center for the Study of Democratic Institutions, Santa Barbara. Vol. II, No. 1, January 1969), pp. 61–74. A somewhat abbreviated version appeared simultaneously in *This Magazine,* III, No. 2 (1969), pp. 40–63.

but I did not know where to begin or how to explain just how many ways she was mistaken. Now, trying to write clearly about education and adolescence, I feel the same way.

For that reason I have chosen an eccentric method of composition, one that may seem fragmentary, jumpy, and broken. This article will be more like a letter, and the letter itself is an accumulation of impressions and ideas, a sampling of thoughts at once disconnected but related. There is a method to it that may disappear in its mild madness, but I do not know at this juncture how else to proceed. Shuffling through my notes I feel like an archaeologist with a mass of uncatalogued shards. There is a pattern to all this, a coherence of thought, but all I can do here is assemble the bits and pieces and lay them out for you and hope that you can sense how I get from one place to another.

An entire system is hiding behind this, just beginning to take form, and these notes are like a drawing, a preliminary sketch. I feel comfortable with that notion, more comfortable than with the idea of forcing them together, cutting and pasting, to make a more conventional essay. I can perceive in myself at this moment what I also see in the young. I am reluctant to deal in sequence with my ideas and experience, I am impatient with transition, the habitual ways of getting "from here to there." I think restlessly; my mind, like the minds of my students, works in flashes, in sudden perceptions and brief extended clusters of intuition and abstraction—and I have stuck stubbornly to that method of composition. There is still in me the ghost of an apocalyptic adolescent, and I am trying to move it a few steps toward the future.

One theme, as you will see, runs through what I have written or thought: we must rethink our ideas of childhood and schooling. We must dismantle them and start again from scratch. Nothing else will do. Our visions of adolescence and education confine us to habit, rule perception out. We make do at the moment with a set of ideas inherited from the nineteenth century, from an industrial, relatively puritanical, repressive, and "localized" culture; we try to gum them like labels to new kinds of experience. But that won't do. Everything has changed. The notions with which I began my job as a high school director have been discarded one by one. They make no sense. What emerges through these children as the psyche of this culture is post-industrial, relatively unrepressed, less literate and local: a new combination of elements, almost a new strain. Adolescents are, each one of them, an arena in which the culture transforms itself or is torn between contrary impulses; they are the victims of a culture raging within itself like man and wife, a schizoid culture—and these children are the unfinished and grotesque products of that schism.

They are grotesque because we give them no help. They are forced to make among themselves adjustments to a tension that must be unbearable. They do the best they can, trying, in increasingly eccentric fashions, to make sense of things. But we adults seem to have withdrawn in defeat from that same struggle, to have given up. We are enamored, fascinated, and deluded by adolescence precisely because it is the last life left to us; only the young rebel with any real passion against media, machines, the press of circumstance itself. Their elders seem to have no options, no sense of alternative or growth. Adult existence is bled of life and we turn in that vacuum toward children with the mixed repulsion and desire of wanton Puritans toward life itself.

As for me, an adult, I think of myself as I write as an observer at a tribal war—an anthropologist, a combination of Gulliver and a correspondent sending home news by mule and boat. By the time you hear of it, things will have changed. And that isn't enough, not enough at all. Somebody must step past the children, must move into his own psyche or two steps past his own limits into the absolute landscape of fear and potential these children inhabit. That is where I am headed. So these ideas, in effect, are something like a last message tacked to a tree in a thicket or tucked under a stone. I mean: we cannot follow the children any longer, we have to step ahead of them. Somebody has to mark a trail.

Adolescence: a few preliminary fragments . . .

(FROM MY STUDENT, V): *yr whole body moves in a trained way & you know that youve moved this way before & it contains all youve been taught its all rusty & slow something is pushing under that rusted mesh but* STILL YOU CANNOT MOVE *you are caught between 2 doors & the old one is much closer & you can grab it all the time but the other door it disappears that door you cant even scratch & kick (like the early settlers were stung by the new land) but this new land doesnt even touch you & you wonder if youre doing the right thing to get in*

(FROM FRANZ KAFKA): *He feels imprisoned on this earth, he feels constricted; the melancholy, the impotence, the sicknesses, the feverish fancies of the captive afflict him; no comfort can comfort him, since it is merely comfort, gentle head-splitting comfort glazing the brutal fact of imprisonment.* But if he is asked what he wants he cannot reply. . . . He has no conception of freedom.

(FROM TAPES RECORDED IN PACIFIC PALISADES, 1966, SEVERAL BOYS AND GIRLS AGED 12–14): *Things are getting younger and younger. Girls twelve will do it now. One guy said I fuck a girl every Friday night. What sexual pleasure do you get out of this (he's very immature you know) and he would say, I don't know I'm just going to fuck.*

or

—How old are you? —*Twelve.* —Will you tell us your first experience with drugs, how you got into it? —*Well, the people I hung around with were big acid-heads. So one day my friend asked me if I wanted to get stoned and I said yes. That was about five months ago and I've been getting on it ever since. Started taking LSD about one month ago. Took it eleven times in one month. I consider it a good thing. For getting high, smoking grass is better, or hashish—it's about six times stronger than marijuana.*

(FROM PAUL RADIN: Primitive Man As Philosopher): *It is conceivably demanding too much of a man to whom the pleasures of life are largely bound up with the life of contemplation and to whom analysis and introspection are the self-understood prerequisites for a proper understanding of the world, that he appreciate . . . expressions which are largely non-intellectual—where life seems, predominatingly, a discharge of physical vitality, a simple and naïve release of emotions or an enjoyment of sensations for their own sake. Yet . . . it is just such an absorption in a life of sensations that is the outward characteristic of primitive peoples.*[2]

Can you see where my thought leads? It is precisely at this point, adolescence, when the rush of energies, that sea-sex, gravitation, the thrust of the ego up through layers of childhood, makes itself felt, that the person is once more like an infant, is swept once more by energies that are tidal, unfamilar, and unyielding. He is in a sense born again, a fresh identity beset inside and out by the rush of new experience. It is at this point, too—when we seem compelled by a persistent lunacy to isolate him—that what is growing within the adolescent demands expression,

[2] Paul Radin, *Primitive Man As Philosopher* (New York, D. Appleton & Co., 1927), p. 12.

requires it, and must, in addition, be received by the world and given form—or it will wither or turn to rage. Adolescence is a second infancy. It is then that a man desires solitude and at the same time contact with the vivid world; must test within social reality the new power within himself; needs above all to discover himself for the first time as a bridge between inner and outer, a maker of value, a vehicle through which culture perceives itself. It is now, ideally, that he begins to understand the complex and delicate nature of the ego itself as a thin skin between living worlds, a synaptic jump, the self-conscious point at which nature and culture combine.

In this condition, with these needs, the adolescent is like a primitive man, an apocalyptic primitive; he exists for the moment in that stage of single vision in which myth is still the raw stuff of being, he knows at first hand through his own energies the possibilities of life—but he knows these in muddled, sporadic, contradictory ways. The rush of his pubescent and raw energy seems at odds with public behavior, the *order* of things, the tenor of life around him, especially in a culture just emerging—as is ours—from a tradition of evasion, repression, and fear.

The contradictions within the culture itself intensify his individual confusion. We are at the moment torn between future and past: in the midst of a process of transformation we barely understand. The development of adolescent energy and ego—difficult at any time—is complicated in our own by the increase in early sexuality, the complicated messages of the media, and the effects of strong and unfamiliar drugs. These three elements are, in themselves, the salient features of a culture that is growing more permissive, less repressive. They are profound, complex, and strong: heavy doses of experience demanding changes in attitude, changes in behavior. The direction and depth of feeling responds accordingly; the adolescent tries—even as a form of self-defense against the pressure of his own energies—to move more freely, to change his styles of life, to "grow." But it is then that he finds he is locked into culture, trapped in a web of ideas, law, and rituals that keep him a child, deprive him of a chance to test and assimilate his newer self. It is now that the culture turns suddenly repressive. His gestures are evaded or denied; at best he is "tolerated," but even then his gestures, lacking the social support of acknowledgment and reward, must seem to him lacking in authenticity—more like forms of neurosis or selfishness than the natural stages in growth.

He is thrust back upon himself. The insistent natural press within him toward becoming whole is met perpetually by unbudging resistance. Schools, rooted as they are in a Victorian century and seemingly suspicious of life itself, are his natural enemies. They don't help, as they might, to make that bridge between his private and the social worlds; they insist, instead, upon their separation. Indeed, family, community, and school all combine—especially in the suburbs—to isolate and "protect" him from the adventure, risk, and participation he needs; the same energies that relate him at this crucial point to nature result in a kind of exile from the social environment.

Thus the young, in that vivid confrontation with the thrust of nature unfolding in themselves, are denied adult assistance. I once wrote that education through its limits denied the gods, and that they would return in the young in one form or another to haunt us. That is happening now. You can sense it as the students gather, with their simplistic moral certainty, at the gates of the universities. It is almost as if the young were once more possessed by Bacchanalian gods, were once again inhabited by divinities whose honor we have neglected. Those marvelous and threatening energies! What disturbs me most about them is that we lack rituals for their use and balance, and the young—and perhaps we ourselves—now seem at their mercy. The young have moved, bag and baggage, into areas where adults cannot help them, and it is a scary landscape they face, it is crowded with strange forms and faces, and if they return from it rattled, without balance and pitched toward excess, who can pretend to be surprised—or blameless?

At times they seem almost shell-shocked, survivors of a holocaust in which the past has been destroyed and all the bridges to it bombed. I cannot describe with any certainty what occurs in their minds, but I do know that most adults must seem to the young like shrill critics speaking to them in an alien language about a Greek tragedy in which they may lose their lives. The words we use, our dress, our tones of voice, the styles of adult lives —all of these are so foreign to that dramatic crisis that as we approach them we seem to increase the distance we are trying to cross. Even our attention drives them further away, as if adolescents perceived that adults, coming closer, diminish in sense and size.

The inner events in an adolescent demand from what surrounds him life on a large scale, in a grand style. This is the impulse to apocalypse in the young, as if they were in exile from a nation that does not exist—and yet they can sense it, they know it is there—if only because their belief itself demands its presence. Their demand is absolute and unanswerable, but it exists and we seem unable at this point in time to suppress or evade it. For one reason or another, massive shifts in cultural balances, the lessening of repression for whatever reasons—economic, technological, evolutionary—those energies, like gods, have appeared among us again. But what can we make of them? The simple problem is that our institutions are geared to another century, another set of social necessities, and cannot change quickly enough to contain, receive, or direct them—and as we suppress or refuse them they turn to rage.

Primitive cultures dealt with this problem, I think, through their initiation rites, the rites of passage; they legitimized and accepted these energies and turned them toward collective aims; they were merged with the life of the tribe and in this way acknowledged, honored, and domesticated —but not destroyed. In most initiation rites the participant is led through the mythical or sacred world (or a symbolic version) and is then returned, transformed, to the secular one as a new person, with a new role. He is introduced through the rites to a dramatic reality coexistent with the visible or social one and at its root; he is put in direct touch with the sources of energy, the divinities of the tribe. In many cultures the symbolic figures in the rites are unmasked at the end, as if to reveal to the initiate the interpenetration of the secular and sacred worlds. Occasionally the initiate is asked at some point to don the ritual mask himself—joining, as he does, one world with another and assuming the responsibility for their connection. This shift in status, in *relation,* is the heart of the rite; a liturgized merging of the individual with shared sources of power.

Do you see what I am driving at? The rites are in a sense a social contract, a binding up; one occurring specifically, profoundly, on a deep psychic level. The individual is redefined in the culture by his new relation to its mysteries, its gods, to one form or another of nature. His experience of that hidden and omnipotent mythical world is the basis for his relation to the culture and his fellows, each of whom has a similar bond—deep, personal, and unique, but somehow shared, invisibly but deeply. These ritualized relationships of each man to the shared gods bind the group together; they form the substance of culture: an invisible landscape that is real and felt, commonly held, a landscape which resides in each man and in which, in turn, each man resides.

I hope that makes sense. That is the structure of the kaleidoscopic turning of culture that Blake makes in "The Crystal Cabinet," and it makes sense too, in America, in relation to adolescents. What fascinates me is that our public schools, designed for adolescents—who seem, as apocalyptic men, to demand this kind of drama, release, and support—educate and "socialize" their students by depriving them of everything the rites bestow. They manipulate them through the repression of energies; they isolate them and close off most parts of the community; they categorically refuse to make use of the individual's private experience. The direction of all these tendencies is toward a cultural schizophrenia in which the student is forced to choose between his own relation to reality or the one demanded by the institution. The schools are organized to weaken the student so that he is forced, in the absence of his own energies, to accept the values and demands of the institution. To this end we deprive the student of mobility and experience; through law and custom we make the only legal place for him the school, and then, to make sure he remains dependent, manipulable, we empty the school of all vivid life.

We appear to have forgotten in our schools what every primitive tribe with its functional psychology knows: allegiance to the tribe can be forged only at the deepest levels of the psyche and in extreme circumstance demanding endurance, daring, and awe; that the participant must be given *direct* access to the sources of cultural continuity—by and in himself; and that only a place in a coherent community can be exchanged for a man's allegiance.

I believe that it is precisely this world that drugs replace; adolescents provide for themselves what we deny them: a confrontation with some kind of power within an unfamiliar landscape involving sensation and risk. It is there, I suppose, that they hope to find, by some hurried magic, a new way of seeing, a new relation to things, to discard one identity and assume another. They mean to find through their adventures the *ground* of reality, the resonance of life we deny them, as if they might come upon their golden city and return still inside it: at home. You can see the real veterans sometimes on the street in strange costumes they have stolen from dreams: American versions of the Tupi of Brazil, who traveled thousands of miles each year in search of the land where death and evil do not exist. Theirs is a world totally alien to the one we discuss in schools; it is dramatic, it enchants them; its existence forms a strange brotherhood among them and they cling to it—as though they alone had been to a fierce land and back. It is that which draws them together and makes of them a loose tribe. It is, after all, some sort of shared experience, some kind of foray into the risky dark; it is the best that they can do.

When you begin to think about adolescence in this way, what sense can you make of our schools? None of the proposed changes makes sense to me: revision of curriculum, teaching machines, smaller classes, encounter groups, redistributions of power—all of these are stopgap measures, desperate attempts to keep the young in schools that are hopelessly outdated. The changes suggested and debated don't go deeply enough; they don't question or change enough. For what needs changing are not the methods of the school system but its aims, and what is troubling the young and forcing upon their teachers an intolerable burden is the *idea* of childhood itself; the ways we think about adolescents, their place in the culture itself. More and more one comes to see that changes in the schools won't be enough; the crisis of the young cuts across the culture in all its areas and includes the family and the community. The young are displaced; there seems no other word for it. They are trapped in a prolonged childhood almost unique.

In few other cultures have persons of fifteen or eighteen been so uselessly isolated from participation in the community, or been deemed so unnecessary (in their elders' eyes), or so limited by law. Our ideas of responsibility, our parental feelings of anxiety, blame, and guilt, all of these follow from our curious vision of the young; in turn, they concretize it, legitimize it so that we are no longer even conscious of the ways we see childhood or the strain that our vision puts upon us. That is what needs changing: the definitions we make socially and legally of the role of the young. They are trapped in the ways we see them, and the school is simply one function, one aspect, of the whole problem. What makes real change so difficult in the schools is only in part their natural unwieldiness; it is more often the difficulty we have in escaping our preconceptions about things.

In general the school system we have inherited seems to me based upon three particular things:

- What Paul Goodman calls the idea of "natural depravity": our puritanical vision of human nature in which children are perceived as sinners or "savages" and in which human impulse or desire is not to be trusted and must therefore be constrained or "trained."

- The necessity during the mid-nineteenth century of "Americanizing" great masses of immigrant children from diverse backgrounds and creating, through the schools, a common experience and character.

- The need in an industrialized state for energy and labor to run the machines: the state, needing workers, educates persons to be technically capable but relatively dependent and responsive to authority so that their energies will be available when needed.

These elements combine with others—the labor laws that make childhood a "legal" state, and a population explosion that makes it necessary now to keep adolescents off both the labor market and the idle street—to "freeze" into a school system that resists change even as the culture itself and its needs shift radically. But teachers can't usually see that, for they themselves have been educated in this system and are committed to ideas that they have never clearly understood. Time and again, speaking to them, one hears the same questions and anguish: "But what will happen to the students if they don't go to school?" "How will they learn?" "What will they do without adults?"

What never comes clear, of course, is that such questions are, at bottom, statement. Even while asking them teachers reveal their unconscious and contaminating attitudes. They can no longer imagine what children will do "outside" schools. They regard them as young monsters who will, if released from adult authority or help, disrupt the order of things. What is more, adults no longer are capable of imagining learning or child-adult relationships outside the schools. But mass schooling is a recent innovation. Most learning—especially the process of socialization or acculturation—has gone on outside schools, more naturally, in the fabric of the culture. In most cultures the passage from childhood to maturity occurs because of social necessity, the need for responsible adults, and is marked by clear changes in role. Children in the past seem to have learned the ways of the community or tribe through constant contact and interchange with adults, and it was taken for granted that the young learned continually through their place close to the heart of the community.

We seem to have lost all sense of that. The school is expected to do what the community cannot do and that is impossible. In the end, we will have to change far more than the schools if we expect to create a new coherence between the experiences of the child and the needs of the community. We will have to rethink the meaning of childhood; we will begin to grant greater freedom *and* responsibility to the young; we will drop the compulsory-schooling age to fourteen, perhaps less; we will take for granted the "independence" of adolescents and provide them with the chance to live alone, away from parents and with peers; we will discover jobs they can or want to do in the community—anything from mail delivery to the teaching of smaller children and the counseling of other adolescents. At some point, perhaps, we will even find that the community itself—in return for a minimum of work or continued schooling—will provide a minimal income to young people that will allow them to assume the responsibility for their own lives at an earlier age, and learn the ways of the community outside the school; finally, having lowered the level of compulsory schooling, we will find it necessary to provide different *kinds* of schools, a wider choice, so that students will be willing voluntarily to continue the schooling that suits their needs and aims.

All these changes, of course, are aimed at two things: the restoration of the child's "natural" place in the community and lowering the age at which a person is considered an independent member of the community. Some of them, to be sure, can be made in the schools, but my sense of things, after having talked to teachers and visited the schools, is that trying to make the changes in schools *alone* will be impossible.

One problem, put simply, is that in every school I have visited, public or private, traditional or "innovational," the students have only these two choices: to drop out (either physically or mentally) or to make themselves smaller and smaller until they can act in ways their elders expect. One of my students picked up a phrase I once used, "the larger and smaller worlds." The schools we visit together, he says, are always the smaller world: smaller at least than his imagination, smaller than the potential of the young. The students are asked to put aside the best things about themselves—their own desires, impulses, and ideas—in order to "adjust" to an environment constructed for children who existed one hundred years ago, if at all. I wonder sometimes if this condition is simply the result of poor schooling; I am more inclined to believe that it is the inevitable result of mass compulsory schooling and the fabrication of artificial environments by adults for children. Is it possible at all for adults to understand what children need and to change their institutions fast enough to keep up with changes in culture and experience? Is it possible for children to grow to their full size, to feel their full strength, if they are deprived of individual volition all along the line and forced to school? I don't know. I know only that during the Middle Ages they sometimes "created" jesters by putting young children in boxes and force-feeding them so that, as they grew, their bones would warp in unusual shapes. That is often how the schools seem to me. Students are trapped in the boxes of pedagogic ideas, and I am tempted to say to teachers again and again: more, much more, you must go further, create more space in the schools, you must go deeper in thought, create more resonance, a different feeling, a different and more human, more daring style.

Even the best teachers, with the best intentions, seem to diminish their students as they work through the public school system. For that system is, at bottom, designed to produce what we sometimes call good citizens but what more often than not turn out to be good soldiers; it is through the schools of the state, after all, that we produce our armies. I remember how struck I was while teaching at a state college by the number of boys who wanted to oppose the draft but lacked the courage or strength to simply say no. They were trapped; they had always been taught, had always tried, to be "good." Now that they wanted to refuse to go, they could not, for they weren't sure they could bear the consequences they had been taught would follow such refusal: jail, social disgrace, loss of jobs, parental despair. They could not believe in institutions, but they could not trust themselves and their impulse and they were caught in their own impotence: depressed and resentful, filled with self-hatred and a sense of shame.

That is a condition bred in the schools. In one way or another our methods produce in the young a condition of pain that seems very close to a mass neurosis: a lack of faith in oneself, a vacuum of spirit into which authority or institutions can move, a dependency they feed on. Students are encouraged to relinquish their own wills, their freedom of volition; they are taught that value and culture reside outside oneself and must be acquired from the institution, and almost everything in their education is designed to discourage them from activity, from the wedding of idea and act. It is almost as if we hoped to discourage them from thought itself by making ideas so lifeless, so hopeless, that their despair would be enough to make them manipulable and obedient.

The system breeds obedience, frustration, dependence, and fear: a kind of gentle violence that is usually turned against oneself, one that is sorrowful and full of guilt, but a violence nonetheless, and one realizes that what is done in the schools to persons is deeply connected to what we did to the blacks or are doing now in Vietnam. That is: we don't teach hate in the schools, or murder, but we do isolate the individual; we empty him of life by ignoring or suppressing his impulse toward life; we breed in him a lack of respect for it, a loss of love—and thus we produce gently "good" but threatened men, men who will kill without passion, out of duty and obedience, men who have in themselves little sense of the vivid life being lost nor the moral strength to refuse.

From first to twelfth grade we acclimatize students to a fundamental deadness and teach them to restrain themselves for the sake of "order." The net result is a kind of pervasive cultural inversion in which they are asked to separate at the most profound levels their own experience from institutional reality, self from society, objective from subjective, energy from order—though these various polarities are precisely those which must be made coherent during adolescence.

I remember a talk I had with a college student.
"You know what I love to do," he said. "I love to go into the woods and run among the trees."

"Very nice," I said.

"But it worries me. We shouldn't do it."

"Why not?" I asked.

"Because we get excited. It isn't *orderly*."

"Not orderly?"

"Not orderly."

"Do you run into the trees?" I asked.

"Of course not."

"Then it's orderly," I said.

In a small way this exchange indicates the kind of thinking we encourage in the schools: the mistaking of rigidity and stillness for order, of order as the absence of life. We try to create and preserve an order which depends upon the destruction of life both inside and out and which all life, when expressed, must necessarily threaten or weaken.

The natural process of learning seems to move naturally from experience through perception to abstraction in a fluid continuous process that cannot be clearly divided into stages. It is in that process that energy is somehow articulated in coherent and meaningful form as an act or thought or a made object. The end of learning is wisdom and wisdom to me, falling back as I do on a Jewish tradition, is, in its simplest sense, "intelligent activity" or, more completely, the suffusion of activity with knowledge, a wedding of the two. For the Hasidic Jews every gesture was potentially holy, a form of prayer, when it was made with a reverence for God. In the same way a gesture is always a form of wisdom—an act is wisdom—when it is suffused with knowledge, made with a reverence for the truth.

Does that sound rhetorical? I suppose it does. But I mean it. The end of education is intelligent activity, *wisdom,* and that demands a merging of opposites, a sense of process. Instead we produce the opposite: immobility, insecurity, an inability to act without institutional blessing or direction, or, at the opposite pole, a headlong rush toward motion without balance or thought. We cut into the natural movement of learning and try to force upon the students the end product, abstraction, while eliminating experience and ignoring their perception. The beginning of thought is in the experience through one's self of a particular environment—school, community, culture. When this is ignored, as it is in schools, the natural relation of self and knowledge is broken, the parts of the process become polar opposites, antitheses, and the young are forced to choose between them: objectivity, order, and obedience as against subjectivity, chaos, and energy. It doesn't really matter which they choose; as long as the two sets seem irreconcilable their learning remains incomplete. Caught between the two, they suffer our intellectual schizophrenia until it occupies them, too. They wait. They sit. They listen. They learn to "behave" at the expense of themselves. Or else—and you can see it happening now—they turn against it with a vengeance and may shout, as they did at Columbia, "Kill all adults," for they have allied themselves with raw energy against reason and balance—our delicate, hard-won virtues—and we should not be surprised. We set up the choices ourselves, and it is simply that they have chosen what we hold to be the Devil's side.

If this is the case, what are the alternatives? I thought at one time that changes in schooling could be made, that the school itself could become at least a microcosm of the community outside, a kind of halfway house, a preparatory arena in which students, in semi-protective surroundings, would develop not only the skill but the character that would be needed in the world. But more and more, as I have said, it seems to me impossible to do that job in a setting as isolated and restrictive as our schools. Students don't need the artificiality of schools; they respond more fully and more intelligently when they make direct contact with the community and are allowed to choose roles that have some utility for the community and themselves. What is at stake here, I suppose, is the freedom of volition, for this is the basic condition with which people must learn to deal, and the sooner they achieve within that condition wit, daring, and responsibility, the stronger they will be. It seems absurd to postpone the assumption of that condition as long as we do. In most other cultures, and even in our own past, young people have taken upon themselves the responsibility of adults and have dealt with it as successfully as most adults do now. The students I have seen can do that, too, when given the chance. What a strain it must be to have that capacity, to sense in one's self a talent for adventure or growth or meaning, and have that sense continually stifled or undercut by the role one is supposed to play.

Thus, it seems inescapably clear that our first obligation to the young is to create a place in the community for them to act with volition and freedom. They are ready for it, certainly, even if we aren't. Adolescents seem to need at least some sense of risk and gain "out there" in the world: an existential sense of themselves that is vivid to the extent that the dangers faced are "real." The students I have worked with seem strongest and most alive when they are in the mountains of Mexico or the Oakland ghetto or out in the desert or simply hitchhiking or riding freights to see what's happening. They thrive on distance and motion—and the right to solitude when they want it. Many of them want jobs; they themselves arrange to be teachers in day-care centers, political canvassers, tutors, poolroom attendants, actors, governesses, gardeners. They returned from these experiences immeasurably brightened and more sure of themselves, more willing, in that new assurance, to learn many of the abstract ideas we had been straining to teach them. It was not simply the experience in itself that brought this about. It was also the feeling of freedom they had, the sense that they could come and go at will and make any choice they wanted—no matter how absurd—if they were willing to suffer what real consequences followed. Many wanted to work and travel and others did not; they wanted to sit and think or read or live alone or swim or, as one student scrawled on my office wall, "ball and goof." What they finally came to understand, of course, was that the school made no pretense at either limiting or judging their activities; we considered them free agents and limited our own activities to advice, to what "teaching" they requested, and to support when they needed it in facing community, parents, or law.

What we were after was a *feeling* to the place: a sense of intensity and space. We discarded the idea of the microcosm and replaced it with an increased openness and access to the larger community. The campus itself became a place to come back to for rest or discussion or thought; but we turned things inside out to the extent that we came to accept that learning took place more naturally elsewhere, in any of the activities that our students chose, and that the school was in actuality wherever they were, whatever they did. What students learned at the school was simply the feel of things; the sense of themselves as makers of values; the realization that the environment is at best an extension of men and that it can be transformed by them into what they vitally need.

What we tried to create was a flexible environment, what a designer I know has called permissive space. It was meant to be in a sense a model for the condition in which men find themselves, in which the responsibility of a man was to make connections, value, and sense. We eliminated from the school all preconceptions about what was proper, best, or useful; we gave up rules and penalties; we refused at all levels to resort to coercive force and students were free to come and go at will, to do anything. What we were after was a "guilt-free" environment, one in which the students might become or discover what they were without having to worry about preconceived ideas of what they had to be.

What we found was that our students seemed to need, most of all, relief from their own "childhood"—what was expected of them. Some of them needed merely to rest, to withdraw from the strange grid of adult expectation and demand for lengthy periods of introspection in which they appeared to grow mysteriously, almost like plants. But an even greater number seemed to need independent commerce with the world outside the school: new sorts of social existence. Nothing could replace that. The simple fact seemed to be that our students grew when they were allowed to move freely into and around the adult community; when they were not, they languished.

We came to see that learning is natural, yes, but it results naturally from most things adolescents do. By associating learning with one particular form of intellection and insisting upon that in school we make a grave error. When students shy away from that kind of intellection it doesn't mean they are turning away forever from learning or abstractions; it means simply that they are seeking another kind of learning momentarily more natural to themselves. That may be anything from physical adventure or experimental community work to withdrawn introspection and an exploration of their fantasies and dreams.

Indeed, it is hard for them to do anything without some kind of learning, but that may be what we secretly fear—that those other forms of learning will make them less manageable or less like ourselves. That, after all, may be one reason we use all those books. Lévi-Strauss insists on the relation of increased literacy and the power of the state over the individual. It may well be that dependence on print and abstraction is one of the devices we use to make students manipulable, as if we meant to teach them that ideas exist in talk or on the page but rarely in activity. We tried to avoid that. When we permitted students the freedom of choice and gave them easy access to the community, we found that ideas acquired weight and value to the extent that students were allowed to try them out in action. It was in practical and social situations that their own strength increased, and the merging of the two—strengthened self and tested knowledge—moved them more quickly toward manhood than anything else I have seen.

One might make a formula of it: to the extent that students had freedom of volition and access to experience, knowledge became important. But volition and access were of absolute value; they took precedence over books or parental anxiety; without them, nothing worked. So we had to trust the students to make their own choices, no matter what we thought of them. We learned to take their risks with them—and to survive. In that sense we became equals, and that equality may in the end be more educational for students than anything else. That, in fact, may be the most important thing we learned. New ways in seeing them were more effective than changes in curriculum, and without them nothing made much difference. But we must understand too that the old way of seeing things—the traditional idea of childhood—is in some way baked into the whole public-school system at almost every level and also hidden in most pedagogy.

In some ways it is compulsory schooling itself which is the problem, for without real choice students will remain locked in childhood and schools, away from whatever is vivid in life. But real choice, as we know, includes dominion over one's own time and energies, and the right to come and go on the basis of what has actual importance. And I wonder if we will ever get round, given all our fears, to granting that privilege to students.

One thing alone of all I have read has made recent sense to me concerning adolescents. That is the implicit suggestion in Erik Erikson's *Young Man Luther* that every sensitive man experiences in himself the conflicts and contradictions of his age. The great man, he suggests, is the man who articulates and resolves these conflicts in a way that has meaning for his time; that is, he is himself, as was Luther, a victim of his time and its vehicle and, finally, a kind of resolution. But all men, not only the great, have in some measure the capacity to experience in themselves what is happening in the culture around them. I am talking here about what is really shared among the members of a particular culture, a condition, a kind of internal "landscape," the psychic shape that a particular time and place assumes within a man as the extent and limit of his perceptions, dreams, and pleasure and pain.

If there is such a shared condition it seems to me a crucial point, for it means that there is never any real distance between a man and his culture, no real isolation or alienation from society. It means that adolescents are not in their untutored state cut off from culture nor outside it. It means instead that each adolescent is an arena in which the contradictions and currents sweeping through the culture must somehow be resolved, must be resolved by the person himself, and that those individual resolutions are, ideally, the means by which the culture advances itself.

Do you see where this leads? *I am straining here to get past the idea of the adolescent as an isolate and deviant creature who must be joined—as if glued and clamped—to the culture. For we ordinarily think of schools, though not quite consciously, as the "culture" itself, little models of society.* We try to fit the student into the model, believing that if he will adjust to it he will in some way have been "civilized." That approach is connected to the needs of the early century, when the schools were the means by which the children of immigrant parents were acculturated and moved from the European values of their parents toward more prevalent American ones. But all of that has changed now. The children in our schools, all of them, are little fragments of *this* culture; they no longer need to be "socialized" in the same ways. The specific experiences of every adolescent—his fears, his family crises, his dreams and hallucinations, his habits, his sexuality—all these are points at which the general culture reveals itself in some way. There is no longer any real question of getting the adolescent to "adjust" to things.

The problem is a different one: What kind of setting will enable him to discover and accept what is already within him; to articulate it and perceive the extent to which it is shared with others; and, finally, to learn to change it within and outside himself? For that is what I mean when I call the adolescent a "maker of value." He is a trustee, a trustee of a world that already exists in some form within himself—and we must both learn, the adolescent and his teachers, to respect it.

In a sense, then, I am calling for a reversal of most educational thought. The individual is central; the individual, in the deepest sense, is *the culture, not the institution. His culture resides in him, in experience and memory, and what is needed is an education that has at its base the sanctity of the individual's experience and leaves it intact.*

What keeps running through my mind is a line I read twelve years ago in a friend's first published story: *The Idea in that idea is: there is no one over you.* I like that line: *There is no one over you.* Perhaps that signifies the gap between these children and their parents. For the children it is true, they sense it: there is no one over them; believable authority has disappeared; it has been replaced by experience. As Thomas Altizer says: God is dead; he is experienced now not as someone above or omnipotent or omniscient or "outside," but inwardly, as conscience or vision or even the unconscious or Tillich's "ground of being." This is all too familiar to bother with here, but this particular generation is a collective dividing point. The parents of these children, the fathers, still believe in "someone" over them, insist upon it; in fact, demand it for and from their children. The children themselves cannot believe it; the idea means nothing to them. It is almost as if they are the first real Americans—suddenly free of Europe and somehow fatherless, confused, forced back on their own experience, their own sense of things, even though, at the same time, they are forced to defy their families and schools in order to keep it.

This is, then, a kind of Reformation. Arnold was wrong when he said that art would replace religion; education replaced it. Church became School, the principal vehicle for value, for "culture," and just as men once rebelled against the established Church as the mediator between God and man, students now rebel against the *public* school (and its version of things) as the intermediary between themselves and experience, between themselves and experience and the making of value. Students are expected to reach "reality" (whether of knowledge or society) through their teachers and school. No one, it is said, can participate in the culture effectively without having at one time passed through their hands, proven his allegiance to them, and been blessed. This is the authority exercised by priests or the Church. Just as men once moved to shorten the approach to God, they are moved now to do the same thing in relation to learning and to the community. For just as God was argued to appear within a man—unique, private, and yet shared—so culture is, in some way, grounded in the individual; it inhabits him. The schools, like the Church, must be the expression of that habitation, not its exclusive medium. This is the same reformative shift that occurred in religion, a shift from the institutional (the external) to the individual (the internal), and it demands, when it occurs, an agony, an apocalyptic frenzy, a destruction of the past itself. I believe it is happening now. One sees and feels it everywhere: a violent fissure, a kind of quake.

I remember one moment in the streets of Oakland during the draft demonstrations. The students had sealed off the street with overturned cars and there were no police; the gutters were empty and the students moved into them from the sidewalks, first walking, then running, and finally almost dancing in the street. You could almost see the idea coalesce on their faces: The street is ours! It was as if a weight had been lifted from them, a fog; there was not at that moment any fury in them, any vengefulness or even politics; rather, a lightness, delight, an exhilaration at the sudden inexplicable sense of being free. George Orwell describes something similar in *Homage to Catalonia:* that brief period in Barcelona when the anarchists had apparently succeeded and men shared what power there was. I don't know how to describe it, except to say that one's inexplicable sense of invisible authority had vanished: the oppressive father, who is not really there, was gone.

That sudden feeling is familiar to us all. We have all had it from time to time in our own lives, that sense of "being at home," that ease, that feeling of a Paradise which is neither behind us nor deferred but is around us, a natural household. It is the hint and beginning of Manhood: a promise, a clue. One's attention turns to the immediate landscape and to one's fellows: toward what is there, toward what can be felt as a part of oneself. I have seen the same thing as I watched Stokely Carmichael speaking to a black audience and telling them that they must stop begging the white man, like children, for their rights. They were, he said, neither children nor slaves, no, they were—and here they chanted, almost cried, in unison—a beautiful people: *yes our noses are broad and our lips are thick and our hair is kinky . . . but we are beautiful, we are beautiful, we are black and beautiful.* Watching, you could sense in that released joy an emergence, a surfacing of pride, a refusal to accept shame or the white man's dominance—and a turning to one another, to their own inherent value.

But there is a kind of pain in being white and watching that, for there is no one to say the same things to white children; no "fathers" or brothers to give them that sense of manhood or pride. The adolescents I have seen—white, middle-class—are a long way from those words *we are beautiful, we are beautiful.* I cannot imagine how they will reach them, deprived as they are of all individual strength. For the schools exist to deprive one of strength. That is why one's own worth must be proven again and again by the satisfaction of external requirements with no inherent value or importance; it is why one must satisfy a set of inexplicable demands; it is why there is a continual separation of self and worth and the intrusion of a kind of institutional guilt: failure not of God but of *the system,* the nameless "others," the authority that one can never quite see; and it explains the oppressive sense of some nameless transgression, almost a shame at Being itself.

It is this feeling that pervades both high schools and college, this Kafkaesque sense of faceless authority that drives one to rebellion or withdrawal, and we are all, for that reason, enchanted by the idea of the Trial, that ancient Socratic dream of confrontation and vindication or martyrdom. It is then, of course, that Authority shows its face. In the mid-fifties I once watched Jack Kerouac on a television show and when the interviewer asked him what he wanted he said: to see the face of God. How arrogant and childish and direct! And yet, I suppose, it is what we all want as children: to have the masks of authority, all its disguises, removed and to see it plain. That is what lies in large part behind the riots in the schools. Their specific grievances are incidental; their real purpose is to make God show his face, to have whatever pervasive and oppressive force makes us perpetual children reveal itself, declare itself, commit itself at last. It is Biblical; it is Freudian; it reminds me in some way of the initiation rites: the need to unmask the gods and assume their power, to become an equal—and to find in that the manhood one has been denied.

The schools seem to enforce the idea that there *is* someone over you, and the methods by which they do it are ritualized, pervasive. The intrusion of guilt, shame, alienation from oneself, dependence, insecurity—all these feelings are not the accidental results of schools; they are intentional, and they are used in an attempt to make children manipulable, obedient; "good citizens" we call it, and useful to the state. The schools are the means by which we deprive the young of manhood—that is what I mean to say—and we must not be surprised when they seek that manhood in ways that must of necessity be childish and violent.

But I must admit this troubles me, for there is little choice between mindless violence and mindless authority, and I am just enough of an academic, an intellectual, to want to preserve much of what will be lost in the kind of rebellion or apocalypse that is approaching. And yet, and yet . . . the rapidity of events leaves me with no clear idea, no solution, no sense of what will be an adequate change. It may be that all of this chaos is a way of breaking with the old world and that from it some kind of native American will emerge. There is no way of knowing, there no longer seems any way of estimating what is necessary or what will work. I know only that the problem now seems to be that our response to crisis is to move away or back rather than forward, and that we will surely, for the sake of some imagined order, increase in number and pressure the very approaches that have brought us to this confusion. I don't know. I believe that the young must have values, of course, be responsible, care, but I know too that most of the violence I have seen done to the young has been done in the name of value, and that the well-meaning people who have been so dead set on making things right have had a hand in bringing us to where we are now. The paradox is a deep and troubling one for me. I no longer know if change can be accomplished—for the young, for any of us, without the apocalyptic fury that seems almost upon us. The crisis of youth and education is symptomatic of some larger, deeper fault in our cities and minds, and perhaps nothing can be done consciously in those areas until the air itself is violently cleared one way or another.

So I have no easy conclusions, no startling synthesis with which to close. I have only a change in mood, a softening, a kind of sadness. It may be, given that, that the best thing is simply to close with an unfinished fragment in which I catch for myself the hint of an alternative:

. . . *I am trying to surround you, I see that, I am trying to make with these words a kind of city so natural, so familiar, that the other world, the one that appears to be, will look by comparison absurd and flat, limited, unnecessary. What I am after is liberation, not my own, which comes often enough these days in solitude or sex, but yours, and that is arrogant, isn't it, that is presumptuous, and yet that is the function of art: to set you free. It is that too which is the end of education: a liberation from childhood and what holds us there, a kind of midwifery, as if the nation itself were in labor and one wanted to save both the future and the past—for we* are *both, we are, we are the thin bridge swaying between them, and to tear one from the other means a tearing of ourselves, a partial death.*

And yet it may be that death is inevitable, useful. It may be. Perhaps, as in the myth, Aphrodite can rise only where Cronos' testicles have fallen into the sea. It may be that way with us. The death of the Father who is in us, the death of the old authority which is part of us, the death of the past which is also our death; it may all be necessary: a rending and purgation. And yet one still seeks another way, something less (or is it more) apocalyptic, a way in which the past becomes the future in ourselves, *in which* we *become the bridges between: makers of culture.*

Unless from us the future takes place, we are Death only, *said Lawrence, meaning what the Hasidim do: that the world and time reside within, not outside, men; that there is no distance, no "alienation," only a perpetual wedding to the world. It is that—the presence in oneself of Time—that makes things interesting, is more gravid and interesting than guilt. I don't want to lose it, don't want to relinquish that sense in the body of another dimension, a distance, the depth of the body as it extends backward into the past and forward, as it contains and extends and transforms.*

What I am after is an alternative to separation and rage, some kind of connection to things to replace the system of dependence and submission— the loss of the self—that now holds sway, slanted toward violence. *I am trying to articulate a way of seeing, of feeling, that will restore to the young a sense of manhood and potency without at the same time destroying the past.* That same theme runs through whatever I write: the necessity for each man to experience himself as an extension and maker of culture, and to feel the whole force of the world within himself, not as an enemy—but as himself:

. . . *An act of learning is a meeting, and every meeting is simply the discovery in the world of a part of oneself that had previously been unacknowledged by the self. It is the recovery of the extent of one's being. It is the embrace of an eternal but elusive companion, the shadowy "other" in which one truly resides and which blazes, when embraced, like the sun.*

THE ALTERNATIVE SCHOOL

Children, Schools, and Utopias

George von Hilsheimer

THE STRUCTURE OF the public education system is now badly out of date and new forms will have to be found, more relevant to contemporary society. The structure we are stuck with at the present time was designed for the mass education of an illiterate, poor, and educationally well-motivated population who lived in close-knit communities where children could get their ethics, their social values and their personality choices from the community around them. Then, centralized schools had a real professional function. Today, on the other hand, they are serving a literate, affluent population conditioned to entertainment and advertising in a community-less society. The time has come, therefore, to re-examine the root assumptions of "comprehensive, centralized, public education."

The key problem with the mass schools today is that they

exacerbate the poverty of real persons in a child's life. While on paper the central school presents a rich display of human (as well as technical) resources, the child, in fact, experiences it as culturally poverty-stricken. He is never treated as an individual and he has no continuing relationships with the adults there who are the only transmitters of culture.

In many ways the child was better off in the one-room schoolhouse. There the teacher had, in most cases, a continuity of years in which to get to know her children, and more importantly, to be known herself. She also had the enormous resource of the social authority of older children to share with the little ones. And she had the tremendous advantage of being forced to leave the children to their own devices for most of the school day thus enabling them to move on at their own pace. Even if a child came from an isolated farm in which he was the only child, he found, in this structure of schooling, a vital and real experience.

Our children today live in a startlingly different world, a world where there is no longer an adult community. For the first time in the history of man children do not associate with adults except in peripheral, stylized, symbolic, and ritual ways which do not teach anything other than the ritual style.

Let's take a look at what has happened in the past twenty years: old urban neighborhoods are being broken up. The magnificent complex of small towns is progressively turned into a series of bedroom communities with limited economic determination for themselves. The neighborhood store and the specialty shop are rapidly disappearing. Jobs are progressively removed, not only in time and space, but also psychologically from the world of the child; jobs are becoming increasingly difficult to explain. Not only are more people crowded into more anonymous dwellings with an increasingly higher background of meaningless noise, but these people have less and less to do with each other on a consistent and personal basis. For the first time in history the majority of Americans are living this way.

Today a child's only adult contacts tend to be with his mother—oppressed and harried as she is in the small-child-raising phase—and a series of vestal maidens in school who must forever remain symbolic and ritual in their importance to him. For a child knows that his teacher is with him only a year or less. In addition, she has thirty other kids to serve and usually has no social contact with the family. Most likely he is attending a consolidated school, far removed from his home—both geographically and socially. It can in fact be argued that the school in America is an alienating experience for children of all social classes, including the middle class which professionally dominates it.

It was different when we grew up. Adults of only thirty years and even younger can remember urban neighborhoods—small enclaves remain in the New York Lower East Side and elsewhere—in which the corner candy-store man was an advisor, counselor, friend . . . or enemy. The druggist, the grocer, the butcher, the greengrocer, the janitor, the neighbors, all played a vital role in the life of the child. They have disappeared or are rapidly disappearing. Most children never see their fathers working. If there *is* an exception, the father's work is usually incomprehensible. Servicemen, salesmen and other adults who come into the child's home are only briefly a part of his life and their work is too complicated to follow. Furthermore, the "respected" character type is one that rejects children's natural interest. Adults have become symbolic, alien, ritual figures in a barren field. Their values are mediated to the child in a distorted, mechanistic way through the school system. To grow up emotionally healthy a child needs a rich culture of adults from whom to select psychological reactions, patterns and values. He no longer has this choice. As a result we have the apathetic, robot-like, nihilistic adolescent of our time.

I

Let's take a look at this adolescent our community-less society has created. I have often thought that if every teacher was forced at the beginning of the year to watch a filmstrip of teen-agers watching the Beatles or the Ladybugs and had time to reflect upon the expressions on the faces of these entertainers, they would be so profoundly terrorized that they might go out and do something.

I recently watched the Ladybugs, who are apparently one of the most popular female singing groups. They sang a song called "The Leader of the Pack." It is very popular. I'm sure it's at least in your subliminal consciousness. It's about a leader of a gang who dies in an automobile crash. The song is full of sound effects and somebody shouts, "Look out." As they shout, their faces don't move. The emotional tone and quality of the voice does not change. At the end of the song, I became a little hopeful because when they were getting applause they did smile, just a little. This is now the cultural ideal of our adolescents. That's why I really recognize myself as a reactionary rather than a radical in education. This is not the control of the Victorians that we are all so much against. This is not the cold Canadian reserve. This is not active, intellectualized control over emotions that enables you to move forward. *It is catatonia!* I haven't seen faces like that other than in the back wards of hospitals for schizophrenics. This is the most precise description I can give of the socially idealized goal of adolescents. The more I have worked with them all over the face of America, the more terrified I am because their goal is to keep cool. To keep cool is not the old Eton idea of keeping your head while the world around you is falling to pieces, but it is NOT TO BE THERE. It is not to possess your body at all, not to perceive at all that the world is falling to ruin, not to be hurt, not to have anger to channelize and focus at the howling savages, not to have any anger at all. It is not even to notice that the howling savages are there but to be detached from reality which is intolerable because there are no exits. This is a profoundly different generation. I think I am the first old man starting to scream at teen-agers, "You will not rebel. You are too damn well-behaved."

What then should a community's relationship to its children be? Ideally, a "school" in a separated sense is not necessary at all, especially our big centralized ones. "School" as presently understood in America was developed for the lower classes. Its infliction on the upper classes is an historic irony that proves some justice is possible in the world. The generation of our founding fathers educated its leadership class at home: tutoring was not simply the job of professionals, but of the whole family. Boys went off to college at twelve or thirteen, and while social discipline was severe, it was surprisingly self-inflicted. Intellectual discipline was almost entirely self-administered at this class level by the time the boy was in his teens.

My proposal, then, is reactionary rather than novel. In a "school" which is really a living community of adults—with a very high ratio of adults to children, ideally outnumbering them—classes would be unthinkable. Children would learn to read and write in their relationship to their mothers, fathers, nurses, peers. They would learn most of their science as they moved freely about in the community. They would specialize and discipline their intellectual abilities in their teens in tutorial relations. Their dependence on adult teachers in the ordinary sense would be negligible by the time they were fourteen or fifteen.

Is my proposal hopelessly Utopian? I think not. That teen-agers can be intellectually and industrially self-starting and -directing should be no more surprising than the fact that some adults are that way, even though our society is aggressively organized to destroy such abilities. A few colleges—Reed, Antioch, Dartmouth, Bard—and most of the monster land-grant colleges demonstrate that American teen-agers even today can be remarkably self-directing. Actually universities like Michigan, Illinois, Ohio State, *et* monstrous *al.*, probably prove the point better than the officially liberal schools. It is simply impossible to police, to inflict a constant social control, in such large colleges. Students either make it or they don't. Of course, the majority don't, but their "successful" fellows prove that self-direction can work.

But let's get back to the public schools as they are today. They have contributed to the creation of the cool generation both by their emotionally and socially impoverished atmosphere and by their program of instruction which places a minimum amount of initiative on the child. The system is based on the assumption that individuals cannot make effective decisions and that those who are older and wiser and more powerful shall make the decisions for those who are weaker, younger, more ignorant. Besides inducing apathy, this approach also inhibits learning. It is a widely held myth that academic excellence, at least, is a result of rigid, authoritarian teacher-and-curriculum-centered education. This simply isn't so. Any research comparing authoritarian versus self-directive teaching methods indicate that the latter is more effective, even using such conventional measuring sticks as grades, college achievement, and success on jobs. Here is a sample of such experiments.

The most impressive comparative study along these lines was done in the 1930's. Several foundations, notably the Carnegie Foundation, put up over four million dollars for a study which is known as the "Eight Year Study."[1] The "Eight Year Study" took in thirty schools, ranging from luxurious private schools to slum public schools. There was a special twenty-point outline for the kind of changes in curriculum and teaching methods that these schools agreed to make. Essentially the changes were in the direction of giving more authority and responsibility to the children and making curricula more flexible. In the most extreme school the teachers refused to teach altogether. They just stayed around as guardians and facilitators for the children, answering their questions, helping them to find books in the library, etc., but refused to tell what to study and would not give lectures. The fifteen hundred children in these thirty schools were tracked down through their four years of high school and through the subsequent four years of college—thus the name Eight Year Study. Next, a survey was made of how they did when they got into the real grim world of dog eat dog, individualism and competition.

The final step was to compare these fifteen hundred children with fifteen hundred children from schools using conventional teaching methods. Each student was matched and paired for age, sex, social background, aptitude test scores, vocational and avocational interests, etc. The results were astounding: on every parameter, on every variable—their grades in high school and college, their academic honors, their leadership capacity, their job attitude while they were in school, and their success in maintaining themselves after they were out of school—the children from the experimental schools were superior to those in teacher-and-curriculum centered schools. The children in the most experimental of the schools, including the one mentioned where the teachers refused to teach, had the highest scores of all.

[1] Commission on the Relation of School and College, *Adventure in American Education* (New York, Harper & Brothers, 1942).

The "Eight Year Study" is a powerful indictment of traditional, authoritarian methods of teaching children. But there are also many smaller experiments that can be repeated by anybody at a very small cost, which are equally persuasive.

1. There are the Lewin experiments in group leadership.

Groups of ten- and eleven-year-old boys were given the opportunity to be released from class for a workshop club period. They, of course, readily responded. A great deal of care was given to the experimental situation. Rooms were prepared so that recordings and photographic records could be made. The leaders of the groups were given careful training in three types of leadership: laissez faire, authoritarian, democratic. The groups led by the laissez faire leader were, of course, not "led" at all in the ordinary sense. They came into a room where an adult was present. He cursorily greeted them, mumbled something about, "Do what you want to; there's stuff over there," and failed further to respond.

The authoritarian leadership was done up very well. The leader stood tall and erect, was dressed in severe and formal clothing. He was domineering, firm and fair. "This is a handicraft group; your name is the Green Dragons; we will make wallets; you will bring the leather, you the knives, you the thread, etc. . . ." The children were quickly organized, and as quickly put to work, which was closely and continuously supervised.

The democratic leader greeted the group informally; he discussed with them the function of the club; he asked them to choose a name; he suggested various possibilities for handicraft and had them choose. After the choice was made, he discussed the implications of the work, where the materials were, what tasks had to be performed. At every point his task was to focus the group on its goal, to bring out of the group its information and skills, and to force the group to make decisions for itself.

There were a number of groups in each leadership category. Each group followed one form of leadership for a time, and then the leaders changed, changing their own leadership style at the same time. Comparisons were made of many things: production of goods, involvement of individuals in the groups, group morale, etc.

The democratic and the authoritarian groups were both high producers of handicraft articles. The laissez faire group, as expected, produced little but mayhem and noise. The significance of the difference in leadership, however, became apparent when the leaders left the group.

When the authoritarian leader would leave the group for any length of time the production of goods in his group would decline to less than that of the laissez faire groups, while their noise and mayhem level exceeded them. In the democratic groups production actually went up when the leader was absent.

When leadership was changed, either simply to another leader or to another leader with a different leadership style, the democratic groups made the easiest transition. They resisted, however, change to authoritarian leadership, not primarily by noise and mayhem, but by retaining their own organic leadership developed under the democratic regime. They simply anticipated and made irrelevant the authoritarian leader. In all important regards, the democratically-led groups were not only better satisfied, more fully involved, but also more efficient than the authoritarian groups, particularly in times of stress, change, or absence of accustomed leadership.

2. There was another experiment done with retention of objective data. Similar groups of students were given

groups of leaves in order to learn the classifications, groupings, names and morphology of the leaves. One set of students was given the leaves in a prepared fashion, carefully packaged in plastic, labelled well, with the most modern techniques of lettering and presentation. The other set of students was simply given a box of leaves and told to see if they could find out the natural relationships of the leaves. Since the classifications are not arbitrary, but based on the evolutionary relationship, the children could, after a time, get the leaves properly organized. They were then told the names, the groupings, and shown the morphology and the developmental relationships of the leaves. Quite naturally the first group—taught by what I call the "entertainment" concept of education—learned the names and so got on much more quickly than the second. However, the groups were taught until both tested with no significant difference. When tested after six months, the first group had forgotten almost all of what they had "learned." The second group retained a significant amount of the data. When retested at the end of the year the first group had no statistically significant recall of the material, while the second retained a useful grasp of the principles and a solid portion of the data.

3. A good friend of mine, an art resource teacher in Richmond, Virginia, reported an excellent experiment with third graders. The children entered the room and found two pieces of construction paper on their desks. The teacher held up a folded fan—the sort we have all made. She asked, "Do you know what this is?" "Yes." "Can you make one?" "Sure." "Well, go ahead." All of the children very quickly folded their papers into little fans. The teacher then had them put the fans on their desks and listen as she slowly read the instructions on how properly to fold a fan. Then she told them to make fans. Not one child could make a fan. She went around the room and tried to get them to go back to their old fan

and make one like it. They could not. The verbal instructions had gotten in the way. This is an easily repeatable experiment, but one I do not recommend because it is damaging to the children. The evidence is already overwhelming that verbal, curriculum-centered instruction is destructive of an individual's ability.

II

Finally, I would like to describe one of my own projects in democratic education, Green Valley School in Orangeville, Florida. Green Valley is a community of teachers and students. It is owned by its teachers. There are no administrators that do not teach. There are no teachers who do not also sweep, saw, hammer, and cook. Teachers join Green Valley only as partners. A lack of "employee mentality" makes a difference both in the atmosphere of the school and how children learn. Green Valley teachers don't go home at 3:00 P.M. or 5:00 P.M. The whole place is sort of a larger-than-life family and school therefore becomes a twenty-four hour process. Students and teachers live together and eat together and struggle together with the problems of both learning and living.

Our school is often referred to as an "experimental school," but Green Valley is not truly an experiment. It is a school that demonstrates a well conceived, adequately proven and essentially conservative philosophy of education which has been neglected and ignored by the main stream in education. It exists in a tradition that includes the Ford Republic, Summerhill, The Gorky Colony, The Ferrer Modern School, Finchden Manor, Prestolee (a Lancashire County School) and many others. These schools are based on the "Commonwealth idea" which makes the following postulates: (1) the adults' legitimate rule-making authority is limited to health, safety, and the requirement of public law; (2) adults and children have an equal voice and vote in the establishment of all other rules; (3) a sort of basic "Bill of Rights" limits the kind of rules the school community can make—no bills of attainder or *ex post facto* laws, etc.; (4) children are not compelled to attend classes; (5) the staff's primary goal is a healthy psychological and social climate, and only incidentally intellectual education.

The "Commonwealth concept" assumes that cooperative, loving, social, and constructive behavior is a natural and healthy potential of children. It does not say that children are *intrinsically* good. Children are not intrinsically anything other than the potentials permitted by their societies. There are societies in which no children, other than those with organic pathologies, are antisocial, but our society is obviously not one of them. Fortunately, there have been a few societies which, like ours, seem to expect all children, particularly adolescents, to be antisocial.

At Green Valley no self-conscious attempt is made to encourage manners, although an adult or a child has a perfect right to ask someone to take offensive behavior out of his room or out of public rooms. No attempt to persuade intellectual interest is made; a teacher may demand discipline as a requisite of a class, but the student does not have to attend. Since we pay a great deal more attention to pedagogy at Green Valley than at some schools, I cannot say that intellectual interest is not encouraged. The encouragement, however, is by competence, relevance and interest. It is not by moral suasion. The only regular complaint about classes at Green Valley is that there are not enough of them—despite the fact that for teen-agers classes go on in the evening as well as during regular school hours.

One of the objectives of the school is to force the responsibility of freedom on the children. This is why we require the student to stay at the school for at least a year—with reasonable exceptions. Children will otherwise seek the escape valve of their often queerly permissive authoritarian home to avoid the responsibilities of freedom. We insist that children not go home for weekends. They will stay up late into the night for a week and then run home where Mama will make them sleep. When they are *required* to face their own need, they begin to discipline themselves. Although it may offend common sense, the disciplinarian family is often the most indulgent. A rigid psychological consistency, if not necessity, appears in those families which most often inflict irrelevant disciplines such as appearance, cleanliness, noise, deportment on their children. These families collapse most easily when a serious conflict such as wanting to leave school, getting married, or buying a car arrives. It is ironic that as a headmaster of a free school I far more often have to counsel parents in how to say "no" than otherwise.

I want to emphasize that the Green Valley philosophy is not a "permissive" philosophy. Nor do I think that it legitimately belongs to the progressive tradition. Progressive education is preoccupied with curriculum and pedagogy. We at Green Valley are preoccupied with community and values.

A teacher at Green Valley must not see herself as a manipulator in community and personal relationships. Technique is valid and necessary in the classroom, but it is out of place in honest friendship. We have increasingly found that our opinions can be safely shared with students. Misbehavior can be openly reported and discussed. A teacher, as well as a student, must be willing to admit her mistakes and accept the consequences of them.

This is the most important difference between Green Valley School and the progressive movement. Progressives, on the whole, cannot stand idly by and watch a child dally in a puddle of water. It must be turned into a "learning experience," which is to say that the teacher must interpose her abstract structures between the child and the reality he is experiencing and learning. The model for education, progressive or traditional, has always been a wrestling match—the student trying to put something over on the superior teacher who must find ways to win him. If he does not learn through drill, then he must through work or through play, but learn he must. Unfortunately, the verb "to learn" has come to mean a quite artificial and abstract kind of talking about the world rather than experiencing it.

For the education of adolescents who have been brought up in Green Valley, there is little the teacher does that is not an ordinary part of interaction of an intellectual community. That is, someone writes, someone produces, someone directs, and someone plays a drama. The events themselves are comparative and evaluative. There is discourse, argument and ego protection. The disciplined, cultured, knowledgeable individuals in the community exercise the authority of their discipline, culture and knowledge. They cannot fake it in this kind of living community. Individuals read and read and read. They talk. They debate. An authority delivers himself of a new idea buttressed by such evidence as he can marshal. The community reacts. Essentially, once a child has learned to read and to compose and to put some distance between criticism of his effort and his personality needs, there is little a teacher can do except to enjoy the growth and cultivation of another unique and precious individual.

There is somewhat more structure in our elementary education. The elementary classroom always has at least two teachers, often as many as ten. The number of students is always under thirty. The room is large and has an easily accessible half-second-story for reading and solitary quiet study, or sloth. The main room is organized with messy corners, book corners and display corners, and it leads into a small shed with a shop and very messy things. The two core teachers establish themselves as active and emotional "poles" in the room.

Without directing the children to either teacher, each teacher moves into his own activity as the day begins. One is active, outgoing, paying loud attention to painting, clay modeling, building, and rambling outside. The other is quieter and more passive—the reader, the writer and composer of songs, and other scholastic activities. It is important that these divisions are not made in a merely mechanistic fashion and that either teacher may perform any task in the schoolroom. Every effort is made to associate books, schooling, reading with relaxed purposiveness.

The children move freely between the teachers or take up their own activity. Reading, writing on paper or on the board, drawing, painting, making things, or simply crooning to the floor go on all the time. Some children seldom, if ever, cross from one teacher pole to the other; most oscillate without self-consciousness or concern. All elementary and kindergarten ages are present.

Reading periods are about the same time each morning. They are sometimes skipped entirely as the teacher senses the tone of the children—or they tell her, "None of that stuff today." Sometimes reading classes consume all day. The smallest children are asked what words they would like. They are printed on a card and given to them, or they are written on the board and the teacher builds a sentence suggested by others, sometimes grammatically and developmentally, sometimes working the sentence out from the middle or ungrammatically. This kind of linguistic analysis goes on from the earliest classes.

Writing is developed in much the same way. Children write what interests them, and they read the writing with others. Tape recordings or transcripts of their own little stories or nonsense or refusals are made, typed or mimeographed, and reading proceeds apace. There is no "Up, up, up, John," at Green Valley. Illustrations of words made by the children, collages of words and illustrations, "dada" stories made up by pasting word cards and other techniques well known to all good teachers are part of our regular armament.

Rather than bringing bits and pieces of the world into the classroom, we make every effort to take childen out into the world. Children are not interested in seedlings in eggshells when they have eggs in eggshells and seedlings in the ground. Nature corners are redundant when an important part of the day is given to rambles with teacher to point, question, prod and leave alone. The city, no less than the countryside, is a vital classroom and this does not mean guided museum tours. Quite young children can see the dramatic change of neighborhood lines, the abrupt economic change at a state line, the significant flow of foot traffic, the flow of vehicular traffic seen from the street and a high building, the difference in taste of commercial bread and home-baked bread or salad dressings. They can ask and answer penetrating questions about reasons for such phenomena.

And above all, we try never to forget that for adolescents and elementary school children alike the role of the teacher is to point, prod, to prick, to question, and always, to draw back from and to look and learn from what the children are seeing and asking. A cultured teacher, living in a community of cultured persons, cannot avoid communicating that culture to children when she is actively involved with the children. The only text books she needs are the ones which she uses herself.

THE HARD-SOFT SCHOOL

Anthony Barton

IT APPEARS that there was an information explosion in the realm of finance before the stock market crash of 1929. Now it seems that there is an information explosion in education.

Pieces of paper are exchanging hands, but the exchange bears less and less resemblance to the real life education of children, most of which now takes place outside the schools. Paper studies, paper seminars, paper diplomas, and paper tapes carry records of student attendance, age and grade: information on which to base provincial grants, not information of help to students trying to learn . . . all this is an overexpansion of credit. The learning which is going on in our schools does not seem to justify the mountain of paper in departments of education and research institutes. If our self-interest does not permit us to put a match to the mountain, let us at least change the schools to permit learning which is more revelant to the present day. Let us have new schools which provide the kind of learning which it is very difficult to obtain in everyday life: the valuable kind. Instead of rationing facts, let children learn ways to think, ways to manipulate concepts, and ways to understand and to work with film, television, and sound: the pen, pencil, and paper of the electric age.

If we can raise the true value of education to something approaching its paper value, we can stave off for another decade the Education Crash, the day when we tear up the journals of applied psychology, attendance sheets, and all the paraphernalia of the Myth.

So we need a new kind of school.
Should it be hard or soft? 5 1-2

HARD

A barred gate in a brick wall opens into an asphalt playground. A notice on the wall reads BICYCLE RIDING, HANDBALL PLAYING, HARDBALL PLAYING, PROHIBITED BY THE TORONTO BOARD OF EDUCATION. Fifth grade children are standing in groups, one or two are skipping. An electric bell rings and a teacher marshals the children into a line. They walk up three steps and enter the concrete school building.

Inside, they are marched down a wide, clean corridor, their footsteps echoing. Private lockers line the corridor, all identical, every one secured by a combination padlock. The children are led into a classroom and seated in alphabetical order at desk-chairs with built-in book racks. After calling the roll, the teacher talks to them about Canadian History for forty minutes, using an epidiascope to project onto a canvas screen some illustrations from the textbook prescribed for the course.

The teacher talks to them about logarithms for the next forty minutes, pausing from time to time to ask questions, to maintain order, and to dictate examination notes which the children write down on the left-hand pages of pre-ruled hardback note books with one-inch margins.

There is a twenty-minute break during which each child consumes half a pint of milk, followed by a practical science lesson in a laboratory with waxed benches, identical stools, identical gas taps, and identical sets of apparatus. During this lesson, all the children perform the same preconceived dummy experiment and write a third-person account under the headings OBJECT, METHOD, and CONCLUSION. This is followed by an art lesson in which each pupil is seated twelve feet from a daffodil and told to draw it. Lunch, prepared by a catering staff, is eaten in a self-service canteen, served in stainless steel trays with compartments for meat, vegetables and dessert.

After the meal there is a compulsory rest period, and then organized team games. The day ends with forty minutes of mathematics drill in a classroom equipped with thirty computer terminals dispensing the same programmed instruction to all.

SOFT

A tangle of mud, trees, grass, and children's constructions leads gradually into a covered, heated area. As the ground changes from mud to linoleum, a wooden grid appears low overhead. From this lattice of unfinished pine, many things are hanging: electronic sculptures, measuring instruments, polyethylene curtains, stage-flats, mirrors, and microphones. The grid carries power and communications outlets and is festooned with mobile lamps and television screens. It is so low that an adult has to stoop, thus it is within easy reach of most of the children, some of whom are climbing about on top of it. In one corner, they are setting up the lighting for a protest play about the slavery of newspaper delivery in their locality. In another corner, a Spasm Band is rehearsing. In the middle of the open area, a group of five talkative children have hung mobile walls in a rough circle to make a projection room. They are discussing some slides which they made on a visit to a potash mine in Saskatchewan. Over on the far side of the area, there are three great bins, the first is full of paperback books, the second is full of scraps of film and tape, the third is a sea of magazines, journals and newspapers. A boy is rummaging in the film bin, and two girls are making a pile of magazines. Several children are lying and sitting by themselves, reading and thinking. The noise is indescribable.

Posters abound. Typewriters, paper, and pieces of circuitry litter the floor. Safety has been built into the equipment and the environment: fire and electricity dangers are small. In the heart of the confusion, a teacher is busy painting a mural of dinosaurs; the children treat him as an equal and seek his advice on various matters from time to time. Close by, there is a computer terminal, a refrigerator and a large gas cooker, all in constant use. People pause in their work to make themselves coffee or to cook a meal for themselves or their friends. Occasionally someone leaves a group to wander outside and roll in the mud, or to gaze up at the sky and dream.

EDUCATIONAL ADVANTAGES

- **THE HARD LIFE**

  prepares children for the illogicalities and hardships of our present-day regimented existence. WAR BUSINESS TABOOS.

  points out the drawbacks of organized efficiency. FORCED TO READ SET BOOKS.

shows how boredom can arise from enforced activity and lead to inactivity. DOZING IN CLASS.

satisfies a child's need for simplified, structured surroundings. YOU KNOW WHERE YOU ARE.

permits nervous teachers to avoid personal relations with children. RETREAT TO THE STAFF ROOM.

- **THE SOFT LIFE**

prepares children for life as active individuals. TRY IT MY WAY.

points out the drawbacks of organized inefficiency. CAN'T FIND MY BOOK.

shows how boredom may arise from freedom, also, and lead to activity. MUSTN'T WASTE OPPORTUNITIES.

satisfies a child's need for diversity in exploratory play. THIS IS JUST A MODEL.

permits teachers to get to know children well, on equal terms. NO TALKING DOWN.

- **THE HARD-SOFT LIFE**

enjoys the advantages of the hard and the soft. CONTRAST.

shows how environment affects people and their work. GRAPH-PAPER AIRPLANES.

allows children to learn how to get the best of both hard and soft worlds. COMPUTERGRAPHIC PAINTING.

demonstrates the need to work in an intermediate zone. DRAMA IN A FRAME.

permits teachers to teach the way they like best. CHALKDUST FOR ME.

The school needs:

- **HARD AND SOFT**

  in equal measure. Both hard and soft have their advantages, both should be a part of everyone's experience.

- **A COMPUTER**

  tapping upon request a vast store of sound, vision, and audiovision. The computer will help to push the information level inside the school above the information level in the television-soaked surroundings.

- **FLEXIBILITY**

  Free access to materials and equipment with which the children can manipulate the modern media.

- **COURAGEOUS ARCHITECTS**

  with the imagination to include purposeless structures and interesting but unlabelled areas in their school designs. Children can learn a great deal by completion: an educational structure should be incomplete.

- **UNTRAINED TEACHERS**

  as well as trained professionals. Artists, scientists, craftsmen, and technologists should be paid to carry out part of their work in the school environment where they can interact with the children. Ideas will flow both ways.

- **LINKS WITH THE WORLD**

  Children should work, but *not* in a classroom to no immediate purpose. Their school should help the community. They themselves should carry out practical projects such as the relief of the elderly or the laying of school sewer pipes. Children need to visit law courts and power stations with an aim in view: to discover the laws relating to the care of the elderly, or the ways to imbed piping in concrete. They are easily bored by conducted tours in which they are mere observers, tiny tourists.

- **COURAGEOUS SCHOOL BOARD MEMBERS**

  These community leaders must be as willing to experiment with buildings as with gadgets and expensive computers to do payrolls.

PROPOSAL: The school should be designed and built with a physically hard area leading to a flexible intermediate zone which in turn fades into a physically soft area.

Alternatively, the school might consist of hard, soft, and intermediate modules in a pattern. The idea is to embody in the design a *complete* spectrum of environments, to help a child learn better how his surroundings affect him and what he does.

An *intermediate zone* seems to be an inescapable part of a hard-soft system. In this zone, hard structures, such as television receivers, screens, and thumb tacks, have to be moved at will. This requires a rigid framework of power and support and we suggest a hard overhead grid made of soft wood.

Where possible, the grid may be extended up and down the walls, to give greater flexibility to the area as a whole.

There should be power and communication outlets at every intersection of the grid.

The hard-soft school might look something like this:

HARD

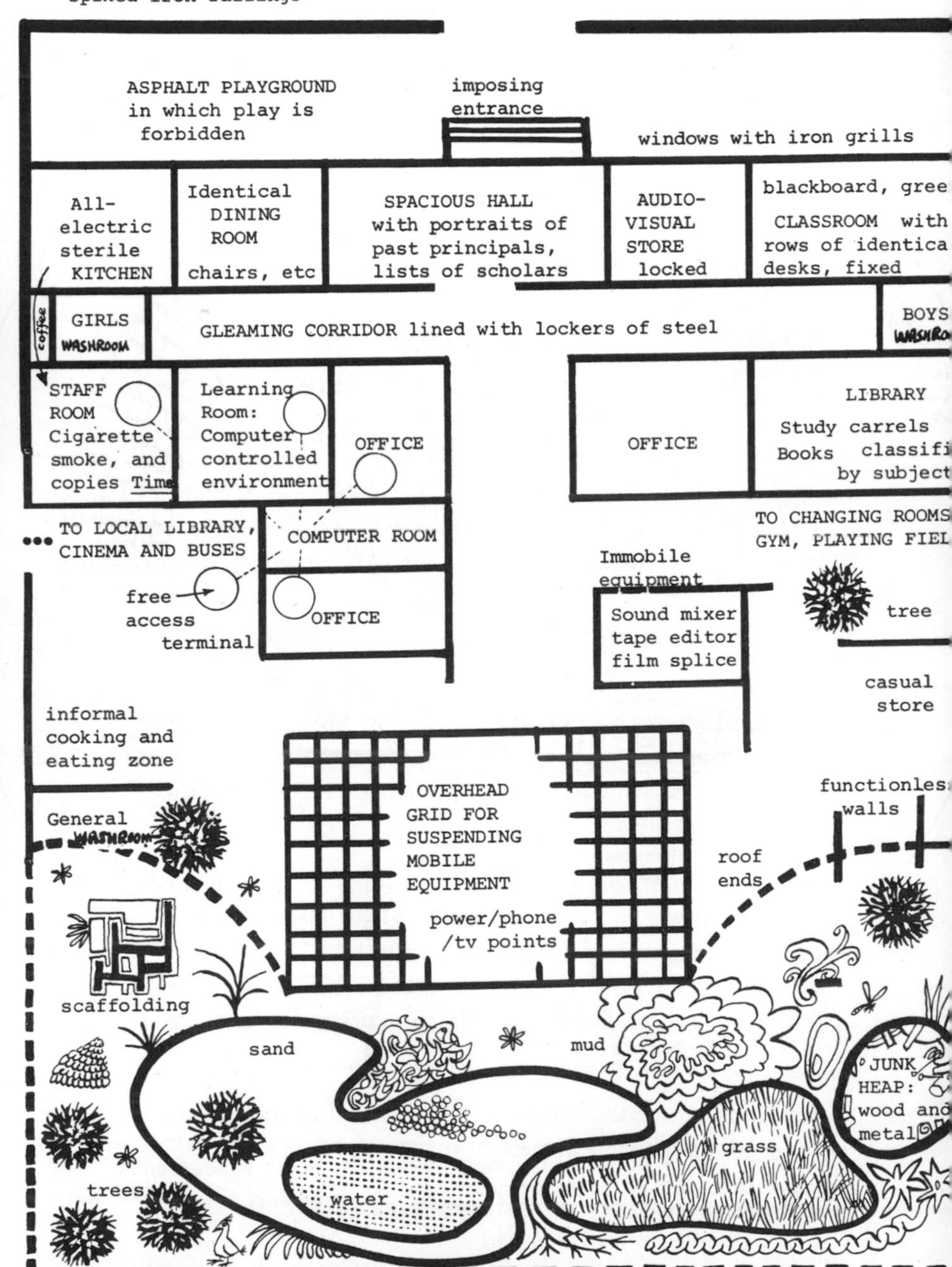

SOFT

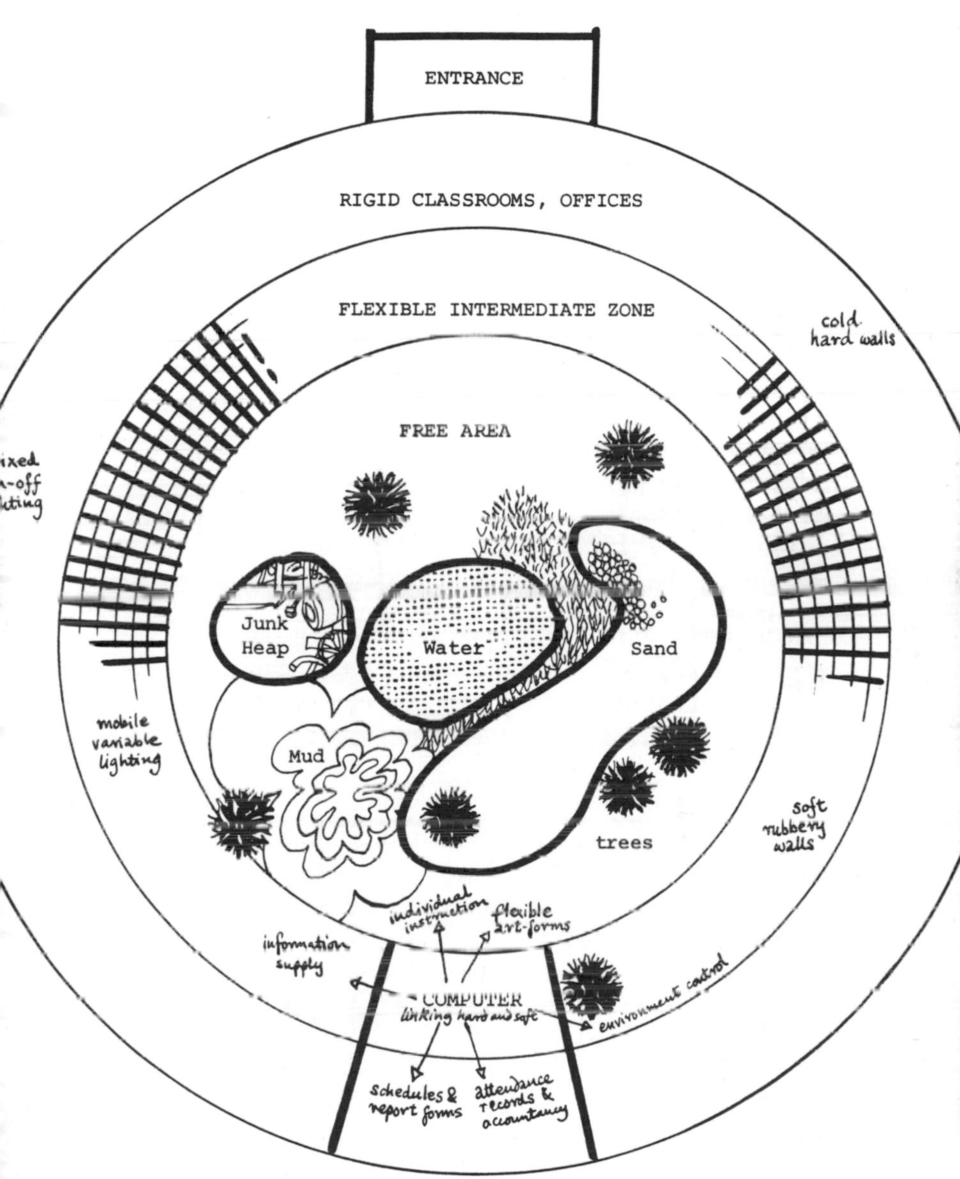

The hard-soft idea can take many forms. It is an educational suggestion, not an architectural one. In the hands of a good architect, surprising things might come of it.

Where Is the Computer in the Hard-Soft School? It Has Tentacles. It would be a mistake to draw clear boundaries between hard, intermediate and soft. The computer itself might have to be situated in the hard zone, but its terminals could be placed in both the hard and the intermediate zones. A terminal or two might even find its way into the soft zone; that would be a milestone in education: a computer terminal in the mud.

The terminals in the HARD zone are used for organizational work, record-keeping, accounting, budgeting, scheduling. (There may be two computers in the computer room, one for this kind of thing and one for educational purposes.) The terminals in the SOFT zone are used for free interaction with the machine, indescribable.

The terminals in the INTERMEDIATE zone are situated in a computer-controlled environment. Each terminal sits in a room of its own and the computer controls the lighting, sound, smell, and tactile surfaces of this room.

Bricks are not enough. What would happen if a hard-soft school were built and placed in the hands of teachers who did not understand it? They would turn the flexible grid into a gymnasium, screw electric bells onto the trees, remove the junk, level the mud, and put up signs saying KEEP OFF THE GRASS. It's a hard life.

So we need new teachers for new schools, people who can change their teaching to match their surroundings, and do it all day. Are there flexible, committed teachers who can splice videotape, discuss the subconscious and climb trees? Yes, there are good teachers.

People are not enough. Good teachers exist, but they have few schools worthy of them. Those that stay in teaching tend to take on slowly the shape of the hard-walled mold.

Build hard-soft. Give them the school's real teaching needs. Half-measures will not do. There is at present a trend toward semi-flexibility which is deceptive in that it is an architectural answer but not an educational one. There is little to be said for a mobile wall if it can be moved only by a teacher. Moving walls is education: children learn when they manipulate their environment themselves, because they want to do so.

HARD-SOFT EDUCATION: A READING LIST

• **HARD**

Circular 14. Ontario Department of Education, Toronto
(Classic document of educational bureaucracy)
The Republic. Plato
(The idea of control as a basis of education)
Teaching Disadvantaged Children in the Pre-School. Bereiter
(The idea of control carried to extremes)
Walden Two. Skinner
(A novel by a behavioral scientist suggesting indirect control)

• **SOFT**

Summerhill. Neill
(Account of a free school forty years old, by its headmaster)
This Magazine is About Schools. Journal
(Accounts of Toronto's own free school, Everdale)
Rochdale College Calendar. Toronto
(Free education at the university level)
Walden. Thoreau
(Life in the woods as a philosophical ideal)

• **INTERMEDIATE**

Island. Aldous Huxley

(Balanced education through experience in a realistic utopia)

Understanding Media. Marshall McLuhan
(Hard formal education balanced by soft TV education in the home)

Misunderstanding Media. Gordon Martin, National Film Board of Canada
(A paper pointing out how the hard school misuses the media)

Émile. J. J. Rousseau
(The idea of allowing the child to develop freely in a hard frame)

Lord of the Flies. Golding
(Novel about hard-reared children thrown into a soft environment)

- **OVERVIEW**

SEF Report El. The Metropolitan Toronto School Board, Study of Educational Facilities
(Quotes from Dewey, many references for further reading)

SOFT BOXES IN HARD SCHOOLS

ANTHONY BARTON

DAVID STANSFIELD and I have been taking a box of multimedia materials on "The Thirties—The Age of the Great Depression" into school classrooms. It is one of our notions that disorganization has positive educational values. The contents of the box are disorganized, and when the children are using the box the classroom becomes disorganized. Here is what one boy had to say about his exposure to the kit:

Student: Well, you know, feeling of security: walk around, do whatever you like. You don't know what's going on, so you make the form for

> yourself. You come into the room. You're not supposed to do anything, but you see all this stuff hanging around, and you say, "Well, it's either going to sit there and do nothing for me or else it's going to sit there and do something for me," you know.

What was the stuff hanging around? Standard equipment from the school audio-visual room plus the box of materials on the thirties. I must explain that the materials in the box are soft in the sense that no attempt has been made to structure them. No labels on the records, no titles on the filmstrips, no captions on the slides, no step-by-step instructions for the student. Just $30.00 worth of raw materials: postcards, stamps, newspapers, letters, all mixed together: over a thousand items. Something of individual interest (we hope) to every one of thirty children in a classroom.

What happens? We have tried the kit in twenty classrooms. In one school, three children are building an airship. A boy in Hamilton, Ontario, is making a movie about the thirties. A girl in another school is *reassembling* "Guernica." There is enthusiasm, involvement: students are staying in school after hours to find out why food prices are so different today. In February, our boxes will go into two hundred classrooms to help follow up four educational television programs on the Depression produced by the dynamic new ETVO team Jim Hanley, Mike Spivak and Don Thompson, who with such programs as "The World of Pieter Brueghel" and "The Career Woman," have begun to give Ontario schools real television at last. It is good that two educational establishment monoliths, OISE and ETVO, are working together.

In some classrooms, the children turn the box into a holocaust of light and sound and recreate the thirties environment as best they can. Trainee teachers will go with the boxes to watch what happens.

David is preparing a Teacher's Guide which will request teachers using the box to say nothing to their students about why and how to use the materials.

Using a portable tape recorder, we have obtained many student reactions, often by asking them to interview one another: their reactions are more varied than those of the teachers, who frequently ask, "For what grade was this kit designed?"

It wasn't. Perhaps nothing should be designed for a specific grade, nor even exclusively for education. To enlarge on that, we have a feeling that there is everything to be said for designing an item of learning material for a child, if you know the child personally; but somehow it does not seem to make sense to design one thing for children, for a mass of children. Take a classroom with thirty pupils and imagine that it is your job to interest every one of them deeply, so deeply that learning takes place. You will never succeed by lecturing, nor by group teaching, nor by showing a film. It is our opinion that your only hope of successfully interesting every child is to provide the class with a range of materials, a range of opportunities, a range of spaces and a range of equipment, and then let them choose for themselves.

NEW NON-STICK PLAN

Choose for themselves is the important phase, for with a range of children you cannot hope to choose on behalf of each and guess aright in every case. So I think there are a couple of lessons for the curriculum planner in our box:

1. *Be more concerned with logistics than design.* Our experiment has driven home to me the disturbing

fact that our schools are starved of information (the libraries, textbooks, and audio-visuals are limited, the information channels with the outside world practically dry) and starved of learning materials (think of the scarcity of creative work-stuffs). It is small wonder that many of the teachers with whom we have spoken have been nervous, strict disciplinarians. Behind the thin layer of chalk on their boards lies a vacuum that year by year grows harder and harder to conceal from their charges. Many of them welcome our grade-less box with open arms without knowing why. Give us more, they ask. Give us more.

2. *Stop trying to measure the child.* It seems to me that if it were possible to plot all his variables, Man would have lost the evolutionary race aeons ago. Concentrate instead upon the real problem of meeting the needs of many children all at once. Do not exhaust yourself attempting to define all these needs in advance, be content to define the wide range of interests that must be excited. Think of the full hard-soft spectrum of the requirements of a crowd of children working as individuals. This spectrum *can* be measured, and I believe that there are fat educational rewards awaiting the first researchers in this field. Take your eyes off the child for a moment and look at his environment. Analyze the variety and scope of the materials, measure the availability of information and of workstuffs, investigate the range of the softness of the walls, lighting and seating. Ask yourself for how wide a range of children does *this* school cater? Why does it not cater for all? What is missing? Bring a touch of Jane Jacobs thinking into the scene. Variety is not the spice of life; it is its very essence.

It's not what you put in, it's what you left out.

No spices.

No enrichments.

Build for the continuum.

Many of the children welcome the box. Some are worried by the lack of instructions, some want an outline on the board. One said:

> I think maybe that—eh—like the first time like this, it's kind of hard, because it's novelty, you know, and eh—everybody's you know, wants to do something or other. But if you did this like, you know, every day of the week, like you have normally in class, you'd have to organize things yourself and you—it would be more of a challenge that way. Where just today, it was just like a novelty, you know.

And another said:

> Well, this was the first time we'd done it—things were kind of chaotic, but we—like we didn't take it seriously, but if we know that it was a matter of our passing or failing or whatever, then I think we'd take it seriously, and in the future if we had classrooms designed for this, like, say with a big index file right in the middle of the room, and then branches off, you know, we could get involved in things—people could work in groups and it would be—I, I'd like it better in classrooms.

THE CLASSROOM WITHOUT CLASSIFICATION

Certainly the box respects the student by treating him as an individual, as a person with a mind of his own. The concept of classifying children arose from this respect for the individual, I feel this. How sad that the educators went on to invent grades and streams, to measure IQs, weights, heights, attendance.

Somehow they lost track of the fact that real learning is a result of deep inward feelings and thoughts, that all else is sham, examination fodder, short-term memory drill. Perhaps the psychologists did not lose track of this, but they were unscrupulous and wished to bare the deep, inward feelings and use them to "motivate" learning, an example of the rat eating its own tail.

Now that grades and suchlike are with us, we cannot sweep them away easily. That sounds as though I were in favor of a rush toward chaos, so let me hasten to explain that I worked for two years writing programs for teaching-machines and those two years convinced me of the value of organizing learning material: I am not an advocate of chaos. I believe ORGANIZED MATERIAL HAS AN EDUCATIONAL VALUE EQUAL TO THAT OF UNORGANIZED MATERIAL, though for any given child one kind of material will be more valuable than the other. What I dislike, and what our multi-media something-for-everyone box is an attempt to escape from, is the impression of order dictated from above, something widespread in all walks of education today. Think of *Circular 14*'s textbook commandments, *Encyclopaedia Britannica's* explain-it-all-away filmstrip captions, the so-much-to-do curriculum and the hop-skip-and-jump timetable. I have met many children who have no need of order, it is criminal to impress it upon them; I have met children who thirst for order and to whom bibliographies, electric bells, instructions, classrooms, teaching-machines, and disciplined lessons should be given whenever they ask for them. Perhaps therein lies an answer to the problem Rousseau groped at but never quite brought into focus.

SMILE, EMILE!

In the preface to *Émile,* he talks of "what a child is capable of learning" and tries to tell us that the book is worthwhile because it concentrates on "the child in the child" rather than "the man in the child." Well, that is commendable, but there are more striking ideas in *Émile*. Authors are blind to their own works and should be forbidden to write about them. George Bernard Shaw would have disagreed, but then in his utopia, in the final act of *Back to Methuselah,* education took place well out of the way. His utopian citizens emerged fully educated, seventeen years old, from giant eggs. No, what seems to me significant about Émile's education is that it is personal. In Rousseau's day it seemed impossible for anyone but the rich to have personal education, but now the speed-up of information flow, the computer, and the new methods of communication born of the electric age have brought personal education within reach of everyone. Yet all that has emerged from *Émile*, and it really came from the Greeks, is the frustrating classroom technique known as "the discovery method." In several teachers' training colleges, our thirties box has been introduced as the latest experiment in the discovery approach, which has annoyed me. The discovery method, to malign it slightly, consists of attempting to turn the members of a physics class into thirty Galvanis by supplying each child with a copper hook, an iron bar and a frog's leg . . . and then standing back with narrowed eyes to await the rediscovery of electricity. I would like to emphasize that there are no pre-planned revelations in our multi-media box; if a child discovers something it is a real event. Ignoring the attempts to administer the discovery method to Émile, we are left with Rousseau's healthy child-centerdness:

> Nature provides for the child's growth in her own fashion and this should never be thwarted. Do not make

> him sit still when he wants to run about, nor run when he wants to be quiet . . . I see little fellows playing in the snow, stiff and blue with cold, scarcely able to stir a finger. They could go and warm themselves if they chose, but they do not choose; if you forced them to come in they would feel the harshness of constraint a hundredfold more than the sharpness of the cold.[1]

Answering a question about reading, he says:

> When reading is of use to him, I admit he must learn to read, but till then he will only find it a nuisance.[2]

The first quotation reminds me of my last visit to Everdale, the free school just outside Toronto. It was winter and outside in the deep snow a child lay reading, unrebuked, absorbed. The second quotation reminds me of a passage in A. S. Neill's book about the world's first free school, Summerhill, which has now been in existence for half a century.

> Tom came to Summerhill at the age of five. He left at seventeen, without having in all those years gone to a single lesson. He spent much time in the work shop making things. His father and mother trembled with apprehension about his future. He never showed any desire to learn to read. But one night when he was nine, I found him in bed reading *David Copperfield*.
>
> "Hullo," I said, "who taught you to read?"
>
> "I taught myself."
>
> Some years later, he came to me to ask, "How do you add a half and two-fifths?" and I told him, I asked if he wanted to know any more. "No thanks," he said.
>
> Later on, he got work in a film studio as a camera boy. When he was learning his job I happened to meet

[1] Jean Jacques Rousseau, *Émile* (New York, E. P. Dutton & Co., Inc., 1911), pp. 50–51.
[2] *Ibid.*, p. 81.

> his boss at a dinner party, and asked how Tom was doing.
>
> "The best boy we ever had," the employer said. "He never walks—he runs. And at weekends, he is a damned nuisance, for on Saturdays and Sundays he won't stay away from the studio." [3]

Education is intensely personal. I sometimes feel that educators, half aware of this, are caught upon the horns of a dilemma. On the one hand they strive to preserve the essential intimacy between child and adult, while on the other hand they strive to deepen their understanding and their control of the educational process by depersonalizing it, by delving for general truths, and by classifying children according to superficial characteristics such as age and IQ. An instance of the depersonalization of education occurred during one of the trials of our box, when eight trainee teachers arrived to study the class reaction to multi-media. They trooped in and sat down at the back of the class, forming a solid row of solemn, trained observers, notebooks out, pencils poised for behavioral notes. The children complained bitterly, pointing out that it was worse than being in a zoo. We agreed, it was more like a circus than a zoo. Great educators like Piaget, excellent

[3] A. S. Neill, *Summerhill* (New York, Hart Publishing Company, 1960), pp. 29–30.

with children themselves, fall into the same kind of trap when they try to map cognitive development and almost accidentally spawn batches of ghoulish kindergarten investigators who tie labels around the necks of four-year-olds and talk as if the concepts of horizontality and verticality were external verities rather than passing reflections of western culture. Even Aldous Huxley slips into the trap of trying to classify children instead of allowing the children to classify themselves. Huxley pins his faith on morphology; it is rather touching.

> "When I was at school," said Will, "the pedagogues did their best to iron out those differences, or at least to plaster them over with the same Late Victorian ideal —the ideal of the scholarly but Anglican football-playing gentleman. But now tell me what *you* do about the fact that everybody's different from everybody else." "We begin," said Mr. Menon, "by assessing the differences. Precisely who or what, anatomically, biochemically and psychologically, is this child? In the organic hierarchy, which takes precedence—his gut, his muscles, or his nervous system? How near does he stand to the three polar extremes? How harmonious or how disharmonious is the mixture of his component elements, physical and mental? How great is his inborn wish to dominate, or to be sociable, or to retreat into his inner world? And how does he do his thinking and perceiving and remembering? Is he a visualizer or a non-visualizer? Does his mind work with images or with words, with both at once, or with neither? How close to the surface is his storytelling faculty? Does he see the world as Wordsworth and Traherne saw it when they were children? And, if so, what can be done to prevent the glory and the freshness from fading into the light of common day? Or, in more general terms, how can we educate children on the conceptual level without killing their capacity for intense non-verbal experience? How can we reconcile analysis with vision? And there are dozens of other questions that must be asked and answered. For example, does this child absorb all the vitamins in his food or is he subject to some chronic deficiency that, if it isn't recognized and treated, will lower his vitality,

darken his mood, make him see ugliness, feel boredom and think foolishness or malice? And what about his blood sugar? What about his breathing? What about his posture and the way he uses his organism when he's working, playing, studying?" [4]

It is myth, thank heavens. The answer lies farther back, in the very idea of classifying people. In a sense, there has to be classification if we are to talk efficiently about what goes on in a school, but who suggested that adults classify children in cold blood? It is too much hard work, and that is one of the system's worst parasites: hard work. Educators are looking for hard work, teachers are looking for hard work, curriculum planners are looking for hard work . . . and all because they went to hard schools themselves and maybe because they read in some psychological journal that persistence is measurable. Children know better than to look for hard work, though we do our best to stifle that knowledge. Children look for interesting work, for activity which leads to learning, to expanding horizons and to adventure. They are busy and so their work is not hard, it is exhausting. Dewey puts it well in his impeccable English:

> Let the child's nature fulfill its own destiny, revealed to you in whatever of science and art and industry the world now holds as its own.
>
> The case is of Child. It is his present powers which are to assert themselves; his present capacities which are to be exercised; his present attitudes which are to be realized.[5]

I think it important that Dewey here says "Child," not "the child." Huxley, too, was groping in the right direction. Children do come in all shapes and sizes, in a variety

[4] Aldous Huxley, *Island* (New York, Harper & Row, 1962, 1968), pp. 208–209.
[5] John Dewey, *The Child and the Curriculum & School and Society* (Chicago, University of Chicago Press, Phoenix Edition, 1956), p. 31.

more splendid than the contents of any multi-media box, and this points to all the hidden, changing shapes and sizes of mind. Huxley's idea of correlating the outward appearance with the inward self is typical of the present run of educational ideas, an idea promising upon the surface but skin-deep because it can be expected to work only in a fraction of cases. There are many, many such half-truths to be found in experimental education today, for the experimenters are unwilling to admit that the human animal is too ambiguous and too complicated to be predictable, that man owes his survival and his place in the evolutionary tree to his unpredictability. Please do not misunderstand me, I feel that education is in great need of experiment. Soon we may have a true science of education, despite the premature arrival of journals, jargon and research institutes. I fancy a true science of learning may come when measurement, the sharpest tool of science, is applied to a previously neglected area: perhaps information retrieval. That measurement has been so far employed in an almost fruitless region, cannot be doubted. Using statistical methods of analysis, educators have been groping for hidden laws underlying the behavior of children, groping for laws that would make learning as easy to control as electricity, as predictable as a magnetic field. We can be thankful that no such laws have been found. Konrad Lorenz would echo our thanks:

> There are few things in the world so thoroughly despicable and deserving of immediate destruction as the fiction of an ideal cause artificially set up to elicit enthusiasm in the service of the contriver's aims. Humor is the best of lie-detectors and it discovers, with an uncanny flair, the speciousness of contrived ideals and the insincerity of simulated enthusiasm.[6]

Lorenz sees humor as the human safety valve. I wish more of us had his insight. During our visits to schools, the

[6] Konrad Lorenz, *On Aggression* (New York, Harcourt, Brace & World, 1966), pp. 294–295.

greatest obstacle to proper understanding of our multi-media box seems to me to have been the teachers' notion that because the children enjoyed playing with it, because they laughed instead of frowned, they were merely entertained and learned little. I am afraid I must report that some of the children also were of the opinion that since it was fun it could not be very useful.

THE THIRTIES MULTI-MEDIA KIT

Order for packing items in boxes:

1 Dust Bowl Ballads
2 German/English Newspapers
1x17 Newspaper Pages
1 Jackdaw C13: *The Great Depression*
15 Notes & Quotes I
15 Notes & Quotes II
1 Blueprint of Dirigible
1 "Guernica"
2 Rivera Mural
2 Adolf & Neville
2 Shirley Temple Eating Puffed Wheat
2 Bethune
2 Pound
2 Hate Page
2 Relishprobe
2 Bank of Montreal
2 Garner Interview
2 Wanted for Murder
2 Callaghan
2 Ships in the Sky
2 Condemned to Starve . . . Compelled to Act
2 Mass Meeting Tonight & Protest for Justice
2 Quotes
2 Illusions
2x2 Vancouver Police Department Letters
2 Help Yourself to our Salad Bowl & Cabbagetown
2 Investigation of Poverty at Russell Sage Foundation
2 Notice from CNR & CPR
2 United Nations
2 Classroom of Tomorrow
2x11 Clippings Pages
1 Prints (1 packet of 20)
2 Canadian Paintings of the 1930's
2 Letter to the Editor
2 Identification Order No. 1194: Charles Arthur Floyd
2 Hindenburg Folder
2 Saint John Hospital Cartoons
9 Phonograph Records
1 Bitter Years
1x36 Postcard Reproductions

1 Audio Tape
1x80 Literature & Science Cards
1 Postage Stamps (1 packet of 20)
1 Mounts for Half-Frame Slides (1 packet of 10)
1x22 Slides (1 bundle in elastic band)
4 Filmstrips
1 Transparency
1 Sheet of Colored Plastic
1 Booklist
1 Guide

IF YOU CAN'T LOVE THEM You can't teach them?

the Warrendale experience

An Interview with JOHN BROWN, Executive Director of Warrendale & MICHAEL WALKER, School Principal

WARRENDALE is one of Canada's oldest private residential treatment centers for children who are emotionally disturbed or mentally ill. It is also one of the most unusual in that its theories preclude the use of locked doors, isolation rooms, and shock treatment. Children of all degrees of disturbance are accepted and no time limit is set for treatment. It is notable as much for its approach to its staff as it is for its work with children: all staff must undergo psychotherapy and no professional qualifications are required for hiring. Above all, its methods bring results—results which one investigator has calculated to be as high as 85 per cent recovery.

One hundred children ranging in age from five to twenty-one live in two centers in the Metropolitan Toronto area. Children live in family-sized groups and their treatment is in the hands of a staff of one hundred and twenty—a remarkable staff-child ratio. Up to this year Warrendale's setting has been a spacious rural area north of the city. In December, 1965, a new suburban center with family-sized houses was added to the program.

Seventy of the one hundred children go to Warrendale School where they are divided into eight classes and are supervised by sixteen teachers. The program is ungraded and all learning is based on individual emotional needs. The school has mushroomed overnight into one of Warrendale's most important projects—last year it was a one-room affair.

John Brown, an ex-American trained in anthropology and psychiatric social work, has been Executive Director of Warrendale since 1951. His teachers have been Fritz Redl, noted author of *Children Who Hate,* and a professor of psychology at the University of Michigan; and Martin Fischer, Warrendale's psychiatric consultant.

But the pupil has long since developed his own style. He has that rare combination of qualities which characterize pioneer experimenters who are successful: an aura of the priest-king, which evokes an almost religious devotion from his staff; and an astute business sense, which has enabled him to manage and considerably expand an institution which costs $7,200 per child per year. (Most children are wards of the Children's Aid Society.) He even finds time to organize other projects on the side—like setting up a network of summer camps for normal children.

Michael Walker, after a B.A. at the University of Chicago, some organizing for the civil rights and peace movements in the U.S. and Canada, and a year of high school teaching, joined the Warrendale staff as a child-care worker in 1964. His gifts were soon recognized by Brown: with children, the ability to be highly intimate and still remain an adult—with staff, the ability to press hard in crises but draw back and trust them day by day. He was appointed school principal last September. In his spare time his hobby is sports car racing.

IF YOU HAD TO SINGLE OUT ONE GUIDING PRINCIPLE IN ALL YOUR WORK WITH CHILDREN, JOHN, WHAT WOULD IT BE?

Brown: The basis of all our work is close human relationship—we are trying to find a feeling communication between people who are out of communication with others or who are dislocated in their place in society.

HOW HAVE YOU GOT THE REPUTATION OF BEING RADICAL? WOULD IT BE IN YOUR METHODS PERHAPS RATHER THAN YOUR THEORY?

Brown: Well, I don't know. Most of the things we do I wouldn't call that radical. Sometimes in the way we go about communicating, we do things that are unorthodox but the purpose of all that we do is not so much to be radical or different as it is to communicate with children who are out of communication. If people perceive it as radical then it's their problem.

COULD YOU GIVE ME SOME EXAMPLES OF THE METHODS YOU USE TO ACHIEVE THIS COMMUNICATION?

Brown: One thing that consistently characterizes Warrendale over the years is the fact that very few of our approaches remain constant. There is a continual change going on. We do start out though on some simple assumptions, such as the assumption that learning at its deepest root, is a taking in and it follows the model of the feeding experiences of the individual in its infancy and the childhood. We believe a child takes in what is palatable, retains what is palatable and rejects or resists what is unpalatable.

ONE THING THAT STARTLES A LOT OF VISITORS IS TO SEE A NUMBER OF OLDER CHILDREN DRINKING FROM NURSING BOTTLES. WHAT'S THE PURPOSE OF THIS?

Brown: Well, when it comes to basic communication with children who are out of communication, we don't rely on the spoken or written word as the major means of communicating feeling. Instead we go back to the more elementary or simple forms of communication such as touch, feeling and taste. The nursing bottle, which is not used by all of our children, is a means of taking a child back to a level of emotional nourishment that was obviously missed the first time round. It is a corrective human experience. Granted the child's basic relationships with the feeding parent were disturbed or dislocated, we go on the assumption that the child's feeling reaction to these dislocations can be unlearned. Our first step in our rehabilitation program is to get into a communication relationship with the child, and then to help the child unlearn negative harmful, destructive, previous experiences. After this is done we can begin to teach the child positively. The giving of the bottle is simply one small technique.

The reason it has such a powerful impact on visitors and on people who work in the program, is that a great many persons have repressed oral needs that they can't find satisfaction for, in the conventions of eating and drinking that are current in our culture, and so the need to suck is strong in many many people. So the people who are upset about bottle feeding are the people who need to have bottle feeding.

WHAT'S THE THEORY BEHIND THIS REGRESSION OF CHILDREN, THIS TAKING A CHILD BACK IN AGE?

Brown: Actually, the proper term is retrogression and the difference is not just technical. We have a simple formulation that was established many many years ago, before there was a Warrendale actually, and it comes out of Freud's concepts. A child may, for instance, be emotionally blocked at an early phase of development, say around the oral stage when he is experiencing the world through the objects he puts into his mouth. Such a child goes on growing chronologically even though he may be emotionally arrested, and at the age of fifteen, sixteen, or twenty the child it not adjusting. We feel we have to go back to the point of the disturbance, to the point of the deprivation and nourish the child emotionally from that point. To attempt to nourish the child at the age of fifteen or twenty would be to provide material for the kid which he couldn't use and this is what you see in so many of the conventional programs, not just in the Treatment Centers and hospitals but, in schools as well. He needs pablum instead of steak and until you give him pablum he isn't going to be able to eat steak, and I think it's just that simple.

WOULD YOU SAY, THEN, THAT YOUR METHODS ARE LARGELY BASED ON FREUD?

Brown: Our methods are a combination of many things and I think this is the thing that most people miss. They glibly pass over our methods by trying to pigeonhole us. We don't exist in a vacuum—what we have learned came out of the roots of many fields of knowledge. I myself trained in anthropology and psychology long before I went into social work. I read widely; I am much more familiar with the work of Pavlov than I am with Freud on a first-hand basis. Any one who knows the work of Pavlov, would see much of Pavlov in our actual practice especially in the reinforcement part of learning.

PERHAPS IT'S TIME TO ASK YOU A QUESTION THAT MIGHT APPLY MORE DIRECTLY TO SCHOOLS. I THINK

THAT A LOT OF TEACHERS WOULD LIKE TO UNDERSTAND WHAT'S BASICALLY WRONG WITH SOME "PROBLEM STUDENTS," BUT THE EXTERNAL SYMPTOMS OF THE PROBLEM TAKE UP ALL THEIR TIME. HOW IN WARRENDALE DO YOU GET BEYOND THE SYMPTOMS?

Brown: Well, the symptoms are simply a sign that something is wrong. How do you get at the problem through the symptoms? You read the symptoms to understand the problem beneath. It's like buried treasure marked by a float. Now if you grab that float and deal with it and flee off to Monte Carlo with your loot, all you have is the symptom and the buried treasure is still down below. This is the problem you see: most places get preoccupied with the symptom. The symptom is simply a marker and it is a marker that there is something wrong at a deeper level. So you follow the symptom back. That's what happens in the Treatment Center that we established and the classrooms that we established, and what we find is that the symptoms fall away because our demand is of a different nature. We create an environment that allows human beings to function at the level of their capacity, and don't set expectations above that.

IN WARRENDALE, IF SYMPTOMS ARE SO EXTREME THAT A CHILD WANTS TO FIGHT WITH SOMEONE OR MUTILATE HIMSELF OR BREAK THINGS AND IN GENERAL LOSE CONTROL, HOW DO YOU COPE WITH THIS, ESPECIALLY SINCE YOU OPERATE WITHOUT ISOLATION ROOMS AND LOCKED DOORS?

Brown: Yes, well there's only one solution. We have to physically and personally, individually or collectively restrain the child by holding him. This involves the full use of yourself; you have to physically contain the child. And you have to do it in such a fashion that he feels safe—safe enough to ventilate feelings that he hasn't otherwise ventilated, to express angers and rage that he isn't feeling safe enough to do without this close human restraint. While you're restraining the child, you're in physical contact with him and communicating a human relationship to him.

DO YOU MEAN THAT THE STAFF ACTUALLY PREVENT THIS CHILD FROM MOVING?

Brown: Yes. In the most extreme cases, in the situations where other institutions would use a detention room or a chemical restraint or an isolation set-up of some kind, we would simply hold the child—generally with the arms folded across the chest, hugging him very tightly to you and trying to prevent him from kicking or biting you.

DOESN'T THIS FRIGHTEN HIM?

Brown: Well, I don't know. I suppose if the child has experienced physical abuse, he might be frightened the first time or the second time, but generally after they've been here for a few days, they've seen other children held, and they know it isn't a harmful or a hurting thing—that it's really a safe thing.

AND WHAT DO YOU HOPE WILL HAPPEN AS A RESULT OF THIS?

Brown: Well, the holding session can be of two types: one, where you simply restrain the child so he won't harm himself or someone else for a period of time when he's out of control; for the other, it's to provide him with the security he needs to vent his anger and rage. And in this kind of a holding session what you get is an uncovering of the tremendous underlying rage, after which the child is accessible and amenable to a quieter verbal approach, so that very often in that pause following the extreme ventilation, he is accessible to insights he wouldn't otherwise be.

YOU DO PUT SOME STRESS ON VERBAL COMMUNICATION THEN?

Brown: We begin to communicate at the most primitive level which is through touch and feeling and we then maybe, some six months, a year or two years, four-five years, later, get around to the verbal level. Now I'll say something to you that will seem a little odd: by the time the child is able to communicate feeling on a verbal level the child is no longer disturbed. If the child has integrated his emotions with his intellect, then you can't honestly call that child a disturbed child and at that point of course you use any conventional method. The child is through treatment by then.

I'D LIKE TO ASK YOU A QUESTION, MIKE, ABOUT WARRENDALE SCHOOL. JOHN HAS BEEN STRESSING NON-VERBAL COMMUNICATION AS A TREATMENT METHOD. A SCHOOL SETTING IS SURELY AT LEAST CONVENTIONALLY A FAIRLY VERBAL SETTING. IS YOURS?

Walker: No, we solve the problem really by not approaching the child at a verbal level. To give an example: in a science course set up for children on a seventh or eight grade level, you find in a standard school system that they expect these children to have already achieved an over-all view of the world and to be breaking it down into various specific categories and areas, to be studying the very specific types of scientific explorations such as biology. Now a child who is emotionally three years old, is not ready to look at the world that way yet, not ready to take in the world as a unified whole and begin to break it down. This child is still trying to unify the world around him. He is still trying to understand it. So if you approach the study of science with this in mind and attempt with a seriously disturbed child to help him to unify the world, help him to see it as all one part of a great picture; he has a great deal more interest in it and he is able to approach the study.

HOW MIGHT THIS BE DONE IN A PRACTICAL WAY? IF THE CONVENTIONAL METHOD IS THE BREAKING-DOWN METHOD AND THE TEXT BOOK, SAY, IS DIVIDED UP INTO CONVENTIONAL TOPICS—MATTER, ENERGY, ETC.—HOW WOULD YOUR APPROACH BE DIFFERENT WITH A SMALL CHILD?

Walker: The difference would be that you wouldn't ask the child to deal with the words in a text book. You would ask him to deal with the world. You would center all of this work in your science classes on explorations of the world around them. By this I don't mean a text book exploration where you proceed from point A to point C. I mean you can begin with a child, and from certain physical matter around him, you help him explore it and you help him to integrate what he has learned to his own experience. You allow him to experiment with it, as he wants.

Instead of expecting him to look at a book and to understand the characteristics of a vertebra by simply reading four pages on them, you help him play with dogs and cats and point out what a backbone is and help the child to see, not that there are forty-seven categories of vertebrae, but that all animals that move in a certain way have a backbone.

Brown: I wonder if I could add something to it? The real point of it is to deal with any child by dealing with what interests the child. The child's scope and perception extends as he is able to learn and incorporate things. Until he can encompass a vast circle of information and knowledge, the emotionally disturbed child has a very narrow vision and experience. And so you follow him in his exploration, help him, assist him, respond to him, give him human relationship while he is exploring the universe around him. I think this is what Mike is saying. Of course, it isn't just for the seriously disturbed child, this is the best kind of teaching for any kid.

YOUR AIMS ARE SO DEMANDING THAT YOU MUST EXPECT EXTRAORDINARY THINGS FROM YOUR STAFF —BOTH YOUR TEACHERS AND YOUR CHILD CARE WORKERS—WHY DO YOU UNDERPLAY THE NEED FOR PROFESSIONAL QUALIFICATIONS WHEN THE WORK IS SO SPECIALIZED AND DEMANDING?

Brown: We are interested in staff who can communicate and you don't communicate on the basis of your specialized training, or your academic degrees—and this applies as much to Mike's teaching staff as it does to the child care staff. I know Ph.D.'s who are not only without language, but are so seriously disturbed that they would have to spend a long time dealing with their own problems before they would be prepared to deal with other people's problems. So it isn't the academic qualifications that we look for. Now this doesn't mean that academic qualifications are not important. I would like nothing better than to have all Ph.D.'s with the most advanced and extensive experience and knowledge in educational methods and techniques from any school, from any philosophy, and bring them in and give them an opportunity to apply it and use it, in the way that we do. This would be ideal, but, of course, we don't find these kind of people. First, because we couldn't afford them and secondly, because they don't exist that much.

So what we are interested in, and the first prerequisite, is: can they communicate emotions, can they feel, can they relate, can they through the use of themselves in the relationship motivate children to feel the world is a safe enough place in which to extend themselves, so they can explore and extend themselves into the universe around?

HOW DO YOU FIND THEM?

Brown: Well, we have a very complicated selection system. If somebody looks good to us we hire them on a trial basis. If they work out, fine. If they don't work out, they usually leave or we help them to leave. It's hard to know. These are things you get a feeling about after a period of time. It boils down to this. You may find a person who you think has the potential, but you can see half a dozen areas where something stands in the way and you say to yourself: if these things can be dealt with, if these things can be removed within a period of six months, a year, a year and a half, two years, this person may be just the ideal type of person to be working in this program. Then you have to decide whether or not you're going to invest in the staff member the amount that is required to make it possible for him to use his potentials adequately. So we are constantly facing this kind of a problem. We are selecting people who may not at the moment be free enough to do this, but through a program of psychotherapy become self-aware enough.

I GATHER THAT PSYCHOTHERAPY IS COMPULSORY FOR THE STAFF?

Brown: It is in our institution. You wouldn't find it anywhere else.

WHY DO YOU BELIEVE THAT IT'S IMPORTANT?

Brown: I think that it is important for a number of reasons. I like to have people who understand themselves and who can separate their emotional problems from the problems of the children whom they are dealing with. I like to have people who have experienced what it feels like to alter yourself, to change, to look at yourself and say: I am dissatisfied, I want to do something to change it and then proceed to do something to change it. This is a painful experience. It is an experience that requires great sensitivity to what the individual is feeling who is undergoing it. Because you see, the person that changes has to give up all patterns of action and defense and these are very dear to him. After all they made the difference between his maintaining himself or not maintaining himself up to this time and you're asking him to go back and review these and give these up. But how can you do it for the child if you can't do it for yourself? This is one of the basic requisites I would say, even before the ability to communicate: you have to indicate that you want to go through a psychotherapeutic experience which means you have to be willing to be introspective about yourself and you have to be prepared to change. Because once you become introspective, it's inevitable that you will change.

MIKE, DO YOU THINK THAT THE TEACHING PROFESSION WOULD BE BETTER OFF TO HAVE COMPULSORY STAFF THERAPY IN OUR REGULAR SCHOOLS?

Walker: No, I don't think so. If you're going to talk about compulsory therapy for all teachers then you might as well talk about a complete change in the entire school system. Ninety per cent of those people teaching shouldn't be teaching. You would have a completely new crew and completely new approach to teaching.

COULDN'T A GREAT MANY OF THEM BE REHABILITATED THROUGH PSYCHOTHERAPY?

Walker: I don't know because I wonder what would put people into teaching in the first place. A good many people that I've seen go into teaching, go into it for very specific reasons: it's satisfying to them to be in complete control of a group of human beings, to be superior to them and have them responsive to their every wish. It fills a need to be the authority, to know everything, to tell the child this is the way the world is. I don't think any one of those things are valid if you want to teach a child.

Brown: But if you take it a step further back, why does he have to be in this position of authority? Why is he more comfortable doing this than say driving a truck or something? There is a deep insecurity in this satisfaction at the root of teaching. So the teacher compensates for it by becoming the boss and by being the authority figure. It may be a reaction to authority from the parents, the family. This is why I say a little psychotherapy might go a long way. Especially in the elementary grades, where the kid first comes into the schoolroom. As with any initial experience, the first experience is the most important experience because it sets the patterns. So if the kindergarten, first, second and third grade teachers could be given a mandatory program of psychotherapy during their training and during their first year of practice, this would undoubtedly improve the quality of teaching and improve the state of mental health. It would be one of the most tremendous programs of prevention.

DO YOU THINK THAT THE GUIDANCE PROGRAMS IN THE SCHOOLS ARE FILLING THIS GAP IN ANY WAY?

Brown: Guidance has nothing to do with psychotherapy. Guidance is advising people. Psychotherapy has nothing to do with advice giving, we give advice in our comments, but we don't give advice in psychotherapy.

MIKE, A PERSONAL QUESTION: YOU TAUGHT IN A REGULAR TORONTO TECHNICAL HIGH SCHOOL.

WHY DID YOU LEAVE THAT WORK TO WORK WITH DISTURBED CHILDREN?

Walker: I left because I found it very unsatisfying in many ways. I had 320 kids in ten classrooms. I taught each group of thirty children three times a week for forty-five minutes and they were just a sea of faces. After ten months of working with them, I didn't know any of them really. I had no feeling for them, they were just little facts in my grade book. Perhaps the most disturbing part of all this was that these kids were in ninth grade and sixteen years old, and most of them were about to leave the educational system. I felt that the school was not preparing them at all to be able to function as adults. It was giving them certain types of knowledge which were not very meaningful to them: it was helping them in certain areas where they were not interested in being helped. In the areas these children were concerned with, in the areas of their emotions and their feeling problems, the kids got no assistance at all from the school. And the school in many ways was more severe with the emotional problems of these kids than the community was.

THIS IS NOT THE FAMILIAR PICTURE OF SCHOOLS. IT'S USUALLY SAID THAT SCHOOLS ARE MUCH PLEASANTER AND HAPPIER THAN THEY USED TO BE: THERE IS NOT THE FEARSOME PRINCIPAL'S STRAP IN HIGH SCHOOLS NOW, FOR EXAMPLE.

Walker: No, because I think what we have done in the school is this: instead of having the strap hanging over the door of the office, the strap has been taken and put in the drawer with a little book and you have to sign in the book every time you use the strap. But the strap is still there and the mentality and train of thought that leads up to using the strap is still there. Principals are getting a little more clever about how to discipline kids. You don't have to hit them any more.

Brown: I certainly agree. The strap mentality still governs the school.

Walker: In these beautiful buildings we have 1,500 children in elementary schools, 2,000 in high schools. Frankly, it is the most frightening thing that a child will ever come up against. Here a child is not expected to function as an individual at all, but as part of a class group. He is not expected to have any personality whatsoever. A kid knows that if he quits school and goes out and runs in the street, at least he will be an individual. The community in many ways is not as severe.

Brown: It is the only way that he can be an individual actually. In a change of dress, or to rebel in some form.

I NOTICE IN YOUR CRITICISM OF SCHOOLS, JOHN, THAT YOU DON'T MENTION THEIR LACK OF STUDENT DEMOCRACY OR FREEDOM—A MORE COMMON CRITICISM MADE BY RADICALS AT THE MOMENT.

Brown: I don't hold with the radical form of democracy that you describe. I don't think that right is necessarily decided by a democratic vote.

If I had left it to democracy, Warrendale would have been voted out of existence in the first year of its operation. If you mean by democracy, that issues get heard and each person has an opportunity to learn and each person is given the facts and has some chance to think about it, come to a position about it, this kind of democracy is a dream.

One always gives and gets a preselected point of view. When I want someone to do something, I tell them what I want them to do. I don't say: now, there are thirty-nine schools of psychotherapy and I want you to select from those thirty-nine schools or create another one. I do say to people I want you to be creative and if you can demonstrate to me—and I expect you to—that you have something new, then we'll go for it. If you can't I won't go for it, and I will reserve to myself this final right of decision. I can be dictatorial as hell about it, both with my board, my staff and with kids. I don't allow a child to have freedom, random freedom. I'm not of the A. S. Neill–Summerhill school in this regard. I think a person needs limiting structures until he is in a position to act in a free fashion.

THEN FREEDOM IS NOT THE KEY TO YOUR WORK? I GATHER IT'S CLOSER TO WHAT YOU CALL ESTABLISHING RELATIONSHIP. DOES THIS MEAN A RELATIONSHIP OF LOVE?

Brown: The way I would phrase it would be that children are born into the world without knowledge and uncivilized. The simple fact is that they get knowledge and they gain civilization from each other; this is how they get their humanness—not from some academic concept and not from some idealistic concept. They get it from direct relationships with other particular human beings who can share themselves—not relationships with humanity in general.

MIKE, WOULD YOU SAY THAT IF A TEACHER, ANY TEACHER, CAN'T ESTABLISH A PERSONAL RELATIONSHIP WITH HIS STUDENTS, HE CAN'T TEACH THEM?

Walker: Well, of course, you can teach them in the sense of instructing them, but I'm not sure what value that has, especially for very young children and for children who are disturbed in any way.

To explain myself I'd like to say something about the basic task of education, what learning really is. To me, education, teaching, learning all mean helping the child to understand the world he's living in, to understand that it's a safe place, that it has a place for him.

Now with an aim like this, there are special problems with our disturbed kids, with young children, or with kids of all ages at certain times. If you're not involved personally with them none of this education gets through. The teacher in our setting has to invest himself in the child, has to show the child he loves him, has to show the child he really cares about that child's relationship to the world.

DON'T YOU THINK TEACHERS IN REGULAR SCHOOLS BELIEVE THAT, THAT TO TEACH WELL YOU MUST LIKE YOUR KIDS?

Walker: They may believe it but I don't think they show it to the child; they don't show that they want to reach out just as good parents reach out to children.

For example, they don't show—or maybe they aren't allowed to show—in the primary grades that they believe relationships with small children are established at the most basic level—touching kids, feeding them. This basic physical communication is the *only* way we can teach lots of our kids, and I believe it would be the easiest and quickest way to communicate with small children in regular schools too.

WHY CAN'T TEACHERS REACH OUT IN THIS WAY?

Walker: I'm not certain why. I think though, notwithstanding my previous remarks about teachers having authority problems, that a great deal of this comes from the school system itself, with the kind of mammoth structure education has become over the years. But even now they could certainly do a lot more in trying for emotional understanding from children and not just intellectual understanding.

I don't deny that at a certain point you have to help children to accept a different kind of relationship than the kind I've been stressing, but this can only come after a child has some integration of his emotions and his intellect.

A DIFFERENT LEVEL MEANING THAT STUDENTS WOULD BE MORE INDEPENDENT OF YOU?

Walker: Yes—that they would not need the constant reassurance of basic communication, that they'd be able to see in my over-all behavior, in the way I look at them, in the way I say good morning, that I care, and that I like them. But if the deep personal contact hasn't come first, all of this independence will be useless—and I mean that literally—independence that the child is incapable of using.

Bob Davis

BEFORE BROWNDALE

1

A FEW WEEKS AGO I spent a day watching six brilliant films about the treatment of disturbed children. The principal film is *Warrendale* which by now has won countless international prizes; and the other five are part of a series which will eventually contain eighteen films, a series of training films called *Children in Conflict*. Because all our readers should see these films, and because I used to teach at the center these films are about (Browndale and Brown Camps Ltd.—formerly Warrendale), I thought I'd review them.

But I had a problem. To show what this center did for me (the place is as important as Synanon and Esalen), I had to tell something of my personal history, and the more I got into this the further I got away from the films.

Of course I hate too much print about film anyway. Suffice it to say that King is a brilliant film artist and so we have here artistic portrayals of a method, not the usual lame and preachy descriptions that training series often are. Furthermore, film is a good medium for portraying Browndale since the center places such importance on moment-by-moment communications of touch and tone. One needs a multi-medium like film to capture such a theatre.

But of Browndale, more later.

2

Ten years ago I used to take these long Greyhound Bus trips all over the U.S. and Canada, and I used to try to park myself beside a "chick" whenever possible in preparation for the heavy make-out scene at night. There was a system to it. You'd talk during the day, establish yourself as a friendly, wandering guy, then when it got dark pretend to fall asleep. After a couple of hours, cough and stretch in my sleep but end up the stretch with my leg against hers. This was test #1. Usually the girl guessed what was up. Next time, cough, stretch, flop, but this time my hands on her knee. Naturally I would also have my coat or my sweater on my lap and, using this cover-up, off we'd go feeling and exploring each other's legs, genitals, blankets, skirts and pants, swallowing any sounds of pleasure, rolling around in that cramped and public space until the sun came up, and the peering eyes of the enemy which included everyone else on the bus appeared to glare as if they'd seen it all. And then we'd both get off at some spot like Durham, North Carolina, or Flagstaff, Arizona, or Lexington, Kentucky, and disappear to separate coffee shops for breakfast.

3

And ten years before that in Quebec City at fourteen the grand discovery of sperm. Fourteen was the Year of Masturbation, not the last year, mind you, but the year when I don't recall anything else happening. Three times a day, morning, noon, and night without fail, in washrooms, in bed, in the Plains of Abraham, the two-finger method, the three-finger method, the wet, soapy hand method, into kleenex, toilet paper, sheets, against the wall, and, I dimly recall that in those days I could hit the ceiling. Last year when I discovered Philip Roth's short story, "Whacking Off," I discovered a new book of the Bible, and roared for days.

4

And more vivid than any other memories, and stretching back further than most, the smells and visions of church, twice on Sunday and often during the week, high Anglican with the smell of expensive wax candles burning and of old cassocks and the breath of old tenors. And clearer than any other memory, my father, looming grand from the altar pronouncing the benediction on us—I can see every bit of gold embroidery and decoration on his glistening priests' robes.

But above all the sounds of music. Especially Gregorian chant, lean and lonely music. And back to Sunday dinner, the very antithesis of Gregorian chant, fat and gregarious meals and visiting ministers for lunch and afterwards banjos and ukeleles and my father's country relaxation and clowning.

And then every Lent trudging down on Wednesday afternoons in freezing Quebec winter to see Dad's set of lantern slides—big, glass ones, some of them cracked and patched up—with one of the unruly boys (never me) running the projector, and the stern moral story of *Pilgrim's Progress* and the story of holy week, the story of the acceptance of suffering. All of this in a rhythm of the seasons—church seasons like Lent and Epiphany—and Trinity which lasted forever—seasons more vivid than the changes of weather, returning securely each year at the same time, "the eternal return," as Eliade calls it.

5

School had no impact, even as the traditional place of knowledge and reflection, let alone in more modern ways as a place of self-understanding, sense bombardment, or the developing of political consciousness. My energies were elsewhere. Having dodged or eluded the bullies, I would tear home for piano lessons or choir practice or other church activities, and on graduation I never for a moment considered attending a university. Instead it was full-time music, practicing the piano eight hours a day, and a scholarship offer to London, England. But here, since I would be leaving home, I reasoned simply: leaving home would be leaving my father, and that would be leaving my source of goodness. But what was *his* source of morality? Religion. So I decided to become a priest and set off to college. This primitive reflection was aided by seeing *Quo Vadis,* a religious extravanganza with a message as subtle as George Wallace but with a finality to me like the personal appearance of the Christ himself.

Six years and two degrees later, the last two away from home at King's College, Cambridge, I had abandoned the idea of becoming a priest. I had some considerable fascination with philosophy and history, but an increasing lack of personal confidence; my ego shrinking fast. In

Cambridge, with acquaintances trying to interest me in politics, in play readings, in intellectual bull sessions, I sat writing letters to my girl, dreary epistles full of Tudor melancholy. In this center of dying English rationalism, I bathed daily in the candles, the robes and the music of King's Chapel, and survived on those fragile sounds made by the voices of young boys.

6

It still startles me to recall that even in 1958, with academic and musical success resting on almost no sense of self whatsoever, I had no capacity to isolate my psychological unhappiness, give it names and do something about changing it. I did not have the terms and certainly not the community to do this in. From my family, church, and schools, I had a strong sense of the aesthetic, communal, ritualistic, mysterious, moral, and theatrical dimensions of life but nothing at all of the personal and the political. Life was a matter of creating and enacting ceremonies together. It was not a matter of changing myself more to my own liking and certainly not a matter of making society more to my liking. Those supreme messages of the nineteenth century—that both the psyche and the polis can be understood and changed—were in neither my books nor my bones.

7

And so in this state I went off to teach in a southern military academy. It was the late fifties; and six miles down the road from us the first sit-ins and bus rides of the civil rights movement were being planned. It all passed by me as I talked till 5:00 A.M. to the sons of the new rich from Atlanta and Baton Rouge—boys now in Vietnam, some of them killed I'm sure. I chalked the whole thing up to "an experience," came close to becoming a full-fledged homosexual, and made the first close friends of my life. The women I went out with didn't work out too well (in that small mountain town they were scarce to begin with). The first told me after our second date that she intended to become a nun, the second went crazy, and the third was a preacher's child even more hung-up about sex than I was. The holidays were the time for my long bus rides with the nightly make-outs followed by crummy breakfasts reading about how much more interesting were Kerouac's times on the road.

8

Two years were enough, though I still have affection for that mad community, and I returned to Canada, met a fine woman, moved to Toronto with her, got a high school teaching job which lasted for four years which I then quit under considerable pressure to stay, entered upon a marriage which lasted for five years which she quit under considerable pressure from me to stay.

I speed through these years which bring me to 1965 not because they are unimportant. The fragile sense of politics I now have, the sense that institutions, like the family and the school, are part of a web of capitalist institutions that must be understood, opposed, and overcome, this sense was forming in those years. But in the area of self and of the strange and primordial forces that loosen or paralyze one as an individual person, in this area these years were a kind of charade of death. They were the rushing, inevitable conclusion of an early life of sexual repression and self-hatred, of the general suppression of strong feeling (especially anger) in our family, of religious Puritanism, and of my worship of my father. I state this in pure Freudian terms because the terms are accurate *for me*. In the end there can be no psychological health within repressive and exploitive institutions, but there is, especially in our cooler Canadian society (for now at any rate), a measure of freedom to liberate oneself from many personal and minor institutional chains. This was the particular liberation I now so desperately needed.

I returned alone to a co-op house my wife and I had left to try to save our marriage, my gorgeous three-year-old daughter was with me three days of every week, every night I drank beer with semi-friends till 1:00 A.M. and ate Chinese food till 3:00 A.M., woke up one of two girls once every two weeks at 3:00 A.M. for a fairly desperate screw—and here is the burden of the last part of my story—worked for two days a week at the Browndale (then Warrendale) Treatment Center for Disturbed Children. The job was to be a side-show to make money, a means of survival, while I spent a year of reflection, oh joy of desperate joys.

9

It was while teaching music and drama at Browndale that I began to discover myself. I'm sure it is a process that for some people has happened with a particular psychiatrist, or by taking a certain job, loving a certain person, becoming political, taking drugs, or maybe by gradual and natural growth.

Not for me. The unique and radical nature of this institution was crucial. Like Synanon, Esalen, Penetang Hospital's therapy community, and some of the free schools, Browndale works with one specific group of people—often a group that society is currently despairing about—builds a firm institutional framework around itself, applies and promotes its method with near religious fanaticism and sends out converts like me. I'm not fooling about the fanaticism. Browndale people feel they have the best and the only method of treating seriously disturbed children, the best and the only method of treating and working with staff in such a treatment center, and they believe that somewhere at the core of this method and experience lies the answer to the screw-up of youth and adults in our entire society. That extreme. Enough to make a good liberal recoil in horror. Enough to make him cry totalitarian, to grasp around for his pluralist groups and his civil liberties, to shout that he owes final allegiance to nobody but himself.

But there's that sermonizing blare again. I wanted this piece to be more personal. What happened lately was that I sat down for a whole day and saw six films about Browndale and the whole experience came flooding back.

The five weeks and forty hours of filming was done in the spring of 1965, the year I worked there. The longest, *Warrendale,* is also the best and the most famous, and I read in today's paper that it has just won the special film critics' prize of the National Society of Film Critics of America. Among many awards it has also won the Cannes Film Festival Prize for the best documentary of 1967, and it shared with *Blow-Up* the International Film Critics' Prize for the best foreign film of 1967. The other five films are the first of fourteen training films, all being put together from the original forty hours of footage.

10

Try to see them if you possibly can. They will not necessarily be the kind of religious and personal liberation that Browndale was for me but they will be an exhilarating experience for any group of teachers, parents, child care workers, social workers—and even students.

11

Naturally the film I was most eager to see was *School* because there I was in a number of sequences with my guitar and tape recorder and tambourines and maracas, sparking a number of things, participating in others. I remember driving to the two different centers each Monday and Tuesday with the back seat of my car full of all my musical and electronic toys.

I was initially a roaring success. Not only were the kids and I having a very fine time, but the particular arts of music and improvised-taped drama, with their primitive pulse and communal sharing and feedback, were also excellent therapeutic devices. There was also an elemental communication here for some kids for whom verbal communication was difficult of even impossible. (I should emphasize that Browndale has many children with very serious emotional disturbances; many are schizophrenic and autistic children who had been bounced from institution to institution and given up on before they arrived at Browndale.)

Things went so well these first few weeks that I was certain I had the ideal part-time job—good pay, minimum involvement. I did have one set-back, but I took it grimly. I fought to be exempt from the weekly compulsory group therapy for staff. I reasoned that I was part-time and besides they were charging me for it. They won and a good thing for me too, as it turned out.

By the third week my classes had started to crack. Music and drama were among the few things that were formally scheduled but kids were free to do other things—more and more kids began doing other things. Some violent ones began buggering up any kind of organized activity with drums and tambourines. A couple of instruments got broken. One boy, fifteen-year-old Dale, hovered between the two nerve centers, the tape recorder and the bass drum, shrieking hysterically when checked, and completely ruined one session while I tripped from machine to machine feeling like a young girl fresh out of teacher's college in her first ghetto class. Apparently the UFT has now got the New York teachers the sacred right to have disturbed children removed from classrooms, but what do you do when all the children are disturbed?

My nicely packaged part-time job was beginning to unwrap. The week after Dale's performance, the classes were total bedlam and I started wondering whether I'd have to quit. My first reaction was to be enraged with the school staff, especially with Mike Walker, the school director, for not giving me more direction on how to approach disturbed children. Should I have different instruments, new songs and records, less of a group affair, abandon the tape recorder? Shouldn't Dale be in a different room during music and drama? Were the drums too tribal, did they stimulate kids too much for these early classes? I surprised myself asking questions this way because they were obviously the kind of leisurely teachers' college talk about classroom techniques that hid the fact that I was now desperately afraid of these children.

In retrospect, what I feared most was the violent boys and the sexy girls, but in those early weeks to see my fears like this would have been too abstract and unwieldy. Mike Walker concentrated in those early stages on something much more surface, but equally potent in the end. I seemed tremendously attached to my collection of instruments and machines, he said. (In fact I had once fantasized arriving in the morning in a moving van filled with every instrument and noise-making machine known to man!) Why didn't I just leave them in the hall the next few times and do something fairly pointless like play a game of cards with a kid or just chat with kids who didn't seem occupied with something else?

What seemed at the time like a small procedural suggestion—why not break the ice with the kids informally?—turned out to be the spark for a self-revelation I still battle with. My sense of self-esteem was largely bound up with my skills: I was the musician, the amateur philosopher, the one with the bag of instruments, the friendly teacher, even the one who was working on the great new magazine.

Which reminds me: we got the first issue of *This Magazine* out the spring I was at Browndale and I remember taking Edgar Friedenberg's complimentary letter to my group therapy session. I wanted to tell them how happy it made me but as I read it my voice started shaking; I started rushing through it, and when I finished I was holding the letter as if it were a piece of wet toilet paper.

12

At the time that experience was pretty staggering for me, but at least I could now do something with it. I started that year thinking that women were my problem. I wanted a woman to love and be loved by, but all the ones I liked fled me. On one level, what I had to discover was the message of all psychology since Freud that all sides of one's personality are put together in a delicate interconnection so that to discover what was happening in my relationships with women I might first have to examine my feelings about my work, and in turn about my father, and in turn about father-figures like Edgar Friedenberg.

Best of all, I was now in a setting where all people were trying to work these things out *corporately* and I needed that kind of support.

13

But it was my feelings for certain teen-agers that caused me most trouble. Most of us on staff at Browndale needed children more than most people do. In my case a screwed-up life with adults, too many unresolved tensions about authority, had probably driven me to those younger and safer. But why this drive to establish contact particularly with the violent boys and the sexy girls? On the surface—to simplify a bit—did it not look as if I wanted to fight and compete with the violent boys for the affection of the sexy girls? What I often got in practice was affection from the boys and rejection from the girls. And here Freud and Browndale were very helpful in making the point that we actually *seek* the kind of failures which recur for us. What I was actually pursuing was sexy boys and violent girls.

Which brings to mind a fairly heraldic incident in my life: It was my second year in Cambridge, England, and I was in London for a holiday. I was at a show in Piccadilly Circus and on my way home I decided to pick up one of the prostitutes who walk the streets of Piccadilly. It was to be an experience but was not planned quite as it turned out. It took very little time to team up with a rather plain, dark-haired girl with a scratchy voice who said in thick Cockney that she was Swedish and would do it for £1. Sounded cheap, but then she wasn't that attractive—maybe that was it, I reasoned. She led me up a laneway, past storage garages, into a warehouse parking lot, and backing against a warehouse door under a wide roof in the shadows, she said to me, "O.K., we do it here, standing up, and give me the £1." This was the catch, I reasoned, but it was an experience after all, and since she had lifted her dress I began to unzip my fly. At this instant, she let out the most terrifying scream I have ever heard in my life. "Peter!!" I swung round, expecting to encounter some enormous pimp armed to the teeth, and this was her cue to swing a heavy umbrella with all her strength across my face right at the eyes. I doubled over, holding my eyes in pain, as she barked that I better get going out to the street bloody fast because Peter was standing by and if I gave her any trouble I'd have Peter to contend with. My parting mutter to her was: "You'll be hearing from my boys and me." Apparently I did not frighten her unduly. She laughed through a gargle of phlegm.

14

Loving boys and violent girls. Such imprints pass slowly. I began to learn at Browndale that a teen-age girl could sit on my lap and we could enjoy each other and she did not conceal an umbrella behind her back. Her hair did not burn if I stroked it and the only person to call me Humbert Humbert was myself. I began to learn that violence and anger, even the volcanic aggression in myself, could be expressed and accepted by a community of people. As some of this anger began dissolving, I was even able to go hunting for my sack of instruments again. You'll see most of them in the film but try to see all the films and make up your own mind about these Browndale kids and these methods. I'm somewhat biased, as you can see.

OPEN POLITICS AND COMMUNITY

An Everdale parent speaks to a school meeting: Feb. '69

STAUGHTON LYND

EVEN BEFORE Barbara expressed herself earlier on the subject of parental interference, I had a sense that I would be laboring under a number of difficulties in talking at this time. First of all, it's four-thirty in the afternoon at the end of a day of talking, and not a time when most people, myself included, look forward to more talking. And I can only apologize to you for that. And secondly, of course, one should always be suspicious of speakers who come on immediately after a discussion of finances. In the third place, I am from the States. And to add one more thing to it, I am really not an expert on the subjects under discussion, and if I need to prove that to you, I might just say that I spent a full half hour this morning discussing with my son whether or not he should leave his right boot unlaced, or whether in view of the fact that parents were coming up, etc., etc., he should finish lacing it up.

I think the reason I was asked to talk is that when Barbara, our daughter, was being interviewed, it happened that I also was here, and at one point the question was asked of me, "What do you as a parent hope this will mean to your children—coming to Everdale?" I said, well, Alice and I had for three years been part of a cooperative community, as Phil mentioned, the Macedonia community—in 1954 to 1957, when we were in our mid-twenties. But even though that community came to an end twelve years ago, it has been for us, ever since, a touchstone of everything that we did, what we were trying to do with the rest of our lives. To find a way to carry forward the same values which had become clear to us at Macedonia. And so I said, when I was asked this question a year ago, I hoped Everdale could be for Barbara something that she would look back on in a way that Alice and I look back on the experience that we had in Macedonia community. Somehow the rest of her life will be a carrying forward of what has happened to her at this place. Now, I could double-cross the staff by saying that only certain early experiences of religious conversion and psychological reinforcement make it possible for me to endure the experience of being an Everdale parent. But the fact of the matter is that I feel great about what's happening to Barbara here insofar as she has condescended to share that with us. But, even before Barbara began her experience here as a student, the moment I stepped onto the place, I had the feeling, "Oh, this is Macedonia." And what I want to try to do is just to say a word about certain things which my wife and I experienced in the cooperative community which I have sensed to be present here. And which we, and I guess I in particular, have also found exemplified in what in the United States is called "The Movement," that is SNCC, SDS, the movement of young people for social change. I want to talk about certain things which I find in all three of these situations: cooperative community, the experimental school, and the movement for social change.

And this is as close as I can come in explaining to you, in an articulate fashion, what it is Everdale was, and what it is I mean when I say, "This is Macedonia." And this is again the same thing I once experienced. One of the things which the community, the school and the movement had in common was the way of making decisions—which SNCC and SDS call participatory democracy, which is sometimes called making decisions by consensus in that one does everything one can to avoid a vote. One waits as long as possible for a common feeling to take hold of all or most of the people in the room rather than pushing matters to a decision by a narrow majority. I think it was that same thing, listening to some of the parents earlier in the afternoon, when they said, "Let's not set up a committee to represent the parents." If there are parents who want to associate themselves with a particular function of the school, parents who feel drawn to taking part in raising money, or parents who feel drawn to taking part in making suggestions for curriculum—that's one thing. That's a functional thing. Those parents are acting as individuals. But let's not set up a panel of five parents and say that this is the channel through which parents will transmit their feelings to the school. And that felt right to me, because each of these three groups that I described function that way. Whenever possible, decisions were made by the whole. And this was not just a question of taste, of preference, although it was that, but for example in the case of SNCC, the southern civil rights movement, the sorts of decisions that were there being made had to do with whether or not a given staff member would go to a particular town in the South and try to do voter registration there. And it was a decision that might well cost that person his life. No one would be part of an executive committee that would assign someone else to carry out that sort of task. And, I suppose by analogy that carries over into situations which are less obviously fraught with the implication for a person's life than a voter registration program which might result in his physical death. The people who are used to making decisions in that way also develop a reluctance to make seemingly much less consequential decisions which would tell another person what it was he ought to do about this or that. Okay, that's one thing.

The second thing which strikes me as common in community and the school and the movement is a certain orientation to experience as opposed to philosophies about experience. And, maybe that's one of the reasons people have trouble getting a statement of education philosophy out of Everdale, because the staff and the students here feel that same way. And let me try to explain what I mean: It happened that the core of the community in which we lived were persons who had been objectors or draft resisters during WW II, and who, when the war was over, tried to find some way of exemplifying positively that which they had stood up for in saying "No, I won't go." Though there was that shared experience of draft resistance, or at least conscientious objection, nevertheless, people came to that experience and came also to the experience of community from very different religious and philosophical backgrounds. I was the village atheist. Other people had come from extremely fundamentalist Protestant backgrounds, and so forth. And we found that when we spun things up to the level of religious philosophy or political philosophy they tended not to go well. Rather, we tended to find ourselves in situations where we would all suddenly feel, "Look, we don't really differ as much as our words make it appear that we do." And we developed it, almost as a rule of thumb, to try to get back to the common experience. What is the experiential content of what we say as opposed to the philosophical or abstract content? Now, oddly enough, in my opinion at least, this is a matter of immense significance in the political movement in the States and also in Canada that calls itself The New Left. I think that one of the differences between the "New Left" and the "Old Left" is that when you had a decision to make in the Old Left, the way you made it was that everybody in the decision-making apparatus, all eighty-seven members of the Party, divided themselves into caucuses or factions, met secretly, each caucus circulated its position paper with appropriate quotations from Marx and Lenin. Finally there was a vote in an atmosphere of mutual denunciation and whichever position was adopted by no matter how narrow a majority became the correct political line for the coming period. That was the way of making decisions, which had little enough to do with experience, and tended to leave people divided and angry at one another, and, very often, not inclined to do anything, no matter what the decision. But in the New Left, with its orientation to experience, it was much more like this: "Okay, we have a general sense that something is important." Before 1961 we had a general sense that it's important to try to register voters in certain predominantly black, rural communities in the South. In the summer of 1966 we had a general sense that it's important to develop groups of people who are prepared to resist the draft and give one another support in doing that. In 1969 we have a general sense that it's important to find ways to resist oppression (legal oppression, political oppression of the movement) in such a way that the movement can go on growing and not consume all its energies in defending itself.

Okay, but having that general sense, rather than going into the kind of caucusing and resolution passing which was traditional as we perceived it as part of the politics of the previous generation, we say, "Fine, now let's cast the seed, let's all of us, as individuals or in small groups, go out and experiment with solving this problem. And then, for example, when one of us, or a few of us, begin to find a solution to that work (when Bob Moses goes to Mississippi), we begin to find ways to gather support in extremely difficult situations. Then people naturally gather around that successful solution and start experimental schools across the face of Canada, and as time goes by select themselves into those that seem to be most fruitful, as parents, as teachers, as students. This was the way we felt it was important to make decisions. So, that a meeting of the movement in the United States would be not so much an occasion (this is not so true of the present, I regret to say, it was more true in the past) the meeting of the movement would not be when people would go at one another, hammer and tongs, to decide who was right, with the implication that everybody else must be wrong, but rather an occasion where people shared experiences with the sense that even the failures were important additions to the common experience. Simply a completely different atmosphere, I think, of folk relating to one another rather than the more traditional method I stopped to describe.

Okay, a third thing, which I think again was true of the community in which we lived, was true of the movement in the United States, and I sense perhaps, in a somewhat different form is also true here at Everdale. And that's what at Macedonia we used to call direct speaking. If you are going to the altar, or for that matter the cow shed, and you discover in your breast you have a difference with your brother, then turn aside and go and straighten the bloody thing out with him. Don't, above all, go to some third person and start gossiping. And if at all possible, don't suppress your feelings with the other person immediately concerned, but say it right out to him on the spot. "Why," to quote an example of last night, "why did you leave your car in the driveway, for crying out loud, so nobody else could get past to come up to this meeting?" And to say it, you see, and the person responds, "You fool, it's obvious why I left the car there, because I wanted to leave the meeting early"; and it's over. It's over! But the other way, you see, over breakfast the next morning with still a third person you say, "You know, I've noticed something about so-and-so." Even the root of not saying it right out, of keeping it back, means that ten days later, at a meeting about something quite different, let's say, when to start planting the garden, you say, "For crying out loud, not only are you wrong about when to plant lettuce, but you even left your car in the middle of the driveway." And by that time, you have to start arguing about the facts of the situation which you've both forgotten in the meantime. And it all becomes more cumbersome and complicated than it needs to be. And I don't think what I'm talking about is essentially a technique. I think it could express itself in quite different forms in different groups of people. I think it's an atmosphere for which I've been able to find no better words than "emotional openness." Is there such a thing as a group in which people expose themselves to one another without trying to protect themselves from the consequences of that exposure? This is a very rare kind of group I think, in our society. This is part of the peculiar genius of this place as of the others I've described. It doesn't necessarily mean earnest, solemn discussions about what we feel toward one another. It can express itself in a kind of humor: sort of understated, in the style, in the way people write or talk to one another. But the important thing is the underlying concept. And that's the third thing.

Now I come to two things that are more, sort of, total, which I will nevertheless take a stab at. In the community we talked all the time about commitment. It simply made all the difference in the world whether you were still there wondering whether you were going to stay, or whether you had put your savings, your car, your mortgage, your emotional problems, the whole of yourself into it. That feeling. Commitment is one way to describe it. In the movement, I think, a very similar thing was talked about as putting your body where your mouth is. "It's very nice, the opinion you just expressed, but I'm not sure I heard you say that *you* were the person planning to do it." "Yes, it would be very good to have a voter registration project in Macomb but when you are leaving?" And which I think Bob Davis was expressing in a different way, just at the close of the last segment of this meeting. "I've been telling you how much we need you parents, but don't make the mistake of believing that we shall stop if by any chance you shouldn't help us. Because, we're going to keep this place going on somehow even if we're all carrying two jobs to do it. Even if there are seven kids rather than seven times seven." And this is what I took from what he said, and I think that's the same quality I'm trying to describe.

Not just that the teachers would have made this kind of commitment in order to bring Everdale into being, but that the graduates from Everdale are people who want to live this way, who insist on living this way, and who won't settle for a life in which people do not give themselves completely to the things that they do. Which means, and I think in our group this morning there at first was a discussion which was inaccurate in its terms, between rebelling against the system and adapting to the system, that these were the two alternatives. If you adapted to the system, you stayed out there, and if you rebelled against the system, of course you came to Everdale. But, it seems to me that what Everdale is about is producing people who when they leave here will create new vocations, will become doctors, lawyers and bricklayers and all the things that people become out there, but with a difference. Doctors who insist on being a different kind of doctor. Lawyers half of whose clients don't pay them anything. Teachers who are fired again and again and again, if I can use my own example, who end up having three part-time jobs instead of one full-time job and no tenure, but much happier than I was when I was still in the academic rat race. It seems to me that the creation of this sort of person who puts his body where his mouth is, who is prepared to take risks through the whole of his life, that Everdale ultimately is bound to do.

And then the last thing is something about what it means to be a community and to turn out young people who will have experienced living in community for a number of years and in this way too won't settle for anything less for the rest of their lives. Now what does that mean? What is one talking about when one says that I can only give a couple of examples? Shortly after we arrived at Macedonia there was an incident with the woodworking shop. Macedonia produced children's toys and created the business that Bob and Phil alluded to that happens on the Bruderhoff, the Community Playthings children's toy business. But at the time when we were at the Macedonia community this business was a very small and struggling thing, as the whole community was. It was all touch and go whether we would get the next order out and make it through the next month. And it happened that a benefactor had given us a planer, the kind of planer that you push boards through. And a member of the community had taken a truck from our community in northeastern Georgia, to somewhere in Michigan to pick up the planer and he drove it back, going day and night and got in about five o'clock in the morning. He went to sleep with the strongest kind of instruction that no one was to touch the truck or the planer until he woke up, because he had directions about how to move it. So while he was sleeping another member of the community, who, like the man who had driven the truck, was also very handy with mechanical things or thought he was, tried to unload the planer. The planer was sitting in the back of the truck. It was lifted by using pulleys with a metal cable which goes up over something and then down to something else. It all went well. The truck drove away, the planer hovered in the air and then the cable broke and the planer came down on its head, like this, and the cement floor cracked. Well, my reaction was: "That's it! The community is over. Let's go back home." Not so much, or only in part because the planer dropped, but also what Dick would say to Ivan when Dick got up. But after a while, I noticed a strange phenomenon. It was true that Dick and Ivan had gone off and had a little discussion with each other, and nobody seemed to be getting ready to leave. As a matter of fact (this was, I think, a Friday or a Tuesday) everybody was going on getting ready for Easter which was three days hence and in a quiet way I scurried about making sure that everyone knew about the disaster which had occurred, because I assumed that once they knew, well of course we would forget about Easter and turn to the problem of the planer. And it finally dawned on me that people there really felt Easter was more important than the planer. And that simply because the planer had dropped they had no intention of dissolving the community.

And as I thought about it, I realized behind that was the attitude that "we are in this together," and the tremendous accession of psychological strength that somehow is created when people say that to one another. It is much more than saying, "Well, we're four, so we are four times stronger than if there were only one of us." It is that each person has somehow had lifted from his shoulders the burden that each of us staggers about with without being fully aware of it—namely that there is only ourselves to depend on after all. Especially financially. And when the push comes to shove, after all, we have to have a bit in the bank for it. We may have a neighbor next door who has a house just like ours, and a car just like ours, and a job not so different. But we don't—if we are laid off, it just doesn't enter our minds to feel that the obvious thing to do is to knock on his door and ask for help. That's not the kind of society we have. But that's what community is about, it seems to me. And it creates the kind of strength that just has to be experienced. I want to say this. I think that can happen in very dramatic and highly charged circumstances, and indeed in circumstances much more highly charged than that of the planer. For example, the group of fourteen people who burned Selective Service files in Milwaukee in September of 1968 issued a statement explaining why they had done that, in which they used the phrase that they had been "delivered into resistance." And then a little later they went on to use the expression "resistance community" as that thing which they were. And it was clear that these were people—not only the kind of single young men and women who are usually involved in the movement—there is Michael Cullen who has three children, there was Doug Marvey who married and gave up a mathematician's job to do this—who had that kind of responsibility which usually leads us to assume that they couldn't possibly be involved in an act of this sort, who were among that fourteen, and it was perfectly clear that none of them would have been able to take that act which involved possible sentences of ten, twenty, thirty, forty, fifty years if both State and Federal government should convict them on all possible charges and give them maximum sentences, none of them would have been able to do that, had they not just had the faith that the children would be cared for. "Yes they are, in a sense, my children," and "No, I do not lightly leave their care to another. Nevertheless there are circumstances in which it is right for me to leave their care to another, and moreover there are others who will care for them." And that's community, in a sense, in an obvious way.

But the last point that I would like to make is that it seems to me community operates much less pretentiously under very prosaic circumstances, such as a group of people feeling that the person who peels the potatoes or drives the bus, or takes out the garbage, is just as important a member of the community as the person who gives speeches at conferences, or the person who usually greets people when they come to visit the community. That in some ways, I think, is just as difficult a thing to achieve as the kind of sharing the Milwaukee Fourteen file burners are capable of. But it's another way of describing what I mean when I am asked, "What is community?"

So! I have not got a dramatic ending. These things that I have talked about are that way that I would like to make articulate what I feel is going on here, and went on in the community I was at, and struggles to go on in the movement for social change in the States and Canada. Now, I must just say that speaking of someone carrying qualities like these from Everdale into later life, this was also my experience coming here the September just after the Democratic convention in Chicago. I felt upset, not because of the way policemen had beaten people at Chicago, but more that our side, our movement, had come to the point where we were calling policemen pigs. That's what I was upset about. Because I felt in that a departure from the atmosphere that I have been trying to describe this afternoon. And I felt having left a community and rediscovering it, as it were, in the movement, finding those same values in SNCC and SDS in the early sixties, it was as if the movement was coming to a place where it could no longer be my community, or only in a much more troubled and complicated sense and I felt very, very alone and upset. And in coming to Everdale I again had the feeling: "Well, all right, maybe then in a different expression, but here it is again, here's Macedonia." And no matter what troubles you've been having since last fall, I assure you that one person who visited you in September has been living off the spiritual capital from that visit from that day to this in a way that it seems to me many of the children who will leave here also will do.

Pacific High

NOTES FROM AN XPERIMENTL SCHOOL

Jack Spicer

THERE IS TALK of making the school a 24 hr. boarding operation next year/building small A-frames or glass domes. Mark feels we would have 80 rather than 40% of the kids' attention/what we would do with it George Leonard only knows. I suppose it would be nice to see a little community humming away in the quiet hills/potters, farmers, plumbers, cooks, eaters, loafers—the interdependency of common necessity. But the only real community is the play of the City. These kids know the City/ they make Kerouac's "geeks" look like Sandburg's farm boys. If anyone was ever lured from beneath the gas lights it was the communitarians.

But then again maybe it *would* be nice. I have seen boarding schools—John Woolman for instance with its farm animals and mountains and building projects—which felt all right. Their kids appeared serene in a curious way to me/as if the school remained a sort of soft blanket—always—just in case. And that soft packing left them brittle/anemic and just a little bitter—at having traded the OUTSIDE for a thumb to suck and a bedtime story.

However what Mark says is true: there are very many unhappy kids at Pacific/maybe they are kids who felt the COLD outside too soon and froze/and for them a little communal warmth would help. But I suspect that the cold is not "out there" but in the way one deals with what's out there. Even a woman is a cold slab when one must "deal" with her/plan, arrange, design—play the architect. And they don't call them intentional communities for nothing/ *intentional*—i.e. consciously limiting the range and complexity of what's out there in order to fulfill a dream. Whether it be Plato's *Republic* or Rimmer's *Harrad* or *1984* it matters not/that state of mind which necessitates intentionality IS cold.

Pacific as it is now seems preferable to a boarding school in the same ways that a novel seems to me better/more "real"/than a movie. While you are sitting there reading *Bros. Karamazov* dinner will be ready, you will have to go to work, a long lost friend will send a letter, you will have to go to the laundromat, etc./maybe for a week. Altho a movie will attract and keep much more of your attention it is really a controlled environment/the rest of your reality will not intrude as it does in a book—sweeping across and between the pages.

I think it would be better for some of the teachers to agree to keep large houses in the city where a few kids could live than to have a boarding school. In a smaller situation the communal mind need not plan and predict how hot the candle will be and when it ought to move its hand. And I suspect the moral heat of the blood needed to change the school would be a little hot for my decadent and aesthetic veins.

I must confess that while I place "planners" and "dreamers" out in the cold those kids that I admire and love for their resilience and I suppose for their humor place me out there too. One day while I was visiting a friend who lives with other kids in a house outrageously free of planning and intentionality I was asking her to talk about the place/tell me how it felt/whether it was good/and she said to me wanly, "Oh Jack, you're so healthy." Brittle & anemic I suppose—but so die we lowly critics & teachers.

An apology too I must make—to adults and planners and other well intentioned persons—for the smugness and facetiousness of the above. When talking to outsiders about Pacific and adolescents it is easy for one to feel as it must feel sitting in the gallery of our Congress while the noble senators proclaim on freedom and liberty/i.e.—speechless. What can you say, "But . . ." and what else? It is all very discouraging to hear a turned-on public high school teacher tell you about the new freedom in his school when you know that a school—a plan—is itself, however "free," total confinement from reality. I have only a sense & a feel for what education and adolescents are really like from which to reply/and the reply is often then smug. Edgar Friedenberg, in a recent *New York Review of Books* issue, replies to the good *intentions* and sterility of George Leonard's *Education & Ecstasy* with a quietly despairing smugness. (I thus place myself among the illustrious & smug.) At any rate, I apologize.

CONTACT

Michael Mason

It may startle some of our readers to find here an article about a treatment program in a hospital for the so-called "criminally insane." When you read Flora Doehler's introduction you will discover one reason we include this piece. Virtually the entire population of Everdale Place (twenty-five students and staff) visited this hospital in Penetanguishene, Ontario, for two days in June 1967 and spent many hours on G Ward with thirty-eight patients there.

The other reason for this article is G Ward. G Ward is a remarkable experiment in a "therapeutic community" inspired by the philosophy of Martin Buber and the experience of men like R. D. Laing in England. It was initiated by a young staff psychiatrist, Elliott Barker, who, like his mentor, R. D. Laing, believes that the psychiatrist's role in a place like G Ward is gradually to disappear and let the patients become their own therapists. This, we can testify from our own observation, has happened to a remarkable degree.

In this account, Michael Mason, a patient in G Ward, speaks from the roots of this experience. His setting is the visit to the hospital of the students from Everdale.

I wasn't scared or anything when we went to G Ward. I had visited Ontario institutions before. After many barred doors and corridors, we came to G Ward, eager to see what "maximum security" was, what all these "bad men" looked like, and to witness their famed therapeutic community.

All of us were paired off with a patient. The guy I was with stammered a lot and was shaking. He was obviously very ill at ease and uncomfortable with me. I tried to joke around with him, hoping this would make him feel a bit better. Anyway, our conversation was cut short because we were now at the end of the ward in the sun-room where people were sitting down and trying to organize us.

So, G Ward and Everdale sat down to have a meeting. We discussed both places. Many of the patients were very negative and hostile towards the school. We discussed that, and a few of the patients said they resented our bounding freedom.

We then were broken up into small groups. In my group were four patients and only one Everdale student.

So I met Peter—a schizophrenic who was handcuffed to Ed because he had been feeling upset. Ed was also schizoid and was very friendly and led our group. Then Joe who was a psychopath and ex-hustler. I noticed him staring a lot at Alan.

We discussed the differences between Everdale and Penetang, and the similarities. Penetang is really a wonderful place. In all the little meetings we had, I really felt as though I'd known those men for years. It was really good to know that the slightest change in facial expression, body movement and voice tones was noticed by them. They wanted to know why, when I spoke of Peter I got all defensive with Alan. Why

I got defensive when talking about beating up my brother. Why I felt obligated and guilty about my brother. Why Alan appeared to be withdrawn on our second visit. Why I was afraid to ask them personal questions and so on. There was really nothing you could hide from them and they didn't miss a thing so it was impossible to put them on about anything.

They all seemed to have gained much insight into themselves and everyone else. It was sad to realize that when these men got out, they would have trouble finding jobs and being accepted by our sick society.

We went around to other wards also. B Ward was "maximum, maximum, maximum, security." A lot of the guys there could have benefited from a therapeutic community but instead they were locked up all day and were very regimented, because of the limited number of psychiatrists who want to undergo such an experiment. As a result, they rebelled as much as they could. They banged lunch trays around, whistled at us, gave out long, deep, put-on laughs, etc.

The A Ward, a lesser degree of "maximum security" was much the same as B except the men were allowed more freedom to walk around their ward. The contrasts, therefore, were so huge that they were depressing. Depressing to know that few beneficial experiments like this are happening. Thirty-eight men in Penetang, a hospital in England, and one in California.

Why must we punish a man who has been punished all his life by a lonely, frightening illness?

—FLORA DOEHLER

Dave inspected the visitors with mild interest. They didn't look like the usual sort who come along to look at ward meetings; this was just a bunch of kids, all long hair and idealism and mini-skirts . . . there were altogether too many meetings on this ward, three a day, three hours every day spent sitting and smoking, and flipping butts into the ashtrays, counting the dots in the terrazzo floor, listening to all the big wheels talking about their therapeutic plans for this and that . . . but there was the one day when they all talked to him. Dave's stomach tightened as he thought of the thirty-seven pairs of eyes all swinging into him; they had very hard eyes, some of them . . . Mike the killer and Ken the rapist . . . very sharp and burning eyes . . . they wanted to know why he had been late at a meeting, but they soon got onto all the other things that Dave did . . . complained when there was no cause, making too much noise on the corridor . . . those guys could make it hot for you, but they were a bunch of hypocrites, really. They didn't care for Dave. . . .

Dave looked again at the visitors . . . they were all listening to Eric describing what LSD sessions were like . . . Eric spat the milk all over the nurse and the patient who had been asking him all those goddamn dangerous questions. They laughed, they didn't get angry at all, and so he strained fiercely on the chains that secured his arms and legs to the four corners of the bed. Then he fell back for a second, exhausted, and stared with wild eyes at the TV camera in the corner of the room. Barker must be on the monitor; the snooping bastard always wanted more and more information. Eric screamed obscenities at the pendulous microphone above his head . . . but now the visitors were here, and it was important to explain everything to them.

"Actually, it's quite hard to understand what living on a Therapeutic Community is really like," said Bruce to the good-looking little blonde girl seated apprehensively in the corner next to Paul, not knowing that she was scaring hell out of him. How would she know Paul had been committed on sex charges. I wonder what she would do if she did know, mused Bruce. "I mean," he continued, "we have a lot of groups and committees, and it takes some time to understand the complexity of it all. . . ." There was complexity, all right . . . the night he was on the treatment committee and John had just had scopolamine and methedrine and he had gone psychotic right in the middle of the corridor . . . Bruce had had to select a team of observers who would sit with John and the other drugged people all night, and that little rat Gerry had asked if he could go down as an observer. A wave of remembered jealousy and fear swept through Bruce. To the sun-room, all night, with John! All night! Over my dead body, thought Bruce. The little son-of-a-bitch just wants to move in on John now that all his defenses are down, and I'll end up getting screwed around . . . somehow. . . .

"What is the purpose of giving all these drugs to patients?" asked a teen-age kid.

"Well, the idea is that their sick defenses are weakened and that means we can get in with our small groups and help him straighten out some of the ideas that are keeping him here," replied Bruce, urbanely.

"But don't you get scared sometimes, and isn't it pretty hard to be watching these guys all the time?"

This is a persistent kid, thought Bruce. Of course you get scared when you see your best friend smoking imaginary cigarettes, and slobbering at the mouth, and looking right crazy. You get scared and tired after half an hour, not after four hours or eight hours; after the first hour you just sort of blank out, and wait for the clock to roll around so you can hand him on to the next observer. Five men at a time, we were shooting with scopolamine-methedrine; five crazy men for four days, shot after shot of methedrine going into them, making them tireder and tireder, keeping them awake all day and night, cutting down their appetite so they can't eat . . . no wonder they go psychotic for a while. Lucky they got put back together again after the four-day blast is over, though. It must be the small groups.

"Small groups," said Joe to the intense-looking little girl who was solemnly asking questions she already knew the answer to, "small groups are set up so the patients can deal with the individual difficulties they get into. . . ." And, dear girl, Joe thought to himself, it seemed more often that the groups made trouble. Five or ten groups a day to talk to individual guys, to listen to the whining and the lying and the stupid defenses, to pry and poke and dig and analyze at what makes a patient tick, why did he commit his crime, what he thinks about his parents, what guy on the ward he is in love with . . . and all that crap. It was always a few guys who did all the questioning in small groups . . . but it was good, thought Joe, when you felt lonely and someone cared enough to ask you why, even if it was just in a group.

"In small groups," continued Joe, "the only thing that we really think important is that everybody should tell the truth about everything, not hold anything back. . . ." Holding things back, thought Gerry bitterly. Why should I have to tell everybody everything. It's crazy. They don't do it on the street, and the people out there are supposed to be sane. Why would they make me scrub the corridor for not speaking up about Mark propositioning me. . . . I wouldn't have done anything, and if I *had* spoken up people would have said I was trying to make Mark look like the bad guy. I like Mark . . . why couldn't we have a dyad like they used to have on the ward. I wouldn't mind being locked in for an hour a day with Mark. We'd have all kinds of things to talk about. My God, they're talking about Mark.

Mike was talking. "Mark looks like a relatively sane sort of guy; you wouldn't think he shot down a couple of people for no reason, would you?" The visitors looked satisfyingly shocked, thought Mark. The way I get talked about on this ward, you would think I was the only guy around who killed somebody . . . a dozen killers, on the ward here, calculated Mark. Twelve killers, a bundle of thieves, rapists and arsonists made good company. They were goddamned hard to suck in, too. Mark had been working on one of the Clarification Committees, and he spent the whole of his month's term working hard for a change. He felt really interested in what these guys were being referred to his committee for, and took a lot of pride in being able to sort out all the motives. There were the guys who just didn't care, there were the schizies who wanted to be punished and the psychopaths who wanted to do the punishing; there was the age-old dilemma of trying to decide which of two false tales was the least false. . . . Mark liked that sort of work; he could sit back and just involve his mind, leave his emotions away in the background where they couldn't bother him or anybody else for that matter. And the month's good work would have him in a good position for the next progress chart. The progress chart committee would be doing a report on his last six months, soon. They might recommend him for a ward conference . . . maybe the guys would recommend a release for him. Then again, maybe they wouldn't; they didn't really care whether he stayed in the hospital or not. He remembered the last sanction he had got from the Sanctions Committee for those two days of tricks . . . they were only little tricks but the bastards said that they were his illness . . . so they made him wear an untearable nightgown all day, made him sleep on the bare floor at night and took away his coffee . . . he would have to be careful . . . next time they might take my tobacco too. That rat Dave will be the one who will think of that. . . .

Dave clasped his hands behind his neck and stared fixedly at the floor, wondering what he was going to say if anybody asked him a question about the Staff Liaison group. Working on the same committee with those other guys was pure torture; they spoke and thought too fast for him and he didn't really understand what was going on at all . . . and he was the secretary, he was the one who had to get attacked at ward meetings if the committee goofed . . . and sometimes it did goof . . . terribly. Ken made too many arbitrary decisions and the other guys on the ward were quick to notice and exploit this. God knows what the visitors might think about a set-up like the one on this ward; he looked furtively across the room to see if the little brunette visitor had spotted him yet; if she looked at me, would she know I was the secretary of an important committee? Even if she knew, Dave guessed, she wouldn't care. Better pay attention to the meeting. The Treatment Committee were feeding back their report. There had been no suicidal risks last night. (They must have forgotten to speak to Roger, noted Dave. Should give them a blast about it when the report is over). Peter was still considered to be a homicide risk . . . poor little Gerry . . . they either want to kill him or make love to him.

No suicide risks, thought Mark. Ha. He remembered the night he had smashed John's coffee jar and tried to fall on it and when that didn't work he slashed himself and then all at once it was too late, and the Attendant was there unlocking the door of his room. He was scared and angry, thought Mark . . . forty stitches. . . . He remembered how he had expected everybody on the ward to be mad at him if he came back from the upstairs maximum security ward. The whole ward had lost a couple of privileges because he had done that, and the whole ward had been given tranquilizers to guard against hysterical reactions to Mark's suicide attempt . . . but he was surprised when they all welcomed him back pretty warmly. . . .

"If you want to know what G Ward is like, then you would have to live here," Richard was saying. Ed was thinking that even if they lived here for a month or so, they would have a lot of trouble understanding. How do you quickly understand what compassion means when you get it from someone who never showed it before? How long does it take to learn what anguish means, more keenly than you know it already; when the intense relationships were stacked so high emotionally that you thought a rejection would destroy you . . . that would take you quite a little while to find out about.

Aha, The Industrial Therapy feedback was coming in. Louis was upset because he had been voted out of his office as foreman of the patient work group that he was in. Joe thought that it was time we started training one another for our "future well-being" by learning auto mechanics or spot welding. Jesus, all the trades training in the world isn't going to make Joe a sane man so he can get out and work. He doesn't know what work is, thought Mike rather smugly. Mind you, in a way we all know. Ninety hours of structured programming each week, hardly any time at all to yourself, just groups, committees, ward meetings, ward meetings. . . . Boredom it was not, but some kind of sickness in the soul, thought Richard: Richard the dreamer, he thought, smiling to himself. Even after two years there still seemed to be so much indifference about one another, and so much, thought Rick, so much of it springs up around me. I didn't know there could be that much despair about not being talked to in a therapeutic community. Everybody else seemed to have a close friend to accept him and comfort him. But not Rick; he was a loner, bound on a wheel of fire, rejected and cast out, just like Lear. He smiled to himself and felt clever. They said it was anxiety that helped people to change, but he found that hard to believe.

The Doctor was talking now. "Every patient is a member of at least one committee or another involved in making decisions about the daily life of the ward. . . ." Fred could just about repeat the whole glossy brochure off by heart. But that would leave out the emotions, and he couldn't convey them to the visitors, and if he couldn't convey the emotions then he didn't want to convey anything. The kids seemed to be too nice for spiels. But the doctor just droned on, anyway. . . .

"About a third of the patient's day is spent in school or in Industrial Therapy. Like all the other phases of the program, this one is compulsory, and it's pretty clear to everybody that any patient who doesn't want to go to an activity is liable to be dragged there if he refuses to listen to reason and be persuaded softly. In Industrial Therapy, the emphasis is chiefly on teaching the basic requirements of the work situation—how to receive instructions and carry them out, how to make decisions, how to co-operate with the others, and how his pathology interferes with these things. We don't try any 'vocational' training, because it seems foolish to teach special skills to a man who doesn't know the basic skill of working with others.

"The theme of all this activity is confrontation, analysis, and change. Having lived together for two years, most of the patients know one another very well. They've also developed great expertise in ferreting out the pathology in any situation. Generally, the ideal is that whatever is private must be made public, whatever can be discussed, should be discussed. In all committees and in all groups, which occupy hundreds of man hours every week, the tendency to examine all behavior with microscopic concentration has become marked.

"Several aids have been developed to assist in this business of mirroring and analysis. A closed circuit TV/videotape recording system has provided a powerful resource for the examination of group and individual dynamics. (Dynamics crap, thought Fred to himself. You mean how people feel.) Group meetings of all sorts can be observed without any intrusion, and played back to the group itself for analysis later on.

"The use of the so-called 'truth sera'—scopolamine, methedrine, sodium amytal, and so on—has become elaborated into a major ritualistic undertaking, since an almost foolproof scheme of observation of upset patients was instituted. At several points in the development of the ward, as many as five patients at a time were disrupted by these drugs for periods of up to two weeks. The effect of such an intensive dosage of defense-disrupting drugs seems to be not the straight reaction of the drug itself upon a particular person, like the effect of an antibiotic on an infection. It seems more that the value of these chemicals is greatest in situations where a ritual heavily charged with emotion takes place. Patients, as helped and as helpers, see much visible madness— the effects of scopolamine are quite startling, for example, and these situations catalyze interactions of a very intense and real nature. This is, of course, usually coupled with the uncovering of more information about the person, which is subsequently fed back to him, but our hunch is that this content part of the whole process is the less significant.

"PT takes place on six days a week, and provides a rich area for looking at hostility and jealousy. Other ancillary forms of treatment are unit conferences in which the patients assess an individual's mental status and make treatment recommendations. Progress charts which provide a written assessment of the patient's progress in the previous six months, and go on his hospital file, are also prepared by a patient committee.

"So for most of the day—for all of it on many days—the patient is exposed to a twofold confrontation—with himself and with others. His role alternates rapidly between worker, committee member, therapist, and patient. In some settings he is treated. In some, he is the treater. Often, he might occupy both roles simultaneously. This sort of alternation is at once an integrative and a disintegrative experience. The individual is forced to pull himself together, sanely, to help someone else. Often in the process his own illness is exposed and pointed out by another, and he is forced to look at that, also.

"But there is the time and there are the safeguards on the unit for each person to be as honest as he can be. In most settings, it would be a heinous crime to tell a schizophrenic patient who is thinking about suicide that as far as you are concerned, he can go and hang himself. On the G Ward unit, there are always enough reserves of genuine caring to allow for the full expression of non-caring. What's more, non-caring is a part of reality with which the mentally ill person must learn to come to terms. Experience also suggests that in a ward of thirty-eight patients no one is ever without compassion from at least one other person."

Carl smiled to himself. He just doesn't know how much lack of compassion you can find in this group of thirty-eight persons. Persons! They're all sick dogs, and just about as capable of compassion as a sick dog. How would he know about compassion or the lack of it, who never got punched in the mouth and never went hungry. . . . He's right, said Vince to himself. The doctor is right, always. . . . I didn't have any friends at all before I came to G. . . .

"But perhaps the most significant aspect of the life in the community," persisted the doctor, "is the one which it is most difficult to describe—the quality of the interpersonal contacts. Most of the patients have seen in others and perhaps—if they are a bit healthier than most—in themselves, the 'worst' or most intimate things that go along with being human. They have talked in ward meetings about their most primitive desires and fears, they have dragged one another down to ward meetings, recommended powerful drugs to control one another's behavior, deprived one another of privileges and comfort, and, in short, have come to know and experience one another in a way that is denied many people."

Drone, drone, drone, thought Peter. I wish I could lose the privilege of pain.

"A certain sort of cohesion has sprung up out of the very fierce friendships and hatreds on the ward, a cohesion generating conflicts, multiplying jealousies and passions, but also providing a relatively stable frame of acceptance for anything that may be produced. With great pain, sometimes the conflicts are accepted, and seem to throw into sharp contrast the good things in friendships. It seems to be no avoidance of the sickness involved to say, for example, that the feelings of love—erotic and agapic alike—that many patients experience for one another may be a valuable step forward from a point at which they felt no love at all.

"So far, the impact of the community has been great for all patients. For many, what takes place in 'Oak Ridge' may seem to be artificial and unrealistic—after all, how far is it the norm to care for people on 'the street'?—but in fact as many patients experience it, the genuine human contact that from time to time takes place among them is the first real contact with life that they have ever had. Although, as you can see, most of these patients are twenty to twenty-five, they are experiencing themselves, perhaps for the first time in their lives, as individuals who are capable of contributing to someone else, contributing, that is, self-consciously, in a way that is self-consciously accepted by, valued by, and effective upon the life of the person they have helped. . . ."

The grand finale, thought Arnold. The touch of poignancy that precedes the touch of the brush-off. He looked around at the Everdale kids—bare feet and long hair—an appallingly healthy and turned-on crowd of children. They had freedom and seemed to be willing to use it, seemed to be free to use it. Arnold wished that his own school had freed him from chains instead of weighing him down with more. As the party line about the community rolled slowly from the doctor's unsuffering mouth, he looked at one of the girls and recognized her for a moment. She was a bit like . . . Auden, like

> Let even the sick rejoice,
> Though buffeted by their illness
> And arrogant with fear
> The sick and the lonely have seen
> For an infinitesimal moment
> (There's a way. There's a voice)
> In another's eye till their own
> Reflection came between
> Singing and dancing.[1]

So Arnold looked at her and made contact with her for a moment . . . and then his reflection came between, and he was lonely.

[1] W. H. Auden, "For the Time Being," © 1944 W. H. Auden. This version of Mr. Auden's verse differs slightly from the standard, as it now appears in *Collected Longer Poems* (New York, Random House, Inc., 1969). The earlier version is reprinted here by permission of the author and of Random House, Inc.

Cabbagetown

Introduction: **George Martell**

IN THE PREFACE to his novel *Cabbagetown* Hugh Garner —who grew up there—says the area used to be "the largest Anglo-Saxon slum in North America." That was before World War II, when the neighborhood was "less than half a mile long and even narrower from north to south . . . situated in the east-central part (of Toronto), its boundaries being Parliament Street on the west, Gerrard Street on the north, the Don River on the east, and Queen Street on the south."

It got its name from the Irish immigrants who used to grow cabbages on their front lawns, even though most of the Irish lived south of the area below Queen's Street in a district called Corktown. Cabbagetown was an Anglo-Saxon slum. White Protestant English and Scots.

Today the Anglo-Saxons still predominate, although the lace-curtained slum of Garner's novel has since been wiped out by the urban renewal projects of Regent's Park, North and South. What is now called Cabbagetown covers a much wider area than before—its earlier boundaries spreading out west to Jarvis, north to Bloor, and south below Queen's now largely coinciding with the City of Toronto's Don Planning District. It holds about 42,000 people. Since the mid-nineteenth century the Don District has been hit by successive waves of immigration, which have cut the percentage of residents of British origin from 96 per cent in 1860 to 55 per cent in 1960.

Of these newcomers the largest group are the French Canadians, estimated a few years ago at about 5,000, and still growing. Mostly they are migrants from depressed areas in the Maritime Provinces (particularly northern New Brunswick) and from northern Ontario.

Unlike the Italians and the Portuguese in the west end, these rural French Canadians brought no culture to the city that can be seen in the streets, only a couple of isolated schools and churches where French is spoken. On a Saturday night in the jammed pubs, pool halls and restaurants of Parliament Street—Cabbagetown's main street—they are indistinguishable from the rest of the crowd. They have no special places of their own. There are no French Canadian ghettos. English is the language of work and public life in the big society: they learned that where they came from. Anglo-Saxon society is where you have to make it. When their children speak English they do so with rarely even a trace of an accent; the kids are fluently bilingual although barely literate.

What the French Canadians brought to the city are their families, and you can't see them on the streets. They are big, tough farm families, who do a lot of marrying into one another. And between the relatives there are very strong loyalties. When you combine these loyalties with their previous experience of poverty and shit jobs, it gives them a real edge in slum survival. (English migrants from the countryside usually don't do as well; and their kids tend to get chewed up in the alleys.)

Clay Borris, the young filmmaker shown in the following pages, is from one of these large French Canadian families.

He's also part of a small night school, Point Blank, which some Cabbagetown teen-agers and myself set up, after they'd all dropped out of regular school in the fall of

1967. [Point Blank School is a free school in a downtown Toronto poverty area. There is an evening program for local teen-agers who have dropped out of school, and a small daytime school for four- to ten-year-olds. It is in its first year of operation as a full-time school. Its objective is to create a community school where students, teachers and local adults participate in the educational process.—EDITOR.]

I met Clay and the other kids in Point Blank (there are eight all told, including two girls and six French Canadian boys) while I was a boys' worker at the local settlement house—Central Neighborhood House—almost five years ago. I continued seeing them and their friends part-time on my own while I was working as an administrator for the Company of Young Canadians, and then as a professor at York University's Atkinson College. No one would pay me to work full-time.

The kids are part of a large group . . . French and English . . . maybe a couple of hundred altogether who either hang out or have the geographic center of reference at a confectionary store called Sam's at the corner of Winchester and Parliament Streets. There is also a key pool hall a half block away where you can also count on meeting your friends. The group is not a well organized gang, although they do sometimes get together to plan robberies and the occasional rumble with some other group, usually from Regent Park, which is down Parliament Street, four or five blocks away.

What I concentrated on at Point Blank, when there were just a few of us, were the creative arts, particularly writing. I thought it was clearly useful to the kids to give their experience form, if only because it kept their pain a little more under their control. I don't think that's a substitute for changing the conditions of poverty and social repression they know, but it's good while it lasts:

BEHIND THE COUNTER

They smile at me
How come a girl like you
    is working at a place like this.
It makes me sad.
I don't know what to say to
    them.
It's the only job
I can get.

—BONNIE LINDSAY
(*from Point Blank*)

I should add that on the basis of his rushes for "Parliament Street" Clay got hired as a full-time filmmaker for the Youth and Recreation Department of the Ontario Department of Education. There he worked on the 16 mm. version of the film he first made in 8 mm.; and he got a lot of professional help. The film is available through the Youth and Recreation Department, 559 Jarvis Street, Toronto, Ontario.

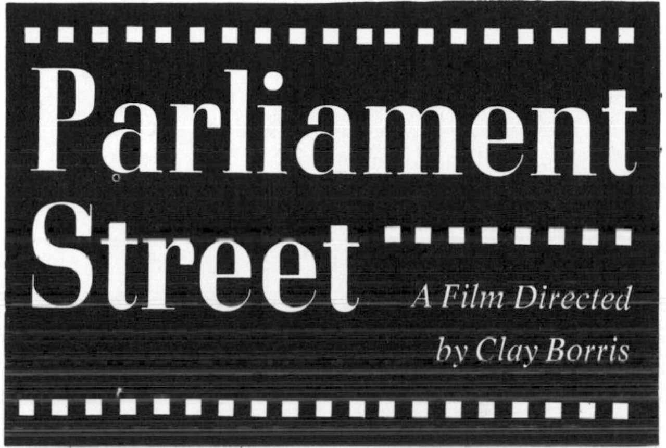

A LEAD-IN

Good morning, Mr. Solway.

He looks at me and nods. When I think about it I hate his guts. Because he's my boss, and he's one of those white-collar people. He's one of those civilized people. That's why I hate him. I hate all of them. But I've got to face it, I'm getting to be just like them. It's happening. They're changing me; I can feel it. I even say "please" and "thank you" and "sorry." A lot of the time I feel like running back to Cabbagetown, back to my friends. I want to get away from these civilized creeps. But I know now, when I'm back with my friends, I feel a little left out. I'm not part of the gang anymore. When I used to hang around Winchester and Parliament Streets all the time I was one of the top guys; everybody respected me,

looked up to me, and I was always one of the first to know about things. I used to make a lot of decisions about where we'd go—to the dance, up to Hillcrest Park. . . . I remember the whole gang used to leave the dances at Central Neighborhood House when I was kicked out. Now I don't have much to say to anyone. I'm not part of it anymore.

I gave it all up for this job at Astral Films as a film repairman. They told me to get my hair cut, to wear a nice clean shirt and tie and to go to night school. "There's no future in Cabbagetown, kid," the man said, "get out while you're still young." I did what the man said, and now I'm caught between two groups of people. I'd love to hang around the boys, to steal with them, have gang fights, but I can't. I'm not one of them anymore. I'm with the white-collar people now, fixing up their films for them, making splices, checking for heavy scratches. I'm a film repairman now, and if I'm lucky in a year or two I could probably be put in the office. I could even get to be manager.

But I don't really want to be manager; I want to be something different. On weekends, instead of going out with the guys, I see every goddam movie in town. I spend the whole weekend in movie houses, which drives my girlfriend crazy because she has to pay her own way and ends up sleeping through most of them anyway. At work the boss lets me take movies home, where I have an old projector and I manage to see these movies on the weekends too. And after I quit acting school—I didn't stay very long—and when I don't go to Point Blank school in the evenings, I see more movies. I don't see much of Cabbagetown.

So I'm at Astral Films, and I feel a lot like I sold out. It was so easy, like I was expecting it. Most of the time I think I'm proud I come from Cabbagetown, but all the man had to say was "do you want the job," and I took it so fucking fast. I'm caught and I want to be. But I also want to find some way of getting back to the guys, some excuse. Which gets me into making this film.

I really wanted to make a film; it'd been in my head for a long time. Now I thought why not make one about Cabbagetown, and I can use the guys. That's it, I'll make a film about them, about what's really going on. I can show the whole world. I know what it's like. I'll show them.

I had a good idea for a film, simple but good. It was about something I'd done in the past with the boys. I knew they'd like it; it's their style. I start it off by having three guys standing at the corner of Parliament and Winchester Streets. These guys are screwed up. They're sick of the life around them, especially the cops—how they hate them. These guys are mad at the world, and what they would

like to do is get it out of their system. How do you do that? You beat the hell out of somebody or something. Here's a square coming out of school. That's who we'll get. So the three guys run after him, catch him, beat the hell out

of him, and then walk away like nothing ever happened. They go back to their corner, and that's how the film ends. It'll be good to have a chase, because that way I can show Cabbagetown. But there's no cops added or any-

thing. I don't want cops. It's like everyone else's story, and it's too phony. The kid wouldn't call the cops. He'd be too scared. And I don't want to add anything at all, because I need something simple where I can just use music for the soundtrack.

Even though I wanted to make this film, George Martell, who teaches at Point Blank, had to push me. I was scared to try it. I didn't know if I could do it. George had to make me promise to go down and figure out where I was going to shoot.

So one night I just went down after work and stood at the corner of Winchester and Parliament and took a pad and a pencil. And I said, "if somebody were running after you, where would you go?" and so I ran and I made a map of where I went, through streets and alleys, to Hillcrest Park, jumped the fence, and then up and down Sandy Hill, along the Bayview Extension and under the Bloor Bridge, where I figured the fighting would take place.

A couple of days later I met Gary Arsenault. He's from Atholville, a little village outside Campbellton, New Brunswick. It's a place near where I'm from. Gary said he'd go in with me and help buy film. We were waiting around to buy it, and one night I went over to George's house. He told us, if we wanted to learn photography he had a friend, John Phillips, who would teach us. We said okay and went over to John's house. When we told him about the film he got interested and said he might be able to get us some free film from the National Film Board. They gave us twenty rolls of super-8 color film but no camera or projector, which we had to rent. When we first got started John helped us with the light meter; we didn't know anything about that. The rest of the time he stood around and took still pictures.

The film making was always on the weekends and it was wild, unbelievable. The first time we went out, the actors weren't there and I had to go to their homes to wake them up. They were hung-over all day. I was using this camera that belonged to Arsenault's uncle. It didn't work out; the automatic light meter was no good. It was really hard filming. A lot of little kids followed us about and everybody in the area knew us, and the actors fucked around a lot of the time. But the acting came out good anyhow. Nobody else could have done any better. They just acted themselves. On Friday nights I used to bring them over to my place and get them stoned. Then they would stay over, and I'd be sure I had them the next morning. We used to drink all night and the next day we'd go on the set. Everyone had a big hang-over, but somehow we got through it okay. I always had to have my aspirins around. I had terrible headaches. I kept yelling all the time. I used to send the little kids who followed us back to Sam's to get more aspirins.

The second time we tried it we had to get another camera. John Phillips helped me pick it out at the rental place. But now we had a good camera, two of the actors were missing, and the guys who took their places weren't right for their parts. I wasn't happy about it at all. I was up on this tree and I was so fucking mad. I knew I couldn't use this film, and I would have to do it all over again. While we were doing the fence jumping scene I asked Greg to take the camera over with him to see what kind of a shot we'd get. On the jump he took both heels off his boots and sprained his ankle a little. So we had to call it all off for another week. It took me that long to talk Pat, who was playing the square, into coming back. In the first scene they really beat him up.

I didn't think I'd have the guts to go through it a third time, but we finally got things settled with the actors. On a hunch the night before I phoned Pat to find out if he was in town and he wasn't. He was in Lindsay, seventy miles away. But I wanted to film so bad that I talked John

into driving me to the cottage where Pat was at. It took a lot of convincing, but finally Pat came with us. We did the shooting the next day, and the color turned out perfect and so did everything else.

I enjoyed every minute of filming, even when the actors were fucking around. I even fucked around with them. I loved it. Gus pulling his pants down, showing his knob to the whole street, everybody, broads and all. "Look like

a roughie, Madge," I'd say for a close-up. He'd get up real close and say, "I'm rough. I'm tough. Give me milk. Put it in a dirty glass. No straw." It half killed me. I just rolled around, couldn't stop laughing. It was like being in the gang again.

WHAT CAN I DO RIGHT NOW?

Notes from Point Blank School on the Canadian Dilemma

George Martell

1

I STARTED THESE NOTES six months ago when I wrote the introduction to Clay Borris' story of making his film *Parliament Street*. Clay had been a client/a student/a friend of mine for almost four years. I hoped that in talking about my relationship with him I'd be able to be clearer about what Point Blank School means to me and why I think it may be one of a number of institutions on which we can build an alternative system to the present governing structure in this country, or at least in English Canada. I didn't get very far in the writing, however, and I soon gave it up. Clay was too close to me and still too far away for me to discuss him without becoming either sentimental or clinical. The same was true of the school. I had no solid hold on it. In the past couple of years I've done so much insane wheeling and dealing—making it up and doing it too, being serious and bullshitting all the while, as everybody does in keeping these places alive—that I was not sure what my feelings were for the place, what it was I loved, and what I cared for elsewhere. I'm still not sure, even though the school continues to be more livable than any place I have been.

I started these notes again after listening to a taped interview Clay made with another eighteen-year-old kid from Parliament Street, Charlie Macdougal. From the age of nine Charlie had spent most of his life in jail or in training school, and on the tape he talked non-stop for almost two and a half hours about the quality of that life: its humiliations, its brutality, its bad sex. For hours afterwards I was angry, and the anger brought me back to realizing the extent to which I believed that the creation of schools like Point Blank was necessary for simple human dignity; they were a matter of justice. The school's reason for being then—in the first telling, anyway—did not require a detailed study of my own survival tactics (which are still unclear to me) or of the personal needs of a very small group of adults and kids I know and care for. This made it easier for me to write these notes: as a response to Charlie, not Clay.

Charlie is very much an abstraction for me. I've never met him. I haven't even seen him about the neighborhood. The kids at Point Blank tell me, for his age, he's one of the toughest guys on Parliament Street. "You otta see him when he gets drunk . . . fuckit, is he ever wild . . . crazy bastard . . . scares the shit right outta me." I don't know how I'd react to his whole person. I've just heard his voice on the tape talking to Clay, who interviewed him. However, while listening to Charlie—intelligent, almost gracious, very cool and hoarse—I knew I believed every word he was saying, even if, as a consummate con man, he made it up. I don't think he did—I think most of the events he relates in fact happened—but whether he did or not finally doesn't matter that much to me. Because the burden of what he says is what every other kid says who's spent some time in our prisons for children. That's important not so much because a lot of other kids back him up and so offer more proof that the objective conditions of prison life are inhuman, but because a lot of kids say the same thing period. That is *what* they say. That is *what* they have to tell us. They don't tell us something else. When Charlie Macdougal talks as he did to Clay those are the only words he uses; they are how he decides to present the world of his prison to us and so also to himself at that time. Whatever the personal and public con involved, the words at that moment are his mind. He has no other.

For me his words are one final reality, one final part of his humanity, no matter how articulate his body may be in love and violence. Without his words and his knowledge that they are in some important sense true, he is a slave and has no chance of becoming a man. If his words do not hold at least one important level of reality for him and for us, the consequences of that fact lead me to greater despair than I am capable of handling. I simply believe that they are true, and hope at Point Blank we can effectively encourage more kids to use words—films, paintings, etc., being words too—in the same way.

Yet finally I don't think that's an adequate reason to be at Point Blank. I don't think you can encourage people to describe the human reality of a corrupt social system and leave it at that, hoping that with some natural dialectic of consciousness they'll do something about destroying that system on their own. It seems to me it's not possible to let others suffer needlessly and do nothing except help them write about it and do a little writing yourself. I don't like the idea of "witness." It seems to me I'm less of a man if I don't put my whole self on the line, and do it in a way that makes a difference to the society as a whole.

To put this another way, I think the society is corrupt enough that I'd like to join the revolution, but I'm not certain what that means. Of course, I'm hoping that maybe one's begun—a revolution that's peculiarly modern—and that somehow I've joined it by being part of the free school movement, but I'm not at all sure, especially in this country.

It may be—and I don't mean to brush this aside lightly—that I am too frightened to look closely at the militant argument that oppression must greatly increase in North America, and soon, and that we all must get ready for violent, confrontation politics: the friends of Ronald Reagan are going to have to be met head-on and killed, or they'll kill us. I don't think that's the situation, mostly on hunch or intuition. I also don't think there are many people on the left in North America who think it's the situation either and actually believe we're going to fight a traditional revolution, with widespread bloodletting and the repression that goes with it. I don't think the left is prepared seriously to take on the police and the army, and I don't think they want to get prepared. The confrontation, particularly in the United States, on the campuses and in the ghettoes, still seems like theater to me—violent theater maybe in which brave individuals stand to lose a lot, including their lives, in making symbolic gestures of defiance—but theater nevertheless, without the potential to go further in the near future. Whatever the chance of a violent revolution in the United States, however, one thing I'm certain about is that a violent revolution will come much later in Canada. The explosive forces in America's cities and in her oppression of peoples of the third world are simply not ones we have to face right now.

But a non-violent revolution is something else. One idea that has been recurring to me lately is that we may actually have more potential for building a base for a non-violent revolution in Canada than in the United States simply because we have more time and space, fewer problems, less immediate government repression. Building a base for a non-violent revolution assumes, of course, that a violent revolution won't happen in the States. If it does, then fledgling institutions like Point Blank will be wiped out as we all pick sides. So I'm assuming America won't be faced with a violent revolution, at least not in the traditional mold. If I assumed otherwise, then I wouldn't be able to do very much, except sit around *and wait for the action to start south of the border.*

When I think about it, I'm not sure of this last point. Even if I did come up with a general analysis that said free schools would likely be historically irrelevant, I'd no doubt go ahead with my present work anyway, because I like what I'm doing, I don't know what else I could do, and my optimism is of a desperate kind. When it comes to large intellectual matters (leaving aside the rest of my life) I'm simply not to be trusted. I've got too much that's personal at stake.

Nevertheless, I would like to put down a couple of general impressions I have about this country that correspond to what my "common sense" (as McLuhan uses that term) tells me are political realities for English Canadians like myself. I want to do so because the argument that emerges tends to support those people who are currently working in the cities, trying to build up, in a miniscule way and without much success, alternative institutions to the present system of government. We can use some support.

The argument is made at the expense of those who take a strong Canadian nationalist stand and are convinced that a humane socialism can emerge in conjunction with a new national spirit. I'm uneasy about this. For while I think that hope is illusionary, the benefits of the forty-ninth parallel in relieving us of some of the burdens of empire, are undeniable. It's a matter of priorities. Maybe it comes down to this: support Mel Watkins[1] in his bid to radicalize the NDP [2] on a nationalist platform, but don't spend the majority of your time at it.

2

The first point I want to make, then, is that it no longer seems likely that a Canadian nation-state can serve as a framework in which something threatening to corporate capitalism can take place. As a country, I believe, we have had it. Our culture, our politics, our economy are almost entirely packaged in the U.S., whether by the radical left or the great corporations. It's not so much we're a colony, we're an integral part of the empire. We're Americans now, and I think we have to begin dealing with that fact; we must think in terms of this continent. The time for polite studies on the dangers of extra-territoriality is past. It's no longer helpful to try to find the touch of Toryism in our bourgeois fragment which is going to lead us through liberalism to Fabian socialism and freedom from Yankee imperialism. It's ceased to be pertinent to speculate on how to man the barricades against the infiltration of American behaviorist professors or how to tap French-Canadian nationalism for English-Canadian radicalism so we can all fight GM together. This kind of discussion has become painfully academic, quite removed from the day-to-day experience of most Canadians. For the game is up. We've been bought, and right now we don't mind

[1] Melville Watkins: Professor of Economics at the University of Toronto, he headed the Task Force that prepared the report on the structure of Canadian industry entitled "Foreign Ownership and the Structure of Canadian Industry."

[2] New Democratic Party: The social democratic party of Canada.

very much. We just don't want to deal with it. "It's okay, all right." The PM has his finger on it, "These are the facts of life," he says openly, "and they don't bother me." Then Trade Minister Jean-Luc Pepin tells us, "We must remember that foreign direct investment involves interdependence more than dependence. While foreign participation in Canadian industry exposes us to external decision-making, we should remember that such exposure does not apply in one direction only. The country and company investing in a foreign land also expose themselves to the possibility of unfavorable foreign actions." The steely-eyed Canadian mouse, roaring in the board rooms of America. And Mr. Trudeau continues, "This is where Canadians can prove whether they are entrepreneurs or not, and whether their assessment of the future is as good as the Americans'. . ." in the "industries of tomorrow."

It's embarrassing to have such patently dishonest leaders, I agree, but do you know anyone who is actually going to do something about preserving this country's independence? What kind of action are you going to get from the U.S. residents who own 60 per cent of Canadian manufacturing, who own 74 percent of Canadian petroleum and natural gas, who own 59 per cent of Canadian mining and smelting, to mention only three prominent areas of control? What about the foreign investors (mostly American) who financed 44 per cent of all net capital formation in Canada between 1954 and 1965? How do you think they'll advise their governments? Do you think there's going to be a strong nationalist stand taken by Canadians whose livelihood depends on this investment? Say by our big businessmen who now operate almost entirely within a continental or an international economy? Or the 80 per cent of Canadian trade unionists who belong to AFL-CIO unions? Or those for whom the increasingly complex apparatus of the welfare state, financed by this investment, provides a job or a handout? What about the political parties financed by the great corporations, the unions and the affluent middle classes? Or the people who run the media and the universities, who get their money from the government and the corporations. How will they act? Or the millions of immigrants who couldn't get into the States? Or the suburbs reading *Time* and *Reader's Digest* (supported by the federal government) and watching Doris Day on the CBC? We have to get serious. It's over! There is not one powerful group in this country, or outside it, prepared to lose anything important to them in order to protect Canada's sovereignty, because, frankly, they don't see that they have anything substantial to gain. Canadians knew what they were getting with Mr. Trudeau, and they are not, as the left likes to make out, all that disillusioned with him. It would have been nice to have had a little more parliamentary glamour, a little more public humanity, but they'll vote for him again. Who else can make it easy for them to lose the country they don't have? Who can do anything other than that?

We don't have a choice, as people like Walter Gordon hoped in 1967, "To do the things that are necessary to regain control of our economy, and thus maintain our independence" or else "acquiesce in becoming a colonial dependency of the United States, with no future except the hope of eventual absorption." And because we don't have this choice it's hurtful to set up the problem in this way, for it always comes down to the question of the "will of English Canada" to survive and then a deluge of exhortations not to be apathetic. It leaves us nothing specific to do, except perhaps protect the forty-ninth parallel (saving our sons from the draft, etc.)—a political border that probably doesn't need much protecting because the Americans will get what they want from us peacefully. For when we get past the question of keeping the Yanks at bay, we turn to mush. Take, for example, Kari Levitt in her otherwise very clear and useful article,[3] the final paragraph:

> In English Canada there exists the possibility that the cultural integration into continental American life has proceeded to the point where Canada no longer is a meaningful national community. Yet here there is the possibility that the current reaction among the younger generation against domination by the efficiency-mongers of big business, big government, or big anything, may revive the "conserving" nationalism which derives from the desire to shape the conditions of life within a community which individuals can control. Only the emergence of a new value system within English Canada can ensure the existence of a nation here. "Man and His World" indicates that the option is still open.

The fact is the "new value system" of youth that is to revive English Canada is at one with the value system of radical American youth, and the emergence of what can be called "youth culture" is a phenomenon that takes in all of North America. I can't imagine Mrs. Levitt denying that; it seems so plain. Just take a look at the lineups outside *Alice's Restaurant*. And the reference to Expo I find as embarrassing as Mr. Pepin's remarks about the possibility of Canadian economic retaliation. When you have to turn (as almost every journalist in the country has turned) to the efficient administration of a world's fair on an artificial island to find the emergence of some unique national soul, you're in considerable trouble.

It seems to me that there is no way out but to recognize that there is only one real question for us now: what kind of Americans are we going to be? Are we going to buy the life-style of the great corporations or are we going to reject it? There are only two choices, and the people who have chosen the second way of acting are that loose col-

[3] Kari Levitt, "Dependence and Disintegration in Canada," *New World Quarterly*, Vol. IV, No. 2 (Mona, Kingston, Jamaica), p. 57.

lection of groups in both Canada and the U.S. called the New Left. In these terms Canada's democratic socialists (in the NDP) are buying the corporate life-style, although they would like it to be considerably more humane—a concern which involves more government control, nicer Canadian entrepreneurs, and better welfare benefits. In the short run, making capitalism run more decently is good because it lessens economic hardship and frees people up to act. But this is finally peripheral (though perhaps a necessary first stage) to the New Left push for a society that is fundamentally opposed to corporate capitalism, a society in which we are controlled by neither the government nor the corporations, and in which we do not have to prove whether we are "entrepreneurs or not," and yet a society which also does not deny our nature as Americans.

3

What does it mean to be an American? First of all, I think it means that we are unalterably bourgeois. In the past our society, like that of the United States, has generally believed that a man's essence is his freedom. We have had no other respectable tradition that has said otherwise. Our society was largely built at a time when the articulation of bourgeois ideals was at its height. Hobbes prettied by Locke was, in the end, the philosopher who counted, and the practical creed that emerged was ideally suited to mastering the frontier. As in America our conservatives are mainly old-fashioned liberals, who have a nineteenth-century version of what it means to be autonomous: to will a destiny outside the destiny of others, and so deny the very notion of destiny.

There is no acceptable Tory or old-line Socialist view that an imposed external order is necessary to put down human greed. What theory of a corporate society some of our ancestors might have brought from Britain had no roots to grow and in the end our loyalists wanted every bit of freedom their Yankee counterparts had to make a buck. When they wrote the BNA Act, with the help of the British government, they had at least the good taste not to deny that. The "Union," they declared, "would conduce to the welfare of the Provinces and promote the interests of the British Empire," and left it at that. "Peace, Order, and Good Government" was necessary to keep the money where it was, and let those people who had it make more of it. The Declaration of Independence still embodied what public ethics there were:

> We hold these truths to be self-evident, that all men are created equal, that they are endowed by their Creator with certain unalienable Rights, that among these are Life, Liberty, and the pursuit of Happiness.— That to secure these rights, Governments are instituted among Men, deriving their just powers from the consent of the governed— That whenever any Form of Government becomes destructive of these ends, it is the Right of the People to alter or to abolish it, and to institute new Government, laying its foundation on such principles and organizing its powers in such forms, as to them shall seem most likely to effect their Safety and Happiness . . .

This statement is still the basis from which we all begin, although many of us may have gone some distance from it. In spite of the enormous extent of their social and economic control, the managers of the corporations still come on with the message that North America is the land of the free enterpriser, that Horatio Alger is alive and well at Standard Oil. It's not that they don't know that everyone is aware that's nonsense, it's just that they can't say anything else. Any defense of a status-quo hierarchy is not considered to be right and defensible. It's not part of the American dream. It goes against the Canadian grain. Even the current bunch of law and order advocates must couch their language in terms of individual freedom; and because our university presidents and our businessmen and our politicians have to bullshit and act against their publicly expressed values, it makes them weak and loses them the loyalty of the young.

Freedom is still the operative value in North America, no matter how perverted, and any revolution that hopes to be successful has to take that into account. It's no longer helpful to think of a revolution, then, as the replacement of one class by another, the conquest of one group by another. From this perspective the confrontation politics in the American ghetto, on the campuses, in the theater will succeed only as a prelude to another kind of revolution in which our experience of freedom is expanded. Americans finally don't like imposed laws, even if the laws result in a more just distribution of goods.

The practical wisdom of the New Left (if I can group everyone from the hippies to the militants under that title) has always appeared to me to lie in their understanding of the necessity of freedom. It seems natural for them to act in a way that assumes an expanded area of freedom is open to them, partly because of the increased democracy in their middle-class homes and warmer, less repressive, child-rearing habits. This is their great political strength: they haven't backed away from bourgeois freedom. In fact, they are pushing it much further than the bourgeois ever expected it to go, and in so doing—with all the pain and the chaos involved—are facing up to what it means for all men to be free, for them to have equal opportunities to fulfil their capacities as men. That means that the New Left has somehow had to deal with the fact of community: that our destinies *are* caught up with the destinies of other men, that all our freedoms are interlocked. A fact our grandfathers denied, and one which bewildered our fathers. The New Left has come at a time when no remnant of the frontier is left, when an urban civilization has to be built in North America or there will be no civilization at all. They are no longer prepared to accept the schizophrenia of the frontier and the new frontier, to live choosing between extreme polarities: moving on and staying put, being individualistic and standardized, competitive and co-operative, pious and free-thinking, responsible and cynical. They don't want children brought up any longer to face the situation in which, as Eric Erikson shows, they are asked at pretty much the same time, to "get the hell out of here" or "stay and keep the bastards out," two of our most sweeping slogans for action. For the first time a large group of people in North America know clearly that things have stopped being that simple.

What the New Left (including the free schools) has been pushing for, more than anything, is some kind of humane social order. They know in their bones that the world has been a madhouse too long. It's no life just to leave your choices open; that finally just burns you out, dries you up. What they are after—as most people have always been after in one way or another—is some new union of freedom and necessity, some order in which they can be complete, in which they can work at what they love. The only way you can get history off your back is to take it all into account. Psychotherapy isn't enough. You have to deal with everybody, a whole society, its present and its past.

4

Why Herbert Marcuse has been the most influential philosopher of the New Left, in spite of his incredibly heavy language, is that he makes the above point very strongly, and puts the current movements for freedom in the context of the past oppression of European thought and institutions. For many, he provides the strongest theoretical basis for what they know everyone around them is feeling, making the present manifestation of the general human desire for unity more intelligible. He is also an old man who has remained a revolutionary and knows that the young are right in demanding an order, now, in which an individual's life instincts are not denied. Any individual. All must be assumed to have equal claim on freedom. You can trust human love to be socially creative. Eros is culture building. Sex sublimates itself. His central argument is this:

> In the light of the idea of a non-repressive sublimation, Freud's definition of Eros as striving "to form living substance into ever greater unities, so that life may be prolonged and brought to higher development" takes on added significance. The biological drive becomes a cultural drive. The pleasure principle reveals its own dialectic. The erotic aim of sustaining the entire body as subject-object of pleasure calls for continual refinement of the organism, the intensification of its receptivity, the growth of its sensuousness. The aim generates its own projects of realization: the abolition of toil, the amelioration of the environment, the conquest of disease and decay, the creation of luxury. All these activities flow directly from the pleasure principle, and at the same time, they constitute *work* which associates individuals to "greater unities"; no longer confined within the mutilating dominion of the performance principle, they modify the impulse without deflecting it from its aim. There is sublimation and, consequently, culture; but this sublimation proceeds in a system of expanding and enduring libidinal relations, which are in themselves work relations.[4]

This non-repressive sublimation, as a reflection of the life instinct, swallows up Freud's death instinct, as that in-

[4] Herbert Marcuse, *Eros and Civilization* (Boston, Beacon Press, 1955), p. 211–212.

stinct's basic objective is the termination not of life but of pain, the absence of tension. So paradoxically, Marcuse argues, the conflict between life and death is more reduced the closer life comes to being pleasurable:

> Pleasure principle and Nirvana principle then converge. At the same time, Eros, freed from surplus repression, would be strengthened, and the strengthened Eros would, as it were, absorb the objective of the death instinct. The instinctual value of death would have changed; if the instincts pursued and attained their fulfillment in a non-repressive order, the regression compulsion would lose much of its biological rationale. As suffering and want recede, the Nirvana principle may become reconciled with the reality principle. The unconscious attraction that draws the instincts back to an "earlier state" would be effectively counteracted by the desirability of the attained state of life. The "conservative nature" of the instincts would come to rest in a fulfilled present. Death would cease to be an instinctual goal. It remains a fact, perhaps even an ultimate necessity—but a necessity against which the unrepressed energy of mankind will protest, against which it will wage its greatest struggle.
>
> In this struggle, reason and instinct could unite. Under conditions of a truly human existence, the difference between succumbing to disease at the age of ten, thirty, fifty, or seventy, and dying a "natural" death after a fulfilled life, may well be a difference worth fighting for with all instinctual energy. Not those who die, but those who die before they must and want to die, those who die in agony and pain, are the great indictment against civilization.[5]

Having said this, however, what do you do if you see, as Marcuse does, that "unfreedom has become part and parcel of the mental apparatus"? How do you react to your knowledge that the majority of citizens are under the illusion that they are free, that their government is demo-

[5] *Ibid.* p. 235.

cratic, that their culture is honest, that the life style of the great corporations is the way to happiness, or at least that they have nothing else to say. In the past, from Plato to Rousseau, the answer to this problem (never carried out in a just fashion) has been the Tory-old-line-Socialist answer: an order has to be imposed to ensure the good life, to ensure that men don't act greedily. What Marcuse says (very much of the New Left) is that "the idea of an educational dictatorship exercised by those who have acquired knowledge of the real Good" is "obsolete." All men can be trusted to be reasonable:

> Knowledge of the available means of creating a humane existence for all is no longer confined to a privileged elite. The facts are all too open, and the individual consciousness would safely arrive at them if it were not methodically arrested and diverted. The distinction between rational and irrational authority, between repression and surplus-repression can be made and verified by the individuals themselves. That they cannot make this distinction now does not mean that they cannot learn to make it once they are given the opportunity to do so. Then the course of trial and error becomes a rational course in freedom. Utopias are susceptible to unrealistic blueprints; the conditions of a free society are not. They are a matter of reason.[6]

While individuals may be capable of handling much greater freedom than they now have, the majority of them don't feel the immediate need of it.

The situation we face is this: "Radical change without a mass base seems to be unimaginable. But the obtaining of a mass base—at least in this country—and in the foreseeable future—seems to be equally unimaginable." The way out, of course, is to go and get a mass base. From there, however, things get difficult because corporate capitalism, temporarily at least, is pretty stable, particularly

[6] *Ibid.* p. 225.

with its increasingly close rapport with the Soviet Union and its tight control over access to the mass media. The result is that you can't meet the establishment head on, except through the theater of confrontation, in which you hope for a widespread expansion of consciousness. Now, useful as that is, it's not enough. What concrete change can be accomplished, particularly when a centralized and co-ordinated movement is neither possible nor desirable? What Marcuse envisages (in a recent speech) is "local and regional political action against specific grievances—riots, ghetto rebellions and so on, that is to say, certainly mass movements, but mass movements which in large part are lacking political consciousness and which will depend more than before on political guidance and direction by militant leading minorities." What Marcuse goes on to suggest is that

> the strength of the New Left may well reside in precisely these small contesting and competing groups, active at many points at the same time, a kind of guerrilla force in peace and in so-called peace, but, and this is, I think, the most important point, small groups concentrated on the level of local activities, thereby foreshadowing what may in all likelihood be the basic organization of libertarian socialism, namely small councils of manual and intellectual workers, soviets, if one can still use the term and not think of what actually happened to the soviets, some kind of what I would like to call, and I mean it seriously, organized spontaneity.[7]

5

I find myself very sympathetic to Marcuse's whole position, but the kind of solution he suggests, a solution many other people suggest also, has to be adapted somewhat to the English-Canadian scene, because our "specific griev-

[7] Herbert Marcuse, in a speech in New York, in the fall of 1969.

ances" aren't half as big as America's. We don't have a war on our hands. We don't have a great racial problem. French Canada we are able to forget in our day-to-day living and for centuries we have so crushed our Indian peoples that they can rely now on little more than our charity. Our cities are still livable, at least for the next ten years or so.

That means that we don't have problems that will rally masses of people immediately to the left, but it also means that we don't have to waste a lot of very good energy fighting for things to stop so life can begin again. I think it means that we can build in our cities—and some people have tried and are trying to build—"small groups, concentrated at the level of local activities," groups that are living institutions, that can provide the basis for an alternative system of government, commerce, and education. We can do it, I think, with a much broader range of citizens than is open to the American radical because the society is not as repressive here. In a very small way we've begun, particularly with residents' associations, the co-op movement, and the free schools, in which the push for a much more workable democracy is fundamental. As they presently stand, these institutions are ludicrously underdeveloped, but in this country they have enormous potential and they can be organized now, within the existing framework of law. They have potential not only as a basis for an alternative system for society, but also as a power bloc within the established system. (If strong residents' associations covered Toronto, say, and controlled the vote at all levels of government, that would mean a great deal.) If institutions like these were organized on a large scale there would likely be considerable pressure from both inside and outside the country to stop their growth. But it might come late, and we might be far enough along the road to have gathered a substantial group of people in Canada committed to this kind of action. This will be strong commitment. You can rely on it because it is built (by people, necessarily, of many classes) on the experience of trying to create a livable world together, and on the knowledge and love of life that comes from that, even if it is mostly the knowledge and love of a life that could have been. As a basis for a movement I think that's good, whatever Canada's fate.

Thinking this, I think also that the energies of the militant students on our campuses are not directed at that sector of Canadian society where they'll do the most good. It's not that I don't buy the radical critique of the universities. It seems to me that universities are a good deal more corrupt than most radicals suspect, and I believe too that the current mode of confrontation with the academic establishment is useful, because the language is not yet hackneyed and so is communicable. However, it seems to me that in its present form, protest in Canada (as opposed to the U.S. where you have to fight against the war) shouldn't take up that much time. Demanding justice from the administration in various ways has many good results, but I don't think anyone should get caught in the bag of trying to take over the administration of the universities. First, because administrators finally do what they're told to do by the people who pay them, and so if you take over their jobs you're then going to have to deal seriously with the corporations and the government; when you do this you'll be doing it without a mass base. Second, and more important really, I haven't found the multiversity to be a place to learn very much, except perhaps some old technology that is useful. I don't believe it's a place where you can learn much that's serious—in the humanities, the sciences, or the arts—no matter how humane the administration becomes or how open the procedure is for choosing and running courses. The form as well as the content is corrupting.

It seems to me, then, that the major thrust of Canadian student radicals should be to encourage students to prepare themselves to leave the universities to go into the cities and work to build the institutions of a livable society. Right now that probably means residents' associations, producer-consumer co-ops, and free schools, although it can mean many other institutions as well. And just as it appears possible to organize a wider range of citizens here than in America under the banner of local democracy, I suspect it may be possible also to organize a wider range of students than on American campuses not when you ask them to occupy Simcoe Hall (which still perhaps should be occupied sometime) but rather when you ask them to go downtown or into the suburbs to build societies that are run by the people who live in them.

In North America powerlessness is felt over a very wide range of classes. What the majority of us want back—and it is a *majority*—is our dignity as citizens. The students who come will not be particularly responsive to a radical ideology. What they will have is a deep but inarticulate sense that something is badly wrong, both in the university and in the society at large. Coming into the cities to work at something they know is good, they will become radicals in their own way, not through well-meaning manipulation, but by living day-to-day in situations where repression is seen and felt, and where they are fighting it for solid long-term ends. The commitment that arises from this experience can be trusted to last considerably longer than the commitment that comes from understanding your university president is a fink and does not care about your personal well-being. Most people knew that before they came.

6

The position I'm putting forward here—and one I hope circumstances will allow me to hold onto—is in all ways a non-violent one, in which the emphasis is placed on building up a new society peacefully. I have an ambivalent feeling about this position. The gestures of those people in the United States (and to a much lesser extent in this country) who break the law and go to jail or get their heads kicked in by the local cops, move me a great deal; and I know these actions are appropriate to the violence and horror of the American empire, of which we are a supporting part. I am frightened of that kind of action, and I have not done it. Partly because of the fear. Partly because I can't convince myself that these actions are worth the risk, in terms of results, in Canada. And partly because I have no real sense of outrage for the issues at stake. If I had I would not be in this country. I would be in Hanoi. Further, while I'm a little sad about Canada's demise, I don't care that much about it. For whatever reasons of personal history and social context, the anger needed to sustain my action on either an international or a national front is not there. I'd like it to be, but it's not.

What it comes down to is that right now, as a Canadian living in downtown Toronto, I do not feel seriously threatened. My imagination isn't very active. I don't sense that I may soon lose something I love, particularly something I love well enough to die for or suffer imprisonment for. If I thought someone was going after my family or my friends or the school, then I'd be prepared to do something pretty serious. But that's as far as I go. Point Blank is the largest social unit I can get solidly angry about. It is the largest abstraction I can imagine fighting for . . . fighting for the whole of it, not just parts of it. It is here—if I can use these terms—that I am just beginning to feel like a citizen who knows he must take into account the larger politics of the polis. We're very new at the school and I may be badly disillusioned, but here I have the feeling that I can consider the general good and not sense that I am betraying what is best in myself in doing so, that I can fuse my destiny with those of others and know, whatever their political opinions and they are many, that I am tied to them. It is my first society, and for all the hassles I am more content than I have ever been in my life.

I have also the sense at Point Blank that by living here (or in whatever arrangements emerge from this group of people or others we join or who join us) I'll be able to develop, as others will, a livable political theory for this continent, assuming we are all pushing in a general way for local control. Right now I don't know what I want specifically from a society, and I don't know what I am capable of giving. Before this time I had had no experience with a fairly large group of people from whom I was not severely alienated, although, like many others again, I kept that alienation to myself out of fear and ambition. The result was I made no commitments, and I ran no risks. I must now make those commitments and run those risks, because unless I do I will not have felt through my capacities as a citizen. Without having done this I will not be capable of responding humanly to the building of the society that must emerge out of the ashes of this one, and I *will* be capable of acting abstractly and tyrannically. Thus, while schools like Point Blank are a matter of justice for Charlie Macdougal, the communities that emerge from them and other institutions like them, are also a human necessity, both for Charlie and for people like myself.

My hope is that in Canada, if we can hold the border long enough and keep the corporations back a little, we may have the chance of building these societies in our cities, both as a political base (which is useful no matter what happens at the top) and a humanizing environment. It's a very long shot, but I think it's the only realistic chance we've got, here in northern America. I believe we should put most of our energies towards it.

THE BALDWIN STREET CLUB

Laura Phillips

INTRODUCTION: SATU REPO

LAURA PHILLIPS *has had an after-school program for kids in her neighborhood, with occasional help from friends, for the past fourteen months. Baldwin Street where she lives is a downtown Toronto street in the west central part of the city, south of the University of Toronto and just east of the Spadina garment district, on the fringes of Chinatown. The area has a mixed population, mainly first generation immigrants. The street looks like a poor man's business street: many single family houses where the ground floor has been converted to a family business of a sort—a corner grocery store, a Chinese hand laundry, an ethnic bakery. Sprinkled liberally through the area are second-hand clothing stores and cheap factory outlets for childrens' clothes and hosiery.*

It is a wide street with generous sidewalks and lots of kids fooling around and cheap rents on top of stores and in the numerous rooming houses. The most recent wave of immigrants seem to be young American expatriots, such as Laura and her husband, John. A group of these people have opened up a colorful Community Store close to the club, with flowers painted on the window and a display of hand-made leather bags and incense and waterpipes and lots of original outfits made of leather and velvet and vintage army surplus stuff.

It is a street with possibilities and it is going through some kind of a change right now: a number of "On Sale" signs and some painting up of house fronts and widening of store windows. There are contradictory rumors circulating in the neighborhood as to what this is all about. Some say that speculators are buying up the street to demolish the houses and put up high-rises. Others suggest that some downtown business men are scheming to transform the area into another Village, complete with boutiques and art studios and sidewalk cafés and hippies rented to sit in front of stores. Be that as it may, one thing is certain: the prices of houses are skyrocketing and it is likely that the club will have to move into another area before long.

The kids that spend their after-school hours and many weekends and evenings at the club range from four to twelve. They are mostly from large families that move around in the downtown area, usually because they are unable to find suitable and permanent housing for the price they can pay. The kids keep changing schools, sometimes several times during the school year, and have a hard time hooking into the school situation. Most of them have not learned how to read and write after several years at school. Many of them are transferred into Opportunity Classes where they are even less likely to learn and which attaches a humiliating social stigma to them. They are the "dumb kids." Last year eight out of the ten children in the Opportunity Class in the local public school attended the club. Seven of these kids belonged to two large families, the Berrys and the Rowes. The Berrys have fourteen children, the Rowes ten. Both the families have moved out of the immediate area since, but the kids had become good friends and continue to come back to the club—some of them walking a considerable distance—the older ones carrying the younger ones.

Although the club began as a drop-in center, it soon shifted its emphasis to a learning situation, because that's what the kids asked for. They decided among themselves that it should be a "school" and that only those who were serious about working were allowed in. They established rules against fighting and fooling around. The club thus became a free school with an emphasis on the creative arts, using tape recorders, typewriters, and photography, as well as painting, sculpture, drama and dance. They also go on trips exploring the city, usually bringing their cameras along. Cooking and sewing are also part of the activities and some of the older girls particularly are making a lot of their own clothes. One favored activity is tape recorded literature: kids dictating poems and telling stories and making up plays. Laura has typed up selections of these recordings and put them in the form of newsletters which she then uses to teach kids how to read. Here are some samples of oral literature that the kids have created, sometimes illustrated with photographs they have taken. The comments are from Laura's journals.

January 5, 1968

Brandy pushed us into action again today. She led the kids into our house. We began our project. I planned to organize the first floor today in preparation of some sort of opening, but here were four kids who wanted to play and to help so I let them in. They washed shelves, put away paper, swept, drew, talked and fought. . . .

January 16, 1968

Hello,

We have recently opened the first floor of our house at 23 Baldwin Street to the neighborhood. You and your family are welcome to drop in—children between the hours of 3:30–5:00 and parents are invited whenever they are free.

We have equipment for photography, sewing, dance and art. Anyone who is interested should come over any time.

There will also be a room open to mothers to get together and talk. Times will be set by mothers who are interested.

Do you have a need for our house to be used as a center for your younger children during the day? If so, please call 364–2630 or come to 23 Baldwin Street.

Sincerely,
JOHN AND LAURA PHILLIPS
JOHN AND JENNY MOFFA

THE CLUB

Once upon a time there was two people living in a big house. They owned the house. They had a big dog. There names were John, Laura, and Brandy. Brandy got up one morning and didn't wake up Laura. One of us kids came over to see if the club was open.

Laura said, "Not yet, come in the afternoon and the club will be open."

So we came back in the afternoon. We played with Brandy in the room and Laura took some pictures and then we were painting all over the room. I made some birds on the windows. Then I did some finger painting. John and Laura went down in the basement to develop the pictures that she took.

One day we had a big play. It was Cinderella and the Bum. Everybody came to watch it. Nearly everybody!

This man he said, "How much does it cost to watch this play?"

Then everybody asked, "How much does it cost to watch this play?"

We said, "Nothing!"

Everybody went away until three o'clock. Then they came back and watched the play.

BRANDY

Brandy went outside one morning.
Laura sprayed some flea spray
on Brandy's skin.
Brandy hated it
but Laura did it anyway.

BRANDY

Every day, when school comes,
Brandy is outside after school
barking at the kids.
The kids go na na na at Brandy
and Brandy barks.
Then Laura has to yell
"Stop it Brandy!"
Then Brandy walks into the house.

—CHARLIE BERRY, AGE 9

February 10, 1968

I am searching for ideas and methods for teaching kids with learning difficulties. They close their minds to anything that in any way relates to school. School is so dull that one really can't blame them. They are humiliated there. I know they can learn. They sew and cook well. It isn't the reading itself that I think is important, but their attitudes about themselves caused by the fact that they cannot read and do academic things that the other kids in the school can do. They need to do things that give them more of a feeling of respect for themselves. They need to find things they enjoy doing, not only at the club but outside it as well.

ON BEING IN OPPORTUNITY CLASS

Debbie: In November she got this letter and she gave it to me and she told me to take it home to my mother to get it signed. It was to go into "Opportunity Class." And I told my mother not to sign it but she did because she thought that it was the best thing for me but I didn't. Then after I waited for a while and Mr. Ingles (the principal) asked me if I had that letter and I didn't want him to find out. He said that I'd better bring it back. So I told my mother and she signed it. Doris was supposed to go in there and her mother never signed it. She wrote a letter and Doris stayed in grade 5. I took the letter back and they put me in there and I didn't like it and I started crying 'cause I didn't want to stay in there. We just didn't learn anything. We had Mr. Ranta for a teacher. I didn't learn anything. It was so babyish. I don't know why they put me in there. Some of the other teachers were saying why did they put me in there. I was too smart for that. Then at the end of the year when everyone was writing autographs everyone said that they hoped that I would go to grade 5 and I thought I was going to grade 5 but I didn't. I went into the opportunity. . . . When I went up for my report card, the teacher asked me if I wanted to go to grade 5. He said: "Does it matter to you if the kids are smaller than you?" I said: "No." He said: "I'll talk to the principal" and he never even talked to the principal. Then this year around November the teacher asked me if I wanted to go to grade 5, and she said that she would

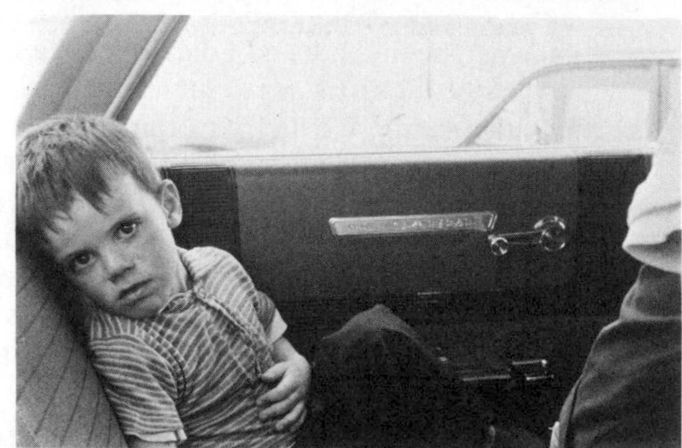

talk to the principal, and she did, and he said that it was all right if I wasn't embarrassed that they were smaller than I was.

—DEBBIE BERRY, AGE 12

March 3, 1968

People often ask me, why I want to work with kids that hate school and learning as much as these kids do. I think that I gravitate towards working with these kinds of kids, because I had similar odds against me when I was their age. I was poor and discriminated against by other kids and I also used to hate school with a passion. Here are just a few things I remember from my first school years:

I began my schooling in a coal-mining town in West Virginia, called Fairmount. What I remember from the first grade is that my teacher made me sit in a closet all day because I didn't know how to add. I remember sitting in that class watching everybody putting down answers and I did not know how to add, so I put down anything that came to my mind. Well, I guessed wrong and the teacher made me sit in the closet for it. The same year I also got hit for reading with my fingers.

The only thing I remember from the second year is that I danced in a school play and didn't have the right color of jeans and got bawled out by the teacher.

In the third grade I began doing anything that I could to get out of school. I stayed at home as often as I could get away with it. My mother would try to force me to go, and I would insist that I felt sick. That year I failed everything on my report card, but got promoted to the next grade just the same. It was a year I really loved to read. When I stayed home I could read all day. Some evenings I would stack up my books beside my bed and hope that I would wake

up sick, so I could stay home and read them. At the end of the year my twin brother and I took our years' work that the teacher had handed back to us and threw it down a hill, and my brother went down the hill and pissed on it. We both felt much better.

In the fourth grade my teacher didn't care whether I showed up much, because we lived over a mile away from school, and she thought it was too far for me to walk in bad weather. I was really scared of this teacher. She would pick up kids by their hair and knock them around the room. She used to hit me for talking in class.

In the fifth grade my attendance was even more irregular. We were particularly poor this year and I didn't have a warm coat until after the January sale.

TROUBLE

ACT I

Mother (*Debbie*): Mary, get up for school.

Mary (*Sharon*): I don't want to.

Mother: Get up. You have to. If you don't get up, I'm going to phone the school and tell them that you just don't want to get up. Now get up.

Mary: I don't want to.

Mother: Come on, get up.

Mary: I don't want to go.

Mother: Get up. I want you to get up and get washed for school.

Mary: I spend six hours in school. School, ugh!

Mother: Well, that's too bad—you get ready. Take your lunch. Don't forget your lunch. Come home after school.

Later, after school

Mother to father: Where could Mary be? I wonder if I should call the school. (pause) There you are! What took you so long coming home from school?

Mary: I ah, I had to . . .
Mother: What?
Mary: I had to help the teacher.
Mother: No you did not. I told you to be home by 4 o'clock.
Mary: I had to. I had to help the teacher.
Mother': You go to your room and you stay in that bed. You don't get any supper. You stay there.
Mary: Ugh.
Mother: Look! Don't talk back. I'll have to rip you up the side of your head.
Mary: I don't even have a room that I can play in. I can't even eat lunch with the other kids, oh brother!
Mother: Shut up! You're always arguing back and forth with me. I'll just really get her, give her a good wallop because she's very bad.
Mother (*to Sharon, Mary's sister*): Come out of your room Sharon. Get in here and watch TV.
Sharon: Goody. Goody.
Mother: You let Mary stay in your room. You watch TV now.
Sharon (*quietly*): Yes, ma'am. Flintstones, meet the Flintstones.
Mother: Stop your noise. I'm liable to rip up the side of your head.
Sharon: I'm watching TV. You said I could watch TV.
Mother: I didn't tell you you could make any noise. You watch TV to see it, you don't make any sounds. Look! Do you want a good beating? Now stop it!! Now go out and eat your supper. And stop throwing the ball up on the thing. Go eat your supper. Now!
Sharon: Oh, do I have to?
Mother: As soon as you finish your supper, you go right into that room.
Sharon: Ah, do I have to?
Mother: Yes. Eat! I might just let you stay up.
(*Sharon makes too much noise eating*)
Mother: Cut that noise out.

Sharon: Oh, I'm sorry. I was just eating. I'm not very loud. I was just eating.

Mother: Get in that room. Stay in.

—DEBBIE BERRY, AGE 12
SHARON POWELL, AGE 12

ACT II

Policeman: (*Darlene*): Is Sharon Powell here?

Mother (*Debbie*): No, she's at school.

Policeman: No, she isn't at school. She's been playing hookey. I'm going to put her in the home.

Mother: I didn't know anything about it. I don't know what I'm going to do about it. When I do get her, she's going to be sorry.

Policeman: I'm putting her in the home.

Mother: No, I don't want that. If you find her, bring her home and I'll be there. I'll teach her not to be bad. OK?

Policeman: All right.

Mother: Would you like to come in and sit down and have a cup of tea?

Policeman: Yes.

Mother: Come in. What would you like in your tea—sugar and cream?

Policeman: Yes, please.

Mother: I really didn't know anything about her playing hookey because if I would have known I would have beat her. You know that. I don't let my daughters play hookey or anybody. If I saw somebody playing hookey on the street I would take them straight to school, if I was in the mood, but if I was tired I couldn't do anything, you know. I don't know where the school is. I didn't know anything at all. If I did know, I would really beat her.

Policeman: Sharon told the teacher that she was going to the washroom.

Mother: Well, she should not do that. When she does

come home, she's going to get the beating of her life. And I'll make sure that she does and if her father finds out, well, I'm not going to tell her father, but if her father does find out, lord help her.

Policeman: She said she had to go to the washroom so the teacher let her go to the washroom.

Mother: You shouldn't let her go to the washroom. Anyone could just run out of the school and you would just forget about where they are. I'll show her when she gets home.

Policeman: So the teacher went down to the washroom and found a girl or boy, we weren't sure . . . all beaten up in the washroom. Then we couldn't find her in school.

Mother: Well, the teacher shouldn't let them go to the washroom so much 'cause that's just what they'll do.

Policeman: That was her first time today.

Mother: Oh, would you like some cookies?

Policeman: No, thanks.

Mother: Would you like any cookies?

Policeman: No, I get my lunch break pretty soon.

Mother: Well, did you tell the principal about this?

Policeman: The principal was the one who phoned us.

Mother: Well, I don't think that she should be put away but when she comes home I'll give her a good beating and I won't tell her father because she'd just get it worse.

Policeman: I'll come tonight and see if she is here. Okay?

Mother: Okay. Goodbye.

Policeman: Goodbye.

—DEBBIE BERRY, AGE 12
DARLENE ROWE, AGE 9

March 28, 1968

The important thing about the club is to make kids feel that it is theirs. This is already beginning to happen. They feel very possessive about it and get very upset if kids come in here that the regular kids didn't know about and if the place gets messed up or even rearranged a little. They like fixing the place up. With some help from me they put up some shelves and painted a blackboard. They have decorated and redecorated the rooms several times. They insist on keeping the place clean. They pick up before they go home each day. They want to wash the floor constantly, but I had to limit it because the floors were beginning to warp.

IN THE MORNING

I don't like to get up in the mornings and my mother always calls, "Emma, Emma, get up and feed the babies." And then I say, "Emm emm," and then I go, "emm emm," like that. I'm really tired and then I get up and feed the babies. I get some milk and I put some hot water in it. Then I put it on the stove and I boil it. Ricky can eat by himself and so can Ricardo. Only Ricky knows how to hold on to the bottle.

I say, "Here Ricky, hold onto the bottle."

Then I change Ricardo.

Then we have to take them outside. My mother kept saying, "Is Ricky awake? Is Ricky awake to take him outside?"

I say, "No."

I trick my mother sometimes when I don't want to do it.

—EMMA BERRY, AGE 7

April 5, 1968

The kids had strange ideas about me first. Emma, age 7, couldn't believe that I was married because I painted with the kids. She said, "But you are not supposed to sit on the floor when you are married." Several months later she was still concerned about what was proper for a married woman. One day I didn't feel like playing tag with her because I just didn't feel like running around that day. She said that it wasn't really because I just didn't feel like it, it was because I had a baby inside me and I didn't want to hurt it. I wasn't pregnant. She assumed that once you get married you are continuously having babies. She comes from a family of fourteen kids.

MY MOTHER

My mother is nice to all of us.
She doesn't hardly hit us.
She likes us.
She always loves us
like your mother loves you too.
except, if you get big and get married
you can not live with your mother any longer
but it's nice to live with your mother
as long as you've got her.
Now say, if your mother didn't live with you
and you never saw her since you were a baby
and your mother came to visit you one day
You wouldn't know who she was now would you?
But if you'd seen your mother before like I do,
I see my mother every day, every night,
because I live with my mother
until I'm big enough to leave her.
But I wish that I couldn't leave her
because I like it there
and my mother wishes that we didn't have to leave her.
Some mothers are mean sometimes;
Our mother is mean and nice, all things
but we love her the best of all.

—DARLENE ROWE, AGE 9

SAY IT OUT LOUD

Say it out loud now, I am black and proud now.
Say it out loud now, I am black and not proud now.
Say it out loud now, I am white and proud now.
Say it out loud now, I am white and not proud now.
If you are black stay black
If you are brown stick around
If you are white you can't fight
If you are white get out of sight.

—PHILIP DIXON, AGE 12

April 22, 1968

One thing that I have always wanted to do is to try to make children's books completely written by kids. I have tried doing that at the club. Since few of the kids can even print their own name, I have had them dictate their stories to a tape recorder. I then copy them down in big print and use them for teaching them how to read. When we added photographs the books really became very relevant and interesting for the child that took the pictures and wrote the story. The pictures are sometimes too limiting. Lately they have been making up the stories first. I am going to try having them make shadow prints to go with their stories instead of pictures.

Many problems arose from this approach to teaching reading. One, in order for it to be successful there can't be a time lapse between the time the story is said into the tape recorder and the pictures are taken and the time that I have the story copied and the pictures printed. Developing film and printing pictures is so time-consuming that it leaves me with little time to do anything else. Still, the kids themselves were very enthusiastic about this project. They keep wanting to make more and more books.

DISCUSSION ON ELVIS PRESLEY

Philip: He's okay in the movies but when he sings, blaa.

Debbie: He's white, that's why you don't like his singing.

Darlene: His wife, you know his wife why she married him?

Debbie: For his money.

Darlene: For show business, that's all she wants and for his money. That's all she likes.

LETTER FROM PHILIP

Dear Billy Berry:

Do you live?

Do you like Darlene BILLY. Not as a girlfriend just as a friend to fool around with.

Billy thinks he is the cool but he is just a fool.

Billy knows that I am not a fool but the cool.

Billy is the cool of the fools.

PHILIP IS THE COOL AROUND THE FOOLS.

May 11, 1968

I have found that typewriters are very useful for teaching reading. The kids write stories, letters, poems, and sometimes just lists of words. I am doing this on a regular basis with Charlie and Emma. They know all of the letters. They don't know that there are spaces between words. I had some difficulty in explaining the difference between letters and words. Looking at a newspaper they couldn't tell me when one word stopped and another one began. It is easy to assume that they know something. Caren, age ten, thinks that she is actually writing words when she just types any letters without even once in a line stopping for space. She asks me to read what she wrote. It will be something like this: Jkdieurjkjjuiuu8374j d.

Charlie thought of an idea. It was to have me sit next to him and spell all of his words for him. It sounds very simple, but it is a perfect time to teach him about letters and to begin teaching him how to read. I sit next to him with another typewriter and he tells me what word he wants to type and I spell it. I think that it is important that I also have a typewriter so that I am not hanging over him exclaiming that he is working wonders or something of the sort.

I spell even the most simple words. Charlie, like the others, will guess at anything. They don't admit that they don't know something, so I eliminate the need for guessing by spelling each word before Charlie has the chance to say how he thinks it is spelled. I point out letter combinations (phonics) and tell him some spelling rules at the same time.

They guess less when their friends aren't around to distract them and to tease them when they get them wrong. They get in the habit of guessing when they are in school. The books that they are taught to read are so repetitive and have so few words that it is easy to memorize them and guess when one is asked to read. If their guesses prove right, it reinforces the pattern. Learning anything at school has guessing in it. When they are tested on the colors in first grade, they have a choice between red, blue, and orange to color something red. Chances are they will get it right. Testing in general encourages guessing. For the kids that never learned when they could guess and when not to, it is most difficult to break the pattern and teach them anything.

A FIGHT

Byron: I don't like black people. I don't like indians either.
Michael: You're a black indian.
Byron: You drink some wine.
Michael: I don't like black men.
Byron: I don't like blue men.
Michael: You don't like white people.
Byron: I don't like white people. They're too ice creamer.
Michael: You're a poop leg. You poop leg.
Byron: You're piss pants.

Michael: You're shit pants.

Byron: Look you nut, I don't want to fool around with you. I'm going to beat you up.

Michael: Look black man.

Byron: Look white man.

Michael: Look black man stop fighting. I'm a cop.

Byron: Well you're a white cop. You're an ice cream cop. . . . Listen boy, I want to fight with you. (Giggling, they began to fight.) Why don't you fight with me? Why do you fight with me. I'll get the gun out of your hand. . . . It's out.

Michael: No, it's not.

Byron: Well, I've got a knife and I'll stab you. . . . You ham sandwich, you white bum. . . . You're a white bum.

Michael: Do you know what you are?

Byron: You are a . . . You are a . . .

Michael: You're a black man.

Byron: You're a farty.

(*The fight stops and Byron and Michael begin to sing and dance together.*)

—BYRON BERRY, AGE 6
MICHAEL ROWE, AGE 5

REACTIONS TO THE DEATH OF MARTIN LUTHER KING

My teacher told me that Martin Luther King was killed and he made peace between the black and white so he got a reward and he died. My teacher didn't tell us how he died and we have been talking to our mothers all about it and we've been watching TV all about it. We saw his grave place. I think that it's very sad. He was a good guy. He was on everybody's side. I think it's very sad that he got killed. I wonder when, what day and what year he got killed. My teacher said that it was this year but I don't know the date. I don't like to hear of this so I hope he goes to heaven. Now Charlie is going to speak. Introducing Charlie.

—DAVID MILLER, AGE 6

Martin Luther King, he was the best man in Ontario. He was a good guy. He was waiting near a hotel for a taxi and a man came up and shot him in the face. Then he died before he went to the hospital. He was rich. He was talking in person on TV. He was the best guy in Nova Scotia and all over the countries. Today they said that Martin Luther King was on television. They said that in the United States when we first heard that he died they said that there were orders to shoot out the street light. The police had orders to shoot out street lights and hunt for the people that killed him.

—CHARLIE BERRY, AGE 10 (*Negro*)

POEMS

I hate caterpillars
I hate snakes
I hate worms
I hate bumblebees
I like ants
I like,
the teeny ants
that crawl up on my hands
I like butterflies
monarchs,
but I'm afraid of them when they land on me

I like flowers

I like to go to the island
I went to the island once

I like tulips

I like and don't like lots of things

I like to do coloring

I like to do projects

I like to do art

I like to read stories to kids

I want to be a nurse someday
You get lots of money for being a nurse

I like to go to Milton's on Sunday
I get either Pepsi or a mini soda
or orange pop or fresca or whatever you call it

I like typing

When I grow up
if I lose one job
and I get another job
and I lose that one
and I get another one
I'll keep that one!

—EMMA BERRY, AGE 7

THE MASTERPIECE

One day there were two boys named Michael and Ricky. They had a masterpiece. It was a funny face masterpiece. It had a face and a mouth.

Ricky wanted it but Michael said, "No! You can't have it."

So Ricky got mad and started to cry. He jumped and he jumped and he jumped all about. He got mad like a Vietnam boy. Oh what a sight! So Ricky got up and he tried to get it.

Michael said, "You can't have it. You're too little. You might break it!"

But Ricky said, "I will not break it!"

And he began to cry just like a Vietnam boy who was crying for food.

Michael started picking at it and he broke the head.

So along comes Gail and she said, "What have you done to my masterpiece? You broke it, Michael, and so I am going to smash you."

And she did and Michael began to cry.

Then my mom came up and she said, "What's going on here?"

Gail said, "Michael has broken my masterpiece that I had made."

Mom said, "It's alright, you can glue it back together."

Gail said, "No this is clay and you can't glue it back together."

Gail began to cry. She went into the house.

She said to Darlene, "Look what Michael did. He broke my masterpiece that I had made at the club and now I have no masterpiece left. What should I do?"

Darlene said, "Go to the club and make another masterpiece."

Gail said, "But there's no more clay left."

Darlene said, "Well make some!"

Gail said, "No that's too hard!"

But later she walked down to the club.

—DARLENE ROWE, AGE 9

January 28, 1969

After working more or less alone with kids for a year, I have got involved with a group of people here in Toronto who are going to set up a full-time free school for the kind of inner-city kids I have been working with. I will be teaching there beginning next September and I hope to bring along a number of kids that have attended the club for the past year. What will this school be like? It is hard to tell exactly, but I am interested in it because of a very positive experience I had myself in grade nine in a school that was run vaguely on similar principles that we have been talking about in this group.

It was a boarding school in Celo, North Carolina, and most of the adults involved in it were Quakers. The emphasis there was put on learning only the things that were relevant. We used some of the traditional school texts, because the teachers were probably afraid to throw them out completely for fear that the school would be closed down or something, but we did not pay much attention to them. We grew our own food. We baked all the bread we needed. We built most of the buildings. We kids thought of it as our school. Classes were held irregularly or not at all, if something important was happening. We spent a week in South Carolina studying the black situation and I did a report on black musicians. We also spent four days on the Cherokee Indian Reservation in North Carolina. The eighth grade class from the reservation came to live with us for a few days and then we went back to their homes with them. I took weaving at the nearby Penland School of Crafts. Other kids took ceramics, copper enamelling or painting. Celo is fifty miles from Asheville, North Carolina, the nearest city. We didn't get a newspaper and we didn't even have a radio. After I had been there for a month the school got a telephone. It was pleasantly isolated. We had frequent visitors that would come and speak to the school. Most of the teachers were students at Antioch College. They would stay for three months and then go back to college. The school had a car and we would drive to the city occasionally for plays and concerts. The people living in this Quaker community were mainly artists and writers. We would also get together with the local mountain people. The school had folk dances on weekends and films at least once a week that the neighbors were invited to.

I really loved that school. Unfortunately it was only for grades seven, eight and nine, and I was in grade nine. So I had to leave, and go back to the public school system and the same old horrors. The only reason I finished high school was because I wanted to go to Antioch College afterwards, so I could some day go back to the Arthur Morgan school to teach.

TRAVELING WITH CHILDREN AND TRAVELING ON

BILL AYERS

One of the major motivations for the people who started the school was that they felt there wasn't a good model of an integrated school: the integrated schools were in many ways as racist as the old segregated model. We're trying to approach integration in a totally new way. Not only do we have black and white kids in the same school, but we don't make any value judgments about either of those groups of kids, because making value judgments turns out to be racist.

In every integrated school I've seen except ours the model for failure is everything that is ghetto or Negro culture. If you dress a certain way, prefer a certain kind of music or food, then you're ignorant. It comes out most obviously in language. When a child says, "I ain't," and the teacher says it's wrong, he's destroying a lot. The child grew up saying that. His parents speak that way, everyone he knows speaks that way, he's learned to speak his way successfully and suddenly he's confronted with a new system that says he's ignorant. In this way the integrated school may be more destructive to both white and Negro kids than the old segregated system.

What we try to do is to allow these groups of kids to learn from each other, to exchange things, throw things away, pick things up, without any kind of value judgments. I think that more than anything it is dangerous to consciously create models for kids to emulate. Most of us have had the experience of a model of what a teacher was and what an adult was, and we found that model, especially as we got older, a very restricting model. When you were sixteen the model didn't screw, didn't drink and didn't mess around and those were all things that you wanted to do, so that the model was unrealistic. Of course we found out later that it was just a model and not true at all. One of the advantages of a school like this is that kids aren't forced to believe in one kind of model: there are a lot of models. The group of people that comes into the school is in a lot of ways very diverse. There are students who come in, community people with all kinds of different ideas about politics, life styles, kids, interests. Kids can learn much more from a number of different models. Everyone says, for instance, that the model of a nice cop is unrealistic for ghetto kids because cops are just not nice in ghettos. We get out of the community a lot by taking trips—as many as five or six trips in a day—and the vital sense you develop in the community of what to expect from different adults gets tested out. You learn that some cops are nice and help you across the street and others aren't so nice. I think they are getting a much more realistic picture of the world. The point is that kids learn by testing reality and not by what someone has decided is the truth they are going to tell them.

PICKED THINGS UP AND THREW THINGS OUT

I don't think you can generalize from twenty-five kids in three years, but I think we have seen some indications that this is a good approach. We've seen every kid come in much narrower than he is today. The white kids came in generally quieter, more academically oriented, more afraid of new situations. The Negro kids came in busting out all over with enthusiasm, excitement, violent play. They enjoyed new situations, meeting strangers; they liked exploring, and of course they spoke differently from the white classmates. We've seen in three years that the white kids have loosened up a good deal, that they now follow the lead of their black classmates; they too explore on a trip, they go off by themselves and ask questions of strangers and kind of snoop around. They do more physical kinds of play, they dance much looser, they've picked up some of the language and thrown some away. The Negro kids today are able to spend a lot more time doing something quiet, they've picked up some of the language of their white classmates. We've seen this exchange completely without our intervention, without us saying these things are good or bad, but just by themselves they have picked things up and thrown things out however they saw it necessary.

The ratio of black and white kids in the school is about half and half. We make decisions when we accept parents of kids to keep a lot of different balances—age balances, sexual balances, race balances—so that in different age groupings there are different kids. Each kid has kids his own age and his own color and sex to play with. It's really hard to do when you only have twenty-five kids—like programming on a computer. One of the problems is that the school is, in a lot of ways, much more oriented towards black kids, or rather the atmosphere that prevails is created by those kids in the sense that many of the things that go on there are dominated by black kids. We didn't consciously make that decision, but the fact is that the black kids are more of a group, they are older and smarter. The black kids have been in the school longer as a group. They tend to be more open and more anxious to get out of their houses and hang around with us. Some of that was certainly conscious. We live in a black neighborhood now. We thought it would be good to be near those kids, because we have been in a white neighborhood before and much nearer to most of the white kids.

Another problem is that we do not have any black staff. That is primarily because we can't afford to pay anybody and there are very few people at the university that are willing to devote time to the Children's Community rather than get a college degree and a job. That is something that really works against us. Parents come, and are encouraged to come as much they can, but that is never regular because they have to work. The first year we had an unemployed black guy who came regularly and we now have a black girl who comes once a week, but it is still one of the big shortcomings.

There is no conflict between black and white kids in the school. There is real openness and acceptance of other kids. But there is a kind of ghetto atmosphere in the school. It is a poor run-down place to begin with, and much noisier than it would be if we had all white kids. Yet that is not a simple matter of class difference. We have wealthy kids who are black and white, and poor kids who are black and white. The spectrum of the school runs from very poor people who can't afford to pay any tuition to people who are professors and make over ten thousand dollars a year. I think the wealthiest kid in the school is black, but he is about the only one that crosses the economic boundaries. For the most part the black kids are poor. The fact is that the white kids who are poor are the sons and daughters of struggling students or new left parents coming out of a middle-class culture. And the black kids whose parents may make more money than those people are still coming out of a ghetto culture. It is hard to talk about the differences economically.

The economic and racial differences between kids are sometimes reflected in the kids' attitudes to each other. When they leave the school, the white kids probably go to their white neighborhoods and the black kids go to their black neighborhoods. But they play together outside of school more than kids from most schools, although not necessarily interracially. Given the fact that they are scattered all over Ann Arbor, for Todd to play with Duke is a big trip, and yet they do it three, four, five times a week. More important than the interracial relationships that are formed (which, after all, are hard to measure) is the fact that exchanges take place in a very free atmosphere that is broadening for all of them.

ON THE OUTSIDE

We see learning as going on every place—unstructured and undefined. When we talk about the discovery approach to learning, or about making learning a total process, we often talk about the cooking we do and the trips we take. We take trips every day certainly. That doesn't mean every kid, but those who are interested in whatever is happening. Sometimes the kids suggest a trip, sometimes we do. If we have to plan it we involve the kids in the planning. We don't consider the teacher suggesting a trip a betrayal of the discovery method. If there is healthy open relationship the kids feel no kind of pressure about accepting the suggestion or rejecting it. Whether they want to go or not has nothing to do with what the teacher thinks of them. We do think that we have a responsibility to make a lot of different kinds of things accessible when available, and that includes materials, trips, even activities we might bring in. For instance, I was reading a book to three kids about fossils, and I discovered through reading that you could find fossils in limestone. Since limestone is plentiful and commonly used in a lot of the buildings around, I suggested a trip to go to the administration building and look at the marble floors and the walls to find the fossils. We did it. It was the kind of thing I could suggest to tie into what they were doing.

APPLES, HAMBURGERS, CARS AND AIRPLANES

A number of times we've gone to an apple orchard and eaten the apples. Once as we were leaving, a truck was loading up with apples. One of the kids wanted to follow it and we did. It dropped off a load of apples at the A & P and we went in and bought some more apples to eat. You could see in that whole process that a real understanding about the economics of apples was starting. Apples are grown, sold, and bought.

Another trip came out of a discussion of meat. Someone in the group said wisely that hot dogs come from a cow you know. Someone else added that hamburgers come from a cow too. I sensed in the discussion that they were fascinated, but didn't have a clear understanding of what they were saying. Everyone knows that meat comes in pieces and packages. When someone asked if it was true that salami comes from a sheep I started to talk about it. I said it was true that meat comes from animals and that we kill a lot of animals every day to get the meat we need. This was very fascinating to them. We talked about going to Detroit to see them slaughter animals. I arranged the trip and took five kids. The only stomach that turned was mine. We spent a couple of hours watching them herd in pigs, electrocute them, slit their throats, hang them up, take them down, cut them up, and package them. The way they talked about it afterwards to their friends and to one another was significantly different from what they had said before. I don't think there is any way this kind of understanding could have been gained through lectures, pictures or adult pronouncements. Perhaps we ought to record some of the discussions, but I would argue that written records are a sort of neurosis of older people, who want to get the understanding spelled out on paper.

Oh yes, I just remembered another great trip. There's a real fascination with cars with a lot of little kids, you know. Interest in cars can lead to any number of things but a couple of kids really wanted to see the way a car was built so we arranged two trips—one to the Cadillac plant in Detroit (of course being near Detroit helps) and one to the largest Ford plant. An interesting thing happened, I think. You see the way I learned about automobiles was through the history of automobiles and Henry Ford and all that, and Henry Ford was a genius, and he did a lot of good for the whole country, and he liberated masses of people with his invention. Now as I got older I started to get a different analysis, and I feel that Henry Ford did more to enslave workers than he did to liberate them. But you know my philosophy of teaching overrides both of these views, and I don't think it's wise to put either one of these on kids—to tell them that Henry Ford was a genius and liberator or to tell them that he was an enslaver.

So what we did was go to the plant. Coming back from the Cadillac plant I had about five kids in the car, I think, and they were concerned with different things. Some of them were concerned with how amazing it was and it *was* amazing to watch the assembly line, it's an amazing kind of thing if that is what you want to see. It's a stroke of genius in a sense to see that all this can come together and make a car—so some of the kids were concerned with this. Another group of the kids were talking about the fact that it stank, that it was noisy, that it was filthy, that it was too long, that the trip was too long, it was boring . . .

Okay, so without me imposing my values on them, or someone else imposing theirs on him, they learned what they wanted to learn and I think that they learned it much more significantly than if we had given them all the lectures about it. You know, in a sense, this says that any kind of social studies that you could possibly teach or write books about has to be alive, in a sense has to be incomplete at least and the point that is often made that these kids know more about sociology and about social sciences than we do—if by social sciences we mean the make-up of society and how one exists in it—that is true.

So I think the car trips were fascinating to us. The airport trips are other ones—kids love airplanes, they all love airplanes but about five or six love them more than others, so there was a while there when we were making about four or five trips to the Metropolitan Airport a week which was getting a little heavy on the gas bills. But you know it wasn't only a fascination with airplanes although that was part of it. It's so many people talking in foreign languages, escalators, movies, little displays that they have all over, cards hung up on the ceiling. And it's big and it's got a big marble floor, and you can run across it and no one gives you much trouble.

But it's also the car ride. It's fun to get in a car with five other kids because that situation is a foreign situation and you can talk and bicker and notice and observe and, you know, carry on all sitting there going someplace. Last week I got in a car with four kids who said, "Let's go for a ride," and I said, "Where?" and they said, "It doesn't matter," so we got in the car—I had a couple of short errands I wanted to do—we got in the car, and we drove around and they spent the whole time fighting, competing, noticing things, singing songs. But that's all they wanted to do for a couple of hours—just ride around in the car, and I think riding in the car aimlessly is sometimes a very good experience.

It's an interesting thing about the Cadillac plant incidentally. There was a public relations guy who showed us around, typical public relations guy, very nice guy, and he said, "Well you know we've never had kids under twelve before," and he was a little apprehensive and he said, "Now the first thing we do is go into this auditorium and I give you a five or ten minute talk about what you're going to see . . ."

So I said, "Well, that's fine," and we walked in and you know there is something magical about stages and little kids, so they saw this stage and twenty of them rushed up to the stage and started to do an impromptu dance and song routine and the guy was just appalled and didn't know exactly what to do. So I rushed over to him and I said—I kind of blurted out as fast as I could that these are little kids and it's very hard for them to learn by you lecturing to them, and so why don't you just lead the way and we'll kind of orbit around you like little stars and if anyone has a question he'll come up and ask you. And it turned out that the guy was just a very nice guy and once he got into it really, he dug it. When it was through the guy said, "Well this is amazing. We might just have to re-evaluate our policy."

THE BOGIE OF STUDENT-STAFF RATIO

People have often said to me, "You have such well-behaved children." My first reaction is to say that well-behaved doesn't mean anything, but then I start to wonder what in the world they mean. By anybody's standards but our own they are really ill-behaved. There is no way in the world that I can control them if they don't want it. But I think a group of kids, even a large group, are well-behaved when they are interested, when this is where they would rather be. In terms of trip-taking our kids have become very sophisticated. Part of it is the way we take trips. We don't make the kids stand in line while a person lectures to them. We don't force them to go from one thing to another, in the museum for instance, and listen to someone talking about what they think the kids should be interested in. We allow our eight-year-olds, considering the amount of experience they have had, to go out by themselves in groups of three or four. We don't have fear about that. In a year or two some of our kids will be taking all kinds of trips by themselves. The teacher who says he can't take trips because he is only one person and the children need a "capable" adult to control them should consider that classes are going to get bigger and that you can't control thirty-five kids unless you spend your time bringing kids back into the group. The only possible solution is to let kids do what they are interested in. You've got to trust them to go off into many different activities at the same time. The student-staff ratio is a big bogie. Successful public school teachers in this country have come to the decentralization of the class through trial and error. They learned that any other way their primary role was as cop, their secondary role was bureaucrat and lastly they might be able to get a little bit of teaching done, though they weren't even sure of that.

USING WHAT IS THERE

Cooking is another of our activities that allows a wide range of learning. Through cooking you have to get to things like reading in its natural setting, and some kinds of chemistry. You can very easily go into social sciences. If one kid makes cheese sandwiches one day, another kid might bring in his mother's recipe for corn bread and chitlings, and you get a whole discussion about cultures. You have to allow food to be used in a lot of different ways, to be messed with, to be thrown around some, used as a weapon, to be played with. Cooking happens all the time. There is always someone in the kitchen, usually a few kids. They love to cook. They come with baloney sandwiches and they fry their baloney before they eat it. They use whatever is there.

BOMBARDED BY WORDS

With all the hysteria about reading, we find that kids learn to read in a million different ways. Some learn to read because they like cars and want to learn the different names of cars. Others learn because they go on a lot of trips and read the signs along the way, they learn to read each other's names, or they read the labels in a store, or they learn to read because they like to. Most of the kids really do want to learn to read. They learn to talk because everyone around them talks. They want to be competent. They want to make sense out of things like everyone else seems to be able to do, so they learn to talk, and the same is true of reading. It is impossible to exist in this world without being bombarded by words on television, street signs, advertising. Kevin, for instance, learned words like Dristan and Stop. Michael learned words like synagogue. These aren't the clean clinically-tested sociological words.

Part of the great sorting-out process of American public education is that a lot of the kids who come through high school don't know how to read. In this sense the school system has failed because it has set itself up as the institution that teaches reading. It really ends up in just teaching a skill, and we are not particularly interested in that. We hope that the kids can do more than identify certain words. We hope they learn how to express themselves, that words have a certain power, and the only way to learn this is to have something powerful to communicate and then to have the opportunity. Learning just can't take place in a situation where you have curriculum guides and authoritarian teachers putting a mass of knowledge into an average student. That isn't real learning at all.

HOW LIMITS ARE LEARNED

We have not sat down and decided what is important for kids to do. They choose what they do and they do what they are interested in. There is no set of values by which we judge cutting up carrots as opposed to doing something else. The kids are already fairly conscious of what is reasonable in relating to society and what is not. They are used to having their hands slapped. But I think they learn more in this kind of environment. What they learn about fighting, for instance, is infinitely more valuable than being told it is not nice to hit. Here they learn over a period of time and a number of experiences. Every day a kid named Kevin would pick a fight with Darlene and always get his ass kicked. There was nothing you could say to him to convince him that fighting with Darlene particularly was going to lead to getting your ass kicked. Over a two-week period it finally sunk in. He learned he was better off not to pick fights with Darlene. Another issue we had was swearing. We didn't want to say swearing was wrong—probably because that's phony, but also because we wanted the kids to learn for themselves what is appropriate. I always used to say when we were going on a trip that there was a good chance we would get kicked out if there was swearing. One day we went out to a printing place, and I told Jonathan that if he swore there was a good chance we'd all be kicked out. We walked in and he looked at the lady and said, "You're a mother-fucker," and we got kicked out. I think he learned from that.

The school has always been in the basement of a church but the kids have been quick to learn the restrictions made by being in someone else's facilities. The main restriction is that we have two not very big rooms. It is difficult to be able to be alone. But we have arrived at an arrangement through a meeting with the kids. You have got to understand that meetings with six- or seven-year-olds are just the most beautiful things. They last about a minute and a half, with everyone very excited, all trying to get in at once. They decided that the big room should be a place where they could ride tricycles and run up and down and play games like frozen tag and so on, and the little room should be crowded with activities like mathematical games, typewriters, books, and art supplies. The little room is very crowded, but a lot of kids spend a lot of time there. This is the closest we have been able to get to a kind of privacy. Occasionally a child will ask to be by himself in a room we can use upstairs very quietly, or one will ask to take a walk with an assistant as a way of being alone. But the last thing on their mind is a nap.

ANXIETIES FROM OUTSIDE

There are a lot of problems with trying to run a school like this, and one of them is the anxiety the kids feel from their older brothers and sisters, from the neighborhood kids about being in a different kind of school. They have a hard time seeing it as a real school. The kids on their block talk about reading lessons, homework, and other things they don't have. Kids shouldn't be faced with the problem of having to defend their school. They should just think that they go to a different school, no better or worse. They don't really understand the differences, and having to defend it simply confuses them. Parents send their kids to the school for all kinds of reasons. They are not all absolutely committed to our philosophy of education, and though we interview them carefully, I don't think we always know whether they think it makes sense. The black parents as a group are fairly authoritarian with their kids. One of the overriding reasons they send them to our school is that they think black kids get a fair shake here, and they wouldn't at another school. We try to avoid being used for kids who are found emotionally disturbed at the public schools. Although the whole philosophy sounds beautiful, when you actually have to deal with all the things that come out in a free atmosphere it's not always pretty. A lot of anger and hostility come out and are allowed to be expressed without retaliation.

The kids have a tremendous identification with the school as a community. There is the sense that it is our school. I think that if we continue to grow at the rate of a grade a year, if we get through junior high, we will have done a great deal. The kids who leave then will be able to make conscious decisions about when they will or won't play the game. People often ask how kids adjust if they have to go to public schools. When you think of what that means, it means doing everything for the approval of the teacher, molding oneself around what other people expect. It's a double-edged knife. The kids who don't adjust get screwed in one way, but the kids who do are just getting molded into that other-directed person. It's a shame.

FUNDS AND STATE BOARDS

I think that the majority of our problems would be wiped away if we had an angel come along with funds. A year ago we had the major problem of not having a full staff.

Now the staff is full and working well together. If we had our own building and the kind of supplies we need it would be golden. We urge other people—groups of parents, community organizing projects—to start their own schools too. We could get some information together about how we got supplies, raised money, and coped with the legal hassles.

We have no enemies now because there is really nobody around who cares a whole lot about what we are doing. At some point when the school becomes more threatening to different groups I can envision a legal hassle. There are a lot of legal things that hang over our heads but have not yet come down. Teacher certification is one. Now we have one certified teacher in a room, and as far as the State Board of Education is concerned she is the only one who is supposed to engage in any kind of learning situation with kids. Everyone is counter to having adults in the classroom and to using the resources of the community. One of the funniest things the administrators of the State Board talked about was the reason we needed an accredited teacher. An accredited teacher is the only one who can make learning decisions. We talked about that. I said, "Well, we have a retired engineer who comes in and does science experiments, is that all right?" And he said, "Yes, that's perfectly fine as long as he does not make learning decisions." Then we have a lady who comes in and dances with the kids. "Is that all right?" "That's demonstration of a skill, as long as the demonstration of the skill is not a learning decision." It became clear that that term just defined itself. We asked about the university students who come in one or two days a week, and they said that as long as the teacher makes the learning decision the assistant can sit down and supervise—as if from that point nothing about learning goes on. I have an idea that the children make more of the decisions than anyone else.

TEACH BLACK KIDS KARATE?

Part of what kids learn in this kind of situation is that adults are different, that they're not always men, not always black, not always white. They don't all blow their tops at the same thing. Some of them never blow their tops. Some of them would never like to sit down and read a story; some of them would never like to go on a hike. That's all good to learn. Rather than confusing the kids, I think it sharpens them.

One of our primary considerations is to fight the monolithic system of American society. We still have the goal that people break out of their ghettos, that they grow and pull in other things. Our model of integration says that there are differences, and you don't have to make judgments about those differences. When black kids are bussed into white schools, you have to ask, "What does it mean for a black kid to ride through the ghetto to the suburbs?" I think it is more damaging to him than when he just existed in his little ghetto school. It says that white schools are better, and white kids have learned better things. America is in a time of crisis and we don't know what kind of society these children will have to live in. But we're not retreatist. Someone argued with me that if you want to prepare black kids for what is coming then you teach them karate, you twist them up and make them hate you. But my feeling is that when you give kids self-confidence, when you create an environment where they can learn who they are and develop a certain amount of pride, and where they can learn about the world in a very realistic sense, then no matter what happens in ten years, they'll be ready. They'll have more of a sense of what's happening in our society than other kids. You don't teach people to deal with difficult situations by punishing them. The kids have some positive ideas about what life can be like, and that's the important thing. That's why you can be involved in this school and find it regenerating for you day by day.

TEACHING BLACK KIDS

I think the original issue is still the issue: Is this society going to educate black children or not? When it took the form of bussing, of Head Start programs, a lot of people got off. Now you see Black Power schools run by black communities. If you read the '54 Supreme Court decisions you get a very clear sense of the whole concept of cultural deprivation before the words were even invented. What does culturally deprived really mean? The Negroes clearly have a very strong culture and it has had a tremendous influence on all of American culture. It doesn't mean that their culture is isolated. The Coleman report says that of all classes taken together, the white middle class is the most isolated from other cultures in America. What "culturally deprived" ends up meaning is "not suitable to this white middle-class culture." So integrated schools were pushed and pushed, and eventually, with the coming of the Coleman report, we realized that we had to confront the failure of integration and start to re-examine some of our assumptions.

Given America today, the reason you have a school like the Children's Community is that kids are forced to go to schools, and why not provide the best possible school? Those of us who are running the school see in it a lot of political implications. We think that by creating this radical alternative and working with this small group of parents and kids in creating a model around which we can do other kinds of political activities, we can become a force for change, not just in schools, but in society in general.

YOU SHAVED OFF YOUR MOUSTACHE

Now I'm going to be running for the school board. Issues have to be raised, you know, like teacher certification, all the issues that could close us—they are really at the heart of what is wrong with American education, and you have to choose a time when you think you have enough support in the community and wherever you can get it, you have to last through a campaign where issues are raised like how you run a school, and you try to force some kind of change. As Skip Taube, one of our teachers, has pointed out: "Either you are going to exist as an isolated wonderful little project or you are going to become a threat." Whenever you become a threat you are risking something but you waive that and you decide to risk that at some point and we have decided to do that now.

Running for the board can raise some questions that wouldn't be asked otherwise. For example, people's attitude to our school can raise some really fundamental things. For the most part the people in the education Establishment think that we are, you know, give us that patronizing stuff about nice idealistic kids trying to do a nice thing and under their breath they are all saying, "Oh, it was tried forty years ago and found to be a failure." One was a dean in the education school and we have argued with him for days, and after a lot of talking we of course realized that in fundamental ways we do differ. In fundamental ways he supports the status quo and in fundamental ways we are working for change. I saw him in the street today and he said, "Oh"—with a couple of patronizing asides—and then he said, "I see you have shaved off your mustache," and I said, "Actually, I didn't. It was shaved off in jail at Christmas by the police and I just haven't had the energy to grow it back." And he said, "Oh, I thought you shaved it off because you wanted to win." So obviously, he already knows about the campaign . . .

What happens is you have a bunch of nice people who push for reforms in the schools, the reforms are absorbed by the system and nothing fundamentally changes. Witness what happened to Dewey—that in a lot of ways all his rhetoric, a lot of the forms that he developed were taken into the public school system and yet nothing fundamentally was changed. But I think one of the interesting things about running a school like this is when you start talking to groups of people about the school and about free education generally, and they start questioning what will happen. I mean, is it possible to have a lot of Children's Communities in this country?—and you start to throw that around. And what kind of kids will develop? and will they be able to fit into General Motors and a Ford plant? In evaluating questions like these, people may start to move, politically, at least in their heads. Because it is clear that the school system that now exists does a pretty good job of channeling people into different places, of fitting kids for the Ford factory and other kids for the executive offices, other kids for politics, and academics, whereas our system doesn't do that at all. Our system has, in that sense, a lot of very revolutionary implications because American society couldn't exist with a lot of Children's Communities, or said the other way, a lot of Children's Communities couldn't exist in America.

So around the issue of education, around the issue of what is a good way to treat kids, you can start to raise a lot of the issues about American society and why the political scene is the way it is. I have seen it happen a lot of times in classes, in groups—just that kind of progression, and that is kind of exciting.

Editor's Note:
I saw Bill again in August and talked to him on the phone in early October. Since he made the tape, he ran for the board and was not elected. He feels it was worth

it anyway, partly for the reason he gave in the interview —in public meetings he felt that by holding firmly to his radical position, the other candidates and the audience were forced to be serious about fundamental questions. Even more, he says it was worth having the chance to do some organizing of Ann Arbor high school students and teachers.

Recently he and two other teachers at the school, Diana Oughton and Skip Taube, took part in the Chicago demonstration. He and Skip were both arrested and their trial is pending. "To be young in Chicago was to be a nigger," he says. He tells of one incident when he tried to get into a hotel but was stopped by police. A handsome McCarthy kid, well-dressed, came along and asked to go in and the police were about to let him. The kid grabbed Bill by the arm and said, "He's my friend—we're both going in," and immediately, "The handsome guy became a nigger too and both of us were kept out."

Bill has changed jobs. He is no longer at the Children's Community but is working full-time on various Ohio and Michigan campuses as a regional traveler for the Students for a Democratic Society. He says that for a year now, as the students have become more mobilized, he has questioned whether the school community in Ann Arbor was making the impact on society at large that it should. "Apart from vague vibrations now and then and my running for the Board, I feel we have been too isolated," he told me. "Schools like ours are still very important, especially as student revolt gets nearer to being successful, but I think I can be most helpful more directly as an organizer. Eventually if there's to be a serious revolution in this country there must be an adult movement, possibly built around professions like teaching. But any such movement must be built on the foundation of the student movement. In building this movement, one serious question we're going to be facing—since the country as a whole is moving more and more to the right—is to choose when we must do things which are good for the movement which in the short run are bad for the country. Chicago, for example, drove the country towards Wallace, but it built up the movement. Lots of unpleasant choices will have to be made.

"The Children's Community is in trouble right now. The fire marshall and the building inspector have said that we can't meet any longer in temporary quarters and we don't have the money to buy a building. The school authorities aren't too pleased about this either but they aren't pushing us. It looks as if we may not be able to open this year."

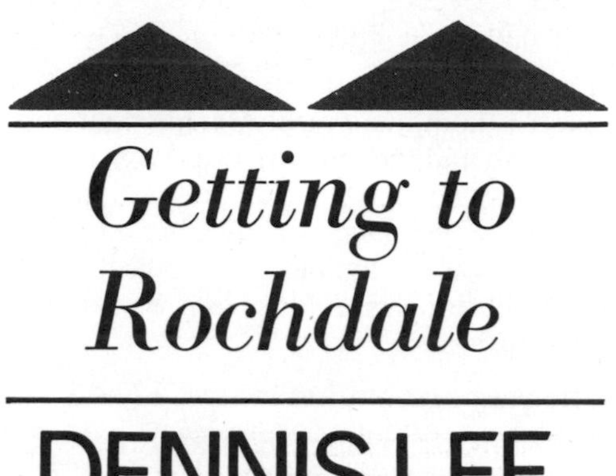

Getting to Rochdale

DENNIS LEE

I. THE LIBERAL DREAM

I REMEMBER sitting in a seminar, upstairs in the cloisters of University College, one overcast day in the autumn of my M.A. year. We were about six weeks into the term. The room was crowded with graduate students and we were listening to two professors of English who were speaking about the movements of twentieth century literature. The subject fascinated me; Yeats I think it was. They were very knowledgeable men, and they spoke well, and I can recall my sense of utter estrangement as I wound my way through the realization that what they were saying had no purchase on me, that the experience of being in that seminar was without meaning for me, that doing graduate work had not become real, and that my entire undergraduate and high school education had been mainly a sham. The room was humming with questions from other students, some were taking notes, some were pushing for recognition by the self-consciously daring leaps of their discussion. This was higher education in the ranking university in English-speaking Canada; and I knew, in the pit of my stomach it was not what education was about. I can still feel the grain of the wood in the table under my hand as I sat waiting, and the sense of a kind of impersonal process by which the people, the words, the situation realigned themselves in a different perspective.

This was no easy recognition for me. I had invested most of my life up till then—I was twenty-three at the time—in academic excellence. And I'd excelled, heading my year throughout high school and university. Moreover, I had broken all the superficial rules as an undergraduate—skipping class, playing games with the examiners, taking years off—but the professors I respected understood what I was fumbling after, that I was trying to play by the rules of the real academy, and they gave me support and were friends. I did far more work than the students who went along with things, and I got the best of both worlds. And I always assumed that the surface of education, which was unaccountably all I could find in the university's version of things, was some kind of an irrelevant intrusion; that you ignored it and got on with what mattered, and in doing so you were in lively cahoots with the spirit of the place. I thought that somewhere in the university—though I would never have said it so naïvely—there must be people who were getting a liberal education. Liberal education had stopped being glamorous for me, since I had gotten into it far enough to know how much of it is dogwork. But that was fine, and I assumed that somehow, somewhere, there were people who were being helped by the university, day by day, in their liberal pursuits.

What I came to in that English seminar, in the fall of '63, was the simple recognition that this class, with its shallow, irrelevant busywork "was" the university. The surface of education, the inessentials of education, the travesty of education was what the university was about. I could get on with what I really cared about, or not get on with it; that was my business. But what the university cared about and insisted on, and gave marks for, was everything that got in the way. Individual teachers and students knew that it was grotesque to have graduate seminars of twenty people, undergraduate classes of a hundred, to set people tearing around the campus for so many hours a week that they never made human contact with one another, to encourage a style of knowing that was clever and cretinous. But the fact that individuals knew this was no longer relevant; their encouragement to the other solitary misfits was generous and humane, but it didn't change anything. And the many splendid minds and imaginations dotted across the staff were almost anomalies; certainly they did not give the wave-length of the education which prevailed. Because, insofar as it professed to be assisting in the day-to-day education of its members, the university was a fraud. And at that point a tremendous resentment welled up in me, resentment that we had jumped through so many hoops for so many years, working at the university for something which the institution did not comprehend and could only surround with barbed wire.

Though I still couldn't articulate it, sitting there removed from the seminar and Yeats, I knew that things made sense from this perspective, the university as a fraud. For when you looked at it as an academy fallen away from its own ideal of liberal education and struggling to find its way back or ahead, it just didn't add up—there was too much that was downright looney. Yet viewed as a different kind of animal, one that had come to manifest a different style of education, a different set of goals, a different ethos, a different logic, different procedures, the university was a thoroughly intelligible place. It merely had little to do with what used to be called "university." It was this shift of focus that had stymied me for so long—the shift to recognizing that the university was functioning quite adequately, but in a different educational universe from the one I thought it occupied. I had kept on asking why no one shot the puck, but it was easy: we were all playing basketball.

The words went on like Muzak in the background, and eventually the seminar was over and we all filed out of the room, down into the bleak Toronto autumn. I didn't feel anything very coherent, but I knew that whatever had been established in those two hours would finally have to be taken into account.

That year I finished the M.A. with high A's, and I taught English literature at the same place for three more years and collaborated again and again with a system which frequently professed its ability to direct students' real education. Sometimes I collaborated by implementing its demands, sometimes by denouncing them along with the students so they could find a pressure release and keep going within that system.

And as I went on supporting the pretense, mainly I guess from a baffled timidity, but also from sheer disbelief, I grew to discover more and more about the internal patterns of compromise. I suppose I can thank the university; it is very chastening knowledge. But I am left with an abiding sense of the grossness of our hypocrisy. It was best summed up for me in the glossy little booklet we gave to incoming students. The one entitled, "Welcome to a Community of Scholars." For it is this sort of lie—welcome to a community of scholars!—which begins by reinforcing the student's undeveloped expectations of the university and himself, and ends by humiliating him internally at his own failure to achieve what hard work was supposed to bring. It is only when he steps outside the zone of the university's version of itself that he comes to himself, he realizes that what it promised him cannot be reached by its methods nor in its spirit. And at that point, I think, he undergoes a double recognition.

The first is a sense of sadness, of compassion even, that the university today cannot possibly come through with what its past and its rhetoric demand, and that so many good men and women are being lacerated there by history. My friends. Myself. It even brings a sense of the perspective from which nothing different could have happened—numbers, technology, democracy—for the decline of the universities has not come about by conspiracy. It is tempting to linger in the inevitability of the inevitable. But we are not talking about the debasing of picnics, nor the abandonment of family bicycling. We are talking about sell-out of the universities, their conversion from places where liberal education was possible though difficult to places where liberal education is discouraged by the temper and method of the university itself. And to acquiesce in that as inevitable when the stakes are so high—I mean, to shrug and give up—can become the coziest way of bartering your remaining self-respect. For those who remain and try to make things better, I have the utmost admiration (though I'm not always sure that they face what they're doing).

The second sense I came to was one of renewed anger, that in the universities' bad time there are so many shallow explainers who can brandish the rhetoric of liberal education—I remind you of "Light for the Mind," or "Welcome to a Community of Scholars"—without an inkling that education has finally to do with the texture and the reaches of our mind and imagination and spirit, and that you do not bandy those things lightly about, or even mention them unless you're playing in that league. And if they are in the process of passing out of existence in the universities, that is the last time to begin reciting this vanishing litany. If there cannot be honest regrets there should at least be silence. That is what there should have been in that English seminar in the UC cloisters—silence, while we M.A.'s and Ph.D.'s and professors contemplated our appalling unfamiliarity with education.

II. THE MULTIVERSITY

So now I begin with a gut disaffection from the university at which I spent ten years, a disaffection which is tempered by the morbid realization that most other universities are as bad off or worse. But while disaffection may be a valid response to the contemporary academy, at least so long as it maintains the pretense of being an academy, a disaffected man cannot continue indefinitely setting out his own critique. Either he pretends to an open-mindedness which he no longer feels, and discusses it all in bad faith; or he simply rehearses the same splenetic indictments on every occasion. At best this becomes a bore, at worse an exercise in self-righteousness.

To put it another way: the convictions which rose from my gut to my head have settled, with some alteration, to my gut again. I have trouble getting at them now; they seem self-evident. Perhaps it would be best if I summarized:

(1) The multiversity is a place where great thought and great research are often possible.

(2) The multiversity is a place from which great contribution can often be made to society.

(3) The multiversity is a place in which the claims of institutional continuity and efficiency come to head-on collision with its educational aims; the latter are normally wiped off the map.

(4) The multiversity is a place in which the education of the vast majority ranges from the mediocre to the pernicious. This fact creates new educational norms which become positive deterrents to the education of any who wish to go beyond the majority. It is for these students—the bright ones, the original or independent ones, the ones who care deeply—that the university is such bad news. It is in the crazy position of obstructing their education.

(5) Education at the multiversity is post-secondary, encouraging the transfer of discreet units of information and theory, rather than liberal, encouraging the contemplation of energizing form in what a student comes to know. And the system of lectures, essay and exams, and the root assumptions of thousands of the university's members, canonize the post-secondary version of education. It is possible to go beyond it, but only by radically dissenting from the university. For the twenty-year-old who does not know what he is dissenting in favor of, this is either very isolating or very undermining.

At this point I think it would be possible to say—in fact I know it would be possible since I've heard the president of my university say it—roughly the following: "Look, you've got a point. Things are not so hot, and they're not going to clear up over night. But I honestly can't see why you're getting so choked up and above all I can't see why you come on with this tremendous sense of having been betrayed. The university is under pressure from society, so it bends. What did you expect—cast iron? But the fact remains that the university is one of the freest institutions left in society; and if you can put up with freshman survey courses and the paperwork, you'll have all kinds of time left for the liberal things you care about. Can you honestly ask for more?"

I raise this case to recognize its weight and indeed its status as a kind of consensus among liberal men in the universities. Let me try to articulate my objections to the liberal justification of the multiversity:

(1) Many of the students who are being processed have little inclination or capacity for the rigors of a liberal education. Fine, but I object to the game of pretending that they would be able to achieve liberal goals within the system we offer if only they tried harder. That is simply not true, and it does bad things to their psyches to encourage them to believe it. It would be far more honest, and I should think more fruitful, to accept most university education as having different aims from the liberal. Once you drop that pretense, in both rhetoric and practice, and you could begin meeting the great bulk of students where they actually are.

(2) Some students at least would be capable of an education far superior to the one the system enforces. They are being positively harmed by their university education, since they have to meet its demands before their liberal (and usually private) pursuit begins. (And before you ask, "Why can't the two coincide?" ask a good student how much of the university's instruction moves him toward the first-hand apprehension of his discipline's coherence and beauty.)

(3) What has been abandoned in the daily processes of education is not something that is peripheral to the university's purpose; it is what the university has professed as its reason for being. But is it really so simple? Do we abandon our reason for being with no more than a regretful shrug? (Many a time in the last four years I have felt like a member of some minor committee who suddenly realizes that the meeting he is dozing through is actually a funeral. He reacts as best he can, letting loose with some ill-timed snivels, and discovers his fellow committee members observing him with tolerant sympathy while they go on matter-of-factly decking out the corpse, unable to see what the fuss is about.)

(4) I resent intensely being told that I at least have more free time to do what I want, even if I have to play mickey mouse games in my working hours to get it. It makes me feel as though I'm being bought off.

(5) In fact, I found that the university had the knack of co-opting much of what I did in my spare time (not to mention the confused effort I put into trying for a more humane and rigorous educative process). Not deliberately, but no less effectively for that. The two compartments weren't watertight the way they were supposed to be.

(6) Furthermore, that bit about freedom for real work isn't true. I shirked most of my institutional responsibility, and I received a great deal of enlightened consideration in terms of courses taught, salary and the like—the fact still was that I "didn't" have a great deal of time to myself and men ten years my senior were practically sending proxies home to dinner or off to the cottage. There is some painful irony here. What's the good of being bought off if all you get is an ulcer?

(7) Finally, whatever the university afforded it did not afford the chance for broad or deep community of the mind. I made some friends at the university but I never found myself—in my working time or in my own time—a member of a group I felt was central to my intellectual, imaginative or spiritual life. I think I was typical.

As these objections came to matter very much to me I had to recognize that the university can only be irrelevant to people like myself. And vice, quite likely, versa.

III. ROCHDALE

What was happening to me during these years was, I was getting radicalized. I still find it a bit comical to swing into the radical lingo, since appreciation of even its point for existing was for so long excluded by the liberal assumptions on which I was nourished. But that's beside the point. Over the last ten years I was getting radicalized, along with many other people. And for some of us now, the attempt to make sense of higher education has come to a focus around Rochdale College.

Rochdale is an experiment in higher education and urban living which opened in Toronto in the fall of 1967. It grew out of the co-operative student housing movement which is very dynamic in Toronto, but it has now become legally independent. I moved along Bloor Street from Victoria College to Rochdale last summer.

At the moment there are some thirty full-time members of the college who come from all over North America, and range from Ph.D.'s to high school dropouts. They are much younger than a cross section of the university, but somewhat older than a cross section of undergraduates. There are another fifty to two hundred part-time participants, mostly students or teachers at degree-granting institutions in Toronto. We occupy six rented houses this year; next fall we'll move into an eighteen-story building which is under construction at the corner of Huron and Bloor. It will house 850 residents who will own and operate the building co-operatively; it will also become a focal point for the college's external members. It is up to each member to determine the extent, form and content of his participation in the college's educational life—including, in a number of cases, none at all.

A governing council is elected by the vote of all members who retain the final say on all major college decisions. The council combines the functions of a board of governors, a senate, and a students' council, since there are not the corresponding distinctions among members of the college. It spends a good deal of time trying to shift responsibility for making and implementing decisions back onto members. This expresses the college's basic assumption, both administrative and educational: the people who make a decision should be the people whom that decision affects, and they should have to live with the results of their decision, modifying it or altering it as they see fit. The principle, of course, is both old co-op and new left.

To get at this assumption more concretely I want to recall an incident—in itself pretty trivial—in the second Rochdale seminar I was at back last September. I had asked people who wanted to work on phenomenology, particularly on Heidegger, to talk in my living room one Sunday evening. (There is no college calendar, at least not in the conventional sense; it is up to the members of the college to define their own educational goals and work out the best way of pursuing them. Thus a seminar, or any other activity, gets started when somebody starts it.) Eight or ten of us were there, trying to piece together a curriculum that would meet our various necessities. Most of us were uneasy about how little we knew but it was an amiable enough evening and we roughed out a common reading list.

About eleven o'clock when things were breaking up, one of the people at the meeting called for an assessment of how we were proceeding. It had been a long night and most of us felt a bit embarrassed—even a bit annoyed—since many had become leery about group narcissism. However, it turned out that Michel wasn't really asking for the scrutiny of souls; he was saying that Peter Anson and I had monopolized the discussion all night and he didn't want us to go on. And he was also saying that his own necessities would be left hanging if we didn't find some way of relating Heidegger or Sartre or whoever to our own ways of being who we were. In effect, that he would feel excluded unless these ten people reopened the question, "What is a seminar?" in very concrete terms.

Sitting in an overstuffed chair in the corner of the room, I felt gathering in my veins a tremendous sense of release. For this, I need to explain. I'm at Rochdale as one of the first year's two "resource people." Everyone involved in setting up the college agreed that this meant nothing beyond people having a desire for us to be there and feeling strongly enough about it that they'd find salaries for us. We were not there as resident experts at large; if we taught anyone anything it would be because we knew something—in whatever sense of knowing—that the other person wanted to know and we wanted to impart. Just as when we learned something from other people, it would be because they knew about it and we wanted to learn. There was to be a shifting teaching-learning role open to everyone, and (apart from the distinction created by salaries) only one status in the college: member.

That was the principle. But it had become obvious even during the summer that we were all pretty edgy about authority, given our past experience in school and society. When is it authentic, when is it merely formal, how many ways are there of deceiving yourself about it? Would Ian Mackenzie (the other resource person) and I start claiming respect because of roles? Or (as seemed more likely) would we get so bothered that we'd balk at gravitating towards leadership in any area at all? And what about other members? How would they react? I think we got paralyzed by all the possibilities.

While Michel was talking that Sunday evening, explaining why the meeting had left him so little engaged, telling me I ought to shut up, I was starting to let go. And I was thinking of all those years in school, at university, the classes and lectures I had sat through, copying words or mouthing words, hopelessly out of the game but unable to challenge the rules. Not because I would be punished but because I didn't know I could—I didn't "know" I could! So I had gone private for years. As we talked out the point, beginning to set our own rules for the education of the people that we were, feeling our way awkwardly towards a viable relation with Heidegger, Sartre, each other, it was a good beginning.

I could speak of other times last fall when people developed new ways of doing things, new things to do; or of the many times we slouched ahead, or simply fumbled around aimlessly. But unless I can convey exactly what Michel's objection meant to the seminar, I will not convey why Rochdale has galvanized the people it has.

In the first place it didn't mean that Michel was automatically right—though as it happens he mainly was. And it hasn't meant that we've jumped to it and started functioning the way he wanted. He didn't know what he wanted any more than we did—not in concrete terms; he only knew what was oppressing him. I still talk too much, as does Peter, and Michel still gripes that we're coasting. But it is now accepted that finding our way—in the coming months, perhaps the coming years—to a seminar mode that works for the people who are seriously committed to it is a normal part of this seminar's project—as it is for other activities.

Normal in that it is what we're doing, and also normal in that it will affect what we understand of Husserl or Merleau-Ponty or Heidegger, just as any other seminar mode would become a mode of knowing. There's no delusion that the answers we find will be unaffected by the form of the questions we ask—including whatever we thrash through to as the format of our seminar. And normal, finally, in that this kind of freedom to explore, which ricochets uneasily from the individual to the group and which can never do more than open up possibilities that remain to be realized—this is the point of Rochdale's existence and the seed of the hope that the model of the academy which the university gives is not the only viable one.

Don't misunderstand me. I do not suggest that seminars which grow with the growth of the members are the only, nor even the main point of the college. (Some people aren't working in seminars at all.) Nor that they are unique to Rochdale. I mean that when we have reopened almost every question, every assumption that underlies the going versions of education, it is this freedom to explore which becomes our reason for being. It is expressed in Rochdale's doctrinaire unwillingness to prescribe or proscribe any activity whatsover as educational for the person carrying it on.

Thus there is no degree, though members can negotiate elsewhere for one if they need it; no institutional curriculum, though members can give or take lectures, seminars, tutorials, make films, agitate on the streets, start construction firms or publishing houses, vegetate; no staff, though anyone can teach; no exams, though anyone can be examined if he can find an examiner; no entrance criteria and no criteria for leaving.

It is not that a permanently unstructured education strikes anyone as a good thing. It is that finding structure yourself to embody your own living necessities, alone or with the advice of people you respect, is the concealed nine-tenths of the educational process. That is the critical dimension, and it is usually presented to students as a containing structure and a *fait accompli*. But at Rochdale, anyone who looks for it from the institution finds a vacuum. And it is by means of this institutional vacuum that the fundamental questions are reopened.

Our experience so far with this principle has confirmed what was obviously true all along: it is possible for some people to get on with challenging work without being motivated by the stuff-and-throttle philosophy which prevails in Canadian universities. It's chancier. But at its best it's vastly more liberating and what is more, it gives scope for far more searching or far more innovative work when people are up to it. For to question authentically is the hardest part of wisdom whether one is questioning with one's mind or imagination or action. And authentic questioning is possible only when the fundamentals are up for grabs.

Needless to say we often respond by burrowing in the sand, because who wants to grow—and when we do start inching ahead it's never with very much savvy or aplomb. We also rediscover things painfully that are taken for granted elsewhere. But none of this lessens the importance of re-opening the questions; nor of coming to see how every item of human knowledge is the result of a decision to ask a specific question, to ask it in a specific way, or to welcome and endure the pathless necessities which bear in on us, or recede from us, when we admit that we do not know what question to ask at all. It is this zone of our education that Rochdale inhabits, for better and worse; this zone which—for me—had begun to settle that Sunday night.

There is a lot to say about what people are doing at Rochdale though three months is too soon for any pronouncements. Some are moving very quickly into specific work; the study of systems theory, or of modern literature or of Greek; development of a ceramics workshop; educational experiments in Toronto slums. A lot of work is going into planning the new building. Some aren't doing much of anything, by conventional standards; this is fine, both because it's their prerogative and because doing nothing can play a vital part in the rhythm of a person's life.

Some are working independently, by necessity or choice; others have found mentors in the college or the larger Toronto community that is in sympathy with Rochdale. Some have gotten pissed off that no one wanted to do what they did, or because no one paid any attention to them at all. These people make me uneasiest because I can't tell when we've done them the discourtesy of treating them like adults, and when we've just been discourteous. Some, I think, have been affronted that what they had been mythologizing in advance as an academic apocalypse turned out to be housed in a series of rather shabby houses, plagued with the usual problems of communication and decision-making, and populated by thoroughly fallible human beings.

But far more important than what we are doing is how we are doing. Not in the sense of success or failure—certainly I know no criteria to judge by at this point. But in the sense of how we are coming to be: what relation we are finding to one another and to ourselves, what ways of getting on we have begun to uncover.

Something happened last summer that has become a kind of model for me of how things can go. When the college started moving into its space, the first thing Ian Mackenzie and I did was to plan for our offices. This seemed eminently reasonable and we were close to having the renovations done when one of the students asked why we needed offices in the first place.

I don't think Ian or I took the question seriously at first; though to be candid, I took it seriously because I thought somebody was sniping at me. After a bit, though, we realized that he was perfectly right. Why should two members of the college have offices to themselves when we are crying for space? And, more important, wouldn't that institutionalize everything we were trying to get beyond—both in other people's responses and in ourselves? Certainly it would. We would set up office hours, we would come and do office work, we would start playing all sorts of roles, not because we felt right playing those roles but because the bloody offices demanded them of us. We canned the idea and instead we've installed a number of desks, with a typewriter and phone, which anyone can come and use (including us) for reading, writing or office work.

Initially, the incident tickled us all because of the brash sanity of the question, and because it helped us to realize some of our ideas about what it meant to be a member of the college. Since then, thinking it over, I've come to see other things as well. They include the way in which our backgrounds—in this case, Ian's and my experience as university lecturers—can make it hard to free up in a more open situation; the way in which a radical response comes most easily as a challenge, an objection, and insistence that something in the "status quo" needs fixing or obliterating; and the way in which this radical reaction, invaluable as it is, gets you not much further than to a different starting point—it does not, for example, give you any clues about what to do in the common space after you've set it up. I'd like to look at each of these aspects, because they seem to me to get at how we are doing. In fact they carry pretty deeply into our ways of getting on. And their real import is not so much a question of experience at Rochdale as of experience in any attempt to make a fresh beginning, to work out a new concrete model of how we might live. What I say derives as much from my limited involvements with the Student Union for Peace Action, the Company of Young Canadians, and the Canadian Union of Students as from the time at Rochdale.

IV. REACTIONARY RADICALISM AND AFTER

My interest in Rochdale has changed a lot since I got involved a year and a half ago. In the beginning I saw it as the place where I could pursue a liberal education in company with people who shared its values. The institution sounded open enough, from what the little band of Rochdale spokesmen kept muttering, that liberal people (like myself, of course) wouldn't constantly have it in our hair. I still hadn't grasped that the only institution would be us.

By "liberal education" I meant any study which liberated a person from unreflecting reliance on the assumptions, structures, models, categories that he had soaked up from his family, school, church, and society. It encouraged him to steep himself so deeply in a discipline—philosophy, say, or economics or theology—that his mind and imagination came to recapitulate the structures and categories and models that inhered in that discipline; at that point his mind had a new order accessible to it—not as an object of study, but of itself—which cast things in a new perspective. And it brought him through the educational processes—I saw them in terms of an idealized Oxbridge education: immersion in the subject, testing conclusions against the mind of a tutor, re-immersion in the subject—by which that initial liberation could be repeated and extended as he pushed into new disciplines, or deeper into one which became his vocation.

I qualified this by saying that I wanted to reunite fragmented areas of knowledge, not so much by interdisciplinary work as by cross-disciplinary work, by which I meant work that would collate the structures inherent in many disciplines and try to arrive at a "structure of structures"; and I qualified that by saying that I wanted to reverse the (bastardized) Cartesian dictum which now rules so much of the academy, *cogito ergo sum,* and make it *sum ergo cogito;* I wanted to set knowing in the context of being and allow the consequent shaking of knowledge's foundations, rather than continue with the existing a-valuative scientism, performing its feats in the limbo of a hypothetically unaffiliated intellect.

I was turned on by Rochdale, then, as a place where people of a particular temperament could do the university's work better than at the university. The first thing I discovered was that everyone else had the same idea, except that it wasn't necessarily liberal education (as I understood it) that was to be foremost. For some, it was individual development. For others it was some form of community. One wanted a base for the liberation of Canada. Several wanted to paint. In each case we agreed that we were unable to do what we wanted elsewhere, but if Rochdale was open we'd get on with it at once.

There's a bit of a caricature. These were pretty aware people, not just roles in search of an environment. Still, to accept us where we were, we began as reactionary radicals: we were largely defined by what we were reacting against. The shortcomings of the mainline institutions had driven us to a root or fundamental rejection, but when it came to building a new institution, all many of us could offer by way of new fundamentals was something that was absent or perverted in the "status quo"—in this case, our discovery of the value of taking a large part in directing our own lives, when so much of our lives is not normally under our own direction. This strikes me as pretty much defining contemporary radicalism, together with one other reactionary value: that of releasing your life impulses directly—of being straight with yourself and with others—in a society where roles often preempt lives. As far as the institution went, this meant that people were often limited to expressing directly the arrogance or mistrust they felt over someone else's attempt to make the institution work. It's a pretty rare case when a committee structure expresses its members' life impulses.

Still these are inestimable values, and beginning to realize them alters your life. Let me give you an example. I differentiated between liberal education, which was a good thing, and liberalism, which in the radical usage is very bad—a shallow, optimistic dedication to method which never raises the question of ends and winds up serving every powerful interest that comes along. But getting to Rochdale made me question whether the liberal education I wanted to pursue and the radicalism which one saw as the base of the institution weren't both shot through with the assumptions of liberalism.

Today liberal education does not consist of apprehending order of knowledge, with theology at its center; it consists of apprehending the order of a discipline. And for reasons which are fairly well understood, though they are too extensive to investigate here, the order which is apprehended is generally conceived to be neutral, a-valuative. I had met this in my own field of literary criticism, but it was in evidence everywhere. There is a noble tradition behind this assumption; but it issues today in a dishonest and shallow pluralism in which the guardians of wisdom themselves disclaim any mandate (or even responsibility) to present truth in anything but its professional sense, yet urge the practitioners and apprentices to engage with the various pretenders to larger truth in an open arena. This is shallow because the possibility of more adequately human truth has already been undercut by this approach, which refers any sense of truth to private needs or traits in the searcher; they need not be engaged during the search for professional truth. But what a view of ourselves! It is dishonest because it tries to mask the intense anguish of this position behind a sophisticated and professional aplomb, which would never discourage the slightly ridiculous pursuits of people whose concern goes beyond the rigorously professional, but would no more be caught talking that language than it would be found at a meeting of the Pentecostals. Because its finest practitioners see knowledge as value-free, then, contemplating liberal education is involved in the central contradictions of liberalism.

The issue which Rochdale raised was this: were we not re-creating a more libertarian version of the same thing, with our attempt to allow people to do what they pleased? If I can write poems and you can do ceramics and John Jordan can read Greek and nobody will ever say us nay, are we not going even further toward making a specious virtue out of our own poverty in the face of the root question, "What is it good to know?"

The first part of the answer is that it's entirely possible that this is what we're up to; or, more to the point, that this may be all we end up achieving—a wider pluralism. For my money that would mean that we'd failed. But I can see how we might go a different route and use what has been instituted at Rochdale in a far different way. In the process we would do more than try to realize some of the university's stated goals that are now unrealized; we would push through to new goals.

Consider the pursuit of wisdom and its application. The multiversity pays lip service to wisdom's pursuit, yet it does not fundamentally believe in it; as a result, it oppresses its best members with the pursuit of method and its poorest with the pursuit of marks. And in its own life, it also pays lip service to the enlightened application of sound insight; yet it allows itself to be governed by businessmen and run by personnel officers while it occupies its academic members at all levels with what is largely busywork.

There are three points where Rochdale might improve on this and challenge the university:

(1) Every member of the college is able to do some rather extraordinary things to keep up his end of the institution. He may be negotiating for millions of dollars of mortgage money; consulting with architects, lawyers, academics, businessmen, artists, on matters that are vital to the college's life; working out the administrative structure of the residence office. People from seventeen to thirty-five are doing these things and often doing them astonishingly well; but that is not the point. The point is that any member has the chance to take a responsible and often a crucial hand in the life of the college. There are real things to do; if he bogs down in mickey mouse work, that's because of his own bad judgment.

(2) The second point is what I have called Rochdale's institutional vacuum. The multiversity makes the same kind of claim, in the sense that the institution does not profess to dispense a truth, "the" truth. But the claim is meaningless because a student's (and teacher's) time is pre-empted by so many arbitrary but inescapable demands that he must either reconcile himself to trying to find nourishment in the kind of truth that is available by these means or get out. For the multiversity to refrain from pushing one version of absolute truth while making absolute truths out of trivia is scarcely something to boast about. (And this is to ignore George Grant's claim that even the multiversity's professed agnosticism is a delusion, and that it has erected the new God of value-free efficiency.)

But if the vacuum is made real, if a member has literally no requirements upon him on entrance, no institutional prescriptions for his education, the situation is potentially very different. The emptiness is now something which actively confronts him, which may in fact enable him to discover the same thing within himself—not accept the rules of a game which lets him spend all his time trying to mask his own emptiness. And at that point if he enters into his own poverty of knowledge and motive and being with honesty, he may learn painfully and at great length how to ask authentically what it is that he should be asking. This is at least one of the routes to wisdom which is open today; for some of us, it is the only one.

The discovery that we can stop finding answers to questions we don't believe in is something a number of people have come to independently, getting to Rochdale. It is liberating, for it enables you to breath deeply again; it's with a delicious sense of bewilderment that people come, full of their long-delayed projects, and gradually realize how little reality those projects have. But as the implication set in it is also terrifying; for after you let go of the projects which are really just tics in your will, you discover that the thing can't stop there: the projects which spring from what you took for your deepest selves are also less than authentic. And you must eventually face the fact that you do not know how to know.

(3) But all this is possible only if we begin to discover our community with one another. Not as chumminess, nor busyness, nor shared malaise, for none of these things stands up very long when someone close begins to explore his own ignorance. It is, I think, my discovery that I stand with you in our mutual ignorance, our mutual quickening yen to be, to know, or at least to question, in a way that we know is for real. This cannot be forced and it can include a great deal of privacy. But without it few of us can move ahead or even endure. It is what I take a community of scholars to be about; and by respecting the void which we share, by laboring together to keep it void and not let it get jammed with irrelevancies, we can begin to appropriate our own mutuality.

If there is something to this, Rochdale could become a good thing: a place for ignorant men, for know-nothings. But it is clear that in the process the assumptions of a person like myself, who has taken liberal education as a norm, must be questioned to their roots and probably undercut. Letting go of those assumptions is harder than letting go of an office, but the two are not separate phenomena.

But if liberal education is called in question, what about the reactionary radical values which struck us as the common ground on which we could do our separate things? Directing your own life and being straight with yourself are beyond reproach, but they are insufficient, they are without content; Gandhi and Hitler both did their own things. How do you tell the difference?

These values by themselves can produce nothing more than a counter-institution: one which replaces a functioning but compromised system with an uncompromised one that won't function. You simply keep cruising for new abuses to object to in a new flurry of self-righteous honesty. In fact, as it works out, reactionary radicalism by itself means the relinquishing of civilization because of the disdain it inevitably feels for slog and rote. If a committee gets to be a hang-up, if you stop feeling it, then screw it—how else can you be honest? And if your life is starting to get wrong vibrations, go make another life somewhere else. (I mean this as a pattern, not just as an act.) This has its own nobility just as it has its own naïveté; but one result is that any commitment running beyond a few years at the outside, and any project in which more types than the rootless middle-class radical are to participate centrally, stop being viable. The purest reactionary radicals I know are poised between nihilism and insanity; one I know is becoming a hermit. None believes in the project of civilization—and I mean as project, not as "status quo."

But it still is not that easy. For even if we courageously accept the impossibility of the civil and social, in any form but ones we refuse to collaborate with, our friends and lovers remain, and it is terrible how easily the reactionary radical in me becomes a shifty, lacerating man who is selectively candid and so busy being human that he cannot stop to be humane. On this route lie the pathological excesses of radicalism. Our necessities become apocalyptic, and the normal play of sell-out and integrity in someone close—or in ourselves—becomes the occasion for another absolute purge. What we say does not stop being true; but our lives stop being true, which is far harder to face, and in the name of openness to live we can become shrill, death-ridden people. Yet there is a fierce integrity in this; and if we surrender the knowledge that we're responsible for our lives, that we have to be honest and that nothing in life can be adequately charted in a plan or a system, what is there left that isn't undercut? Our shared inauthenticity.

As we moved beyond the naïve identification of our own goals with those of Rochdale, then, we got into deep water. Creating the college was not the same thing as pursuing the individual goals we began with (though the two are not separable); we had to keep re-creating the vacuum out of which people could claim their own freedom by their educational decisions. But the new-left model of freedom means that something like a mortgage payment can become a metaphysical freak-out, and community a kind of cannibalism; while the traditional co-op model of freedom seems to be so mesmerized by voting majorities and efficiency that it never gets to the important questions at all.

How create a radical institution? My own answer is that we can come to share the experience of impoverishment and detachment, that we can discover the mutuality of our ignorance and our inauthenticity; and that because this ground is really common—it is not something we have to persuade ourselves of—we can build upon it. But this is not everyone's way, and it is more likely that Rochdale will take its basic direction from people who aren't as deeply skeptical of our knowing as myself. It also seems likely that bureaucracy as play, rather than bureaucracy as outcome of detachment, is for most people a more viable resolution to the issues of structure and organization that we've come to. Hence the aspects of Rochdale that interest me most—the institution as vacuum, for example—will not necessarily be dominant, though they'll be constantly accessible. This strikes me as a sane arrangement.

I think often of Christ's advice to his apostles, that they were to be as crafty as serpents and as innocent as doves. Not because I know a way of being both, but because I have not heard better advice for living in the world. Along with the Hindu dictum—everything matters, nothing matters. It is not a question of reconciling positions taken by different people—the radicals with their aggressive innocence, the liberal bureaucrats with their uncomprehending know-how. That is sometimes the only way to tackle the problem because most of us allow ourselves to be defined by one or the other position, particularly when a decision must be made. But the deepest way through is for us to make the acquaintance of both strains in ourselves, and of the many others that jostle with them; and, with a sense of humor that only angels are reputed to have, to live our way through the blitzes and shack-ups that ensue as they come together. We don't need a reconciliation of personality types, we need a deeper exploration of who we are and how we can be together. Of our bafflement before the question, "What is it good to know?" it is only if we can grow to the measure of that question that we will be able to create the institution. That is where I take us to be at Rochdale now, inching into the early stages of that exploration, though I do not suppose that we know where we are going nor that we have any qualifications for being where we are.

I write down words, and they fix one set of confusions as a norm. And I don't know what to do with such norms, particularly those of my own making. But I do know that our concrete inquiry—how can we create an academy we will respect?—has become as important as anything else we are doing, in our education. And far from being lethal (though they are very wearing no matter how we understand them) the fissures and tensions that rise become a kind of celebration. Not in the short run, because some of them are stupid and we feel silly even the next morning. But the discovery that we can push into questions which we don't even recognize at first, and live in them as they start to take shape around us and exert their pressure on our lives is at a profound level exhilarating.

It's clear that Rochdale has found its way to issues which it hasn't even raised properly, let alone resolved. But that is token that there "are" questions to reopen, sometimes with great risks, and that those risks will never stop being our life contexts until the questions are denied. Which is why I find Rochdale a good place to be.

—November 1968

PART III

THE INSTITUTIONAL PUT-DOWN

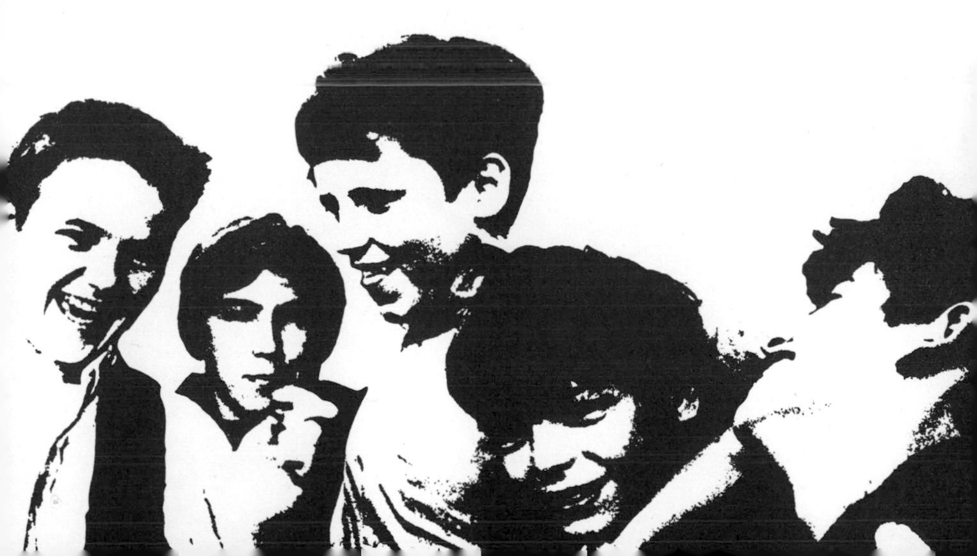

ELECTRONICS AND THE PSYCHIC DROP-OUT

Marshall McLuhan

THE MOVEMENT IN EDUCATION during the past fifty years or so has been a movement towards specialization, each expert burrowing in depth into a particular segment of knowledge. Today all this has changed. Specialization won't work any more as a means of learning. The only technique today for obtaining depth is by interrelating knowledge, whether it be in physics or anthropology or anything else. When a man attempts to study anything, he crosses the boundaries of that field almost as soon as he begins to look into it. For example, in physics in the last decade big discoveries have all taken place by benefit of biology and the models of structure borrowed from other areas altogether different from physics.

Information not hardware. Under present-day electronic conditions the total human environment becomes made of information. The electronic bomb, for example, is almost pure information. In terms of hardware it only weighs a few ounces, but the whole power of the thing and its whole relation to mankind is informational circuitry. They represent the real strength and the real power of our time. The moving of information has become the task and the occupation of almost all of mankind, whereas a scant fifty years ago most men were engaged in making and conveying hardware hither and thither or across national boundaries. At the same time, information levels have risen spectacularly and the amount of information needed to conduct oneself in the most ordinary jobs has risen tremendously. It is that that causes education to become appreciated and enormously stepped up in its scope. One way of testing this is simply to look into the matter of how much research and higher education is considered normal in the business world today or in the military establishment. Ten times the money is being spent on higher education inside the business and military establishments compared to the community at large. And there's no ideal behind this, no educational goals whatever, simply a pressure of daily need and urgency.

Small children can now do top level research. Now this has some strange implications for the community at large. One of them is that higher education is going to be forced downward into the elementary schools. In other words, we're going to have to re-program the whole of our educational establishment for discovery rather than for instruction. Instruction is something that will have to be taken for granted under the new conditions of electronic information and movement. We have to realize that more instruction is going on outside the classroom, many times more every minute of the day than goes on inside the classroom. That is, the amount of information that is embedded in young minds per minute outside the classroom far exceeds anything that happens inside the classroom in just quantitative terms now. And this is going to increase enormously. In the future basic skills will no longer be taught in classrooms. They can be taught by gramophone records or by tape records or video tape playback machines. When video tape becomes available to the ordinary household as it will shortly, there will be a revolution in education comparable with that which took place with the coming of the printed book. As long as education depended upon access to manuscripts, it was a very slow and painful process. With the coming of the portable, privately owned, printed book, the whole educational process took on a new character. This is going to happen with video tape machines, because it means then that anybody can have top-level surgeons, biologists, physicists, philosophers, poets—anything for his own private use on all subjects and at his own time, his own leisure and in his own space.

That is why all the talk about instructional aids in the classroom from electronic means is nonsense. You cannot introduce electronic forms into the classroom without rescheduling the whole process of instruction, and this is impossible under our unwieldy, fragmented conditions of classroom use. But we're on the verge of a complete decentralization of instruction.

Children and adolescents a backward country of the mind. As the levels of information rise in the total community, it means that very small children have access to very high learning indeed. And as the whole community becomes structured environmentally by information and knowledge and circuitry, it means that quite small children can do top level research by team methods co-operatively. Robert Oppenheimer has been saying for years that there are small children playing here on this street who could solve some of his top problems in physics because they have modes of perception which an adult has lost a long time ago. This awareness of the perceptual modes that enable people to participate in various types of high level research as much as anything they could be taught or anything they could learn instructionally, is only beginning to filter through. Edmund Bacon, for example, the head of the town planning commission in Philadelphia, a few years ago became world famous overnight when he enlisted the aid of the elementary schools in solving some of his top problems in town planning. He got children in the early grades to study the plans for Philadelphia and to discuss them among themselves and their parents and neighbors, and to study their communities physically and geographically, and they came up with some of the top solutions to the whole problem. It is clear that we are just beginning to recognize that children and adolescents are a kind of backward country of the mind that's been deliberately suppressed for centuries in our Western world. They are now an underdeveloped country that have to be brought into the picture. It means educationally, of course, that our whole system of grading is useless in the schools. Because if you live in a community where the information levels are very high—just in the sense of the amount of data moving on the radio and TV and movies and so on—then the idea that you should use your school system as a means of eliminating half or three quarters of the community from higher education is ludicrous.

Mere literacy won't do any more. The task of community education ought to be to lift the entire community up to the level of the technology the community is using. Otherwise the whole society collapses. The only reason that we ever had universal literacy was quite simply that the industrial tycoons demanded that the labor market be flooded with people who could read and write. And the military likewise demanded that the entire population be able to read and write so that they could be available for military service.

What we still call a backward country is an area where most of the population is illiterate. That means that we cannot lay our industrial hands on them: they are immune to our manipulations. As soon as they can read and write they are completely in our grasp. We can do anything with a literate population that we want, whereas an illiterate population is relatively immune to our type of operations. On the other hand it is not free from the atom bomb, which is pure information that has become environmental—and can affect any area and culture on the globe.

But in our world where our typical environments are now made of information, and high level information, mere literacy won't do any more. We now have to teach literacy on many levels; pictorial and electronic forms of knowledge have to be imparted in order to enable people to live and work. Automation will wipe out the narrow specialist: a machine will be more effective in storing information and making deductive calculation on the basis of it. And this will have a profound impact on the educational system.

The psychic drop-out is probably 100%. Canada is still almost entirely a nineteenth-century country. It has very little relation to the twentieth century. Its educational system is anachronistic: students are still being processed through the old fragmented specialist chopper, and they might as well be on a carousel or a merry-go-round in some entertainment park. Our youngsters at school are reacting to this, and dropping out of school is one response. The youngsters coming out of a highly integral electronic environment go to school and are confronted by a fragmented, specialist environment of subjects and hours and instructions which baffle them. They know that this form of fragmentation does not correspond in any way to the world they're living in. They've already been deeply imbued with this new electronic world from the cradle, from the time they begin to look at TV. When the school fails to make sense of their environment, they drop out, either physically or psychologically. The psychic drop-out far outnumbers the physical drop-out which also is on the increase. The psychic drop-out is probably about 100 per cent.

The failure to relate one's needs and one's actual environmental structure to any educational procedures is something that can happen only during periods of very rapid change. And we live in a period of such a rapid change that change itself has become the only form of stability we know. We relate everything to the fixed point of change. An educational system that tries to hold a line is making the Maginot Line mistake. What happens to Maginot Lines is that people ignore them and go around them. The drop-outs are just people who are going around the Maginot Line of our educational system, looking for some other source of entry into the territory of their times.

An age of feed-back . . . an age of involvement. We have to become aware of the fact that the whole effect of electronic technology is to bypass our older mechanical, fragmented ways of organizing society. We have moved suddenly from the age of the wheel to the age of the circuit. Whereas the wheel merely conveyed materials and data, the circuit interrelates and is a thing of feed-back. From an era of transmission we move into an age of feed-back which is also an age of involvement.

Now, when I'm talking about involvement, I'm not talking about ideals. I think that sort of visualizing of distant goals belongs to a much earlier period. When you are deeply involved and participate in the life of your time, you don't have goals. The man who is involved doesn't have ideals. A mother does not have a job; she has a role, she has about forty jobs at once and she doesn't have any ideals whatever. She is thoroughly involved. It's like a man and his hobby; he doesn't have any ideals about his hobby; he is involved in it. Anybody who is involved in what he's doing doesn't have any goals or ideals whatever; he's just with it. He's doing something that takes every ounce of his energy.

Instead of a specialist job, people now have to go back to roles in depth in all levels of work and employment and study and knowledge.

A probe, not a package. Education on all levels has to move from packaging to probing, from the mere conveying of data to the experimental discovering of new dimensions of experience. The search will have to be for patterns of experience and discovery of principles of organization which have universal application, not for facts. An example of this, if you like, is the psychopathology of everyday life: every child now understands the patterns of the Freudian slip—this is a probe, not a package. In some circles this is called "mature learning," a learning for discovery rather than mechanical learning. This kind of learning, in the end, has nothing to do with an age level: there is nothing to stop small children from becoming very adept experimenters, graduate probers, explorers. It is the orientation of the society that matters, and our whole world, in shifting from the old mechanical forms to the new electronic feed-back forms, has already shifted from data packaging to probing of patterns.

What the Schools Do

EDGAR FRIEDENBERG

WHAT DO SCHOOLS REALLY DO? If you watched them, as a very, very intelligent Uganda native of the eighteenth century might watch a dynamo, would you say that they were in the society for the purpose of doing something you thought was desirable?

In the first place, under what circumstances do we have schools?

Look, for example, at the New York City teachers' strike. One of the most extraordinary aspects of the strike, it seems to me, is that fact that according to the press reports there was almost universal consensus among the people of New York City that some dreadful emergency had arisen because the schools were closed. Now as the teachers' strike continued, the garbage collectors also went out on strike, and that *is* an emergency: you don't notice the change very rapidly, but ultimately you can't get down the street any more and then you really do have to make other arrangements. The police were also on strike, and that is a situation that has, after all, the qualities of its defect. What people did was lump the strikes together, believing that the police, the garbagemen and the schoolteachers ran institutions which had not only legitimate, but also indispensable, purposes. Thus for all the strikes there was great urgency to settle.

With the school strike, the urgency of settling became as great as it did because nobody thought to ask, "Look, what do these schools do anyway besides baby-sit?" And if we can't get along without that for a while (which may be true in a society so organized that both parents have to go out to work to have a decent living) then you ought to look at that situation instead. However, instead of asking this question, the city went ahead and endorsed the teachers' assumption that education is something cumulative, that each day missed in school was a slice off the child's learning life. If you think back to the moments at which you learned relatively important things in your life, you'll find that the things that are, let us say, of grade B importance on the usual scale of twenty-six you learn in about a second. And the things that are of grade A importance, of course, you don't even know you know; you couldn't even say when you learned them. The notion of the cumulative effects of educational routine, however, is rooted deep: you should never miss a day.

The question immediately arises: Why so much concern about the effects of cumulative education if the important things in life are known outside this process? What do the schools really do?

In the first place, let's remind ourselves that the school is a relatively new kind of institution. At least a school which is supposed to include any very large proportion of the population is a relatively new kind of institution; but I don't think I have to modify the first statement that much. In the U.S. in 1870—with the Kalamazoo decision—there wasn't any question of compulsory attendance at high school. The only question was whether you could pay for it out of public funds for the people who had the money and the marks to go. Obviously, there have been other social changes that make the high school a more . . . here I hardly know what to say . . . I started to say a more useful institution, but if you're an elephant obviously you need a trunk, but this doesn't mean you have to be an elephant.

Let's say that social evolution has developed in such a way that the society certainly wouldn't work without wide-spread public compulsory education. There is no large industrial society, whether in the free world or in the Eastern world, using the conventional designations for these, that can get along without compulsory school attendance. They all seem to have agreed on a fairly similar number of years' limit on the age range.

The question is then, what do schools do that requires compulsory education? That requires cumulative education? What are their social functions?

1

The most important social function of the schools, it seems to me, is in defining *youth as a social role*. I would like you to consider what that may really mean. We generally think that youth is a natural category. There aren't any natural categories, however. There really are not *any*. I mean, if you are reasonably comprehensive in your survey of anthropology, you will find that even the living and the dead do not constitute for all societies, all cultures under all circumstances, two distinct categories or groups. In fact, with a different view of the supernatural there may well be little attention paid to the distinction. Obviously, a corpse presents certain practical problems, but they are not insuperable. The transition may be looked on as something having very little significance in the relationship of what we would call the survivors and the persona of what we would call the departed. The difference between men and women seems to be relatively more stable, but by no means always certain. The difference between races, however, is notoriously artificial. There are no Negroes in any part of Africa except Liberia and The Union of South Africa; for the rest of it there are black people who become Negroes if they fly to New York.

Youth is very much the same thing, and one reason that youth is youth is because (as with black people) it is subjected to certain specific, invidious, legally institutionalized distinctions, of which the school is the major source.

For example, since the war between the States, in my country, it has not been unlawful simply to be anywhere because you are black. But this is obviously not true of young people either in Canada or the United States. It is an offense to be anywhere but in school during school hours. Since it is an offense, you can be and will be apprehended, and you can be sent away to what we call a Juvenile Hall or Detention Home; the names vary. At any rate, there isn't any way you can hang loose. This isn't true of any other element of the population. It has even been elaborated in some jurisdictions in the States in ways that still astonish me. What compulsory school attendance does is to define young people as a subject category, and puts on both their movements and their perceptions certain kinds of restrictions which no one else is subject to at all. It does so, moreover, in a way which is remarkably total since even a veritable Samson has not the strength to grow out his hair within two hours between three and five in the afternoon when he may want to pursue some activity among his own peers, for which long hair is a desideratum.

The schools manage by virtue of manipulation of the authority invested in them by the education code. In other words they usurp or intrude upon their students' life space—not just his time in school—and this action they justify. In Canada this action is likely to be justified as character building. (I get this impression from talking to a group of Ontario school principals—a rather less hostile group than I often get in the States because they were so confident; *This Magazine* published an account of the conversation a little while back.) In some ways the States is getting a bit more liberal and the explanation of character building doesn't go down well in a society as heterogeneous as ours. It would have thirty or forty years ago, but there have been a few court decisions on the question, and American schools are not supposed to go around building your character without your consent. They have to say that long hair is so distracting that it interferes with the educational function of the school. The wife of one of the students who came with me to Buffalo from California, and who is now teaching in the schools of a lower middle-class suburb of Buffalo, had the odd experience of having the principal come into her room a few days ago and ask her to search a young girl. The principal said he was being distracted beyond his capacity to perform his duties by the fact that somewhere on her person this girl had a bell. She knew she wasn't supposed to wear a bell at school, so she put it under a sweater or something; but he could still hear it tinkle. It was found and confiscated.

It is reasonably clear that the hegemony of the school situation is really a good deal grayer than it would be if it was only a place to which you go of your own choice because you want to learn something you are curious about or that is useful to you for purposes of your own. Once you put it in the context of your being the client (society supporting you in this definition of your own role) then it seems obvious that education takes on a totally different function than defining a social role for youth.

2

The second major function of the schools, one which is obviously related to the first, is the legitimization of a form of economic discrimination. The best piece of writing on this subject is by John and Margaret Rowntree in an article called "The Political Economy of Youth." It's in the May 1968 edition[1] of another Canadian journal that competes with *This Magazine* and is somewhat older, called *Our Generation*. (It is published in Montreal under the guidance of an editor with the formidably bilingual name of Demetrios Roussopoulos.) I very strongly recommend this article to you. It is a cool, clear analysis of the way what the Rowntrees call the "education and military industries" make use of the role definition of people below twenty-five as young. Their arguments seem to be directed to the workings of capitalist society, although I think they can be equally well applied to the industrial societies of the East.

The main thing the school is supposed to do for children is to guide them in investing in their own future. Once you get people to agree to this then you can avoid the question of having to pay students for what is, after all, a form of involuntary servitude. By assuming that what goes on in school prepares young people to earn more money and have higher social status in the future, you can get out of any implication that they ought to be paid

[1] Vol. 6, No. 1 and 2.

for the labor of doing it: the school, the argument goes, is already contributing to what the students are laying aside, if you regard their higher income as a return on capital investment; and what else could a good North American regard a higher income as? This makes everything perfectly just and okay.

However, pieces begin falling off the above little model as soon as you begin turning it around so you can look at it closely.

Now all the books on the subject of income, status and schooling, even the relatively sophisticated ones, will say that one thing about schooling is that it does indeed assist you in getting a higher standard of living; it contributes to social mobility; it is necessary if you are going to get ahead in the world. The best of the books may be rather wry about that and say, "Isn't it a shame that our traditional cultural faith in education seems to come to so little in comparison to the nitty-gritty issues of everyday life, and we wish people really were interested in ideas, but maybe we can't expect that. . . ." Yet once you've shown a tight correlation between the number of years of schooling completed and the average income for the rest of your life and particularly, of course, for the highest level of income achieved, what have you really proved?

What you've proved, it seems to me, if you've proved anything, is the existence of a conspiracy. Because you are faced on the one hand with a very widespread agreement that you are not going to hire people who don't have the credentials, and on the other hand, if you don't hire people who don't have the credentials you'll never find out if they could have done the job or not, with no alternative ways of earning the credentials on the job. Increasingly we have no way outside the school system of legitimizing participation in the process of growing up, much less getting a license for a trade everyone agrees you need a license for.

What we need to justify educational participation is not the correlation of higher income to higher levels of schooling, but rather some direct indication of where or what the skills really are that enable a person to make it through life, and to what extent the school does in fact contribute to learning these skills. Further, if there are such skills, and there is no other place than school to get them, that still does not really prove that schools are the best method of passing on these skills. In fact, the argument that schools are the only channels for opportunity in American culture is a little bit like the argument that David would have made a suitable and pious husband to Bathsheba. There is still the question of his complicity in Uriah's fate and whether there would not have been something even better available except for what he did. In this case it isn't the schools themselves that provide the economic and social rewards, but then, in the biblical story, David isn't the murderer either. He's simply the influential administrative official.

If this were not enough to weaken the argument for schools as places for getting ahead, there is the fact that the statistics are interpreted in a kind of phony way. In the first place, most of the arguments linking higher incomes and schooling are directed toward high school, concentrating on those who have or have not completed high school. The data for completing high school includes everybody who completed high school, which means people who go on and get university degrees. When you look at those who completed high school and didn't go on to college and those who didn't complete high school the difference in earning potential isn't very great. It averages out to something like an extra $20.00 per month for those who completed high school; not enough probably to make up for the aggravation.

Of course, you can say, "Yes, but we think everyone should go to college, and you can't do that unless you go to high school." But then you are faced with a couple of other things that a reasonably bright lawyer would raise in countering such an argument in a court of equity. You see, the financial value of a high school degree was great only at a time when the high school degree was relatively scarce and was a symbol of an elite position. So again we do not know that it was the high school education that caused the higher income. All we can say is that the people in the top 10 per cent of the society, with the resources to not earn money and go to school, are likely to earn more money over the long run than those who didn't have the resources and didn't go to school. Further, when education becomes universal, everyone going to college, then it's possible that its fiscal utility will diminish; this seems, in fact, to be what does happen. You can't, I think, use any part of this argument to conclude anything with certainty except that the schools are a sentinel. They provide the check points along which you progress.

From the point of view of the corporations, however, the schools do perform a useful function: they instill or induce you to develop certain characteristics which are marketable, the kind of characteristics that allow you to work comfortably within the corporation. Of course, if you have a mind to, you can then argue that this means that the schools constitute a subsidy for so-called private enterprise provided by the tax-payers' dollars. So maybe students ought to get paid much earlier, and by the people who use them.

3

I think probably in order to understand the relationship between our corporate society, our schools, and our students in a general way—as to how schools do what they do—there is no better source than the sage of Toronto and two of his most familiar aphorisms.

In the schools, more than in most of the other mass media, it is indeed true that the medium is the message, which is one reason I haven't said a word about curriculum. What is taught isn't as important as learning how you have to act in society, how other people will treat you, how they will respond to you, what the limits of respect that will be accorded to you really are. What the schools teach is the experience of being a school child, and once you get used to that it's unlikely you will run amuck among the inhabitants of Yorkville.

The other McLuhan point that seems to me to provide an even deeper source of insight is the observation that we don't know who discovered water, but we're pretty sure it wasn't the fish. What I mean by this is that the schools, by providing a continual social substrate—a kind which is, in effect, a caricature of the society—makes the society seem so natural that you don't notice the awful things that it does. In fact, even your ways of fighting the school are determined by what it teaches you to regard as propriety—or obscenity—whichever you happen to want to employ. In any case, it's essentially true that what the schools do is teach you how "it's spozed to be," particularly in a liberal democracy, where the schools embody the society's central contradictions.

In America, for example, we have a written constitution to which the first ten amendments constitute the Bill of Rights. Most states have laws—laws made before the Supreme Court went over to the "communists"—that compel you to teach the constitution. However, if you learn the constitution in the American public school system, you certainly are not going to go around thinking that the Bill of Rights applies to you. There has been a little research study, as a matter of fact, on what children really think the pledge of allegiance to the flag means, and there was a very wide divergence of opinion. A master's degree student, who was more imaginative than most, simply went around and asked children to tell him what the pledge said, to repeat it for him. The nicest result, I think, was: "One nation indivincable, with liberty and death for all." We have been trying to fulfill that promise all right, but when it comes to promises, say of freedom of speech in situations in which it creates real social disruptions, we've been less than careful in keeping our word. I don't want to put down the quite remarkable and creditable degree of freedom of speech in the United States in the sense that you are unlikely to be subjected to official sanctions for anything that you say. The point is that the function of the school is to teach you about the unofficial sanctions, to prepare you for the blacklist, to make sure you understand the implications of being labelled a "trouble-maker," which is the worst thing a school can call you.

The schools perform this kind of function, it seems to me, in a society that is lying about its traditions. A nicer way of putting it is to say the society still honors or likes to draw from components of its tradition that are nobler than it can in fact hope to institutionalize in everyday practice. But it still comes out lying.

One of the reasons this has happened is that we have included into the social process, with some degree of influence, people who would in an earlier, more conservative organization of society, been déclassé and non-voting. Here, I think, we are at the heart of the matter. The schools have succeeded in becoming mass organizations, serving a much larger proportion of the population, and are as bad as they are because of their response to this process. The problem is not that they are serving people now who have less ability than before, but that they are serving people who in earlier days were treated by decision-makers as victims. When a society becomes more democratic and no longer feels comfortable about treating people as victims, yet still retains essentially the same exploitative social arrangements, then it has to create institutions that will induce people to choose to be victims. Choosing out of anxiety or out of a lack of sense of what their own resources might be or out of a realistic sense that they might not be smart enough to be rulers if they don't choose to be victims.

In the most general terms then the schools, like the society, hold in tension the contradictions of the liberal tradition as it grew out of British and later, American society. They emphasize both the individual and the sanctity of getting rich, and so they obscure moral issues and at the same time tend to favor continual enlargement of the ingroup.

There is real conflict, it seems to me, between provision through the school of increased economic opportunity and the support of cultural values that might treat all people more generously. The schools have been set up to avoid this conflict, although lately they don't seem to be having so much success. A serious polarization seems to be happening in America, for which I am glad, but then I'm not a liberal. The schools have tried to evade this polarization by defining the difference between the rich and the poor, not in terms of their relationships to the means of production and the consequent real conflicts of interest, but rather in terms of cultural deprivation. They take the sting out of this deprivation by making the authority of the things that really are associated with what is left of high culture so tenuous and so ridiculous that there wasn't much left but the implication that, of course, you must learn this culture just as you have to learn to put on a coat and a tie and comb your hair and have it short, because otherwise you won't get a job. Thus not having this culture doesn't have to mean you're inferior to anyone else. Now, it seems to me that a more valid human message would have been that you have the right to dress in a way you think becomes you, but no matter how you dress, it may indeed be true that you are inferior to other people. And this inferiority may be a consequence of experiences that happened so early and that were so intense that they will never be reversed. No school can be magical. There will be some things that you don't understand, that you will never understand, that certain kinds of schools could help certain other people understand if you would shut up. You have been permanently deprived of something that is of inestimable value.

The possibility of such deprivation we can't face up to. We are very suspicious of the cultivation of the kind of subtlety that builds only on antecedent association, very suspicious of going off with a few people to explore meanings that might be private, letting these people select themselves. You get everyone up-tight if you form a self-selected group to talk about issues of importance to you. In American society this is a real violation. The whole thing is set up with the schools as a prime part of it, to keep anyone from fearing that there may indeed be a hidden treasure that they aren't going to find. As a result, it may have been destroyed, at least the one that came down through high culture.

The kids, on the other hand, aren't buying this loss and are rebuilding other modes of communication. Here we get into the best of folk-rock, the sound of groups that are communicating private experience. They are put down as hippies because the experience has to be private rather than political. Yet it is privacy that is being destroyed, not isolation. What we have increasingly lost is our social right to do our own thing with our own kind of people. Society's institutions are there to stamp it out. The result is that new forms of personal experience have to come in from areas that are not legitimized. If they were legitimate, they would be seized and democratized. It can only be done the other way—by working with materials which were assumed to be of no value until they are finally noticed, and one hopes that it will take years as it did in the case of the Beatles. With them it was finally noticed that

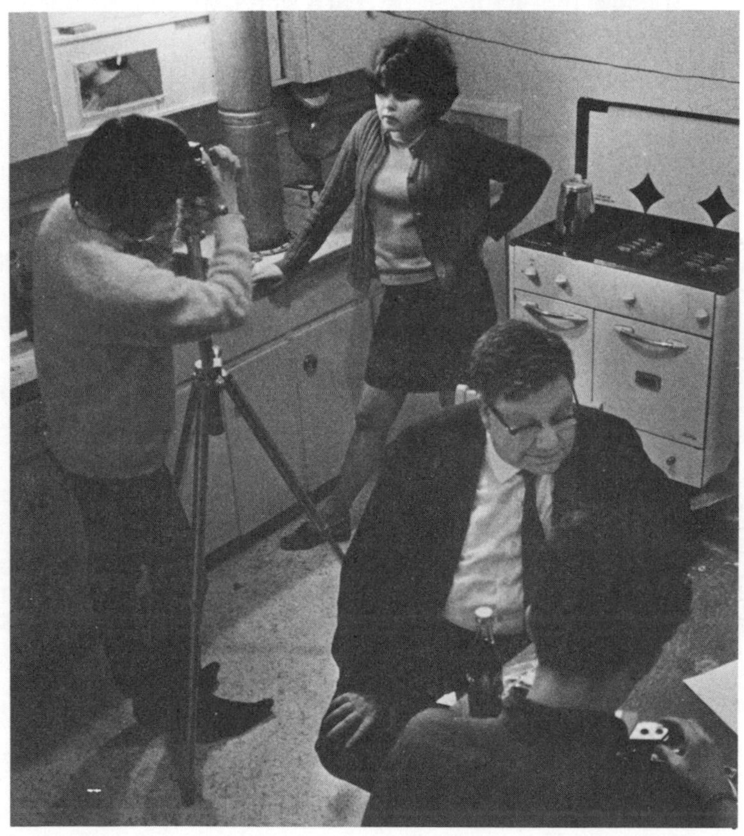

there were enough people who shared their illicit longing for subjective communication to make someone rich. At that point the thing falls into the commercial pile and you have the Maharishi appearing, Brian Epstein committing suicide. In this way Western Civilization is carried on.

THE PSYCHIATRIST: A Policeman in the Schools

THOMAS SZASZ, M.D.

> We are full of scruples but have no ethics. This is especially true in the intellectual world, where scientific investigators, teachers, medical men, psychiatrists, pollsters, purveyors of tests, surveys, and news, commit with internal impunity breaches of faith and acts of indelicacy which in another age would have brought private shame and social ostracism.
>
> —JACQUES BARZUN

I

THE PUBLIC SCHOOL system is one of our major social institutions. Like all such institutions, it is the repository of certain kinds of social force deployable for social action, and also a powerful vested interest.

The aims and functions of this institution are of two

kinds. First, in common with other large-scale bureaucracies, Parkinson's law is at work: the institution seeks to enlarge its size and scope by increasing its personnel, its budget, the range of its services, and so forth. I shall not be directly concerned with this aspect of the problem. I mention this characteristic of large institutions here to help explain why they rarely reject opportunities to expand, even if doing so jeopardizes their primary functions. In the case of the public school system, this has meant that school boards, administrators, and teachers have generally embraced the "help" offered them by psychologists and psychiatrists.

Second, there are the socially acknowledged and codified aims and functions of the schools: to teach and to socialize. In our society these are largely antagonistic to each other.

II

Is there evidence for this view? Or shall we rather assume—or assert, as many do—that these are not two functions but one, two faces of a single coin?

Personality development is a complex biological, cultural, social, and personal affair. The kind of personality an individual develops depends partly on the kinds of values his family and his society cherish and despise—by word as well as by deed. The kind of personality modern western man has grown to value in the last few centuries is embodied in the religions, laws, morals, and customs of this civilization: it is a person, adequately socialized, but possessing an authentic individuality. However, the precise proportion of the two ingredients necessary for a suitable balance is variously defined; and, regardless of the proportion, the achievement of such a balance is an exceedingly delicate task. This is why the concept of a "normal man"—or, more generally, of life as a well-executed dramatic production—is so elusive.

We must therefore try to be clear about the nature of the conflict between teaching and socialization. Of course, children are instructed in what society expects of individuals; in this sense, the process of socialization is part of teaching and learning. But this is trivial: what else could socialization be but an instructional enterprise? Moreover, teaching that does not go beyond socializing the pupil is better called indoctrination. In other words, only the simplest, psychologically most unsophisticated kind of teaching aims at socialization. In this type of teaching the student is required to imitate: the final aim is a performance that reproduces a standard model. A child may thus learn to use English words, or to eat with a fork, or to control his bladder. Though such learning is essential, it is by no means representative of the scope of education. On the contrary, the broader aim of education is not so much socially correct performance as creative innovation with its own fresh standards of value. Particularly from the early teens onwards, the more serious and sophisticated the teaching, the more likely it is to create diversity rather than homogeneity among the students.

Nor is this the end of the process of education. The highest ideal of the teacher is nothing less than *subversion*. (I use the term advisedly, and with intentional precision.) This is not a new idea. Great teachers—from Socrates, through Jesus and Luther and Spinoza, to Marx and Freud and Gandhi—were all critical and, in this sense, subversive, of the existing socio-ethical order. To be sure, they were not nihilists: their subversion was but a proximal goal, or a means, to a distant end, the creation of a more rational, more just, more peaceful social order. Thus, teaching, especially critical teaching on a high level of competence and personal devotion, fosters many qualities and values antagonistic to those of simple socialization.

III

Let us look at the actual operation of mental health services in educational institutions. The psychiatrist in the school, like the psychiatrist in the public mental hospital or clinic, faces a conflict of interests. We know only too well that, in the latter situation, the individual patient and the psychiatric institution are often in conflict. When they both are, the psychiatrist cannot serve the interests of both. The upshot is that he sides with the more powerful party to the dispute: he helps the system, and harms the patient.

When psychiatric services are introduced into the school, the psychiatrist finds himself in a similar position. In general, the conflict is between the student and the teacher, or the student and the school administration. As an employee of the school system, it is hardly surprising that the psychiatrist should take a position antagonistic to the student's (self-defined) interests. The literature on school and university psychiatry supports this contention.

IV

The effectiveness of psychiatric programs in schools is difficult to assess.[1] But some of their effects are clear enough. We know that being cast in the role of mental patient is a form of personal degradation: it is a kind of stigmatization, like being classified as Negro in Alabama or Jewish in Nazi Germany. The psychiatric cant may be that the aim of school psychiatry is to help the child: but the very definition of a student as someone in need of psychiatric help stigmatizes him. And the question is: which person's assertion requires fresh proof—the one

[1] N. Jaffee, "Counseling Fails in Delinquency Test," *The New York Times,* February 20, 1965, p. 1.

who claims that a public diagnosis of mental illness is a stigma, or the one who claims that it is not?

The advocates of mental health practices in the schools ignore the stigma inherent in the mental patient role and the coercion which they, as therapists, propose to employ. Here are some excerpts from a typical paper on psychiatric services for public school children:

> The classroom teachers, along with principal, school physician, school nurse, and visiting teacher, frequently call to the parents' attention the existence of a problem requiring psychiatric evaluation. The nature of the behavior which is symptomatic of deeper underlying disturbance is manifold, but may be grouped into several broad categories which rarely occur separately.
>
> 1. Academic problems—under-achievement, over-achievement, erratic, uneven performance.
>
> 2. Social problems with siblings, peers—such as the aggressive child, the submissive child, the show-off.
>
> 3. Relations with parental and other authority figures, such as defiant behavior, submissive behavior, ingratiation.
>
> 4. Overt behavioral manifestations, such as tics, nail-biting, thumb-sucking . . . (and) interests more befitting to the opposite sex (such as tomboy girl and effeminate boy).

There is no conceivable childhood behavior that a psychiatrist could not place in one of these categories, thus classifying the child as requiring psychiatric attention. To categorize as pathological, academic performance that is "under-achievement," "over-achievement," or "erratic performance" would be funny were it not tragic. When we are told that if a psychiatric patient is early for his appointment, he is anxious, if late he is hostile, and if on time, compulsive—we laugh, because it is supposed to be a joke. But here we are told the same thing in all seriousness.

Here are additional excerpts from this essay, to indicate the kinds of social action that psychiatrists feel justified in using after detecting so-called psychiatric symptoms in a child.

"In most instances a careful history and clinical examination of the child and parents will be sufficient." It does not seem to occur to this psychiatrist that a physician retained by the school system has no business "examining" parents; nor that parents may reasonably object to such an "examination," since it affords no protection for their privacy and confidences. On the contrary, the author asserts that an "important reason for carefully considering the child-parent unit is to ascertain who the patient is. . . . In some instances only the parent may require therapy." In an abstract, psychoanalytic sense, this may be so. But we have long known this: What is more important here, it seems to me, is whether it is any of the school's business to psychiatrically diagnose, much less treat, adult persons who also happen to be the parents of school-age children. Again, we ought to be clear about the issues. For if membership in the group of persons called "parents of school-age children" justifies involuntary mental diagnosis and treatment by an agency of the government, why not also membership in other groups, such as the unemployed, or teachers, or judges, or Jehovah's Witnesses?

I use the term "involuntary" here to describe not only psychiatric procedures ordered by courts, but also psychiatric manipulations of people enforced by informal coercions (for example, by corporations, governmental agencies, schools). Most parents are economically dependent upon the services of the public school system. Because of this dependence, and because of the social-psychological authority of the school, any service recommended by the system will be experienced by the parents (and the children) as an order to which they must submit, rather than as an offer which they are free to accept or reject. In other words, if the parents have no alternatives, if they cannot send the child to a parochial or private school—they can easily be coerced by the public school system. This situation is often exploited by school psychologists and psychiatrists; however sincerely and in the "best interests" of the child they may do so does not matter.

The power of the public school to coerce, especially in matters of morals, is of course well recognized. It is one of the reasons why religious training is barred from such schools. For the same reason I believe that the public school is the last place, not the first, for a psychiatric service.[2]

The psychiatric invasion of the family contemplated, and actually carried out, by the school mental health team knows no bounds. Members of the

> clinical team . . . acquire detailed information about the child and his family through social case-work, psychological interviews, home visits, and psychiatric observations—all in an endeavor to understand not only the individual personality of the varied constituents of the family but also the manner in which members interact with one another in both healthy and neurotic fashions. *After an investigation and subsequent under-*

[2] The basic issue is the use of the social power of the school system: should it be deployed for the promotion of "mental health"? The arguments justifying the placing of psychiatric services in schools may be applied to any interest or value that society might wish to promote (for example, birth control). If we wish to attain a particular social goal, it is often easier and more "effective" to coerce people to behave in a certain way, than to provide them with alternatives among which they may freely choose. Liberty has a habit of getting in the way of social planning.

> *standing of the family has been completed, a total plan for the child and his family is formulated.* This usually includes individual and/or group therapy of the child; social case-work, group therapy, or psychiatric contacts with at least one parent; periodic meetings with teachers . . . [italics added].[3]

If all these glorious "therapies" are provided by a marvelously enlightened community for the benefit of families, why connect the service with the public school? Why not offer the psychiatric services in a separate setting, and let the families take advantage of them, if they wish. Could it be that the services provided are not really desired by the families affected? Indeed, that they are a means for manipulating the "clients" and for this the coercive power of the school is necessary?

The views I have cited are typical of those held by the advocates of community mental health, social psychiatry, and school psychiatry. According to Gerald Caplan, the main task of the community psychiatrist is to provide more and better "sociocultural supplies" to people. This is accomplished by reviewing "the conditions of life of his target group in the population and then influencing those who help to determine these conditions so that their laws, regulations, and policies are modified in an appropriate direction. . . . The most obvious example of social action for the provision of sociocultural supplies is that of influencing the educational system." [4]

Caplan justifies this procedure as follows: "If the preventive psychiatrist can convince the medical authorities . . . that his operations are a logical extension of traditional medical practice, his role will be sanctioned by all

[3] Sherwin S. Radin, "Mental Health Problems in School Children," *The Journal of School Health,* Vol. 32, No. 390–397 (1962), p. 395.

[4] Gerald Caplan, *Principles of Preventive Psychiatry* (New York, Basic Books, 1964), pp. 62–63.

concerned, including himself. All that remains for him to do so is to work out the technical details." [5]

Is Caplan aware that he proposes nothing new, but, on the contrary, advances the most discredited plea of the collectivist technocrat? The problem that confronts the community psychiatrist is the traditional problem of the politician and the moralist: it is a problem of ends, not of means. It has always been, and it still is, useful to deny this. For, as Isaiah Berlin so eloquently observed:

> Where ends are agreed, the only questions left are those of means, and these are not political but technical, that is to say, capable of being settled by experts or machines like arguments between engineers or doctors. That is why those who put their faith in some immense, world-transforming phenomenon, like the final triumph of reason or the proletarian revolution, must believe that all political and moral problems can thereby be turned into technological ones. That is the meaning of St. Simon's famous phrase about "replacing the governments of persons by the administration of things." [6]

V

I wish now to describe the operation of the psychiatric service at Harvard University. Because of the eminence of this institution, its mental health practices are likely to command wide respect and to serve as models for other schools and colleges.

The principles of "educational psychiatry" have been set forth by Dana L. Farnsworth, the director of the Harvard University Health Services. The following excerpts convey the essence of his views:

[5] *Ibid.*, p. 79.
[6] Isaiah Berlin, *Two Concepts of Liberty* (London, Oxford University Press, 1958), p. 3.

> It is vitally important that nothing a student says to a college psychiatrist in confidence be divulged to any one without the patient's permission. Of course, if a student is overtly psychotic, suicidal, or homicidal, the safety of the individual and people in the community must take precedence over maintaining confidence . . .[7]

In other words, whether or not the psychiatrist chooses to protect the patient's confidences depends on his judgment of what is "best" not only for the patient but for the community as well. As we shall see later, the college psychiatrist does not in fact protect the student's confidences.

Indeed, Farnsworth refers to a truly confidential psychiatrist-patient relationship in tones of condescension: "A psychiatrist who is comfortable only in the one-to-one relation with patients would not enjoy college psychiatry." [8] What then, is the purpose of college psychiatry? Says Farnsworth:

> If the only purpose for having psychiatrists on the staff of a college health service were to treat those persons who become mentally ill, then they might as well not be there. Colleges could carry on their responsibilities by referring sick students to private psychiatrists. . . . The presence of psychiatrists in a college health service is justified more because they learn about the institution, become familiar with the pressures encouraging or inhibiting maturity and independence, and thus *become able to consult with faculty members and administrators* in a constructive manner about any matters in which *abnormal behavior* is an issue than because they treat disturbed students. [italics added] [9]

It, is of course, not "abnormal behavior" in the abstract about which college psychiatrists consult administrators;

[7] Dana L. Farnsworth, "Concepts of Educational Psychiatry," *Journal of the American Medical Association,* Vol. 181, No. 10 (September 1962), p. 818.

[8] *Ibid.,* p. 816.

[9] *Ibid.,* p. 816.

nor—and let us be candid about this—is it the "abnormal behavior" of faculty or administration that concerns them; their business is only the "abnormal behavior" of the students. Farnsworth admits this much when he observes that: "If they (i.e. the college psychiatrists) confine themselves to treating disturbed students only and *do not share their findings with the faculty, with administrators.* . . . Then they might as well remain in their private offices and have those students who need help come to them there." [italics added] [10]

Is such a physician then a kind of psychiatric policeman and spy? According to Farnsworth he is just the opposite: a liberator.

> A basic goal of psychotherapy should be to free the individual from crippling inner conflict by *inculcating* the kind of honesty, sincerity, and integrity in him that will enable him to act with confidence and a sense of competence. In situations involving *inappropriate response to authority, such consultations between college officials and psychiatrists* have great value. [Italics added.] [11]

So much for the principles of "educational psychiatry." Its practices at Harvard University are described by Graham Blaine, Jr., one of the leading psychiatrists at the college, from whose article I shall now quote.

"The college therapists," states Blaine, "have a responsibility to the institution they represent, the parents of their patients, and their government, and they must also be protective of their patients." [12] The order of responsibility is interesting—the patient is last.

[10] *Ibid.*, p. 816.
[11] *Ibid.*, p. 818.
[12] Graham Blaine, Jr., "Divided Loyalties: The College Therapist's Responsibility to the Student, the University, and the Parents," *American Journal of Orthopsychiatry,* Vol. 34, No. 3 (April 1964), p. 481.

After noting the importance of confidentiality in psychotherapy, Blaine states that the college psychiatrist may:

> give blanket promises about confidentiality that he may later regret . . . we know that in the life of a college psychiatrist instances arise almost daily in which some kind of information about a student is asked for by others and in many of these instances the requests are legitimate and necessary. In the vast majority of cases it is in the best interest of the student to comply with these requests. Often professors want to know whether they can honestly excuse a student because of his emotional illness, or a dean may want to refrain from taking action if he knows that a student is earnestly working in therapy.[13]

The psychological implications and social effects of limiting communications in psychotherapy to therapist and client, as against diffusing them over third, fourth, and nth parties in accordance with the wishes of either or both participants, is a familiar problem and I shall not dwell on it. Suffice it to note that even at this outstanding university it is considered the legitimate function of the school psychiatrist to obscure rather than to clarify, to compound rather than to separate, his loyalties to the student, his family, his school, and his government:

> Over the years at Harvard we have been able to establish certain customs that have contributed greatly to our effectiveness as therapists to individual students *and* the community at large. Important among these is a *medical administrative lunch* held weekly and attended by the therapy staff of the psychiatric service, members of the medical and surgical service, deans who are concerned with the students or the problems on the agenda, members of the local ministry who counsel students, our psychiatric social worker, the psychology staff, representatives from the student counseling offices, and the

[13] *Ibid.*, p. 481.

> *chief of University Police.* Originally, this meeting was kept more or less *secret from the students,* but now it has become so well recognized as a forum where the students' interests are well served that it is openly discussed among them and an individual will ask his therapist to discuss his problems at the "doctor's lunch." [italics added] [14]

If the meeting served the best interests of the students, why was it originally kept a secret from them? And why does Blaine interpret the students' acceptance of the "doctor's lunch" as proof of its moral legitimacy and psychotherapeutic value, rather than as a symptom of the students' acceptance of their debased role and of their attempt to turn it, however pitifully, to their own advantage? Did the presence of the Jewish *Kapo* in the concentration camp mean that the camp served the best interests of the inmates? Or the presence of the American POW who collaborated with his North Korean captors mean that the prison guards were really protecting the "best interests" of the prisoners? The total denial, by even as prominent an authority in the college mental health field as Blaine, of the school's *power* over the student, and the implications of this fact for therapy carried out under the auspices of the school, is astonishing. Most likely it is a sign of the moral capitulation of the expert: the college psychiatrist seems to have acquiesced in his role as an arm of the university police. He is a psychiatric spy. To be sure, he may try to "help" the student, if it is possible to do so without coming into conflict with the university: but if it is not, the physician's loyalty is clearly to the school first, and to the student last.

How do we account for the existence of such a service, especially in an area like Boston, where there is no shortage of private psychiatrists? One would think that many, perhaps most, of the students at Harvard could afford

[14] *Ibid.,* p. 482.

private psychiatric therapy. Why, then, does the university provide them with psychiatric help? Blaine suggests that it is because the university psychiatric service is a means of keeping tabs on the students: "In the medical school and the divinity school all first-year students are interviewed for evaluation and also introduced personally to the therapist to whom they can turn later should they need help."

Let us remember that we no longer deal here with children (not that I consider such procedures justified with them), but with young adults, many of whom are only a few years younger than junior faculty members. Why are there not similar "services" provided for Harvard faculty members (and their families), including compulsory psychiatric interviewing of all new teachers? I believe the answer is, again, that the students are a captive patient-group in a way that faculty members are not, or at least, not yet.

The best way to illustrate the role of power in this type of psychiatric work is to cite some case material presented by Blaine.

A graduate student was taken into treatment following a suicide attempt. During therapy, he became depressed again and the therapist wanted to hospitalize him. The patient refused to go to the hospital; instead, he "wished to be allowed to return to his room and to make his own decision as time goes on about whether to live or die. Several different therapists interviewed the patient, but were unable to persuade him to go to the hospital. Finally his department head was asked to speak to the student, and *by showing him that his future career at school depended upon his cooperation* with the mental health service, convinced him that he should follow our advice." [italics added][15]

[15] *Ibid.*, p. 483–484.

Are we really expected to believe that, in such a case, the Harvard University Student Health Service is concerned only about the student's "best interests," and is not also deeply concerned about the effect of student suicides on the public image of the school? The fact is that if such a student is committed to a mental hospital and there kills himself, his death may not even be mentioned in the local newspapers; but should he jump out of the window of his dormitory room the news of his suicide is likely to be front-page news in Boston and be carried over the national news wires.

In this example, the college psychiatrist feels justified in using the school authorities to force a student to accept a type of "psychiatric treatment" he does not want. Surely, this does not solve the basic moral and psychiatric dilemma: has the psychiatrist acted as the agent of the student or of the school? Has he helped or harmed the patient?

Another case is that of a "model student and good athlete (who) was caught stealing a small item in a local store. The college rule is that students caught stealing are required to withdraw for one year and then may be allowed to return. The dean requests our opinion about levying such a punishment on this boy. He asks, 'Is not such sudden uncharacteristic behavior evidence of illness rather than evil intent?' "

Did Blaine suggest that if the dean did not like the rule, he might propose to the administration that it be changed? Or that if he did not like punishing students for infractions of rules, he might resign as dean? No. Instead, he acceded to the technocratic collusion proposed:

> After interviews and psychological *tests* we were able to tell the dean that this student was suffering under a combination of stresses at the time of the stealing epi-

> sode and that the *deed was a symptom* rather than an innate character trait. . . . We made no recommendation about disciplinary action but did suggest that *psychiatric treatment was indicated.* [italics added] [16]

Blaine seemed to be greatly pleased with his restraint in making no *direct* recommendation about disciplinary action. But is indirect action not also action? Indirect communication, not also communication?

The role-diffusion of the college psychiatrist and the corresponding diffusion of psychiatric information which Blaine considers justifiable have few limits. Not only does such a psychiatrist owe loyalties to the students, the parents, and the school—he must also cooperate with the FBI:

> An FBI agent calls to discuss a former patient, and has a signed release from the student who is now applying for a responsible government position. [Clearly, from the point of view of the ethics of autonomous psychotherapy such a release is meaningless: the applicant must sign it to qualify for the position he seeks.—T.S.] While in college this boy sought help for homosexual preoccupation. He had engaged in homosexual activity in high school and once[17] in college.[18]

The FBI agent wants to know if the student has engaged in homosexual practices. "This is a difficult problem—one involving loyalty to patient and to country," says Blaine. His solution is to hedge, to double-talk—in sum, to inform on the patient, while, at the same time, telling himself that he hasn't really done so, but has instead protected the "best interests" of both student and country:

[16] *Ibid.,* p. 484.
[17] Blaine seems to think that the psychotherapist really knows how many times such an individual has had homosexual intercourse.
[18] *Ibid.,* p. 485.

> We have found that questions about homosexual practices usually can be answered in context without jeopardizing security clearance. Pointing out that an individual was going through a phase of development which involved him in temporary homosexual preoccupation and even activity does not seem to alarm these investigators.[19]

I find this a dismal picture, indeed, and a terrifying example for other schools to follow. The Harvard University Health Services claim to be genuinely interested in providing psychiatric care for their students. But would the services agree to distribute reprints of the paper from which I have quoted to all who apply for psychotherapy or are coerced into it? Or are the students at Harvard University not sufficiently intelligent or "mature" to receive complete and accurate information about the "medical" service supplied to them by the college? [20]

VI

Jacques Barzun, one of the most perceptive and incisive critics of our educational system, has perhaps said all there is to say about the twin aims of the school—education and adjustment. The moral imperative of equality on the one hand, and the practical necessity of assimilating

[19] *Loc. Cit.*

[20] Insofar as student health services do not adequately protect the confidences of their clients, their practices pose legal as well as moral problems. The lack of confidentiality in this kind of psychiatrist-patient relationship represents a special risk for the client (as illustrated above). The courts have held that the physician is negligent if he undertakes the treatment of a patient without his "informed consent": "A physician violates his duty to his patients and subjects himself to liability if he withholds any facts which are necessary to form the basis of an intelligent consent by the patient to the proposed treatment. Likewise the physician may not minimize the known dangers of a procedure . . . in order to induce his patient's consent." (*Salgo* v. *Leland Stanford Jr. University Board of Trustees,* California Appellate, 1957).

a steady influx of immigrants on the other, made it "inevitable that our schools should aim at social adjustment first. . . ." This being so, the schools were easy prey for the purveyors of psychological and psychiatric scientism. Thus:

> The notion of helping a child has in the United States displaced that of teaching him. Anyone who tries to preserve the distinction is obviously unhelpful, and is at once known for a declared enemy of youth. The truth is that even apart from its hostility to Intellect, systematic coddling is as dangerous as it is impertinent.[21]

The aim of the public school curriculum, continues Barzun, "is to round off edges, to work moral specifications —in short, to manipulate the young into a semblance of the harmonious committee, in accordance with the statistics of child development." Given this character of the American elementary and secondary schools, is it not sheer madness to make them the purveyors of psychiatric services as well? What, after all, do we want our schools to be: houses of knowledge where the child acquires the discipline of learning—or day hospitals where he is lulled into believing that the best identity is no identity?

The pressures that force and the enticements that lure the growing child into relinquishing the risks of striving for a sharply defined personality, and, instead, taking refuge in the opacity of non-identity, have been discussed by many sociologists and writers—most eloquently, perhaps, by Edgar Friedenberg in *The Vanishing Adolescent*. We have long encouraged the growth of what Ortega y Gasset called the "mass-man" (the other directed or heteronomous personality). The introduction of formal psychiatric services into the schools is therefore

[21] Jacques Barzun, *The House of Intellect* (New York, Harper & Row, Publishers, Inc., 1959), p. 102

not so much the cause of this process as it is a symptom of its final afflorescence.

The phrase, "My house is my castle," may have accurately expressed the beliefs and values of our forebears; today it is virtually meaningless. In days past, it signified not only the sanctity of the home for the individual as person, but also the security of the mind as the abode of the soul. Solitude, however, is a source of comfort and strength, only for the autonomous personality: for the mass-man it is just the opposite, a calamity and a threat. Those used to being watched by Big Brother expect to be on stage; they know how to hide there behind a mask of impersonation. Alone, without an audience, with no one watching, they meet themselves—and, having met a ghost, are properly frightened.

Institutional psychiatry, whether in the mental hospital or the school, is perhaps the finest technique developed so far for driving the soul out of man. Mentally ill man is often said to have lost his mind. The cure institutional psychiatry offers is to give him back his mind—empty. The hospitalized mental patient hounded by the specter of electric shock treatments, and the child harassed by psychological testing and the threat of invidious psychiatric labelling, are exposed to the same dehumanizing influence. Usually they accept the solution the system offers them: to adopt a rounded, rather than an edgy, identity, so that, like greased pigs at a rodeo, no one can catch and subdue them. But, having become shadows, they cast no shadows. Social survival is their spiritual death.

It is pertinent, in this connection, to quote some of the things Friedenberg says about this problem.

> It is easier, and less damaging, for a youngster to face bad grades, disappointment at being passed over for a team or a club, or formal punishment than it is for him to deal with gossip about his character or his manners,

> with teachers who pass the word along that he is a troublemaker or that he needs special patience and guidance because his father drinks.[22]

The central developmental task of adolescence, according to Friedenberg, is self-definition. As Freud saw it, and practiced it, psychoanalysis—voluntarily sought by adult clients—served the purpose of helping the individual sharpen his self-definition. In another context, a similar method may serve the opposite purpose: to confuse and undermine self-definition. In my view, regardless of its aim, this is the effect of school psychiatry.

Nor should this surprise us. The surgeon's scalpel can heal or wound—depending on who uses it and how. Similarly, if psychiatric and psychotherapeutic methods are effective (as indeed they are), we cannot naïvely suppose that they may not be put to various uses, depending on the aims and values of those who employ them.

> A society which has *no purposes* of its own, other than to insure domestic tranquility by suitable medication, will have no use for adolescents, and will fear them: for they will be among the first to complain, as they crunch away at their benzedrine, that tranquilizers make you a square. It will set up sedative programs of guidance, which are likely to be described as therapeutic, but whose apparent function will be to keep young minds and hearts in custody till they are without passion.[23]

This is a rather dark image. Is it correct? Perhaps feeling disheartened by his own vision—which, however, may well be twenty-twenty—Friedenberg added: "We have by no means gone so far as yet: but the sort of process of which I speak is already discernible."

I think we have gone very nearly as far as Friedenberg has indicated. If there is hope, as I believe there almost

[22] Edgar Friedenberg, *The Vanishing Adolescent* (Boston, Beacon Press, 1959), p. 9.
[23] *Ibid.*, p. 15.

always is, it does not lie in the moderation of collectivists; rather, it lies in the resistance of some of the victims in whom each new assault on individuality seems to generate fresh determination to defend the individual. Though no doubt more complicated in its genesis, I surmise that the recent vast increase in the use of illegal drugs among college students—often sensationally labelled "addiction"—is related to the increasing psychiatric surveillance of the youngsters. If political oppression provokes political resistance, why should we be surprised if psychiatric oppression provokes psychiatric resistance?

Of course, psychiatric therapy need be neither oppressive nor anti-individualistic. But, as Friedenberg himself so clearly saw, the school is not the proper setting for a client-valuing therapy. Noting that it is normal for a youngster to face crises in formulating his identity, and that such a child might well benefit from psychotherapy, he stated that what he needs is the services of a

> skilled psychotherapist, not of a petty official. A civil service, in dealing with him, is most likely to constitute itself a Ministry of Adjustment; however sophisticated its staff may be about psychodynamics, its basic interest will be in the kind of problem the student creates for the school and for other people. This will serve as the real basis for classifying him and disposing of his case. It is almost impossible for a school guidance counselor or dean [or school psychiatrist—T.S.] to believe that his function in dealing with a particular student may *not* be to promote adjustment, but rather to help the youngster to find rational rather than destructive *alternatives* to adjustment, in circumstances where adjustment would cruelly violate his emerging conception of himself and the basis for his self-esteem.[24]

Thus has Freud's subversive psychotherapy been domesticated in America: an instrument for liberating man has been transformed into yet another technique for pacifying

[24] *Ibid.*, p. 83.

him. "That psychotherapy should be devoted to the ends of adjustment, rather than growth," comments Friedenberg, "is a tragedy that the indomitable Freud would have found ironical: but it is perhaps inevitable in a culture in which one must have an acceptable personality to succeed, and one must succeed to have self-esteem."

In this I cannot fully agree with Friedenberg. To be sure, the culture must share in the blame. But the psychiatrists and psychoanalysts who use psychotherapy in this way—are they not also responsible?

VII

I have said it before and would like to say it again: I am not opposed to sound psychiatric practices. Just as the person critical of torture as a means of extracting confessions from alleged criminals is not opposed to law and order—so I, opposed to the practices of psychiatric fascism, and not opposed to the practices of psychiatric humanism. Psychoanalysis, individual therapy, group therapy, family therapy, remedial counseling—all these and many other methods that students of psychotherapy have developed and may yet develop have a legitimate place in a free and pluralistic society. But, in my opinion, they have no place in social situations where they may be used as instruments of psychological coercion and torture against captive, unconsenting, or unwilling individuals. Hence, such procedures have no place in the schools.

If society desires to make psychotherapeutic assistance available to those who cannot afford it themselves, the way to do so is obvious: whether through philanthropy or through funds supplied by the government, society must supply a service for the client. But he must be left free to use it or reject it: Such a society must be ready and willing to underwrite the services of a "private" therapist for the individual (or the family), and must not try to use the therapist as its spy or policeman. To be sure, society needs policemen (and perhaps spies as well). But it had better not use its psychiatrists and psychologists for such work, unless it wishes to liquidate the individualistic uses of these professions.

THERAPY & THE POWERLESS

Memoirs of a Social Work Student

SATU REPO

> If growing pains are never sickening, heartbreaking and terrifying, it is equally true that heartbreak, terror and a sense of insult and violation contribute nothing to growth. They stunt it and twist it and the grower is more or less deformed.
>
> EDGAR FRIEDENBERG[1]

THE YEAR I spent as a student in a School of Social Work is still the most painful and humiliating experience I have ever had, and in the past I have deliberately attempted to forget as much about it as possible. In particular, I have wanted to forget my eagerness, my innocence, and the good will and faith I had when I entered that institution. Although I have experienced war and refugee camps and even spent a short time in a mental hospital, it was at a

[1] Edgar Friedenberg, *The Vanishing Adolescent*, p. 35.

School of Social Work that I finally lost my social innocence: the feeling that social institutions are rational and benevolent, working in the best interest of all citizens, and that, broadly speaking, the interests of all individuals are in harmony with each other and with the goals of society. I was twenty-eight years old at the time and I feel in retrospect that I ought to have known better. It was a year of such profound alienation that it has contributed more towards making me a radical—forcing me to question the very roots of our social organization and beliefs—than anything that has happened to me before or after.

I have waited nearly three years before writing about this experience because I was hoping that time and further experience would enable me to see the year in a better prospective, that I would stop feeling so "emotional" about it. Unfortunately time did not manage this trick. The world and society never again seemed as well-meaning. And the school in retrospect seems as oppressive as ever.

Initially my reasons for wanting to understand what happened that year were quite narcissistic: I wanted to account for the almost uncontrollable anger that I felt during that year and that I still feel when I think back on it. I have had very few experiences of being angry. Having many rather classic neurotic characteristics, I tend to face conflict by internalizing it, examining in what ways "it was my fault." I used to think that there was something virtuous in this approach: it sounds so Christian, not looking for the mote in your brother's eye. But this process of becoming personally responsible for more and more aspects of adverse reality had resulted in a psychotic breakdown a couple of years before I entered the School of Social Work, and I had been encouraged both by therapy and personal insight to react to environmental pressures in less self-destructive and more extroverted ways. Lately, however, I've become more interested in seeing the extent of my social innocence and the kind of difficulties it got me into at the school.

Society in the past had seemed reasonable to me, because people in authority had always treated me well. I am the oldest child in a family of five, four of whom are girls. I was my mother's favorite against whom she measured the performance of her other children, who tended to fall short on the criteria she applied: school success, creative interests, respectable friends. As I was a studious and reflective person who liked the company of older and more "serious" people, there seemed to be little conflict between what she wanted and what I felt like doing myself. The same thing happened at school and on jobs I held. Not only did I get away with what I wanted to do; I usually got approval for it. I realized that my younger sisters and my school mates often felt quite differently about the benevolence of those who wielded power, but this was caused, I thought, by their rather regrettable emotionalism and inability to see things "in a larger perspective."

In believing that society was reasonable, I also thought that it was *quality of work* that really counted when society measured you up. At home, at school, at university, at work, there had been a great deal of explicitness and very little ambivalence about expectations. They were all performance-oriented and left you alone as long as you "delivered the goods." The goals might have been cynical or banal—like my mother's desire for personal glory, the school's ambition to excel in national exams, the university courses solely aiming at fulfilling professional requirements—but there was no bullshit about them. There was a franker selfishness about your personal goals and what the institutions expected from you. There would be off-guard moments when your teachers might admit to you that the institution or society or even he himself did not have as "high ideals" as they ought to, but usually the discussion was terminated with a philosophical monologue about "the selfishness of man" or "the survival of the fittest."

I entered the School of Social Work after working a year in a social agency which seemed to fit the previous frameworks I had been used to: my performance was again esteemed and my eccentricities were tolerated. It was possible to have frank, if resigned, discussions about the shortcomings of the service we were offering and about general weaknesses in society.

When I entered the School of Social Work I entered a different world. My initial interview with a staff member was pleasant enough, although I was puzzled by some of the undertones. "Now why would a person that seems to have so many interesting life opportunities want to go into social work?" was one of the implied questions. "I hope you realize that the school will not have much to teach you?" was another. "Will you be able to tolerate the social injustice that you will be exposed to as a social worker?" was the third. But I, all aglow with my year's experience in the field, thought that he was merely putting me on—trying to make sure that I had not developed absurdly idealistic notions about the profession and what it was able to accomplish.

When I became a student and met other members of the staff, I sensed a new kind of reaction to myself, which I found very disturbing. A kind of ill-defined hostility that manifested itself in the alertness and suspiciousness and very aggressive compliments which seemed to arise from nowhere: "—of course there are very few people in this world that have as good a mind as you, Miss Repo—," "—you certainly have an outstanding academic past—," "—your success in the agency may bring you some adjustment difficulties—," "—you may find some of the courses repetitious, but I hope you realize that the other students do not have your background—"

It took me quite a while to realize that the very qualities that were generally esteemed in the world—academic success and relevant experience—were, in the context of the school, considered drawbacks. I wasn't given compliments at all; I was receiving warnings. The never-quite-articulated position was that intellectually astute individuals make poor social workers, because they tend to "intellectualize problems" rather than getting to their emotional core. They tend to find glib, rational answers to complex emotional problems and do not have the patience to let the casework process unfold itself and offer the client the healing qualities of a professional relationship. There might have been some truth in this general observation, although I have not found it verified in my experience of social work and social workers; but like most generalizations pervading the school, it had ripened into a dogma which was impossible to refute. The fact that you were considered intelligent meant *ipso facto* that you were somewhat retarded emotionally: you lacked compassion, sensitivity, ability to relate to people, etc. It was also probable that you had authority problems.

Experience had similar nasty connotations. If you had worked in a social agency before entering the school, the chances were great that you were "rigid," had "preconceived notions" about social work and a tendency to "resist learning." The irony of this position did not seem to bother anybody: the same agencies that so distorted the perceptions of their "untrained workers" were used for field placement to train students while they attended the school. Somehow the assumption was made that a person with my background would be hostile towards what the school stood for, and I was given oblique warnings that the school would not put up with that. (This is, of course, pure hindsight on my part. At the time I felt like K. in Kafka's *Trial*. I spent the whole year trying to discover what I was being accused of, but without success.)

I had known in advance that the school attempted to combine teaching and therapy in some ways. The school had a Freudian psychological orientation, and it was considered important that the basic principles of psychoanalysis should not only be taught but experienced in some ways. In addition, there was a general belief in the importance of knowing yourself and becoming aware of your reactions. After all, self-awareness was essential if one wanted to help others in making sense of their experiences, which was considered to be one of the goals of social work. This seemed to me a goal that was both reasonable and laudable. In the social agency where I had worked we had attempted to do pretty much the same thing. At the School of Social Work our field supervisors attempted to get our personal reactions and associations arising from our experience with clients we were seeing. Our faculty advisors tried to draw us out about our general reactions to the school, the staff, our peers, and our current personal life.

I might never have perceived the contradictions in this kind of set-up, had I not run into difficulties in my relationship with my field supervisor very early in the year, which kept me alert about this issue for the rest of the time. During my first evaluation in November she suggested that I might not be a suitable person for casework—giving a one-to-one personal service to seekers of help. When I asked her what she based her judgment on, she told me that she was worried about my ability to relate to clients. As this had been considered my special strength in the agency where I had previously worked, and as my present "clients" seemed to trust me and talk freely about themselves, I asked what evidence she had of this. She cited back some adverse comments I had made about clients during our supervisory sessions. I had compared individuals and said that I found such-and-such a person more likeable or making more sense than another, and we had traced some of these reactions of mine back to my own earlier experiences. A procedure not unlike what had happened when I was receiving psychotherapy. I had neither felt nor expressed violent dislikes or hostilities, but had said, for instance, of an unfortunate Mr. L., who was single, in his sixties, and still living at home with a bossy mother, that "mother-ridden, passive men really make me depressed."

"Fortunately for you," said my supervisor, "you have not expressed any hostility either towards me or the school as an institution, or I would recommend that you be advised to leave right away. But I certainly expect considerable improvement over next term." When I pressed her, she admitted that actually my relationship with the clients wasn't the only thing that worried her. She also did not consider me respectful enough of her and her experience and her judgment. I treated her more like a colleague than a superior, arguing with her interpretations about the clients, etc. Again, I felt utterly bewildered, because I thought I had behaved no differently with her than I had with other authority figures in the past, yet the result was very different. We adjourned, after a four-hour session which became more hostile and more opaque by the hour. I felt extremely shaken up after this encounter, and decided that I had better discuss the whole situation with the administration. I did not think that either my "capacity for casework relationships" nor my "ability to accept authority" would substantially improve in the next few months, and I wanted to ask the vice-principal whether it would be wiser for me to withdraw from the school at this point.

The vice-principal received me the next day politely and listened to my rather breathless story without interrupting. After I had finished he asked one question: "Do you want to stay at the school or would you prefer to leave?" I told him that I wanted very much to stay and complete the course. He smiled and seemed more relaxed. He said that he could not see that there was a real problem here. Obviously I felt very upset, and he was glad that I had come to talk about this, when it was so much on my mind. However, he had recently had a conversation with Miss Smythe (let us call my supervisor that) and she had not said a word about possible expulsion. On the contrary, she seemed quite satisfied with my progress. He knew Miss Smythe very well, she was in fact a *very* good friend of his, and he could assure me that she never could have mentioned expulsion. It must have been that in my anxiety I had heard something that really hadn't been said, just because I dreaded that something like that *might* happen. There was a deep, therapeutic smile in his voice at this point, and he gave me examples of situations such as accidents when several people "see" something quite different in the same event. Having spent a sleepless night worrying about my future—I had an agency scholarship that I would have to pay back if I did not successfully complete the year—I felt sufficiently cowed even to consider the possibility that I had just been hallucinating, and nodded silently. The vice-principal promised to get in touch with Miss Smythe and phone me back the same night.

When I received the phone call that evening, the vice-principal still sounded cheerful and reassuring, but not quite as positive. It appeared that Miss Smythe herself was sufficiently angry not to accept the political decision that he had made: that the whole incident had only taken place in the mind of an agitated student. He had to admit that Miss Smythe seemed to have certain reservations about me, but nothing that couldn't be remedied by serious application on my part. The school, he assured me, was quite pleased with my progress, and would definitely like me to continue on the course. I decided to stay and completed the year. Miss Smythe never brought up the issue of expulsion again, but from now on we were both aware of the power distribution in our relationship and she had a considerably less confident and outspoken student.

I am not describing this incident to vindicate myself. For all I know I really was an intolerably arrogant student. My aim is rather to draw attention to the conflict between therapy and authority which prevails not only at the School of Social Work but wherever the attempt is made to combine concrete service (usually financial assistance) with some form of psychotherapy. As one of my classmates used to say "this teaching and shrinking is a real bind."

The first thing to realize is that in this situation the relationship between the student and the teacher or the social worker and his client is only superficially similar to the psychotherapeutic relationship. The three cornerstones of the therapeutic situation are missing:

1. The patient voluntarily seeks out the therapeutic situation and can withdraw from it at any time.

2. The psychiatrist is a "disinterested individual." He has no power over the patient except as a therapist. The patient's livelihood or scholastic success cannot be endangered by anything he says to his therapist because:

3. There is a guarantee of confidentiality. The patient knows that nothing he says will go any farther. Any social worker attempting to get information from a privately practicing psychiatrist, even with the patient's consent, knows that it is like pulling teeth, and in the end you have not learned very much.

Now a situation which is set up to "test out" the individual at the same time as he is encouraged to open up and be spontaneous, is likely to produce more anxiety than confidence. The situation is filled with possibilities of treachery and bad faith, and the theoretical model is "combat" rather than "disinterestedness." The person on the receiving end knows that it is not in his self-interest to be frank, yet he is forced to play along, because he is not in the position to withdraw either, without serious repercussions. The situation has more in common with a police interrogation than the classic fifty minute hour.

Somebody will probably object that this is an unnecessarily paranoid view. Surely what happens is in most cases in the best interest of the client or the student. If your therapist is nice he will not tell on you. I myself have every reason to believe that my faculty advisor, who was both respectful and loyal, kept my confidences. But this is like arguing for slavery by demonstrating that most slave owners treat their slaves in an exemplary fashion. THE POINT IS RATHER THAT THEY CAN AT ANYTIME UNILATERALLY CHOOSE TO ACT OTHERWISE. You become dependent on their personal integrity; there are no institutional or structural guarantees. The individual has no rights, except perhaps the right to walk out of the situation and forget the concrete services that he is in desperate need of: money, clothing, a degree, etc.

In addition, a person's vulnerability is increased in an institution pervaded by psychotherapy, because "facts" have a way of totally disappearing among projections, fears, hopes, fantasies. He cannot resort to the kind of defense that he could if he was accused in a legal court; witnesses, alibis, etc., are useless. AND WHAT IS REALITY AND WHAT IS FANTASY IS ALWAYS DETERMINED BY THOSE IN POWER, as was shown in my exchanges with the principal.

The other cornerstone in social work theory, besides Freudian dynamic psychology, is the belief in the healing qualities of the relationship that the social worker develops with his client. I could hardly put it more eloquently than one of our textbooks:

> The relationship is the soul of social casework. It is the principle of life which vivifies the process of study, diagnosis and treatment and makes casework a living, warmly human experience. It would be hard to exaggerate the importance of the relationship in casework, not only because it is essential to effective casework, but also because it is the practical living out of our basic convictions about the value and dignity of the human person. It is based upon a philosophy of life which is both realistic and idealistic, which encompasses matter and spirit, reason and faith, time and eternity.[2]

The study of this relationship is broken down to examining—and affirming—qualities said to be inherent in it, such as "non-judgmental attitude," "client self-determination," "confidentiality." Again, when I was first exposed to these concepts I felt both excited and enthusiastic. At the time I only objected to the prose in which they were expressed.

But again, reality stubbornly refused to accommodate itself to the principles we had drawn out. It turned out that the clients were not necessarily as keen on this relationship as the professional social worker. It was often necessary to either "take them by surprise" or apply some reality pressures to get them involved. In practice, therefore, both the school personnel and the agencies were forced to treat their clients in a rather high-handed way. And I continued to aggravate my supervisor by trying to take the principles of "self-determination" and "confidentiality" as seriously as I had attempted to take the therapeutic teacher-student relationship.

The agency where I was placed for field practice was a public agency giving financial assistance to indigents. The workers in the agency used to handle caseloads of three to four hundred families and did not usually make home

[2] Felix P. Biestek, *The Casework Relationship* (Chicago, Loyola University Press, 1957), p. v.

visits more than once every two or three months. The visits consisted of unannounced spot checks to discover whether the clients were carrying on "indecent living" or perhaps augmenting their income by illegal means. From the files of this agency a number of "promising" cases were selected for the students, and they were asked to find out what problems the people had and to get involved with them therapeutically. The students were asked to tell the welfare recipients that they were new workers for the agency, working part-time only, and having rather more time to help individual people. Not a word, of course, about our being students, lacking in experience and staying only a certain number of months, or about the detailed records we kept on our interviews with them.

I must confess that my first unannounced, unsolicited home visits to offer casework help were not easy. I felt like a friendly cop, and certainly that was the way I was treated, too. These regular weekly visits that we made were often seen by the welfare recipients—harassed as they are by many authorities—as just another spy job by society. They were anxious and often eager to please, insisting that we look at their rent receipts and food bills, telling us how grateful they were to the city for the assistance they were receiving. Some students, sensing the absurdity of the situation, finally told their clients that they were university students doing field practice, and this usually put people more at ease. In our own underdog position our loyalties naturally gravitated towards the clients. Probably the more housebound individuals—deserted mothers and elderly people—quite looked forward to our visit and the "serious talks" we attempted to get them involved in.

Our difficulties as students began when we were faced with having to write "verbatim" reports of our home visits, and had to decide what part of the dialogue had to be suppressed and what could safely be brought into the open. In addition, our supervisors tended to be very directive when it came to diagnosing the client's problem and recommending solutions. This often involved us in further deception, if we had any respect for the client and his right to do what he wanted. Attempts toward reconciliation of broken marriages were often recommended. We were told that wives were usually more "unreasonable in these situations." If they had not acted in such a hostile and rejecting fashion toward their drunken, violent and spendthrift husbands, the marriages would have stayed together and the city would not have had to come in for financial support of the family. Maybe there is some truth to this generalization, but it is not an easy approach to take when you visit a mother who is all by herself attempting to bring up half a dozen children on a meager welfare allowance.

Interestingly enough, students placed in private social agencies where casework therapy was mandatory and *sine qua non* for financial assistance, usually encountered more initial hostility from the clientele, who seemed to have a deeper and more passionate resentment of their agency than did the public welfare recipients. The welfare recipients had evolved a live-and-let-live relationship with their harassed workers: neither party bothered the other very much and both parties liked to keep it that way. But those receiving aid from a private agency often felt very resentful about having to sing for their supper and become subjected to all kinds of "exciting" new treatment methods, group therapy, family therapy, therapy for unemployed fathers and so on. When they realized that the students were in many respects in the same boat as they, they spent a lot of their energies abusing the agency and its workers in very colorful language. (One of the more innocent stories is the one about the client who phoned in and asked if he could come in and just pick up his check this week and get a double dose of "that other stuff" next week.)

However, the moment this kind of reality was introduced between student and client, it added to the difficulties in the supervisor-student relationship. The student—having after all to deal with the clients face-to-face—could not take quite the detached and cheerful attitude that seemed to characterize the experienced worker. The individuals whose misfortunes they had to listen to never quite seemed like "teaching aids" to the students. They could not get as excited as their superiors about the opportunity to encounter a problem of desertion or illegitimate pregnancy or terminal illness. The supervisor seemed to be most interested in how the student reacted in encountering such and such a situation, and what her reaction revealed about her as a person. The student, on the other hand, was quite caught up in the human tragedies that they were facing during their casework visits.

Most of the approximately one hundred students in our class were recent university graduates. The great majority were girls. These girls came predominantly from middle-class or upper middle-class homes, not unlike the general undergraduate population. They were intelligent enough, but not academically oriented. Most of them had made B's rather effortlessly through college, to their own great surprise. There was, in general, a sweetness and wholesomeness about these girls that makes one think of young nurses, but they seemed to have somewhat more differentiated personalities and perhaps a more assertive common sense. They were lovely looking girls, most of them, and extremely marriageable, quite unlike the general stereotype of social workers.

The men seemed to come mainly from working-class homes and had usually not done well academically. They were conscientious and modestly upwardly mobile, the kind of individuals one encounters as public school principals, postmasters in small towns or firechiefs. Among them were a few boys from the upper middle-class who for various reasons had not found the more traditional professional careers feasible. The male students were not a very colorful group and seemed somewhat over-anxious in front of authority, eager to discover "what was expected from them."

One's over-all impression was that the students were a solid, common-sensical group of young adults who had enough emotional reserves—or, in some cases, social ambition—to take a lot in their stride. They wanted to work with people in some kind of constructive capacity, but were not overly idealistic and were certainly not prone to social criticism. The collective hysteria and paranoia that the school created in them was therefore that much more startling.

The school officially admitted that the first year of the two-year course was "very hard on the students." They were forced toward self-examination and exposed to class differences which they had not had to face before, creating anxiety and a kind of "culture shock." I admit that there is some truth in this statement, but most of the anxiety came from an entirely different source. It was mainly created because of the tension between appearance and reality which I have discussed previously, and particularly because of the "therapeutic approach" to learning. The double bind of "teaching and shrinking" made life almost unbearable. It meant that you spent a great deal of your time with superiors highly skilled at drawing people out, while your very existence at the school was jeopardized any time you expressed an honest opinion. The students sensed these opportunities to "unburden themselves" as combat situations which they were quite unprepared for and which frankly terrified them; few of them had my naïveté about ever attempting to open up. In order to feel safe in these situations many students went to great lengths to invent problems that would seem innocuous and yet keep them talking (such as "having a problem about looking too young" or "feeling shy with older male clients") in order not to be caught off guard and forced to discuss real difficulties they might have had. But not only did they have to guard against showing their real feelings at any time, they also felt obliged to take on the job of protecting their clients, both from arbitrary directives from their superiors and from disclosing what these people were in fact thinking about the agency. The latter became as much of a problem as the former, because we were supposed to write "verbatim" reports on our interviews, and deception was again only possible by invention: we were often forced to fabricate dialogues and then remember them well enough to discuss them when the report was no longer with us.

The students were anxious because they felt very vulnerable. There was a great uncertainty about the standards which were used for determining whether you were "suitable for social work." Academic criteria were not very relevant, for the course work demanded little intellectually, and it was rare for anybody to receive a mark below B. Students were usually expelled for much less definable reasons. Usually they were considered to have a wrong kind of personality for social work, with some oblique hints about "authority problems." It was generally believed by the students—and admitted by at least some staff members—that expulsions primarily took place as a result of personality conflicts with your superiors and the most likely person to get in conflict with is your field supervisor who sees you most and is therefore also your chief shrink. Seeing as most of us had pretty serious objections to how we were treated personally and how clients were handled, we feared we would be found out and expelled any time.

The thought of expulsion was made the more forbidding, because most of the students were receiving rather substantial government grants which they had to pay back if they failed the year.

Because of all these feelings of uncertainty and powerlessness, the students developed a collective resentment toward the staff which almost defies description. Most of us would spend several hours a day over and above our very full schedules sitting together in nearby coffee shops and bitching about the school. There was no crime or perfidy that we did not think the staff capable of. Endless examples of tyranny, arbitrariness and bad faith were brought up and circulated with glee. Husbands of married students complained that they had to listen night and day to these stories and started to suspect their wives' sanity at times.

At no point were any of us able to convince "outsiders" that things were as bad as we claimed. The hysteria and paranoia would be such that incredible rumors would start sweeping back and forth—that our private mail in our mailboxes at school was being read, that the common room or our offices were "bugged," that spies were planted in the coffee shops. (I am not suggesting that we actually believed in these rumors, but we did not entirely disbelieve them either.)

We would also indulge in fantasies of revenge and revolt, but not a great deal. A favorite activity was to describe in front of an appreciative audience "what I really felt like telling that bitch," to make up for the sweet reasonableness that we simulated in the presence of a superior.

The conclusion is inevitable: we were behaving like powerless people anywhere, cringing, without dignity, full of resentment. We were reacting to a new kind of tyranny with the helplessness of those who are totally unprepared and almost incredulous about what is happening to them.

Our explanation mechanism had broken down; we could no longer go through the process of finding rational reasons. Our experiences made no sense and we felt out of control. We had no experience of accommodating ourselves to the irrational, except by not believing it, and this was no longer possible. As the year progressed, an increasing number opted out even from anger and withdrew to a kind of apathy or numbness or total nihilism.

The year seemed to be dragging towards its inglorious end. But just before final exams something happened which promised to unite the students enough for some kind of showdown with the staff. John de Bohr, the most outspoken and critical of the male students, was told that he had failed his field practice which meant that he would fail his year. John was a sharp and very entertaining fellow, usually quite prominent in our coffee shop sessions, and most of us had a clear image of him as a good guy. What outraged us as students was that apparently he had not received any warning about this possibility, so that he could have withdrawn earlier. During the previous evaluations no suggestions had been made that his work was below standard. In fact, a couple of weeks before he was told that he had failed, he had been asked by the agency he was doing his field practice in whether he would work for them during the summer.

The president of the student council (who, like other council executives, saw his position as that of a *mediator* between student and staff rather than *representative* of the students) seemed to rise to the occasion. He circulated from table to table in the coffee shop, asking whether we thought that a petition should be drawn on John's behalf. The feeling ran high for a petition, and he finally came to my table where a dozen of us were sitting together, and asked whether I would draw one up, after getting all the facts and details from John. I agreed to do it.

When I was typing up that petition the same night, I felt rather elated. It was clear that we had a very straightforward case of miscarriage of justice and a lot of student opinion and the student council behind us. I predicted that an overwhelming majority would sign it, and that we would be able to force the staff into some kind of honest confrontation and explicitness. I did not trust the members of the student council, but thought that if we got enough signatures, they would be forced to represent the class, even against their own desires. The next morning I circulated the following petition in class, after showing it to John and getting his approval (All names have been changed.):

TO WHOM IT MAY CONCERN

We have been led to understand that John de Bohr was told by his Faculty Advisor, Dr. Middleton, on April 1 1964, that he had failed his field practice, which is tantamount to failing the year. Our class, which has known Mr. de Bohr as an articulate, dynamic individual and an active participant in class events, well-liked and respected by all, was rather dismayed by the news and particularly by the late date of its announcement.

A question many of us have been asking ourselves is: Why, if the school judged Mr. de Bohr to be unsuitable for casework, did it wait until so late to announce its decision? Was Mr. de Bohr in fact forewarned, or did it come as a surprise to him as well? After talking to Mr. de Bohr it became clear that the decision had come as a total surprise to him. Mr. de Bohr has communicated the following items to an official representative of the class:

1. There was no expression of criticism of his field work during the first term by his supervisor Mrs. Wiener. Mr. de Bohr received a Mid-Term B– mark for Field Practice, but, according to his supervisor, she had estimated his performance considerably higher.

2. No criticism was expressed during the spring evaluation either.

3. On March 12, 1964, Mr. de Bohr saw both Mrs. Wiener and Miss Goodman, his Field Consultant, who both assured him that he had nothing to worry about. Mrs. Wiener asked if he would work for the agency for the summer. On the same day Mr. de Bohr received a phone call from his Faculty Advisor, Dr. Middleton, asking him to come and see him.

4. On March 13, 1964, Dr. Middleton told Mr. de Bohr that he was doing extremely poorly in his field work and it was likely that he would fail.

5. During the following two weeks at Field Practice, Mrs. Wiener expressed encouragement about Mr. de Bohr's work habits. He was given three new cases.

6. On March 31, 1964, Mr. de Bohr was called in by Mrs. Wiener for a five-minute interview. He was told that "things were not going to work." His field practice was going to be terminated. Mrs. Wiener told him that she regretted that because Mr. de Bohr was a very accepting, sensitive and non-judgmental person. Unfortunately he did not get involved enough with his clients. Mrs. Wiener said she did not have time to elaborate any further on the reasons for her decision, but would see Mr. de Bohr on April 2, 1964, if he so desired.

Needless to say, we are puzzled by the above events as they have been related to us. Moreover, a substantial number of us feel that the de Bohr case is only a symptom, albeit an extreme one, of a deeper problem in faculty-student relationships: a very basic lack of communication which has resulted in a widespread feeling that there is a disturbing degree of arbitrariness in judging who is and who is not suitable to become a member of the social work profession. There is a suspicion that we hope is not justified, that any intelligent, critical examination of the methods and content of the training program as it is presently constituted is widely discouraged, and individuals expressing such criticism will experience great stress in their relationship with the staff and their capacity to become full-fledged social workers is seriously questioned.

> Questions and doubts of this nature can have serious consequences in an institution of higher learning for which the life-line presumably is two-way communication. If criticism is stifled, it goes underground and expresses itself in widespread apathy and cynicism, if not nihilism, which certainly is no climate for learning and discovery. We therefore wish to draw to the attention of the faculty the feelings that John de Bohr's dismissal has created in the class. It would seem that nothing less than an official clarification of what happened to John de Bohr could dispel the heavy cloud of suspicion and unease that has gradually developed.

About thirty people signed it during the morning class, but it was clear from the tense and harassed expressions of the student council members that they had, by now, second thoughts about the matter. After the class, the student council president got up and asked everybody to refrain from taking a stand on the matter until the student council had met. It was Friday and he suggested that we have a class meeting on Monday. Somebody told me that the president had become worried about the idea of a petition the previous night, and decided to consult the faculty for advice. He had seen the vice-principal, who had thought that a petition was an extremely bad idea, and had suggested that any students who were dissatisfied ought to drop in and have a talk with him.

During the breaks between classes the petition was debated in rather hysterical tones. Some felt that it was too extreme, others said it didn't go far enough. Somebody suggested that we drop the general part, somebody else was for leaving John out altogether and having a pétition about student-faculty relations only. The student council members spent their energy trying to dissuade people from the whole idea of a petition. They argued that:

(a) any clarification needed was a private affair between John and the staff, and it would be "unfair" for the student body to get involved, and

(b) in any case, how could we ever be assured of the facts of the situation well enough to take a stand for or against John's dismissal? Was it not possible that John "in his anxiety" would have distorted the facts to put himself in a better light?

Those defending the petition pointed out that we were not asking for John's reinstatement, but only for clarification on the part of the staff. There was a lot of excitement in these informal sessions, but not much exuberance. Both those that had signed the petition and those who hadn't felt torn and vulnerable.

When it became clear that the student government was "chickening out" (the president had informally disclaimed that he ever asked for the petition—I had, in his words, "volunteered" to draw one up), those who had put down their signatures began to get worried about their own safety, and asked their names to be omitted until there was a class decision. A rumor went around that the student council president—on the vice-principal's request—was planning to show a copy of the petition *prior* to the class meeting, and some loyal supporters of the petition quickly confiscated all the copies and handed them to me.

Usually after Friday classes we went *en masse* first for coffee and then for beer. This Friday the whole class dispersed instantly, as if a great calamity was in the air.

I spent a tortured weekend trying to decide what to do myself. It became clear that my integrity—or at least what was left of it, after the compromises I had made in order to survive—demanded that I back up the petition I had drawn. I still thought that, despite the student council, we could make a minority representation to the administration. I decided to draft another statement to clarify the situation. I still felt fairly confident that we would be able to get about 25 per cent of the class to sign it.

I circulated the following statement in the Monday morning class:

CONCERNING THE STATEMENT CIRCULATED ON FRIDAY ABOUT JOHN DE BOHR, ETC.

Hi Everybody:

A lot of you may have wondered how I, not being an elected representative of the class, got involved in drafting a petition for the class. This is how it happened: on Wednesday when John learned from Dr. Middleton that his field practice was terminated, Vance approached me and asked if I had heard what had happened to John and whether I felt, like many others, that we should draw up a petition on his behalf. I said that it sounded like a good idea. He then asked me if I would like to draw up the petition and suggested that I see John first and find out how he felt about it and get the facts from him. It sounded like an interesting task so I accepted it and went ahead. I talked to John and got his story and I also talked to a number of other students placed in the same agency as John, to find out what their views were on the matter. All the information I received supported John's story. I then drew up the statement you saw on Friday. The responses, I must admit, have been mixed. Vance disassociated himself from the whole idea of a petition, and before finding out how the rest of us felt about it, had a couple of interviews with the staff, which seem, from what I can gather, rather inconclusive. Some people felt that they could support the first part of the petition but not the second, and vice versa. However, quite a substantial number were willing to sign it, there and then, as it stood. Showered with suggestions and countersuggestions, I decided to postpone any further action on the matter until I could give it good thought over the weekend.

I must say that the whole thing has given me a terrific headache. Although I accepted the suggestion to draw up the petition in all innocence, I have discovered that I cannot disassociate myself from it without a considerable loss of innocence and something else that I cannot quite define, maybe integrity. Somehow, willy nilly, I got involved, as all of you who have read the statement are. I am usually as good as the next guy in passing the buck, but I don't know quite where to pass it now. The cynic in me says, what's the point in getting into trouble when probably nothing will happen anyway? Why not leave it to Vance? I have struggled through an exhausting year, I have financial commitments and besides, a family to support; why take any chances? On the other hand, even the experience of this year has not completely obliterated the reasons why I went into social work: It seemed at that point—light-years ago—like one of the few professions left that I could engage myself in without loss of meaning and integrity. It began to look as if I was trying to play a rather grim joke on myself.

To make a long story short, it seemed when I thought about the whole affair that a much more important survival was at stake than passing the year. I have therefore decided to back up the statement I presented to you on Friday, substantially as it stands, and if necessary, take it personally to the Principal. I am passing the list so that those of you who have arrived at a similar conclusion can sign your name to support the petition. Those of you who would like to come along to see the Principal, please do. There is comfort in numbers.

SATU R.

The president got up after the class, and said that the student council was unanimously against the petition. Anybody who signed it was doing it at her own risk. When the petition was returned to me it had collected seven signatures.

I felt humiliated and shaken and realized that I had to revise my preconceived notions about "just causes" uniting oppressed people. I also had to revise some grandiose notions about myself as a popular leader. Having in many institutions of my past played the role of the student council members—although, according to my recollections, in a more Robin Hoodish spirit—I was pleased that this time I was "one of the people." This year was my first experience of group participation, and I had become rather high on it. I had forgotten that affection, trust and camaraderie existed because we were united in misery. It was safe, and in any case, there was not much else to do. Acting against oppression makes you stand out; you become an individual and a highly vulnerable one. You have to be very clear about what you are after and what you want to give up for it. Also you probably need a leader that you can identify with. People enjoyed talking to me because they found me "different" and "interesting." But that didn't mean that they were prepared to follow me to any brink and over, if necessary.

In some sense the students were also, despite their youth, more worldly-wise than I was, because of my different background. The agrarian and semi-feudal Finnish society where I was brought up aligned me with two breeds which, according to Edgar Friedenberg, are vanishing from this continent—adolescents and aristocrats. I still held some quixotic views of honor that in this vague, anonymous mass society seem to make very little sense. (Shotgun weddings, at least in some parts of Finland, are still taken quite literally.) My classmates, on the other hand, "knew" that the cards were hopelessly stacked against us, and did not believe in futile gestures.

The petition had, in any case, cleared the air somewhat. The eight of us who signed it felt rather good about it and started drinking coffee together. We did not present it, naturally, because it was only backed up by 5 per cent of the class. The debate about the rights and wrongs of the issue went on until the end of the year and even spilled over to the second-year class which, so far, had ignored us. The eight of us had a number of interesting discussions with second-year students who backed our position. A critical note was introduced by the second-year class president, who seemed anxious to talk about the issue any time he bumped into me. He was very worried about me and my friends, he said, and also about the general negative spirit in our class. Why did we not have more trust in the faculty; why did we always suspect them of malicious intent? He had had some difficulties himself in first year, in fact he had to start seeing a psychiatrist in order to get through the year. But, he realizes in retrospect, the difficulties were due to his own wrong attitudes. Did I not think that there was something paranoid and almost pathological about the resentment our class harbored against the staff? The last time I saw him, he left me a copy of a university publication with a picture of him shaking hands with the Principal of the School of Social Work.

What happened to John de Bohr? The student council sent a group of safe class representatives to discuss "the issue" with members of the staff. I don't know what happened in that discussion, except that at least one of the girls who had participated in it told me afterwards that it was "the most frustrating and humiliating experience in her life." There was a general class meeting with staff members, organized by the student council, ostensibly to discuss John, but he was never mentioned. Instead the students voiced a lot of outspoken criticism about the lack of periodicals in the library, the number of essays to be written, the inconvenient hours and the new regulation of compulsory class attendance. Some people argued that many of the courses would require a different approach. Many more seminars should be introduced.

Others were equally persuasive about the uselessness of existing seminars and suggested that they all should be scrapped. The staff members were friendly and very conciliatory. They admitted that there was room for improvement and promised to revamp the courses. Some papers would be dropped, the reading lists would be revised.

John himself did not challenge the school's decision on him, having been totally cynical about the outcome from the beginning. He dropped in to see us in the cafeteria after he had picked up his papers from the registrar's office. "The last laugh's on you guys," he said. "The registrar just told me not to feel too badly. In any case, I was too intelligent to become a social worker." But the smile did not reach his eyes.

Neither John nor I returned to the school the following fall. We belonged to the 70 per cent of the class who had decided to drop out at this point.

CONTRIBUTORS

Gail Ashby is a Toronto artist and designer. She was the original art editor for *This Magazine is about Schools* and has also been involved in setting up two free schools in the Toronto area, Everdale and Superschool.

Bill Ayers was a teacher at the Children's Community in Ann Arbor in 1968, an organizer and on the national executive of S.D.S. in 1969, and is currently a member of the Weatherman revolutionary group.

Anthony Barton does research for the Department of Computer Applications at the Ontario Institute for Studies in Education. His current project is a multi-media perception kit to be used in Ontario schools. He is a frequent contributor to *This Magazine is about Schools.*

Clay Borris is a young film maker from Cabbagetown, Toronto. He is a member of Point Blank School.

Bob Davis is an editor of *This Magazine is about Schools* and a teacher at Everdale.

Edgar Z. Friedenberg is a professor of Sociology and Education at the State University of New York in Buffalo. His books include *The Vanishing Adolescent* and *Coming of Age in America.*

George von Hilsheimer is the headmaster of Green Valley School in Orange City, Florida.

Herbert Kohl has recently been director of an experimental program in the Berkeley schools, called "Other Ways." He is the author of *The Open Classroom, 36 Children, The Age of Complexity,* and the pamphlet "Teaching the 'Unteachable.' "

Dennis Lee is a Toronto poet and publisher. His major works are two collections of poetry, *The Kingdom of Absence* and *Civic Elegies.*

Staughton Lynd is an editor of *Liberation* Magazine. His books include *The Intellectual Origins of American Radicalism; Nonviolence in America: A Documentary History; Reconstruction; Class Conflict, Slavery and the United States;* and *The Other Side* (with Thomas Hayden). At present he is working on a history of the draft resistance movement to the Vietnam war and teaching at a school for community organizers.

Charlie MacDougal is from Cabbagetown, Toronto. He spent a substantial part of his childhood and adolescence in reform school and jail. He is living at home now and is unemployed.

Marshall McLuhan is the Director of the Center for the Study of Culture and Technology, University of Toronto. His books include *The Gutenberg Galaxy* and *Understanding Media.*

Peter Marin is a Visiting Fellow of the Center for the Study of Democratic Institutions in Santa Barbara, California. In 1967–68 he was the Director of Pacific High School, an experimental private school in the Santa Cruz mountains outside Palo Alto, California.

George Martell is an editor of *This Magazine is about Schools* and a member of Point Blank School.

Michael Mason was a patient in the experimental G Ward at the Penetang Hospital for the Criminally Insane. He is currently a graduate student in psychology at York University, Toronto.

Wilfred Pelletier is an Odawa Indian, born in the village of Wikwemikong on Ontario's Manitoulin Island. At present he is on the staff of the Institute for Indian Studies at Rochdale College, Toronto.

Laura Phillips is a young American photographer living in Toronto. She has over many years been involved in setting up afterschool programs for downtown kids, concentrating mainly on the creative arts.

Satu Repo is an editor of *This Magazine is about Schools* and a member of Point Blank School.

Jack Spicer teaches at Pacific High School in Palo Alto, California.

Sarah Spinks is the managing editor of *This Magazine is about Schools.* She has done community organizing in downtown Toronto and is at present an active member of the Women's Liberation Movement.

Thomas Szasz is a Professor of Psychiatry at the State University of New York in Syracuse. He is also the author of *The Myth of Mental Illness* and *The Law, Liberty and Psychiatry.*

Nomi Wall works for the Toronto Draft Resisters' League.